Beyond Toleration

Beyond Toleration

The Religious Origins
of American Pluralism

CHRIS BENEKE

OXFORD

UNIVERSITY PRESS

2006

OXFORD
UNIVERSITY PRESS

Oxford University Press, Inc., publishes works that further
Oxford University's objective of excellence
in research, scholarship, and education.

Oxford   New York
Auckland   Cape Town   Dar es Salaam   Hong Kong   Karachi
Kuala Lumpur   Madrid   Melbourne   Mexico City   Nairobi
New Delhi   Shanghai   Taipei   Toronto

With offices in
Argentina   Austria   Brazil   Chile   Czech Republic   France   Greece
Guatemala   Hungary   Italy   Japan   Poland   Portugal   Singapore
South Korea   Switzerland   Thailand   Turkey   Ukraine   Vietnam

Copyright © 2006 by Oxford University Press, Inc.

Published by Oxford University Press, Inc.
198 Madison Avenue, New York, New York 10016

www.oup.com

Library of Congress Cataloging-in-Publication Data
Beneke, Chris (Christopher J.)
Beyond toleration : the religious origins of American pluralism / Chris Beneke.
p. cm.
Includes bibliographical references and index.
ISBN-13 978-0-19-530555-5
ISBN 0-19-530555-8
1. Freedom of religion—United States—History—18th century.   2. Religious
pluralism—United States—History—18th century.   I. Title.
BR516.B39   2006
323.44'20973—dc22   2005034383

9 8 7 6 5 4 3 2 1

Printed in the United States of America
on acid-free paper

To my wife, Christa
And my parents, George and Cathy

Acknowledgments

From the beginning, this project inspired a great deal more doubt than faith. It elicited more rejection letters from nonprofit foundations, national funding agencies, and dissertation fellowship committees than I care to remember. But the rejections led to major revisions and the revisions to what I hope is a better book. The manuscript gained a few (semicommitted) adherents along the way.
I am especially grateful to those whose kind words or tough criticism either buttressed my own wavering assurance or supplied a well-deserved kick-in-the-pants.

The earliest stages of the project were developed amid heated discussion with the late Robert H. Wiebe. His imagination and discipline were both justly renowned. Since Professor Wiebe's death, I have been fortunate to enjoy the counsel of the ingenious and humane James Merrell. Early on, James Oakes freed me from many foolish misconceptions and persuaded me of the importance of liberal thought in early America, while T. H. Breen asked the skeptical "so what?" questions that forced me to reconsider central aspects of the study. Recently, I have again enjoyed the sage advice of my undergraduate adviser, R. Laurence Moore. During the early summer of 2004, both he and Richard W. Pointer took time from their very busy schedules to give the manuscript a careful reading. Rick Pointer surely ranks among the scholarly saints. He provided voluminous comments without ever having met me. Pauline Maier may have later regretted her kind offer to read a few chapters, but her critique was essential to the transformation of an esoteric dissertation into what may be an accessible book. Like the good friend he has become, Thomas S. Kidd supplied a last-minute reading of some important material.

At various stages, I have also profited from the insightful comments and suggestions of Josef Barton, Ruth Bloch, Patricia Bonomi, Steven Bullock, Jon Butler, Martin Burke, Stephen Foster, W. Clark Gilpin, Christopher Grasso, Timothy D. Hall, Philip Hamburger, Leo Hirrel, Thomas William Heyck, Daniel Walker Howe, Mark Noll, Douglass Sweeney, R. Stephen Warner, Gordon Wood, and Alfred Young. Friends—James Brennan, Seth Cotlar, Marcus Cox, Ryan Dye, Louis Ferleger, Christopher Front, Patrick Griffin, Michael Guenther, George Huppert, Richard Kraft, Karen Leroux, Karen O'Brien, Graham Peck, Ross Rosenberg, Meredith Rusoff, Chernoh Sesay, and John Howard Smith—extended numerous kindnesses, while enduring countless bad ideas and repeated bouts of intellectual churlishness. During these last months, Cynthia Read has proved an exceptionally encouraging and patient editor. Her editorial assistant, Julia TerMaat, skillfully shepherded this project from the acquisitions stage through final production. Renee Leath did a splendid job of copyediting the text. I would also like to thank the anonymous readers at Oxford University Press for their invaluable suggestions.

Bentley College has provided a welcoming community and a stimulating research environment. My colleagues and friends here, especially those in the History Department—Beverly Astourian, Marilee Crofts, Richard Geehr, Robert Hannigan, Joyce Malcolm, Bridie Minehan, Clifford Putney, Jeremiah Schneiderman, Marc Stern, Cyrus Veeser, and Cheryl Weiser—have provided endless advice and unceasing support. Bentley's crack ILL team of Robert Ross and Donna Gouldson obtained many of the obscure texts that made this project possible. This book simply could not have been written without their tireless assistance. Given how many items I returned late, I also thank them for their forbearance. Catherine Cronin, Sheila Ekman, Kimberly Morin, Joan Morse, and Barbara Rayburg have (cheerfully) done more to make a business college library accommodate an early American historian than I ever would have dreamed. Graduate assistants Bien Galang and Bethany Sweesy probably did not anticipate that acquiring their master's degrees in business would require the photocopying of eighteenth-century newspapers and pamphlets, but they should be praised for their diligence. I am also obliged to my gracious former colleagues at The Citadel who welcomed me to my first academic job, provided munificently for my research, and did not seem to resent it too much when I returned to the Northeast.

My extended family could very well serve as a model of how a religiously diverse community can function. The majority are Catholics, but there is also a significant remnant of Protestants and Jews among us. My mother- and father-in-law, Jean and William Von Ancken, have demonstrated again and again that sincere faith is compatible with tolerance. My own parents, George and Cathy Beneke, have always served as examples of hard work, piety, and charity. I have only myself to blame for having not practiced what they always preached and practiced themselves. My sister, Amy, who endured her older brother's constant teasing without altering her gentle demeanor, is a tribute to their parenting.

No one has worked harder to ensure that this project was completed than my wife, Christa. Her love, patience, and, perhaps most of all, her laugh have sustained me since high school. And her endless labor in real jobs has permitted me to pursue this less than lucrative career. I hope she knows how grateful I am. Finally, I would also like to thank Billy and Bryan for making these last two-and-a-half years an absolute joy. It's "all done" boys.

An earlier version of chapter 1 was presented before the Omohundro Institute of Early American History and Culture's colloquium. An earlier version of chapter 2 was presented at the Newberry Seminar on Early American Culture. An earlier version of chapter 3 was presented at the Newberry Seminar on American Religious History. A few of the arguments advanced in chapter 5 were first presented at the meeting of the Society for Historians of the Early American Republic and later posted online at "The American Religious Experience" (http://are.as.wvu.edu/index.html), though the majority have changed significantly since. Various parts of the manuscript were presented at the meetings of the American Historical Association, the Historical Society, the American Society of Church History (twice), the Southeastern American Society for Eighteenth-Century Studies, the Midwest Society for Eighteenth-Century Studies, and the Midwest History of Education Society.

Generous support for this project came from Northwestern University, the Citadel Foundation, and Bentley College. I am also grateful to the American Antiquarian Society and the Massachusetts Historical Society for the opportunity to use their collections.

Contents

Introduction, 3

1. The Plague of Dissent: And the Rise of Toleration, 15

2. Partial Judgments and Divided Churches: America's
   First Great Awakening, 49

3. Open to All Parties: The Ordeal of Religious Integration, 79

4. "None Are Tolerated": The Rise of Religious Liberty, 113

5. "Equality or Nothing!": Religious Pluralism in the Founding
   of the Republic, 157

Conclusion
"[M]ingle with Us as Americans": Religious Pluralism
after the Founding, 203

Notes, 227

Index, 295

Beyond Toleration

Introduction

Can two walk together, except they be agreed?

—Amos 3:3

During the late spring of 1791, an unusual visitor strolled the streets
of Boston. Recently appointed as the nation's first Roman Catholic
bishop, John Carroll had traveled from his home in Baltimore to settle a dispute between clergymen of his own church. Dressed in plain
black clothing, Carroll probably offered few outward signs of his religious affiliation. But his faith could not have remained a mystery for
long. Boston's Protestants would have been sensitive to the presence
of a Catholic prelate in their midst. After all, until just a decade and a
half before, they had celebrated "Pope's Day" by parading around
grotesque effigies of the pontiff every November 5th. The merriment
concluded with the burning of either the North End or the South End
Pope. Fortunately for Bishop Carroll, he enjoyed a much different
reception. Taking a moment to write a friend, Carroll noted that the
religious atmosphere in Boston had altered considerably. He testified
to the "great civilities" extended by his local acquaintances. The
magnitude of the change may not have been apparent until the bishop
was told that, in years past, his fellow pedestrians would "have crossed
to the opposite side of the street rather than meet a Roman Catholic."
Now, important members of the community walked alongside him.[1]

An even more notable event for contemporaries occurred three
years earlier, on a gray July Fourth morning in Philadelphia. Perching

upon an ornate carriage next to a framed copy of the newly ratified Constitution, the chief justice of the Pennsylvania Supreme Court set out near the head of a mile-long column. Members of every major occupational group marched behind him with tools in hand and livestock in tow. Groups of farmers, tailors, coopers, printers, potters, hatters, and harness-makers passed by eager crowds who lined the city's doorways and leaned out its windows. Thousands marveled as horses wheeled a replica warship over the bumpy cobblestone streets. The three and a half-hour affair was suffused with symbolism. An immense columned dome (each column representing a state) emblematized the federal union. Blacksmiths diligently stoked the "flame of liberty" and a rider carried a reminder of the revolutionary union with France—a white flag decorated with three fleurs-de-lis and thirteen stars.[2] Even more gratifying to the organizer of the procession, Francis Hopkinson, was the "universal love and harmony" that evidently prevailed on this day. That spirit, he wrote in a newspaper account of the event, was illustrated "by a circumstance which probably never before occurred in such extent"—the sight of seventeen clergymen, representing various religious faiths, walking three and four abreast, arms locked together. Nor was it just Christians who walked side by side through the streets of Philadelphia. Proceeding arm in arm beside two ministers was a rabbi. "May they and their flocks so walk thro' life!" Hopkinson gushed.[3]

Obviously, there was more to the spectacle of the seventeen clerics than their exhibition of professional skill. No one asked the clergymen to bring their writing desks and pulpits. Instead, they were expected to display a more universal, though less tangible, talent: an affectionate regard for people of other faiths. "Pains were taken," Benjamin Rush recalled in his description of the event, "to connect Ministers of the most dissimilar religious principles together, thereby to show the influence of a free government in promoting christian charity." In case anyone missed the significance of the performance, Rush explained it. "There could not have been a more happy emblem conceived of that section of the new constitution," he wrote, "which opens all its powers and offices alike, not only to every sect of christians, but to worthy men of *every* religion."[4]

In our cynical age, we might wonder at the Catholic bishop who was impressed by modest gestures of respect from his fellow citizens. We might also mock the pretensions to religious inclusion that the seventeen clergymen were supposed to represent and ask how Jews really benefited from "christian charity." In 1788, we might point out, Jews and Catholics were still denied access to civil offices in several states within the federal union and neither outright anti-Semitism nor anti-Catholicism was unknown to contemporaries. Yet if we ignore the delight and surprise that came upon John Carroll and those who witnessed the clergymen of different faiths walking arm in arm, then we will have failed to recognize the momentous importance of these events.

To avoid that fate, we need to consider the bishop's visit and the Philadelphia parade from a late eighteenth-century perspective, rather than our own. We have to remember that the history of Europe and America had, until this time, been distinguished by a long train of bigotry and persecution. We have to recall that most early modern governments treated dissenters from their state-sponsored church establishments as criminals. Religious minorities could be imprisoned, exiled, or even whipped, branded, and hanged; their property could be confiscated, and their churches closed. This meant that Bishop Carroll and the gentlemen who marched in the Philadelphia parade were not much farther from the brutal persecution of dissenters than we are from the lynchings of African Americans. Nor were they any farther from the exclusivity practiced by most colonial governments in the early eighteenth century than we are from the de jure racial segregation that persisted until the 1960s.

Viewed in such a light, the image of clergymen from various denominations walking arm in arm assumes the gravity it warrants. Even in Philadelphia, where religious minorities had been free to worship privately since its founding, there was nothing natural or easy about forging this particular symbol of religious ecumenism. Benjamin Rush's words should be emphasized: "*Pains were taken* to connect Ministers of the most dissimilar religious principles together." Perhaps the parade's orchestrators met resistance in the attempt, or perhaps they just expected the ministers to display the perfectly human inclination of walking alongside those whom they knew best or agreed with most. In either case, a self-conscious effort was made to bring men of distinct religious persuasions together. We can imagine an analogous plan to bring black, white, and Hispanic marchers together today. There may have been no more interreligious harmony at that time than there is interethnic harmony in our own time. Yet, then as now, inclusion, equality, and cooperation among different groups mattered deeply. But then, unlike now, it was religious inclusion, religious equality, and religious cooperation that concerned people. Though still practiced inconsistently in the late eighteenth century, these ideals had become incontestable. The history of their controversial emergence is the history of America's first great attempt to accommodate diversity, its first experiment with pluralism.

Two revolutions, one in law and one in culture, made it possible for men of different denominations to walk together in the streets of Boston and Philadelphia during the late eighteenth century. The first, a better-known revolution, took place in the statute books. By the 1730s, major American dissenting groups across most of the colonies had gained the right to worship privately and to direct their tax payments toward the support of their own ministers. Many also gained the right to participate in politics. They obtained what contemporaries called "toleration." In more than half of Britain's mainland colonies (as in Western Europe), however, these rights had to be squared with the prerogatives of the established churches and the public's contempt for dissenters. The policy of toleration relieved religious minorities of some physical punishments and some financial burdens, but it did not free them from the indignities of prejudice and exclusion. Nor did it make them equal. Those "tolerated" could still be barred from civil offices, military positions, and university posts. In colonial Virginia, dissenters still had to petition for the right to preach dissenting doctrines, while Massachusetts's Quakers, Anglicans, and Baptists still had to go through the unpleasant ordeal of obtaining state certification before they could be freed from the religious levies that benefited other groups. The outright persecution of small, marginal churches continued until the last third of the century. European governments generally went no farther in the eighteenth century. But in America, the legal revolution did not stop at toleration.

As gradually as colonial governments adopted the legal practice of toleration, they suddenly abandoned it between the 1760s and the 1780s for something that is usually called "religious liberty." From Georgia to New Hampshire, the barriers that had prevented white Americans from practicing their religion freely and speaking their views openly gave way during the revolutionary period. The new state governments either could not or would not maintain the discriminatory policies that continued to characterize European societies. By the end of the 1780s, traditional religious establishments had been either pruned back or completely eliminated. When the United States Constitution was signed, it prohibited religious tests for federal office. The First Amendment, ratified four years later, precluded a national religious establishment.[5]

Momentous as this statutory revolution was, a revolution of equal importance and lesser fame took place in the realm of ideas and public norms. Eighteenth-century America experienced a rhetorical or ideological transformation—a shift in discourse—that moved it well beyond the language of toleration and toward a much more egalitarian mode of addressing its religious differences. The way people discussed their faiths in public changed dramatically between the first and the last decades of the eighteenth century. Through a process much like the one we have seen in the modern movement toward racial equality—following the establishment of equal standing before

the law, proceeding with the inclusion of different groups in the same cooperative endeavors, and culminating with self-conscious gestures of respect
between different groups—eighteenth-century Americans stumbled their way
toward something usually called "pluralism." Through both concentrated
effort and historical accident, they created a society defined by integrated
social and political institutions, public deference toward different beliefs, and
repeated assertions of equality. If living peacefully among a great diversity of
people with roughly equal rights signaled a new direction in Western culture,
so did the changes in language and behavior that made some degree of unity
and cooperation possible. In both respects, late eighteenth-century Americans
distinguished themselves from the persecution of the past and established
important precedents for the future.[6]

The latter, cultural, revolution will receive the most attention in this book.
The legal changes that brought toleration and religious freedom to the United
States have been well documented elsewhere. But no one has yet explained
how it was that eighteenth-century Americans managed to accommodate the
religious differences that produced so much bloodshed in the past. The ensuing chapters first explain how the right of private judgment gained the
status of an unquestioned assumption, then how the print trade expanded its
meaning, and how a series of evangelical religious revivals transformed it.
They go on to recount the subtle changes in public language and social behavior that occurred as official persecution ceased and social institutions became integrated, as toleration first became law and then became irrelevant, as
religious establishments crumbled and an ambiguous concept called "religious liberty" triumphed. They examine the move away from the assumption
that dissenting faiths were merely permissible and toward the conviction that
all faiths deserved equal treatment. They explain how it was that a people who
still cared deeply about the fate of their immortal souls could manage to live
with those who held significantly different beliefs about God and the church.
They seek to show, in other words, how Americans learned to live with differences in matters of the highest importance to them.[7]

At this point, it might be worthwhile to stop and ask: Why should the study of
pluralism's origins be confined to religious differences? Why not political or
ethnic differences? For anyone interested in the origins of American pluralism, there are several good reasons to focus on religion. First, and perhaps
most obviously, a considerable amount of religious diversity existed in the area
that became the original United States. On a church census taken in 1775, the
number of congregations in the original thirteen colonies appeared as follows:
Congregational, 668; Presbyterian, 588; Anglican, 495; Baptist, 494; Quaker,

310; German Reformed, 159; Lutheran, 150; Dutch Reformed, 120; Methodist, 65; Catholic, 56; Moravian, 31; Congregational-Separatist, 27; Dunker, 24; Mennonite, 16; French Protestant, 7; Sandemanian, 6; Jewish, 5; Rogerene, 3. The major port cities—especially New York, Philadelphia, and Charles Town (now Charleston)—hosted a broad array of religious groups. Reporting to London officials on the eve of the American Revolution, Charles Woodmason noted that the capital of South Carolina was home to two Anglican churches, "A Presbyterian Meeting," "An Independent-Meeting," "A Baptist Meeting," "A Quakers Meeting," "An Arian Meeting," "A Dutch Lutheran Church," "A French Calvinist Church," and a "Jews Synagogue."[8]

These kind of denominational calculations are misleading because they give the impression that the proportions were constant throughout the colonies. In fact, there were large concentrations of Congregationalists in New England, large concentrations of Presbyterians in the Middle Colonies, and large concentrations of Anglicans in the South. But denominational diversity tells only part of the story. In many areas—particularly New England and the Middle Colonies—these denominations were divided among themselves. That is because the formation of a new church represented a preferred method of resolving doctrinal disagreements. Early Americans' seemingly limitless capacity for separation continually extended an already impressive religious diversity. Choices have proliferated and differences have been multiplied ever since. By 1850, there were four distinct varieties of Methodists and eight distinct varieties of Baptists in the United States. Thus, from the mid-eighteenth-century onward, most Americans would have to live amid a range of faiths, all endowed with similar legal rights.[9]

If the range of churches in early America provides one reason to focus on the issue of religious pluralism, the contemporary importance of religion offers another. Even though church membership rates stayed low (less than one in five) through the eighteenth century, a much larger percentage of Americans (perhaps as many as eight in ten) attended church regularly. At the same time, printed sermons and theological treatises were widely purchased and widely read. There was, moreover, hardly an occasion in either private or public in which God was not invoked. It may not, then, be shocking to learn that serious consideration was given to religious diversity long before it was given to ethnic or political diversity. Several decades before they imagined the formation of open, organized party competition, and two centuries before the emergence of ethnic multiculturalism, Americans wrote extensively about the importance of getting along with those whose religious beliefs were quite distinct. If political and ethnic diversity were not regular topics of public discussion, neither were the rights of political dissent or the preservation of ethnic autonomy especially valued ideals. Though private religious liberty was often an object of sacred reverence for eighteenth-century Americans, political opinions and ethnic affiliations garnered no comparable protections.[10]

There is a third reason to focus on the development of religious pluralism. The success that early Americans had at maintaining civil peace and encouraging cooperative endeavors between different religious groups provided a reassuring template for those that followed. In whatever form pluralism surfaced thereafter, it usually began with the popularization of roughly equal rights in speech, property, and assembly, continued with the integration of social and political institutions, and was always characterized by a shift in public rhetoric toward some kind of equal recognition. In this way, the political egalitarianism prevalent by the 1840s, like the ethnic pluralism and gender consciousness developing by the late 1960s, followed a well-trodden path. For ordinary white men of the early nineteenth century and white women and African Americans of the late twentieth century, the achievement of formal legal equality made integration possible, while integration made respectful language necessary. Today we distinguish ourselves as right-thinking people by our inclusive rhetoric about race and ethnicity. Mid-nineteenth-century folks did it by displaying their reverence for the common man. Eighteenth-century Americans demonstrated their "liberality" by making ecumenical statements about religion.

Indeed, it's not hard to locate some striking resemblances between the development of late eighteenth-century religious pluralism and the development of modern multiculturalism. Although eighteenth and early nineteenth-century Americans usually did not celebrate diversity as a positive good or insist upon the preservation of every unique identity, they nonetheless found ways of addressing important religious differences in ways that exceeded toleration. If they did not accord legitimacy to the most culturally distant religions or the most suppressed, the egalitarianism they articulated demanded the same sort of cultural leap that multiculturalism has required from those living at the beginning of the twenty-first century. Throughout early America, standards of public expression changed to accommodate the unprecedented diversity of beliefs, practices, and institutional affiliations that made up the nation's religious landscape. Along the way, the bounds of mutual respect and the expressions of solidarity expanded dramatically, and began to include previously marginal groups and unorthodox beliefs. Like the toleration that preceded it, such recognition may have been offered begrudgingly, it may have often been insincere, and it may have been generally confined to Protestant Christians, yet the very fact that it needed to be given at all is testimony to the momentous change that had occurred. Eighteenth-century Americans extended what the philosopher Charles Taylor terms "a presumption of equal worth" to a wide range of beliefs and institutions.[11]

Developments of this nature should probably not faze us. A casual observer of our own culture could tell you that a diverse society in which individuals are treated as the legal equals of one another may require a different set of norms for behavior and speech. In the case of eighteenth-century Americans, the religious integration of their society prompted a newfound inclination to find points of fundamental agreement and a newfound sensitivity to the harm caused by aspersions cast upon other faiths. Outside judgments, indeed, any kind of religious authority, stood on increasingly tenuous ground. Just as they removed the legal barriers that prevented them from practicing their religion freely and speaking their views openly, early Americans increasingly deferred to the descriptions that individuals and churches offered of themselves. In short, as people acquired greater freedom to define their own religious experiences, their liberty to criticize other people's diminished. A pluralistic society required nothing less.

One could justly argue about the extent of these achievements. And it would indeed be a mistake to think of late eighteenth-century America as some inclusive nirvana. The routine denigration and occasional persecution of eighteenth-century Catholics presents one of the more glaring exceptions to the argument being advanced here. Anti-Catholicism possessed a long and venerable tradition within Anglo-American culture, and remained vibrant into the revolutionary period. Almost everywhere in colonial America, Catholics were denied civil offices, militia service, and voting rights. They were taxed to support Protestant churches and routinely harassed. Yet before we draw the conclusion that Protestant tolerance for other Protestants was insignificant, it should be remembered that the vast majority of white American colonists belonged to a wide range of Protestant denominations. Catholics, meanwhile, made up a very small proportion of the colonial population—probably no more than one percent. Of the fifty-six known Roman Catholic churches established in the colonies at the time of independence, the vast majority were in Delaware, Maryland, and Pennsylvania. Moreover, the legal disabilities that Catholics suffered, and the indignities they endured throughout much of the eighteenth-century must be seen in the light of a long-standing Protestant hostility toward Catholicism and a longstanding suspicion of Catholic political motives. Eighteenth-century Americans feared that Catholic armies, accompanied by their Indian allies, were ever poised to strike and that, in such a conflict, only Protestants would prove reliable citizens and soldiers. When the threat of imminent attack faded, so did much of the anti-Catholic animus. During and

after the American Revolution, Catholics enjoyed a reprieve from the heretofore unrelenting charge of "popish" intrigue. For several decades thereafter,
they were frequently accorded the same deference Protestants enjoyed.

Native Americans and African Americans enjoyed no such reprieve.
Those called "heathens" by their white contemporaries were consistent objects of Christian proselytizing. Seldom did the traditional beliefs of either
group receive public acknowledgment, let alone respect. With a few important exceptions, white colonists simply had difficulty viewing those outside
the monotheistic faiths as religious. While some devout missionaries managed to muster admiration for Indian believers, even they professed contempt
for Indian beliefs. From the very beginning, Native American religions were
equated with witchcraft and devil worship. Traditional African beliefs and
rituals fared no better in European opinion. Part of the explanation lies in
the fact that neither Native Americans nor African Americans confronted
Europeans with the confident, carefully structured networks of belief that
Protestants would have associated with alternative religious systems, such
as Catholicism, Islam, or Judaism. The authority of Native American shamans and belief in the efficacy of customary spiritual remedies were deeply
shaken by the devastation wrought by European-borne diseases. African faiths
fared still worse—as religious systems, they simply did not survive colonial
American slavery. By the late eighteenth-century, Native American faiths
survived mostly in fragments, while West African faiths persisted only in
traces.[12]

European contempt for Native American and African faiths was embedded within an even more encompassing disdain toward non-European cultures. In fact, the persistent refrain that Native Americans and African
Americans needed to be civilized before they could become Christians, as well
as the continued deprecations of their religious practices and beliefs after they
did convert, might lead us to the conclusion that early American whites were
not genuinely interested in bringing their faith to non-Europeans. The Reverend Hugh Jones of Virginia, for example, suggested that it was a "Prosti-
tution" of the baptismal sacrament to extend it to "wild Indians and new
Negroes" who seemed attached to "their own barbarous Ways." By the end of
the colonial period, Christian teaching had been made available to only a tiny
fraction of blacks and Indians. Nor did Christian baptism (a practice usually
neglected) bring release from slavery or other forms of social oppression.
African American and Native American church members almost always occupied subordinate roles within the churches, just as they did within the
larger society. The former were sometimes forced to sit so far back in the
meetinghouses that they could not hear their minister's sermons. For a time,

upstart evangelical churches, such as the Separate Baptists and the Methodists, treated black worshipers like brothers and sisters in faith. Yet as the
status of their churches improved, even these groups succumbed to the racism that stood in marked contrast to the religious equality that so many white
Americans professed to embrace.[13]

We can locate still more exceptions to the general pattern of religious
pluralism in the nineteenth century. During the 1830s and 1840s, the
founders of the Church of Jesus Christ of Latter-Day Saints, or Mormons,
were continually harassed and beaten. At approximately the same time,
Catholic churches and convents were burned. And, of course, throughout the
twentieth century, Jews, Buddhists, Hindus, and, more recently, Muslims
have endured repeated rounds of discrimination. All of this has been sufficient to convince some that eighteenth-century Americans were far from
pluralistic. Even those who do concede that America has developed into a
religiously pluralistic nation push its appearance back to the late nineteenth,
or even the late twentieth century. According to the leading scholar of modern
religious pluralism, Diana L. Eck, America maintained its exclusionary approach to religious differences until roughly 1965.[14]

As vital as Eck's work has been, it underestimates the religious pluralism
that emerged in eighteenth-century America and the capacity of Americans to
maintain it ever since. The fact that eighteenth-century religious pluralism
was generally extended only to white Protestants should not obscure its significance. When we measure the intra-Protestant ecumenism of the late
eighteenth century against the intra-Protestant persecution that had prevailed
across much of northwestern Europe and colonial America for the previous
century and a half, the change is stunning. Until the beginning of the eighteenth century, religious differences had always been treated with disdain if
not violence. But by the end of the eighteenth century, Eck's description of her
own Christian pluralism—it is "incumbent upon Christians" to "witness to
their faith," but "not fine for us to bear false witness against neighbors of
other faiths"—would have found many sympathetic ears. As early as 1753, the
New York essayist and politician William Livingston wrote: "I Believe, that to
defend the Christian Religion is one Thing, and to knock a Man in the Head
for being of a different, is another Thing." Livingston's blunt statement was
not all that distant from Eck's. Few would be startled to learn that pluralistic
ideals were first applied to white Protestants by white Protestants. Fewer still
would be surprised to learn that many white Protestants acted in a manner
grossly inconsistent with those ideals. Yet, as Bishop Carroll's experiences and
the Philadelphia parade of 1788 suggest, the civil treatment of Jews and
Catholics was already evident at the founding. Since then, the scope of

American religious pluralism has certainly extended much further. Nonetheless, its basic premises have been with us since the beginning.[15]

A note must be made regarding the subjects examined on the following pages. Every first-year graduate student in history will readily point out that the "Americans" to whom this book refers are almost exclusively adult, white, and male—and, very often, ordained clergyman. However, it's worth observing that if there were standards of public discourse in the eighteenth century, adult, white, male Protestants articulated them. Ministers represented the largest professional group of writers in the American colonies. They possessed a virtual monopoly when it came to religious publications. In this way, as in others, eighteenth-century ministers were the intellectual leaders of their communities. They were the ones who would have attended Oxford, Harvard, or William and Mary. They were the ones who purchased large collections of learned tracts and corresponded with friends in other colonies or in Great Britain. They were the ones to whom local parishioners were compelled to listen—in some cases, several times a week. It was they who spoke on the days when militias drilled and voters gathered to cast their ballots. They were the ones who shaped the social and cultural assumptions that had to be accepted, brashly resisted, or reluctantly endured. And while their opinions may have sometimes been ridiculed and their instructions often ignored, most of them were dependent upon their parishioners for their positions. These self-described shepherds could not stray too far from their flock's fundamental assumptions.[16]

One further caveat is in order. The audience for eighteenth- and early nineteenth-century religious writing was largely male. But the audience for the sermons that ministers personally delivered on Sundays would have been heavily female. In fact, throughout the years examined here, the majority of members in most colonial churches were probably women. Except for the Quakers and a few short-lived separatist groups, however, the churches forbade females from regular preaching and church elections, just as contemporary governments excluded women from civil offices. And no colonial-era woman was known to have contributed regularly to the newspapers or the pamphlet literature. Nonetheless, the early modern history of female piety and religious dissent may have shared a good deal in common. It is clear, for instance, that women's speech was curtailed throughout the colonial period. There is also evidence that female religious leadership was equated with religious heterodoxy. Moreover, the research of historian Catherine Brekus has revealed that female preaching became much more widespread and far less controversial following the disestablishment of America's churches during the founding period. Unfortunately, we do not have enough information to say whether the same rights of private judgment and, later, full religious liberty, applied to women *within families*. That is, we do not yet know to what extent early American women could dissent from their husbands' beliefs and practice. There is another whole book to be written on the topic. The present work will focus on those differences that preoccupied religious institutions and civil governments between the seventeenth and nineteenth centuries: the conflicts over doctrine and practice, between churches and within them, which had once resulted in great wars and inspired countless executions.[17]

Ultimately, the following pages offer readers a brief introduction to the kinds of problems that arose when a culture premised upon uniformity gave way to a culture premised upon diversity. While they have not addressed the entire range of early American opinions on the subject of religious differences, I hope that they have at least recovered the major questions that these issues presented, as well as the general tenor of debate and the core of assumptions that would be employed in developing the answers. This is, after all, a story about our own time as well, of great hope and great uncertainty. For if religious pluralism represents one of the most laudable features of the modern world, it also ranks among the most difficult to achieve and maintain.

I

The Plague of Dissent

And the Rise of Toleration

All the days wherein the plague shall be in him he shall be defiled; he is unclean: he shall dwell alone; without the camp shall his habitation be.

—Leviticus 13:46

The Believer's private judgment of discerning, implies a supernatural ability, of knowing what he judges, to be certainly true; and therefore such a private judgment, is always right...no man ever had a right to judge wrong, and many men that have a right of judging, do abuse it, to make wrong judgments.

—Hugh Fisher, *A Preservative from Damnable Error* (1730)

As he approached the gallows on Boston Common in the late winter of 1661, William Leddra may have experienced a glimmer of relief. Leddra was probably aware that his impending death would be neither painless nor short. Once his body dropped from the tree limb, the noose would tighten around his neck, cutting the air passage through his trachea until he died of strangulation. Leddra probably also knew that he might very well expire in a convulsive fit, emptying his bowels and foaming at the mouth. Yet having spent the winter shackled to a log in a cold, damp prison cell, this devout Quaker must have also anticipated a glorious afterlife where his sufferings would be redeemed. Offered an opportunity to recant and avoid such a terrifying end, Leddra refused. He would neither forsake his faith and join one of the established Congregationalist churches nor stay out of Massachusetts. He remained as committed to the absolute truth of his faith as his persecutors were to theirs. So on March 14, 1661, William Leddra passed from this world.[1]

Leddra's hanging marked the last of four that occurred over a two-year span. The executions confirmed Massachusetts' reputation for intolerance from London to Providence. Contemporary observers were appalled. The colony's authorities, however, saw no alternative. Quakers had been coming together for unauthorized religious gatherings, publishing tracts favorable to their sect, and proselytizing among the Congregational laity. Every one of these actions constituted a punishable offense. To this point, however, cropped ears and public floggings had produced no discernible change in Quaker behavior. Quaker missionaries remained stubbornly determined to spread the truth they knew, even if it meant interrupting Congregationalist meetings. Instead of keeping their heretical thoughts to themselves, they displayed a seemingly irrepressible inclination to impose them on others.[2] The Massachusetts General Court felt it had exercised every other recourse. If a man could not be blamed for protecting his family from "persons infected wth the plague of pestilence or other contagious, noisome, & mortall diseases," neither could the legislature be blamed for protecting its subjects from this spiritual plague. In executing these afflicted souls, the Court claimed, it had done what any responsible father would have.[3]

Never again in American history would government officials hang a person for his or her religious beliefs. The horror that the Quaker executions evoked among outsiders was shared by later generations of New Englanders. The recently restored king of England, Charles II, brought a rapid end to the executions. Thirty years later, the British government would force the Puritan Commonwealth to accept a policy of toleration. Yet in its zealous persecution of the Quakers, the Bay colony had followed a long-accepted formula for dealing with religious differences. Most seventeenth-century European and American governments suppressed dissent. In their role as guardians of public order and spiritual uniformity, they confined minority beliefs to private settings, denying them the public access and recognition that established faiths enjoyed. An increasingly widespread commitment to religious toleration would emerge during the second half of the seventeenth and the first half of the eighteenth centuries. Nonetheless, legally sanctioned assemblies of worshipers, open proselytizing, and religious publications—not to mention public dignity—remained the preserve of established clergymen and churches. The idea that these figurative fathers should treat dissent like a plague, that they should quarantine what they could not destroy, survived many decades past William Leddra's body.[4]

The Religious Settlement of British America

Beginning students of American history often make the forgivable mistake of assuming that Britain's North American colonies began as cradles of religious freedom. It would be more accurate to say that many of the early colonies began as sanctuaries for religious *dissenters*, particularly those seeking to escape the impositions of established churches in northwestern Europe. Whether they protected religious liberty was another matter. Almost right from its founding in 1682, Pennsylvania was known throughout Europe as an asylum for persecuted minorities. New England represented a "City upon a Hill" for the English Puritans who could no longer endure the spiritual "corruption" or the legal disabilities they encountered back home. And the southern colonies attracted oppressed Protestants (known as Huguenots) fleeing the oppression of an absolutist French monarchy. Yet only a minority of European migrants settled in colonies where extensive religious liberties prevailed from the beginning. Moreover, some of these dissenters proved perfectly capable of systematic intolerance themselves. No sooner had the Massachusetts Bay colony been established as a Puritan refuge from the Church of England than Rhode Island was established as a dissenting refuge from Massachusetts Puritans. The Quakers who were hung on Boston Common between 1659 and 1661 illustrated what might happen to those who challenged the orthodoxy that former dissenters had created themselves.

Early modern authorities on both sides of the Atlantic possessed a perfectly good reason to suppress religious dissent: they knew they were right and the dissenters wrong. They operated under the reasonable premise that there could only be one legitimate form of religious truth. For this tradition they owed something to the Roman Catholic Church, whose beliefs and institutions had structured religious affairs in much of western Europe for centuries. There was, according to the conciliar decrees of 1215, one universal church and no salvation outside it. The Church was never as universal as it hoped and rarely as oppressive as critics later claimed. Yet, for an entire millennium, it squelched every serious challenge to its religious rule. The heresies of the Cathars, the Waldensians, and the Hussites all met dismal fates. Dissenters confronted the severest repression from the thirteenth through the seventeenth centuries as the Church tracked down errant souls and—barring a torture-induced decision to repent—delivered them to the flames. To be sure, few if any persecuted groups should be revered as patrons of religious pluralism. In the opinion of historian Perez Zagorin, the heretics would have established their own faiths and imposed their own forms of intolerance had they been in charge.[5]

At the start of the sixteenth century, one dissident movement finally succeeded. An uprising of discontented ministers and laypeople, which would become known as the Protestant Reformation, broke the Catholic Church's grip on western Europe. Condemning the mediation of priests, the corruption of bishops, and the abuse of the sacraments, the German monk Martin Luther fomented a revolution in the name of sincere faith, plain scripture, and the individual's right to read the Bible in his own way. But neither church establishments nor the ideal of uniformity disappeared. In place of the one, universal, Catholic Church, the princes and kings who ruled northern Europe created their own exclusive church establishments. When the Peace of Augsburg brought a temporary end to religious warfare between Protestants and Catholics in the middle of the sixteenth century, the parties involved agreed to recognize whatever church each state called its own. Confessional boundaries would conform to political boundaries. The Latin phrase, *Cuius regio, eius religio,* encapsulated the resolution upon which most of Europe would arrive: "as the ruler, so the religion." If you were a resident of Florence, you lived under the political rule of the Medici, and you took your religious instructions from the Vatican. If you made your home in northern Germany, you lived under the rule of Lutheran princes and paid for the support of the Lutheran Church. Of course, all this might very well change when your prince was deposed or decided to embrace a new faith.[6]

Catholic or Protestant, Lutheran or Calvinist, all the states of eighteenth-century Europe bestowed exclusive privileges on a favored church. Offices and tax revenues were shared. Theological doctrines and political ideologies were fused. Those who differed from the established church were usually suspected of political disloyalty as well. The perpetuation of a single theology and a single ecclesiastical system was the ideal to which most religious and political leaders aspired and toward which some made considerable progress. Even in the famously tolerant and diverse Dutch Republic, the Reformed Church remained established to the end of the eighteenth century. Dissenting ministers relied upon their own congregations for support, while Dutch Reformed ministers enjoyed the largesse of a government whose revenues were contributed by people of every denomination. Dutch religious dissenters could neither hold public office nor freely voice their grievances.[7]

The story was similar in the nation from which most of the American colonists migrated. England's religious affairs were dominated by the Anglican Church, which achieved its independence from the Roman Catholic Church in 1534. In England, a growing reform movement had coincided with Henry VIII's unrequited desire for papal annulment of his marriage to bring about the separation from Rome. Queen Elizabeth's Act of Uniformity (1559) reinstated the Protestant Church of England for good and prescribed penalties for nonconformity. Like other seventeenth-century states, England punished a number of religion-related offenses, including blasphemy, atheism, and heresy. It also prohibited sincere dissenters from holding civil or military office, worshiping openly, or preaching where they pleased. English Catholics received especially harsh treatment. With them, the connection between dissent and political subversion seemed more than an abstraction. Partly in response to actual plots against the monarchy, the government required an oath of allegiance to the crown, which compelled the Catholic faithful to renounce the pope's injunctions to overthrow excommunicant princes.

Here, in brief, was the background for the religious settlement of British North America. At the end of the sixteenth and the beginning of the seventeenth centuries, European governments were not the powerful imperial institutions that they would become in the eighteenth century. So when the challenge of establishing colonies in North America arose, the task devolved upon a range of proprietors and joint-stock companies, and each colonial enterprise came to be distinguished by its own particular religious institutions. Consequently, the tapestry of church-state relations in Britain's North American colonies defies easy description. None of England's mainland settlements imposed religious tests or articles of belief as did most of their counterparts in Europe. Yet because of the decentralized character of early settlement, faith would long remain a largely local affair—highly segmented and internally uniform.[8]

Before they could establish their own peculiar forms of religious life on North America, of course, European settlers had to displace the Indian souls that dwelled there. Colonial accounts of the European-borne diseases that wiped out entire villages within a matter of weeks were notable for the callous disregard they displayed toward Native Americans, as well as for their confidence that God had a hand in such seemingly fortuitous developments. An example was the revisionist history of Rhode Island and Providence Plantations published by the Baptist minister John Callendar in 1739. This influential tract extolled the tradition of religious liberty that distinguished Rhode Island from almost every other part of the Western world at the time. Noting wryly that early Massachusetts' authorities had (as was the custom of the day) suppressed heretics so "that they might not infect the Church, or injure the publick Peace," Callendar went on to assert that God had readied an "Asylum" for Massachusetts' exiles to the south by killing the Native Americans who inhabited the region. Though these dissenters had experienced hardship in their new home, they had been spared the diseases that afflicted local tribes in the years before white settlement. The military annihilation of the Pequot had helped, but the key to English success in Rhode Island was the spread of "infectious Distempers" among the native peoples. Callendar recounted how the Indians were so weakened by their illnesses that "the Living sufficed not to bury the Dead, and the Ground was covered with their Bones in many Places." "This," he proclaimed, "wonderfully made Room for the *English*."[9]

Two decades prior to the English settlement of Massachusetts and Rhode Island, God made room for English colonists on the southern shore of the Chesapeake Bay. The Virginia Company, which established a fortified outpost on the James River in 1607, immediately established the Church of England throughout the region. The accoutrements of a typical church-state alliance remained in place through much of the eighteenth century in colonial Virginia. Parish vestries were entitled to collect taxes from their communities, property-owning male Anglicans enjoyed exclusive access to political offices, and Anglican ministers were called upon to deliver public addresses. Anyone who differed from the Church of England was categorized as a schismatic, a divider of the church, and was punished accordingly. A mid-seventeenth-century Virginia law declared that those "schismatical persons" who "out of their averseness to the orthodox established religion, or out of the new-fangled conceits of their own heretical inventions, refuse[d] to have their children baptized" would be subject to heavy fines. Anglican establishments were eventually erected throughout the South—in Maryland, South Carolina, and eventually North Carolina and Georgia. Though usually less severe in enforcing conformity, these colonies developed the same basic establishment scheme that prevailed in Virginia.[10]

Tens of thousands of so-called Puritans settled in New England during the early 1630s because they could not abide either England or its established church. They complained of too much worldliness in the former and too much Catholicism in the latter. The Puritans were reform-minded Calvinists. In other words, they were zealous Protestants who condemned church decorations, ecclesiastical hierarchies, and many traditional Christian rituals, as well as the notion that salvation had anything to do with good works. Eventually the Puritans gave up their hope of purifying the Church of England and became known as Congregationalists. Sometime before departing for the New World, they managed to have the Massachusetts Bay Company's charter transferred to North America. This awkward arrangement left a group of embittered dissenters from the king's church to run the king's colony. The Congregationalists who would have been denied the right to worship freely in Jamestown discriminated against dissenters in Massachusetts and Connecticut. In those New England colonies, compulsory taxes flowed into Congregational coffers and public legitimacy graced Congregational acts. Well into

the eighteenth century, the descendants of the Puritans suppressed unconventional opinions and guarded the colony's Calvinist orthodoxy. As a consequence, groups such as the Baptists, who thought that baptismal immersion
should wait for the consent of believing adults and that the state had no
business meddling in church affairs, were welcome neither on the banks of
the Charles River nor along the shores of Connecticut.

Because of a series of equally unlikely historical accidents, the European
dissenters who made their homes between Rhode Island and Maryland enjoyed
unprecedented freedom from church establishments. Those who associate colonial America with liberty of conscience usually have Pennsylvania in mind,
where the absence of a state-supported church and generous provisions for
religious minorities gave that colony a reputation for tolerance throughout the
Western world. The peculiarities of Pennsylvania's religious settlement bore the
same marks of serendipity that characterized settlements elsewhere in the colonies. During the late seventeenth century, England's King Charles II repaid a
debt to one of his admirals by donating an immense tract of land west of the
Delaware River to the officer's son, a Quaker leader named William Penn.
Pennsylvania would soon become a haven for all varieties of European faiths.
The distinct territories of East and West Jersey were also awarded to Quaker
proprietors. They later united to form New Jersey, which continued to protect
liberty of conscience. Though no religious establishment was maintained in
either of the Jerseys or in Pennsylvania, Quakers exercised a large measure of
control over local culture and politics until the middle of the eighteenth century.
The Quakers were a small persecuted minority in England, distinguished from
their fellow Protestants by their refusal to appoint ministers, their commitment
to plainness of dress and speech, and their opposition to violence. Their dominance in Pennsylvania would eventually end because of the generous freedom of
worship they offered to all Protestants. Liberal immigration laws and the
promise of religious toleration drew a flood of newcomers during the early
decades of the eighteenth century. Large numbers of Presbyterians, Anglicans,
and German Lutheran migrants eventually made the Delaware Valley one of
the most religiously diverse regions in the entire world.[11]

New York was already religiously diverse when, in 1664, a small English
fleet captured the Dutch colony that was then called New Netherland. The
colony's new rulers formalized the informal Dutch tradition of tolerating
dissent. New York's earliest laws guaranteed that Christians would have
neither their private religious meetings nor their individual modes of worship
disturbed. At the same time, the religious parochialism that already characterized so much of Europe and colonial America would also take root here. By
the end of the seventeenth century, the Anglican Church had been tentatively

established in four southern New York counties. Arrangements in the remaining counties were determined by local circumstances. New York permitted any church to act as the established church in its town, so long as it could obtain the support of the residents.

Thus, in New York, as in much of early colonial America, the structure of faith depended on where you lived. Well into the eighteenth century, European Americans generally conceived of religious belief and practice in specific geographic terms. Each town or parish was orthodox unto itself. In this way, they continued the Old World tradition of assigning established ministers to individual parishes and conferring upon them the "responsibility for propagating and maintaining Christian practice and belief among the entire population, not just among a few knowledgeable and loyal believers." Practical considerations helped ensure the vitality of religious parochialism. Even where religious support was voluntary, as in Rhode Island, it was often too expensive for a town's population to support more than one church and one minister. Consequently, while early eighteenth-century ministers understood their own beliefs to be absolutely true and universally valid, they also worked under the assumption that particular forms of faith had particular, geographic lines of demarcation. To early modern minds, religious belief was no mere abstraction. It was inscribed in their buildings, their civil institutions, in every ceremony their church required. The church's calendars organized the months, its clocks organized the days, and its rituals organized both individual and collective action. Whether you loved the parish minister or hated him, he would usually perform your marriage ceremony. In turn, you would usually pay taxes for his support. Public notices might be posted on the established church's door and election results read from its porch. Within such a context, dissent was more than wrong. It was seditious.[12]

The persistent ideal of uniformity throughout much of colonial America ensured that disagreements would still count as "dissent" and that those who disagreed with official authorities would remain "dissenters." Take the 1730 pamphlet titled *A Letter from a Minister of the Church of England to His Dissenting Parishioners.* In this tract, the New York Anglican James Wetmore laid down two propositions that must have seemed preposterous to his non-Anglican readers. First, he claimed that they, "His Dissenting Parishioners," were obliged to receive him as their minister. Second, he declared that they were obliged not to attend any others *"in Opposition"* to him—meaning their own ministers. By the standards of the Presbyterians, the Congregationalists, or even the Quakers, Wetmore maintained, he qualified for ministerial service. Moreover, as an Anglican divine, he enjoyed the sanction of apostolic succession, which brought all of these groups within his jurisdiction.[13]

Wetmore shared his perspective with the Connecticut Anglican, Samuel Johnson, who, in 1733, published a tract with an identical heading: *A Letter from a Minister of the Church of England to His Dissenting Parishioners*. Johnson requested an opportunity to demonstrate how erroneous his "Dissenting Parishioners" were. He promised to reveal how badly they had erred and why they should return to "the Church"—as if these Congregationalists had just packed up and left the Church of England the previous Sunday, rather than a century before. Those to whom Johnson addressed his epistle had probably never entered an Anglican church. But they were nonetheless "His Dissenting Parishioners," and Johnson chastised them for their complaints of oppression when they well understood that they had had been tolerated for the last fifty years. He also counseled these dissenters to "shut your Mouths."[14]

Non-Anglicans always professed to find such Anglican pretensions baffling. The Rev. John Graham wondered to whom Johnson referred when he used the phrase "His *Dissenting* Parishioners." It could not have been the Anglicans in his own church. That would have been absurd. But neither, Graham continued, could "it properly be the Presbyterians [a term used synonymously with "Congregationalists" in Connecticut] for these are here of the established Church." It was as "absurd to call a Presbyterian, a Dissenter" in New Haven as it was in Edinburgh. Johnson must have mistaken America for England. In Connecticut, the Presbyterians were as established as they were in Scotland. Moreover, he contended, only the Toleration Act secured Johnson's right to preach. It was Johnson, in fact, who dissented. This Anglican minister, not his non-Anglican "Parishioners," required the indulgence of the colonial church establishment.[15]

Who dissented? Whose church was established? The issue was debated from the very earliest years of colonial settlement. Sometimes the debate took the form of abstruse theoretical discourses and sometimes it took more concrete forms. In early eighteenth-century Rhode Island, for instance, an Anglican minister named James MacSparran disputed a local Congregationalist minister's claim to land granted "for the use of an Orthodox Person." MacSparran argued that he, as an "Orthodox" minister, was entitled to the land. In old England, he would have enjoyed an undivided right to the title because the Anglican Church was the established church there. But he enjoyed no such privileges in Rhode Island. MacSparran lost his case before the Rhode Island Supreme Court, as well as his appeal to the Privy Council in London, which ruled that the Church of England *should* have been treated as the "Orthodox" church, but that the grant had been clearly intended for a Congregationalist. Similarly, when the Baptist merchant Thomas Hollis offered to endow a professorship at Harvard in 1722, it was on the condition that adherence to the doctrine of adult baptism not disqualify any candidates. Apparently the grant also stipulated that the individual maintain "sound and orthodox" principles. To the Congregationalist overseers who ran Harvard, of course, "orthodox" meant non-Baptist and so they stipulated (undoubtedly to Hollis's chagrin) that only those committed to infant baptism (in other words, no Baptists) would be considered.[16]

Who dissented? Who was orthodox? Johnson, Wetmore, and Graham all made the traditional assumption that someone had to be orthodox and that anyone who disagreed was a dissenter. In many parts of British North America, however, this framework never quite worked—and it would become even less relevant as the eighteenth century proceeded. The confusing mélange of church-state relations in America would long remain a source of aggravation to pastors who were accustomed to the comforting privileges of establishment. Worse still, they found that as the number of dissenting groups multiplied, the inherited ideal of uniformity became untenable. During the middle decades of the eighteenth century, Virginia Anglicans witnessed an influx of Presbyterians and Baptists; New England Congregationalists watched the construction of dozens of Baptist and Quaker meetinghouses; and Quakers contemplated the loss of their hegemony in Pennsylvania as Scots-Irish Presbyterians and German Pietists poured into their colony. This explosion in the size and variety of the colonial population proved instrumental in widening the chasm between the inherited ideal of uniformity and the actual conditions in which people lived. The change was particularly evident in the realm of print. The increasing number of literate individuals with different religious affiliations raised the odds that a writer would be read by an audience made up of individuals from different religious backgrounds. By midcentury, readers became less familiar with the authors they read, and writers lost the sense of intimacy that they had once had with their audiences.[17]

It would take some time, however, before the imaginations of America's religious leaders were conditioned to the realities of a land that could contain many churches and a world of printed, public discourse that would recognize them all. Until then, disagreement would retain its association with dissent, and dissent would retain its association with rebellion against church, state, and God. Even amid the complexities of colonial governance, church establishments maintained their hold over religious language for many decades. Old habits die hard and the institution of established religion was indeed an old habit. Throughout colonial America, as in early modern Europe, vocal religious dissent continued to carry the same metaphoric associations as political criticism. Both appeared to operate through subterfuge. Both seemed to threaten the foundations of church and state. And, as the volume of news-papers, pamphlets, and books swelled, both seemed on the verge of an epi-demic expansion.

The Disease of Dissent

For the first few decades the eighteenth century, not much changed when it came to the understanding of religious differences. Most early eighteenth-century religious commentators wrote with the traditional conviction that church, community, and audience were indeed the same thing. According to prevailing opinion, church authorities had the obligation to do as the Lord said unto the servant: "compel them to come in, that my house might be filled." They were responsible for maintaining the community of believers in the one, true mode of faith. The answer to the Prophet Amos's question—Can two walk together, except they be agreed?—was a resounding "No." Indeed, it was be-lieved that God would eventually unleash his wrath upon heretics, as well as any people that permitted heresy to flourish among them. Well into the eighteenth century, most of those who published their thoughts were orthodox ministers in what were often established churches. These men usually wrote with the assurance that dissenting beliefs were wrong beliefs and that dis-senters were obliged to "come in" to their houses of worship. And they usually assumed that their audience agreed with them.[18]

On the established view, dissent from the church was a subversive ac-tivity; it threatened to undermine the very hierarchy upon which the authority of orthodox ministers rested. To justify his claims, Samuel Johnson cited imposing institutions and authorities. "That you are my Parishioners," he wrote, "is as true, as it is that I am appointed Minister of this Town and the Places adjacent, by the Honourable Society incorporated by Royal Charter for providing Ministers for the Plantations, and by the Bishop of *London* to whom the Ecclesiastical Government of them is committed by the supreme Au-thority of our Nation." Then he added: "And for this I can produce my Instructions." The insistence that religious disagreement could be settled through official instructions or doctrinal conformity, the idea that ministers of other denominations constituted some form of opposition, and the assump-tion that authoritative arguments on ecclesiology might "shut...Mouths," distinguished the writing of the seventeenth and early eighteenth centuries from that which came after. When a contemporary declared that "we think it more consistent with the spirit of the Gospel, to forbear opposing private Opinions to publick Authority" he expressed the spirit of his age.[19]

Within the imagination of the late seventeenth and early eighteenth centuries, dissent lurked menacingly outside the walls of the church. Like a plague, it threatened to deprive the inhabitants of this community not of their mortal bodies but of their immortal souls. The metaphor of plague, or infection, applied to a wide range of nefarious mechanisms during the early modern period, but seemed particularly well suited to the description of religious dissent. Deadly contagions were no distant memory for those living in the eighteenth century. Early modern society was continually beset by the ravages of communicable disease. As late as 1721, over one-half of Boston's population was stricken during a smallpox outbreak. Especially malicious epidemics could depopulate entire towns in a matter of weeks. Until the introduction of sanitary measures, isolation, exclusion, even execution seemed the only viable remedies. As much as it said about the persistent ideal of the purified church, the metaphor of disease aptly represented the early eighteenth-century sense of how erroneous opinions were transmitted. It suggested, in fact, that error was conveyed corporally, by the very proximity of its source. It suggested too, that the ordinary mind was helpless in fending it off. The best hope of escaping a contagion of corrupt opinions lay in the possibility that the disease itself might be quarantined, that its bearers might be banished, or its corrupting tendencies contained through the purification of its membership. Wherever it was found, religious heterodoxy needed to be purged.[20]

Accordingly, England's first permanent North American colonies, Virginia and Massachusetts, maintained a rigorous system of exclusion. In Virginia, the legislature imposed a fine of one hundred pounds sterling upon ships' captains who gave passage into the colony to Quakers. The publication of Quaker books was forbidden and any members of that sect discovered in Virginia were to be locked away without bail. To maintain "the purity and unity of doctrine & discipline in the church," all nonconformist ministers were to be "suspend[ed] and silence[d]" and then, if they persisted in their teaching or preaching, to be sent away from the colony as expeditiously as possible. The Virginia minister Hugh Jones conveyed these purgative sentiments in 1724. Reflecting upon the state of the contemporary church in the colony, Reverend Jones noted that Anglican ministers currently enjoyed a substantial amount of autonomy within their own parishes. While such "Liberty without Restraint" might not yield any bad consequences at present, it would make it difficult for "any heterodox, libertine, or fanatical Persons . . . to be eradicated."[21]

Puritan New England proved especially hospitable to the epidemiological analogy. When Roger Williams, the great advocate of religious liberty, accused the established ministry of persecution, John Cotton replied that "there be

some unsound, and corrupt opinions, and practices...which are more infectious, and contagious, then any plague-sore." In such cases, he noted,
banishment, or even death, might be warranted. John Winthrop's published
account of the antinomian crisis that struck the Massachusetts Bay Colony
during the mid-1630s was titled *A Short Story of the Rise, reign, and ruine of the
Antinomians, Familists & Libertines, that infected the Churches of New-England.*
Fittingly, after their concerted efforts to convince Anne Hutchinson of her
"dayngerous Opinions" failed, the General Court banished her to Rhode Island. As we know, Hutchinson was fortunate compared to the Quakers who
were hung after returning from their forced exile in Rhode Island. Almost a
century later, the rector and tutors of Yale College warned that two brothers
who had embraced a lay preacher "might Infect and Corrupt" the school. The
brothers were to be publicly castigated and, then if they continued, expelled.
Early eighteenth-century New Englanders might not have understood much
about the actual mechanics of disease, but they did understand that it was
wise to keep the infected out of their communities.[22]

When dissent proved infectious, no good could come from debating erroneous doctrines in the open air of public discussion. The best a minister
could do was prevent his congregants from even considering such errors. In a
1733 indictment of Quakerism, John Graham wrote: "Every Error is a plot of
the Devil to suppress some Truth, and is very spreading & infectious." Graham referred to his injunction against being *"carried about with divers &
strange Doctrines,"* as a "dehortation"—as an attempt at *dis*suasion. His aim
was not so much to persuade his audience of the delusion that called itself
Quakerism as it was to inoculate his listeners from the ravages of such diseases. Those with corrupt opinions, Graham dehorted, must be cut off even
from conversation and other forms of ordinary social interaction; nor should
their books be read or their ministries attended. Children, those least firm in
their understanding of doctrine, were most susceptible to infection. Indulging
his disease metaphors, Graham observed that "[i]f Parents are poisoned, the
Children are exceedingly exposed to infection." The best that parents could do
to preserve their children was to remain fixed in their orthodox beliefs. They
themselves "must not be Children in understanding, ever learning, never
coming to the knowledge of the Truth." For Graham, the value of any belief
was directly proportional to the fixity with which it was held. There was no
time to reflect impartially on the evidence that impressed itself upon us, as
some liberal writers recommended. Nothing good came from an indifferent
attitude toward the evidences before us, from a state of suspended belief.
Indeed, it was at that moment, in the bleak nothingness of indecision, that
Satan conducted his business.[23]

Viewed from the orthodox perspective, a dissenter could best serve himself and his community by keeping his contagious thoughts to himself. When dissenting forms of faith were permitted in seventeenth-century America, they were often required to remain "behind closed doors"—that is, out of the conforming public's hearing. In Maryland, which was originally founded as a refuge for persecuted English Catholics, "all Acts of the Roman Catholic Religion [were] to be done as privately as may be" and Roman Catholics were "to be silent upon all occasions of discourse concerning matters of Religion." Maryland's policy toward Catholics was replicated throughout the Anglo American world. Even when granting liberty of conscience to all groups, state officials and religious commentators urged believers to ensure that their private judgments remained private. Rhode Island's liberal charter, for example, granted religious freedom to the colony's inhabitants (for their "private opinions") on the condition that they behaved "themselves peaceablie and quietlie."[24]

Weighty orthodox tomes for adults and didactic texts for children could themselves serve as antidotes to the poison of heretical beliefs. John Graham's pamphlet was "[r]ecommended as a seasonable Antidote, to all those into whose Hands" it might land.[25] Likewise, the child's catechism, which consisted of rudimentary questions and answers on the nature of faith, was designed to help children avoid the plague of erroneous opinion. It was necessary, contemporaries thought, for them to obtain a right understanding of the Bible—as soon as, or even before, they were capable of articulating the questions themselves. In the introduction to the catechism he originally published in 1708, the Congregational minister Cotton Mather contended that error must be combated as if it were an enemy army. Employing the martial metaphors that substituted easily for the metaphor of disease during this period, Mather insisted that the *"Armour of Christianity"* was required to fortify the young *"Christian Souldier"* against the multiplying errors that would besiege his soul. As Mather described the procedure, the head of the household "would Read the *Questions* unto his capable Young People, and ask *their Opinion* of the matter therein mentioned; Then Read the *Answers* with the *Proofs*, and Lead them to, and Fix them in, the *Right Opinion.*" The *"Proofs"* contained in his book, Mather suggested, could be employed to bridge the gap between the child's opinion and "the Right Opinion," between the child's wavering, uninformed individual judgment and the truth, which never changed. Of course, he concluded, "[w]ere the Truth more Practised, it would be less *Disputed.*"[26]

The fantasy that dissent from the Truth might be so easily contained is probably as old as organized religion itself. But here, on the threshold of an age that witnessed the blossoming of printed debate and the proliferation of doctrines and modes of worship, this fantasy took on particular significance. Conversations that had once been confined to the home or resolved within the church were increasingly conducted before a wider audience. Newspapers, books, and short polemical tracts, known as pamphlets, were becoming increasingly common in colonial America. Into the eighteenth century, each medium served as a powerful vehicle for orthodox ideals. For many years, in fact, newspapers included the phrase, "Printed by authority," on their mastheads. But by 1720s, the volume of printed works had become too great and their authors too diverse for public authorities to fully control. Contemporary ambivalence over the use of print was best expressed by Jonathan Dickinson who chose to employ what he called an "interlocutory way of writing" in defending Presbyterian ordination. Dickinson was optimistic that the printed word could be harnessed to the cause of religious unity. Properly applied, he suggested, it constituted just one more instrument of true faith.[27]

Real dialogue with actual dissenters was considerably riskier as the Connecticut Congregationalist John Bulkley learned in his 1727 debate with the Baptist leader Valentine Wightman. The Baptists were only now beginning to make inroads in this notoriously orthodox colony. They had discovered Connecticut to be an inhospitable place for dissenters. Wightman, whose grandfather had been burned at the stake more than a century before (the last English nonconformist to perish in that fashion), established the colony's first Baptist church in 1705. A second was organized five years later. Until the late 1720s that had been it. Recently, however, a young Baptist minister was called to preach by a New London congregation. When ministers of that faith made arrangements to meet in New London "for the propagation of their opinions," the standing clergy requested a debate.[28] Like other colonies at the same time, Connecticut was beginning to taste the religious diversity that would soon become an integral part of American life. The orthodox would have to act quickly if they wished halt this contagion. Among those who rushed to meet the Baptists in New London was none other than Cotton Mather, famed inoculator of bodies and souls.

The events leading up to the debate provide a glimpse of the asymmetrical relationships and the callous language that characterized interactions between established clergymen and their dissenting counterparts. A preparatory conference was marked by the plaintive requests of the Baptists and the haughty refusals of the Congregationalists. This dispute would be carried on, like religious life generally, by the rules of the orthodox clergy.[29]

Yet, there was trouble brewing here for the established authorities who had agreed to join in public debate. Bulkley himself expressed a reluctance to participate. That was, until he discovered how impudent the "Sectaries" had become. The very use of the designation "Sectaries" conveys the disdain with which dissenting individuals were treated. To be a sectarian was to occupy a subordinate role within society, to be something not entirely legitimate, to think and act with the double consciousness—that is, always being forced to see oneself through other's eyes—that W. E. B. DuBois ascribed to African Americans at the beginning of the twentieth century and Simon de Beauvoir to women a few decades later. Perhaps it was a vague inkling that his print audience might include some who did not share his assumptions that prompted Bulkley to define the term. "By Sectaries," he wrote:

> there intend certain persons among us of a various and uncer-
> tain Principle & Denomination, and who, perhaps, agree not
> among themselves in many things, besides an Opposing the Truth
> and them that stand for it: And are therefore ordinarilily [sic] spoken
> of under the different Denominations of Seventh Day, First Day and
> No Day Baptists, Quakers, Seekers, &c.

Bulkley thus denied the Baptists a single name, assigning them an identity that was both plural and indeterminate. As he viewed it, they were as little inclined to agreement among themselves as with those whom they opposed; their principles were as diverse as they were doubtful. To Bulkley, the Baptists—like all dissenters—seemed united only in their opposition to the truth. "Sectaries" served as an umbrella term for the babble of dissenting groups whose names communicated their theological confusion.[30]

For the moment at least, standards of traditional religious language prevailed. It appears that Bulkley's group successfully quieted the carping "Sectaries" and returned the community to religious health. Bulkley noted that when he asked the Baptists in attendance if they could "Answer...the Arguments offer'd," they spoke "not a word...but all remained in a Dead Silence." But something had changed. For Bulkley hinted that neither he nor his established brethren had needed to justify their principles until the debate. "[B]y what is contained in the fore-going Pages," he wrote, "its hoped Persons will see We of the Established Ministry in the Country, have something to say for our Opinion and Practice in those Points..." The idea of a single voice left speaking, even a voice spoken in anticipation of dissent, is illustrative of a cultural perspective that left little room for differences of opinion. If the Baptists were indeed reduced to dead silence by his authoritative words, it was their increasingly conspicuous dissent that had compelled his speech—as well as Bulkley's published account of the proceedings. There would be many such instances over the coming decades. With greater and greater frequency, orthodox clergymen would find their authority challenged by a growing numbers of "Sectaries." As the presses expanded and opened their pages to a variety of religious opinions, a final word in any dispute would soon become the rarest of luxuries. The disease of dissent was about to infect every region of colonial America.[31]

The Divine Right of Private Judgment

Both Bulkley and his Baptist opponents were well accustomed to state interference in church affairs and to the active suppression of nonconformists. In Connecticut, those who differed from the Congregational (sometimes referred to in that colony as "Presbyterian") churches were treated as second-class subjects. Until 1729, Bulkley's dissenting neighbors would have paid taxes to support his ministry. In that year, Connecticut's Baptists were granted a modicum of legal equality. Pressured by authorities in England, the colonial government had begun issuing certificates to Quakers, Baptists, and Anglicans that exempted them from taxes. Although the Baptists would remain dissenters from a well-entrenched standing church and suffer all the indignities that accompanied such a status, they were now tolerated and would enjoy something that contemporaries identified as the "divine right of private judgment."

In the early eighteenth century, "freedom" was not something that people commonly demanded. Nor did they talk much about "equality." Those were late eighteenth-century ideals. When defended in the early eighteenth century, a dissenting opinion was usually justified as an instance of the *right of private judgment*, a phrase sometimes used synonymously with "liberty of conscience" and "religious liberty." Two centuries before, the Protestant Reformation had elevated this concept to a sacred ideal. Martin Luther insisted upon every believer's right to interpret scripture independent of outside authorities. In practice, however, Protestant authorities limited the right to worship freely to those with correct principles. Luther himself recommended that those who refused to conform should be handed back to the pope, or "the devil himself" (to Luther, it was pretty much the same anyway). Queen Elizabeth's Act of Uniformity prohibited Catholic worship in private houses and even took aim at the "memory" of Catholic worship by mandating the destruction of Catholic icons. Protestants who did not adhere to the Book of Common Prayer were subject to fines and imprisonment. For the dissenters who lived in seventeenth-century England and America, the right to private judgment meant just that. When they did not exile, jail, or hang dissenters, established authorities tended to permit nonconforming Protestants, Jews, and Catholics to worship in private. Dissenting churches were excluded from the benefits of government sponsorship, prohibited from public exercises of their faith, and even forbidden from "worship[ing] in buildings that looked like churches." On the other hand, dissenters were forbidden to remain so private, or secretive, that the authorities could not keep watch on their activities. Ironically, religious meetings that took place behind locked doors were forbidden under English law.[32]

The ideal of toleration for private judgment and private worship first emerged as a pragmatic measure to keep scrupulous consciences quiet, to keep unhappy dissenters from raising disturbances, to keep private judgments private. More often than not, toleration was an instrument of prudent statecraft, a means of heading off conflict within a particular polity and—in an age when princes fought on behalf of their faith—of negotiating peace with one another. In other words, early modern regimes frequently employed toleration as a defensive practice. Policies extending toleration were usually not granted from motives of altruism, theological relativism, or a commitment to equal rights. Though persecuted dissenters usually gave more idealistic justifications, those seventeenth-century Europeans who advocated toleration usually did so as a step toward achieving civil peace and prosperity.[33]

As the seventeenth century turned into the eighteenth century, however, toleration was given a powerful new ideological justification. In England, especially, a radical political ideology known as liberalism introduced a principled defense of toleration into public discourse.[34] Liberal writers such as John Locke made an influential case for liberty of conscience that was largely independent of its utility to the state. The order and stability of government and society still mattered, of course. For Locke, however, the conscience was an inviolable possession of the individual. State compulsion was of no avail in altering the convictions of the mind. Even if the individual was forced to say what he did not truly believe, the belief itself would not change. Locke's writings on government and epistemology gave additional impetus to the tolerationist position. In his *Two Treatises on Civil Government*, he developed an elaborate theory of the social contract, which implied that all legitimate institutions were formed through the voluntary consent of their members. In another series of influential treatises, Locke attacked the philosophical doctrine of innate ideas, contending that what we know about both the natural and the supernatural is the product of impressions made upon our senses and ideas forged by our rational minds. Locke's work fostered the growing suspicion in the late seventeenth and early eighteenth centuries that error was an ineradicable characteristic of the human mind and that disagreement was an ineradicable characteristic of human communities. After all, if our under-standing of the world is empirical—if it is derived from experience and the use of reason, rather than the recognition of eternal verities—then agreement could seem like a fortunate coincidence, rather than an absolute necessity.

The implications of these Enlightenment ideas were far reaching for the way the colonists treated religious differences. In America, the liberal defense of individual rights in matters of faith and the commitment to voluntary con-sent in public institutions reinforced both the Protestant commitment to the right of private judgment and the Calvinist commitment to churches formed by the consent of their members. The most outstanding colonial example of a pre-Lockean, Calvinist commitment to religious liberty was the iconoclastic minister Roger Williams. Banished from Massachusetts on the grounds that he had "broached & divulged diverse new & dangerous opinions," Williams founded a colony to the south that would develop some of the most generous provisions for individual conscience the world had ever seen.[35] That unique bastion of both liberty and eccentricity became known as Rhode Island. The free and fragmented character of religious life there reflected Williams own separatist inclinations. In a famous plea for religious toleration, Williams explicitly refuted the claim that heretics "ought to be put to *death* or *banished*, to prevent the *infecting* and *seducing* of others."[36] Yet he himself could bear no corruption (by which he often meant attendance at Anglican services) in his fellow worshipers. Williams's inability to tolerate others' spiritual infirmities was renowned. "Abstract yourselfe," he once wrote to John Winthrop, "with a holy violence from the Dung heape of this Earth."[37] For Williams, religious voluntarism was so sacred a principle because the individual's quest for the true church—even if that ultimately turned out to be a church of one—was so pressing an obligation. Extreme though it was, Williams's fidelity to the right of private judgment and ideal of a voluntary, gathered church reflected the predispositions of many of the Calvinists who settled in British North America. So did his quest for ever greater spiritual purity. Still, Williams probably exercised very little influence on the development of colonial reli-gious discourse. He simply lived too early and separated too regularly.[38]

The same cannot be said of Locke, whose major works first arrived more than a generation later than Williams. Eighteenth-century Americans some-times paid formal deference to the man referred to as "the celebrated Lock." More often they just appropriated such ideas as their own. If not the most sophisticated philosophers in the Atlantic World, colonial Americans may have been the most receptive to Locke's philosophy.[39] Their English coun-terparts also proved ready to practice Lockean principles. During the late seventeenth and early eighteenth centuries, government policies throughout the empire were gradually reshaped according to these ideals. The English Toleration Act of 1689 formally suspended the penalties imposed on dissenters and, in 1718, the Occasional Conformity and Schism Acts were repealed. Though it was still defined as a crime, dissent was no longer treated as one. Over the next four decades, the Toleration Act was applied throughout the empire. Those colonies that were initially hesitant to grant rights to the heretical were eventually compelled to. By the late 1720s and early 1730s, colonial governments from Massachusetts to South Carolina had eliminated some of the harshest penalties upon religious dissent and implemented a degree of legal equality. Bills that passed both the Pennsylvania Assembly and the British Parliament (and thereby applied directly to all of the royal colonies, including Virginia, Maryland, North Carolina, South Carolina, and Georgia) in 1731 conferred property rights on all Protestant religious societies.[40] In 1727, Massachusetts, like Connecticut, relieved Anglicans, Quakers, and Baptists of the obligation to pay taxes toward the support of Congregationalist ministers. During these same years, New York began to scale back the privileges enjoyed by the Church of England there. When a group of Anglicans seized a building belonging to a local Presbyterian congregation—upon the presumption that theirs was the established church in the province and that all public monies raised for religious purposes were rightfully theirs—a New York court ordered that the building be returned to the Presbyterian congregation. The court also ruled that the Presbyterians were entitled to the future use of local tax monies.[41]

Such changes in property and tax law may seem trifling when we consider them in light of the Church of England's well-entrenched establishment in the southern colonies and the Congregational churches' dominance in New England. The Toleration Act was, as one group of midcentury Anglicans put it, "not designed to introduce separate congregations but to give them a permission to continue, after they were unfortunately formed." Nonconformist meetinghouses still had to be registered with the state and ministers still licensed by official bodies. In Massachusetts, Quakers, Baptists, and Presbyterians still had to seek a special exemption from the burden of such taxes. Dissenting preachers were still harassed and dissenters were objects of scorn nearly everywhere. And yet, the playing field had been leveled considerably. The Hanover Presbytery of Virginia acknowledged the change in a later petition, claiming that the church had "been considered and treated upon an equal footing with our fellow subjects" since 1738. In a certain sense, they were correct. Virginia's Presbyterians were beneficiaries of a pragmatic policy adopted in 1727 that encouraged dissenting groups to settle in the western parts of the colony. There, Virginia and English officials hoped, they might stimulate trade, protect the colony from Indian marauders, and yet present no threat to the established church. To us, these limited provisions for dissenters seem far from equality, but it was as close as many groups had ever come.[42]

Thus, after some prodding from imperial authorities, early eighteenth-century Americans were doing more than simply embracing the right of private judgment in theory, they were actually practicing it. Seemingly minor changes in the law gave substance to the Toleration Act and the Anglo American language of toleration. In most places, of course, the right of *private* judgment continued to exclude *public* expressions of dissenting faith. Toleration certainly did not imply that every believer and every religious group could do and say whatever they wished. Dissenters were still expected to keep a lid on their religious opinions, only worshiping "privately," "soberly," and "indoors." Furthermore, those who did the tolerating remained loath to admit the legitimacy of the beliefs they tolerated. New England Congregationalists were particularly reluctant to concede that local Quakers and Baptists were sincerely committed to their professed beliefs. The historian Thomas J. Curry notes that in Massachusetts:

> the law exempting Quakers and Baptists from ministerial taxes referred to an "alleged scruple of conscience," and when, in 1743, Massachusetts finally got around to substituting an affirmation for an oath in the case of Quakers, the statute described its beneficiaries as "Quakers [who] profess to be in their consciences scrupulous of taking oaths."

Likewise, one turn-of-the-century Virginian pointed out to British readers that his colony granted "liberty of Conscience" to all of the non-Anglican "Congregations *pretending* Christianity, on condition they submit to all Parish Duties" (emphasis added).[43]

The idea that believers were equal in their beliefs remained a hard sell in Virginia even into the 1770s. Until then, Quakers, Baptists, and Presbyterians would still have to petition for the right to worship publicly, and then still have to pay taxes toward the support of the established church. Until then, itinerants would still go to jail for violating parish boundaries, and particularly defiant preachers might still be horsewhipped. As in England, so in this royal colony. Formal adherence to the principle of toleration was no more a guarantor of egalitarian social norms here than it was across the Atlantic. The appearance of isolated pleas for religious equality in the Chesapeake region's sole newspaper, the *Virginia Gazette*, during the late 1730s and again in the 1750s testifies to the increasing diversity in that colony and to the (more gradually) increasing opportunities for dissenting groups to enter printed debate. However, the uncharitable nature of responses suggests that the public culture remained hostile to nonconformists. When a group of Virginia Quakers politely appealed for a release from parish levies in 1738, one of the paper's offended patrons offered the readers a recipe for making a Quaker. The ingredients included the "Herb Deceit," "the Seeds of Hypocrisy," and "the Spice of Babylon." A decade and a half later, when an anonymous author in the *Virginia* Gazette made the case for religious equality, he was met with scorn and ridicule. "Philo Virginia" contended that the colony could attract large numbers of hardworking, loyal settlers if it only extended tax relief to respectable Protestant sects. Philo's arguments appeared absurd to at least two readers who sneeringly asked why the colony would not, upon the same logic, simply free the slaves, or tolerate Roman Catholics? One commentator contended that the presence of black slaves already constituted a significant threat to social stability and colonial security. Virginians would only invite more trouble by encouraging "the deadly Symptoms" of sectarianism. A second author agreed with the first on the threat posed by "Negroes, and Sectaries." "They are each of them," he continued, "Disease enough in any Government; but together would invigorate, and complete the Malignity of each other."[44]

Yet even where liberty of conscience was not welcomed with enthusiasm, even where its beneficiaries were still regarded with suspicion, it could no longer be denied. By 1717, the prominent Massachusetts Congregationalist, witchcraft theorist, and scion of the Puritan establishment, Cotton Mather, spoke at a Baptist ordination ceremony, where he argued that every man was entitled to "Liberty of Conscience." Of course, Mather and nearly every other writer on the subject excluded the blasphemous, the profane, the Catholic, and the atheist, who "deserve[d] to be used as the Brute Beasts made to be taken and destroyed, or to be driven from Men, and have his dwelling with the Beasts of the Field."[45] Nonetheless, the general tendency was toward full toleration for the private religious judgments of sincere Protestants. Throughout early eighteenth-century America, this right came to assume the kind of incontrovertible status that equality would take on after the Revolutionary War and that diversity has taken on in our own time. It formed the premise from which larger conclusions were drawn. It was the principal subject in the grammar of midcentury religious discourse. Commentators opposed it at their peril. At the time, the right of private judgment, or liberty of conscience, merely provided justification for individual opinions privately thought and forms of worship discreetly practiced. Over the next few decades, however, it would sanction displays of public dissent that would have appalled any good seventeenth-century conformist.

Early Eighteenth-Century Debates over Private Judgment

In the 1720s, the tolerationist consensus that was coalescing across the British Atlantic made a striking appearance among the Presbyterians of Charleston and Philadelphia. In both places, it met significant resistance. The controversies that embroiled America's Presbyterians present a useful case study in part because Presbyterians were committed, like their Congregationalist counterparts, to a stringent Calvinist theology that brooked no mediation between themselves and their God. As such, the right of private judgment was extremely important to them. Yet they adhered to a centralized ecclesiastical system that invested substantial authority in regional presbyteries and kirks. The Presbyterians also present an interesting case study because they arrived in the colonies well schooled in the intricacies of debate over religious liberty. Their ancestors had led a violent rebellion against King Charles and his attempt to impose Anglican worship in the late 1630s. More recently, their coreligionists in Scotland and Ireland had been engaged in bitter quarrels over the legitimacy of requiring subscription to the Westminster Confession of Faith. To the American colonies, they brought both a tradition of resistance to Anglican ecclesiastical authority and bitter divisions between conformists and nonconformists. While Presbyterians of all stripes acknowledged a right of private judgment, the actual content of this liberty was the source of substantial disagreement. In a number of ways then, these seemingly minor denominational debates reveal a great deal about the problem that religious differences posed for contemporary Americans.[46]

We turn first to Charleston. There, the conservative minister Hugh Fisher encountered the emerging right of private judgment dogma when he delivered a sermon to the presbytery at some point in 1729. In attendance was a New England transplant by the name of Josiah Smith, a Congregationalist, who thought he heard Fisher deny "a Liberty in People to judge for themselves." Appalled, Smith promptly crafted a short discourse of his own that vindicated the right of private judgment, noting its importance to the Protestant Reformation and lamenting that there were those who left the Bibles in "our Hands" only to "pluck out our eyes." When word spread that he had spoken a "Heresie," Smith published the sermon. Denying that any earthly being was capable of infallible judgments, Smith claimed that humans have little choice but to rely on the probable knowledge that everyone might acquire. The imposition of rigid creeds, he argued, interfered with the obligation of every Christian to examine scripture faithfully. His opponents, Smith contended, had reduced the act of scriptural inquiry to a mere affirmation of authority. By contrast, Smith suggested that ministers should "*search* the Scriptures, and then . . . give their Hearers the Reasons," for their interpretation of it. If the right of private judgment meant anything, it entailed diligent, autonomous investigation. To peremptorily declare the creed correct and the nonconforming believer wrong was to empty this right of all content.[47]

While acknowledging the existence of a right of private judgment, Hugh Fisher maintained—as the Puritan governor John Winthrop had a century earlier, that no man had a right to judge wrong. The "right of judging, contrary to the true doctrines of the Gospel . . . was no more than a right, to perish everlastingly, for their unbelief of the Gospel." Those who opposed mandatory subscription to the creeds contained in the Westminster Confession of Faith were but skeptics who assumed the pretense of faith. Fisher denounced the liberal Lockean idea that truth was something to be determined by the rational subject, rather than something that need only be recognized by the faithful. Those blessed with God's grace could judge scriptures with unqualified certainty, and were therefore entitled to demand orthodoxy. By contrast, those without God's grace "have not the Antidote against . . . Errors, which is common to all true Christians." The unregenerate could be identified by their errors of judgment and measured by their distance from church orthodoxy. Smith's "right of private judgment," then, amounted to little more than "a right to declare, or vomit out Blasphemous Sentiments against our Blessed Saviour." In Fisher's view, to dissent was to criticize, and to criticize was to blaspheme. One who experienced doubts regarding "a truth," he allowed, might "propose his difficulties in order to be instructed," but possessed no right "to declare, that in his opinion, the thing is false." To dissent openly from the church was to reveal one's own iniquity, to demonstrate beyond a doubt one's unworthiness for communion. Only true believers possessed the privilege to declare their opinions publicly because only they could pronounce the truth with unfailing accuracy.[48]

The liberal Smith seems to have lost the contemporary debate. In a pamphlet published the following year, he insisted that those who abandoned his communion had done so because of the principles that were unjustly attributed to him. Smith's defensive tone throughout suggests that he came under a good deal of criticism for his failure to subscribe to all of the articles mandated by the Presbytery in Charlestown. But, it was Fisher who stood on a shaky foundation in the emergent cultural climate. If all were capable of certain judgments, then what reason was there for not making private judgment the rule of every institution? Those who argued on behalf of creeds would have to find another justification for their position—perhaps one argument grounded in liberal principles. And, eventually, they would.[49]

In Philadelphia, a similar story was unfolding. By the late 1720s, a dispute like that conducted in Charleston had been raging within the Presbyterian Synod for almost a decade. In 1722, and again in 1729, this body grappled with many of the same issues confronted by the Charleston Presbytery. Jonathan Dickinson, a pastor in the northern New Jersey parish of Elizabeth Town, articulated the nonsubscriptionist position in both 1722 and 1729. Human meddling, and not scriptural misinterpretation, he maintained, was responsible for the growing divisions between Christians. Unnecessary impositions had turned religion into "a subject of Debate." Like Smith after him, Dickinson maintained that ministers should merely point their listeners in the direction of true belief, without obliging them to walk toward it. Clerical authority added nothing to scriptural truth.[50]

The Philadelphia Synod made do without a confession of faith until 1727 when the issue was again raised by the Irish-born minister John Thomson. Thomson proposed his overture as an "Antidote against Division" as a means of bringing the body to "one Mind, and one Judgment." For him, there could be no church without unity, no unity without uniformity, and no uniformity unless the Word of God were fixed in its "proper Sense and Meaning." Ecclesiastical governments, like other "Politick Bod[ies]," required a substantive "Bond of Union," which the Synod now lacked. Neither the volume nor the stridency of dissenting opinions seems to have worried Thomson. Instead, he feared those private judgments that remained undisclosed and unspoken. Thomson urged vigilance against "secret Bosom Enemies to the Truth" lurking within. "[B]y searching them out, discovering them, and setting a Mark upon them," their nefarious ends might be thwarted. If indeed their silence preserved them, then they should be compelled to speak. The problem, as Thomson saw it, was not bold speech but quiet dissent, not excessive fervor but cowardly indifference. Ever changing, the erroneous belief traveled furtively from corrupt mind to corrupt mind until it was exposed to the knowledge of the truth. From these premises, it followed that the Synod could not be purged of dissent until the dissenters were identified, and with them the pestiferous errors that otherwise eluded detection.[51]

In this, as in so many other things over the succeeding centuries, the Presbyterians of Philadelphia felt it best to come down somewhere near the middle. The compromise, which passed the Synod in 1729, required ministerial subscription to the Westminster Confession and Catechisms. However, it permitted subscribing ministers to profess whatever "scruple[s]" they possessed at the time of the declaration. As long as the Synod or Presbytery judged that "his scruple or mistake . . . be only about articles not essential and necessary in doctrine, worship, or government," the individual could be admitted to the ministry. This Act would thus provide both the substantive bond of union that Thomson sought and the right of private judgment that Dickinson defended—and would, like the child's catechism or a limited dose of small-pox, immunize the church from an epidemic of erroneous opinions.[52]

Historical developments seldom divide themselves into discrete periods. Nonetheless, the debates within the Charleston and Philadelphia presbyteries marked the end of an age when religious dissent could be treated as entirely illegitimate. Systematic public debates on the rights of conscience would not occur again until there was another ideological break in the 1760s and 1770s—when the principle of "mere toleration" would itself stand on the verge of irrelevance. By the late 1730s, it was no longer acceptable to deny liberty of conscience, or private judgment, throughout most of British North America. There were exceptions, and contemporary writers could still ridicule any talk of legal equality, while authorities could still throw an itinerant minister into the stocks. But the rule held. From this point onward, religious differences would have to be negotiated within a culture that accorded the highest value to the right of private judgment. Even the most reactionary of colonial writers usually stopped short of comparing the views they disliked to malevolent plagues. Fisher and Thomson would not be the last ministers to hold that liberty of conscience was compatible with the authority of churches to impose heavy obligations upon their congregants; nor were Smith and Dickinson the first to hold that truth was the product of free inquiry. Seldom again, however, would the tensions between the older network of assumptions, which emphasized the necessity of excluding, isolating, or eliminating dissent, come into as sharp a contrast with a newer, liberal ideology.

Benjamin Franklin, the Expanding Press, and the Right of Private Judgment

The principle of toleration and private judgment might have attained ideological preeminence, but the debate over the nature and extent of those ideals was far from over. It could be said that the first sustained controversy within the American Lockean liberal tradition took place in 1735, shortly after the arrival of the Irish immigrant minister, Samuel Hemphill. According to a reputable observer, Hemphill "delivered with a good Voice, & apparently extempore, most excellent Discourses, which drew together considerable Numbers of different Persuasions, who join'd in admiring them." Within a few months of his first sermon in the colonies, Hemphill's "erroneous teaching" had drawn the ire of the Philadelphia Synod, which prohibited Hemphill from preaching in its churches. On the grounds that their earlier agreement had permitted individuals to note their reservations at the time they offered their confession of faith, Hemphill claimed a right to voice his unorthodox opinions, which attributed far more free will to human action than the Philadelphia Presbyterians were willing to concede. In April, 1735, the Synod brought formal charges against the popular preacher. The ensuing controversy revealed the contours of the new religious framework. No one would deny Hemphill's right to maintain his own private differences with the rest of the church. But neither would any respectable Presbyterian allow him the right to express those dissenting opinions publicly—and certainly not in front of believers affiliated with other different denominations.[53]

There was one man in Philadelphia, a nominal Presbyterian at best, who did believe that Hemphill possessed just such a right. In the wake of the Synod's charges, the ambitious young Philadelphia printer, Benjamin Franklin, rushed to Hemphill's defense. In a July 1735 pamphlet, Franklin contrasted the secretive methods of the Synod with its counterpart in Scotland, whose members "debate amongst themselves publickly, and the Members of which it is compos'd do separately give Reasons for their Opinions. . . ." It may have been the chance to prod what he saw as a stodgy ministerial elite as much as his sympathy for Hemphill that stirred Franklin to action. If that was the case, he succeeded. Franklin's attack prompted Hemphill's opponents to respond with *A Vindication of the Reverend Commission of the Synod*, justifying the proceedings that ultimately led to a guilty verdict for Hemphill. The primary author of this tract turned out to be Jonathan Dickinson. According to the Vindicators, the Church of Scotland did not customarily debate amongst themselves publicly, but instead convened privately when judgment was to be rendered, although the Philadelphia Synod had, until that point, conducted their business in the "most publick manner." The Vindicators argued that a society, like an individual, possessed a "natural Right . . . of Judging," a (private) right to differ with one of its own members, and express its "Opinions."[54]

The modesty of the Vindicators' language reveals more than just their capacity to assume a shrewd rhetorical posture. It also illustrates the extent to which the ideal of private judgment had penetrated this society. Pennsylvania had officially guaranteed its inhabitants liberty of conscience for over fifty years by 1735. But the chasm separating a culture that tolerates private judgments and a culture for which private judgment functions as a governing principle is vast indeed. When a dissenting member of the church could only be excluded on the grounds that he was offending its "Right to Judge" for itself, an important conceptual leap had occurred.

The Vindicators' words suggest a fundamental tension within the liberal ideology that protected private judgment—between the rights accorded private societies and the rights of their individual members. It is significant that Jonathan Dickinson, who had opposed the imposition of the Westminster Confession of Faith during the 1720s, played a leading role in the Synod's opposition to Hemphill one decade later. Throughout the controversy, Dickinson insisted on the rights of societies to make their own judgments. As he saw it, there were some utterances that religious societies could not forbear. Without the right to place limits on its members' speech and to exclude those who did not comply with its rules, no church could survive. "Liberty of *private Judgment*" was due to "all religious Societies in the World" as well as "all Men." At the end of his pamphlet, Dickinson cited no less an authority on rights than "the accute and ingenious Mr. *Lock*, in his *Letter* concerning *Toleration*." Locke had maintained in the seventeenth century, as Dickinson now did in the eighteenth, that religious societies enjoyed the right to determine their own membership. For Dickinson, the liberal Lockean right to form societies trumped the liberal Lockean right to practice one's sincerely held beliefs.[55]

Dickinson's writing revealed the limited freedom offered by the language of toleration and the right of private judgment. Indeed, it proved perfectly compatible with a rigid intolerance toward the public expression of unconventional doctrines. Among the other claims advanced in his pamphlet, Dickinson argued that the apostles had suppressed erring ministers. Those spouting "false Doctrines," he observed, "were ... Silenced, that the destructive Gangreen might be stopt." Likewise, the Vindicators condemned Hemphill's efforts to curry popular favor. Within their conceptual universe, vocal dissent, theological uncertainty, and popular credulity were inextricably linked. The biblical passage John Graham cited in his assault on Quakerism— "Ever learning, and never able to come to the knowledge of the truth"— appeared on the pamphlet's title page. Moreover, the authors confessed that they did not know why this Irishman left his homeland, but they had "Silenc'd him in America."[56]

The dispute between Franklin and the Philadelphia Synod elicited two contrasting visions of colonial America, as well as two very different conceptions of the liberal right of private judgment. For the authors of the *Vindication*, America represented a refuge from "the Epidemical Corruption of the Age." Until Hemphill's arrival, they had hoped that "these remote corners of the Earth" would escape those pestilent "Errors that have overspread so great a part of the Church." For Franklin, America was a refuge from another sort of European-born contagion, that of "slavish and arbitrary Principles." But even in these "remote Parts," Franklin lamented, people seemed susceptible to the disease. Fortunately, he noted:

> In this free Country, where the Understandings of men are under no civil Restraint . . . there is nothing more easy than to shew that a Doctrine is false, and of ill Consequence, if it really be so; but if not, no Man, or Set of Men can make it so, by peremptorily declaring it unsound or dangerous. . . .

Like Josiah Smith, Franklin was confident that open examination would lead to the truth. He expressed the wish that religious disputes might be conducted as civilly as scientific controversies. In Franklin's America, public debate rather than clerical condemnation would subdue error. For him, securing toleration meant establishing the right of private judgment in law. Securing the truth meant airing those private judgments in public.[57]

What we have here then are the two sides of the new cultural ideal that was gaining credence in American culture, which—at a minimum—guaranteed toleration for private judgments. With Jonathan Dickinson's narrow Lockeanism, individual rights were equated with the sanctity of individual conscience, privately maintained, and nothing more. With the expansive Lockeanism of Benjamin Franklin, we have the radical conviction that true liberty of conscience could only be exercised through public discussion. Instead of being a debate about the legitimacy of private religious judgments, which everyone accepted in some form, the Hemphill dispute resolved itself into a debate about the legitimacy of making private religious judgments public. Franklin and the members of the Synod professed many of the same principles, including a commitment to the "right of private judgment." But Franklin thought that only in the open field of public debate could a dissenting judgment be fully exercised. Meanwhile, the Vindicators regarded the promiscuous spread of dissenting opinions as the height of irresponsibility. Would they allow someone to consciously spread a disease?

Unfortunately for Hemphill's opponents, this infection had not one carrier but two. In addition to Hemphill's "good voice," there was Franklin's press. In more ways than one, Franklin represented the incipient publishing industry that would render it increasingly difficult to silence any person or group and transform his public-minded, liberal Lockeanism from an argument into a fact. In effect, Franklin's contrarian sentiments complemented his professional ambitions. His role as a printer immersed him in the language and practices of the medium within which religious disputes would increasingly be argued. He was in the business of providing new forums and larger audiences for different kinds of written address. Appropriately enough,

Franklin's initial experience in newspaper publishing came in 1721 amid the smallpox epidemic that convulsed Boston. In that year, his older brother, James, founded the *New-England Courant*. The *Courant* was the first in colonial America to be printed without the government's imprimatur. It was also the first to substantively critique government policy. Among other hazardous endeavors, James Franklin's paper offered a venue for Dr. William Douglass, whose opposition to inoculation had gained the ire of New England's leading theologians. The *Courant*'s impertinence soon landed the elder Franklin in deep trouble with the Massachusetts government. While James stewed in prison, Benjamin acted as the publisher.[58]

James Franklin's brief imprisonment in 1722 symbolized the press's constricted role during the first three decades of the century. At a time when only large colonial towns were fortunate enough to have a printer, the scope of published debate remained limited. The officials who subsidized early eighteenth-century presses expected them to serve as the mouthpiece of civil and religious authority. Printers had good reason to comply. After all, a large proportion of early printing involved official documents. Few could resist the allure of easy profit that came with the distinction of serving as "government printer." In addition, throughout most of the eighteenth century, criticism of state institutions still constituted a criminal offense. Not long after the Hemphill dispute broke out, the New York publisher John Peter Zenger was charged with having libeled the governor. A local jury acquitted the printer. Nonetheless, Zenger's celebrated trial testifies to the persistent association of criticism with sedition. New York's chief justice instructed Zenger's jury to only consider whether he was responsible for printing the offending articles, not the verity of the criticism contained therein. No matter what its content, public opposition to political authorities, like the denigration of an established minister or the denial of God, was inexcusable. John Peter Zenger paid for his own violation by serving eight months in prison. A decade earlier, Massachusetts authorities had reacted to the anticongregational pamphlets of the Anglican convert John Checkley "by harassing him, trying him for propagating material that reflected badly on 'the ministers of the Gospel Established in this Province,' and fining him L50 and costs." Although prosecutions for seditious libel had been on the decline for several decades, the principle endured into the eighteenth century: by its nature, criticism diminished the dignity of the religious or political office and weakened the ties that bound every community together. Early eighteenth-century restrictions on the press were strikingly consistent with the early eighteenth-century treatment of religious dissent. Hemphill's public dissent, like political criticism, posed a danger to every member of the community. The Synod's defenders thought it their duty to exorcize this infected portion of its body lest the whole be contaminated. To forbear Hemphill's mischievous practices would expose everyone to the eternal injuries that such societies were established to prevent.[59]

Franklin's approach to the Hemphill case reflected a quite distinct set of presuppositions about the treatment of dissent. It also anticipated the more liberal approach to religious beliefs that would soon emerge along with a more open and inclusive print trade. In a well-known 1731 editorial, "An Apology for Printers," Franklin had insisted that the printer occupied an unenviable position. His craft required him to print opinions, and opinions always offended someone. It simply could not be helped. Merchants and artisans in other trades suffered no penalties when they transacted with "People of all Persuasions." But the printer operated in an unusually sensitive business where opinions themselves were the medium of exchange. Furthermore, the printer had an obligation to "serve all contending Writers"—as long, of course, as they paid well. Printers were "educated in the belief, that when Men differ in Opinion, both Sides ought equally to have the Advantage of being heard by the Publick." In other words, the printer had no choice but to publish offensive ideas. His own perspective, Franklin added, was irrelevant. The printer had no business deciding what opinions were right or wrong, good or bad. His only business was to publish as many as he could. (Though Franklin thought he might "live a very easy Life" if people would only begin paying him "as much for not printing things they don't like," as he could from pieces that actually appeared in his papers.) Franklin always wrote as if it were up to his readers to determine the worth of an opinion. Furthermore, he always seemed confident that they were more tolerant of religious dissent than his orthodox adversaries would let on. At one point in the Hemphill controversy, Franklin observed that Philadelphia alone was home to "half a Dozen, for aught I know half a Score, different Sects." And, he continued, "were the Hearts of Men to be at once opened to our View, we should perhaps see a thousand Diversities more."[60]

The contrast between Franklin's assumptions and those of orthodox ministers is revealing. Whereas John Thomson treated the exposure of private opinions as an means of achieving doctrinal uniformity, Franklin thought this kind of openness made transparent differences that had not yet even been articulated. Whereas Cotton Mather subscribed to the position that a child's erroneous opinions could only be corrected when they were spoken in the presence of an orthodox authority, Franklin indicated that the true extent of Philadelphia's diversity would only become evident were everyone's sentiments expressed autonomously. Whereas both Thomson and Hugh Fisher had observed that "heretics" should be publicly marked with their "proper names and Characters," Franklin noted that only the believers themselves could properly describe their own faith.

We should, of course, be careful of drawing too stark a contrast. People are seldom characterized accurately as either progressives or reactionaries. Indeed, clergymen who might have once been confident that the public discussion of religion was their exclusive domain, who might have once reviled those with different views, were instrumental in bringing about the transformation to a pluralistic religious culture. Change came gradually, through arguments and counterarguments, never in the triumph of a transcendent principle. Yet there is no denying that Franklin's perspective provides a glimpse of a new culture in the making.

As Franklin's experience suggests, the emergence of toleration and the spread of the print trade proceeded apace through the early and middle decades of the eighteenth century. The first semipermanent colonial newspaper was born with the establishment of *Boston Weekly News-Letter* in 1704. Not for another fifteen years would the second, the *Boston Gazette*, appear. Then, just as toleration and the right of private judgment gained universal credence, the number took off. Ten papers, including James Franklin's, made their debut between 1721 and 1739—three more in Boston, two in New York, two in Philadelphia, one in Germantown, Pennsylvania, one in Williamsburg, Virginia, and one in Charleston, South Carolina.[61] Book and pamphlet publication experienced comparable growth. An important consequence of the surge in print was that the orthodox religious authorities who had once monopolized printed discourse could no longer do so. This was particularly true, as James N. Green notes, once a second printer (like Franklin himself) appeared in a town. When that happened, state and clerical control declined precipitously.[62]

Wherever an active print trade emerged, toleration, or even full religious liberty, was among those topics that received a public hearing. In fact, less than a year after the *South-Carolina Gazette* (which was partially owned by Benjamin Franklin) began publication in Charleston, an anonymous contributor, who assumed the name "Moderator," appealed for lenience from men "of any Religion" toward peaceful men "of every Religion" and argued that every sincere believer "must chuse his own Priest." A considerably less liberal author, perhaps the local Anglican commissary, derided Moderator's seeming indifference to religious truth. At the same time, he affirmed the conventional tolerationist position that "all Christians" should "peaceably [sic] and quietly enjoy" their own forms of worship. After the appearance of Moderator's second piece, the *Gazette*'s editor announced that he would "suppress" the remainder of the author's correspondence because of the

"Offence" it had caused "to some serious People." Despite the offense caused, Moderator's positions would be defended by a third essayist on the front page of the *Gazette* for the next two months. In Charleston, as in Philadelphia, New York, and Boston, a forum for dissenting opinions had emerged. The orthodox would still have plenty to say, but perhaps even more to be offended at. Their words would no longer go unchallenged.[63]

To those who wished to keep the pestilence of religious error contained, this explosion of print must have appeared as troubling as fresh carrion and unwashed hands are to epidemiologists. Such anxiety would not have been unfounded. Colonial printing performed a service similar to that of Franklin's liberalism—giving voice to a thousand expressions of individual conscience, explicitly appealing to an interdenominational audience, and eventually separating people from the harm that had once been ascribed to their opinions. The cultural function of print thereby complemented the radical strains of Lockean philosophy. Like Franklin himself, both served to create a social and ideological space for individuals to express unorthodox views and to draw together people of different persuasions. Samuel Hemphill's trial represented one of the first uses of that space in colonial America. It would not be the last.

As the extent of published opinion continued its torrid expansion, and colonial courts quietly stopped enforcing their seditious libel laws, religious differences became a normal and conspicuous part of colonial life. Within a few decades, surprising numbers of colonial Americans would embrace Franklin's idea that each believer possessed a faith that only he or she could properly describe. But traditional assumptions died slowly. Liberal ideals of individual judgment and mutual consent acquired widespread currency in a society that continued to evince a great deal of hostility toward disagreement. Indeed, influential figures, even those enamored of the celebrated Locke himself, would continue to conceive of differences in terms of toleration and dissent. This was particularly true when it came to the differences *between* denominations, rather than within them. In the dusk of its existence, the shadow of the established church proved difficult to escape. For the next several decades, Protestant dissenters in both the New England and southern colonies were prosecuted for itinerant preaching, nonpayment of church taxes, and failure to acquire state certification. And nearly every colony denied equal religious privileges to Catholics.

But whether or not eighteenth-century Americans made consistent and concrete provisions for the right of private judgment, there was no disavowing it. The ascendance of this ideal coincided with the expansion of printed debate and a growing awareness of the religious diversity that printed words addressed. The deluge of pamphlets, newspapers, and books simply could be not be contained within the confines of orthodox religion. Nor could audiences for these texts ever be fully anticipated. By the second half of the century, those who wrote about religious issues would often do so with diverse readers in mind and, increasingly, upon the premise that every believer deserved equal recognition. In the intervening years, however, a religious revival swept the Anglo American world. This "Great Awakening" sent both preachers and laypeople across church boundaries in search of spiritual satisfaction. Their movement would upset the fragile consensus that accorded rights to individual judgments and pose yet another problem for colonial American culture: What if dissent did not present itself in the form of a contagious error transmitted from person to person, or even by means of the press, but in the sheer movement of people themselves?

2

Partial Judgments and Divided Churches

America's First Great Awakening

I hear that there be divisions among you; and I partly believe it.
—1 Corinthians 11:18

Let not such powerful arguments as I think, I am afraid, I believe,
and I verily believe, hinder us from thinking and believing for
our selves....
—John Caldwell, *An Impartial Trial of the Spirit
Operating in this Part of the World* (1742)

Crowds gathered by the thousands. Conversions occurred by the hundreds. Laypeople of every rank, gender, and denomination declared that they had experienced a "new birth." They rejoiced in the knowledge that they had been liberated from the weight of their accumulated sins. They rejoiced in their capacity to view the world in a new light. After years of lamenting the sorry state of their souls, after decades of listening to clergymen cajole, admonish, and upbraid, countless numbers of mid-eighteenth-century Americans excitedly participated in, what they called, the "great revival of religion."

Since the nineteenth century, historians have referred to the religious revivals of the mid-eighteenth-century as *The* Great Awakening. We now know that revivals occurred intermittently between the mid-1730s and the mid-1750s and that they were often independent of one another. Nonetheless, contemporaries recognized a pattern of religious enthusiasm that seemed to have enveloped the entire north Atlantic. The first glimmerings of a general revival had appeared in 1734 with the conversion of a few anxious young souls in the small Massachusetts town of Northampton, where a minister named Jonathan Edwards presided. Word of these extraordinary occurrences spread southward through the Connecticut River valley, then eastward to Boston, across the Atlantic to London and Edinburgh, and south along the colonial coastline to New York and Philadelphia. Similar outbreaks of religious enthusiasm took place over the next decade from Cambuslang, Scotland, to Germantown, Pennsylvania. By 1739, a large proportion of northern ministers and laypeople were talking about an awakening of faith throughout the Protestant world. Over the next several years, the newspapers carried endless accounts of revivals and the itinerant preachers who so often inspired them.[1]

Not everyone was impressed. Opposition increased as the excesses of the newly converted became evident and as criticism of established clergymen mounted. The skeptical asked potentially devastating questions: Were these events an authentic manifestation of God's grace? Or, were they the product of deluded imaginations? Across the colonies, opinions were sharply divided. On the one extreme were those convinced that such an outburst of sincere religious activity could signal nothing less than Christ's return. On the other extreme were those who believed that the so-called revivals were inspired by a few self-aggrandizing itinerants who made a living of seducing weak-minded females and inspiring disobedience among enslaved African Americans.

Whatever an individual's evaluation of these events, no one denied their importance. A new era in American religious life had dawned. In the near constant movement of itinerants between towns, laypeople between old parishes, and church minorities into new parishes, colonial Americans became acquainted with the evangelical style of faith that would eventually prevail across much of the continent. The emergence of so many spiritual alternatives and the appearance of so many open disagreements prompted colonial Americans to actively challenge religious authority. Laypeople emboldened by such choices, and fiery preachers animated by their faith routinely badgered the institutions and the people that appeared unresponsive to their pleas for a satisfying religious experience. Churches and ministers confronted questions for which they did not always have ready answers. Clergymen were subject to unaccustomed criticism as the movement of people and the explosion of new churches generated novel grounds for (sometimes invidious) comparison. To their opponents, the volume and stridency of these judgments approached epidemic proportions.

The Great Awakening represents a watershed in the history of religious differences in America. It elicited both the first sustained justifications of individual equality and, in response, the last sustained attacks on religious dissent. By the conclusion of these first major revivals, colonial religious authority had been profoundly shaken. At the same time, upstart ministers and ordinary laypeople had acquired a newfound sense of their worth as Christians. Even if they were burdened with a greater sense of their sinfulness before the eyes of God, lay believers seemed to feel more secure in the eyes of men—especially clergymen. At the same time, their pastors would display a newfound willingness to overlook differences. Irreverence for established authority and disdain for formal distinctions go far in helping us explain the pluralistic religious culture that emerged during the second half of the eighteenth century. The venerable right of private judgment meant little when the individual could not (or would not) judge differently than his minister, dissent from his church's creed, move between parishes, or change religious affiliations. Thanks in large part to vocal dissent and the physical movement that characterized the Great Awakening, that old ideal was about to assume a radical new meaning.

The New Birth

Early eighteenth-century colonial ministers fancied themselves learned men, abreast of their times and relevant in their doctrines. They generally embraced what Cotton Mather called a "Reasonable Religion" and Jonathan Dickinson a "Reasonable Christianity"—a hybrid of traditional Calvinism and the Enlightenment theology that Europe's elites had been tending toward since the latter part of the seventeenth century. A significant number also displayed a fondness for the work of the Anglican rationalists, John Tillotson and Samuel Clarke. Following these modern trends, early eighteenth-century American clergymen took pains to distinguish their faith from superstition. Increasingly, they invoked science (in addition to providential fury) to account for earthquakes, and employed vaccines (in addition to repentance) to ward off disease. The God of the early eighteenth-century minister still operated in the world, but less conspicuously and less often. He was also less inclined to predestine a few for heaven and the majority to hell, and more inclined to work through natural causes. He extended grace more broadly and appealed to human reason more regularly.[2]

To the growing number of American clergymen who immersed themselves in the work of modern science and natural religion, the dreams of their ancestors began to look quaint and their pious exclusivity like sectarian bigotry. By the end of the seventeenth century, a more "catholic" or latitudinarian approach to religious differences had begun to make its way into colonial culture. By the fourth decade of the next century, even the descendants of New England's Puritans had grown comfortable with the practice of toleration. Consequently, what had seemed like an unthinkable indulgence to unrepentant blasphemers could now be viewed as a necessary concession to tender consciences. The Congregationalists, Presbyterians, and Anglicans who dominated contemporary religious life did not abandon their theological heritage, but they did make more allowances for the pious behavior that even wrongheaded neighbors might display. Encouraged by the late harmony prevailing among the various Protestant denominations in Europe, and inspired by philosophers such as Locke and theologians such as Tillotson, they conceded that dissenters should not be punished (at least not too severely) for what they could not help believing. In a very gradual way, the standard of orthodoxy was giving way to the standard of reasonableness. To the ministers who shaped early American thought, upright behavior began taking precedence over the religious state that motivated it, faith was losing ground to morality, and the right of private judgment was becoming more sacrosanct than ever.

Boston Congregationalist Charles Chauncy ranked among the more influential popularizers of rationalist thought in colonial America and, in 1739, he published one of the few systematic defenses of individual conscience to appear in the eighteenth-century provinces.[3] At the core of Chauncy's tract was the contention that when Christ directed a servant to "compel them to come in" (Luke 14:23), he enjoined nothing more than "Compulsion by sound Reasoning, good Argument." He was not, as religious persecutors had long maintained, sanctioning the coercion of dissenters. Echoing seventeenth- and early eighteenth-century English writings on behalf of toleration, Chauncy insisted that the mind and the body required distinct modes of compulsion. While the body might be moved through physical force, the mind was subject only to the "gentle Methods of Persuasion." The decision to accept or reject gospel truths, Chauncy contended, resided exclusively with the *"free Choice"* of "rational, free Agents." As John Locke had written, you could compel a man to remain in a particular church, but you could not possibly make him believe anything that was said there. The rational mind went wherever the preponderance of empirical evidence and the logic of a good argument led it. Religious coercion was therefore as impractical as it was unjust.[4]

Chauncy's was not a terribly radical position for the time. Few contemporaries would have suggested that anyone should be forced to attend a particular church or listen to a particular minister. And that is probably why so few Americans felt the need to articulate such sentiments. By the late

1730s, hardly anyone denied the "right of private judgment" or the value of toleration. While Chauncy's indictment of the clergymen who still zealously imposed creeds might have ruffled a few feathers, his endorsement of individual choice and his insistence on an ontological divide between body and mind would have only reinforced what most people already believed.

But ideas have a nasty habit of getting away from those who articulate them. In the years after Chauncy's defense of religious liberty appeared, countless churches divided, hundreds of new churches came into existence, and dozens of itinerant preachers made their way between legally distinct parishes. As a consequence, Chauncy's insistence upon the sanctity of religious choice acquired a disquietingly concrete character. In town after town, new spiritual choices erupted onto the plane of colonial Americans' social and intellectual existence. Judgments that had been securely anchored to particular places, confined by particular institutions, defined by particular people, would come to roam as ceaselessly as the bodies that traveled to hear different preachers and attend different services. In place after place, geographical location no longer served as a barrier to spiritual satisfaction. To use a common contemporary expression, the Spirit was quite literally "moving" through the land.[5]

During the late 1730s and early 1740s, religious boundaries in colonial America came under nearly unrelenting assault—and established ministers under nearly unrelenting criticism—as "New Light" preachers spread across New England and the Middle Colonies. The term "New Light" was applied to those who embraced the overwhelming sense of grace that the awakenings inspired. For the New Lights, faith was measured by the experience of sincere commitment rather than doctrinal knowledge or conformity to conventional practices. They were also moved less by the salvation that Christ's sacrifice promised to all than by the personal assurance of salvation that was granted to individuals. When struck by God's righteousness, they dropped to their knees and cried out for mercy. When affected by his mercy, they sang hymns through the streets. On the whole, they evinced an unusual interest in divine matters. There was something truly different about those born again. Once turned toward God, the New Lights claimed to see the world anew. Their view of both spiritual and worldly things became largely incompatible with that of the unregenerate. They just could not see things the same way anymore.[6]

Thousands were brought to the New Light faith through the preaching of itinerant ministers who sailed back and forth across the Atlantic and rode up and down the Atlantic coastline. The itinerants' physical movement and their blatant disregard for parish lines complemented the New Lights' general contempt for theological forms and church affiliations. The reborn gladly subordinated the obligations of church allegiance and social decorum to the delights of sincere faith. Those whose isolation prevented them from hearing certain preachers could read about them in the many printed works that appeared at the time. Connecting the itinerants' promiscuous visits with the explosion of print, the Anglican minister Timothy Cutler grumbled: "The presses are ever teeming with books and the women with bastards."[7]

By the 1730s, Middle Colonists and New Englanders had learned to accommodate the sincere, preferably quiet, dissent of a socially and geographically distinct minority. And they had begun to relax the doctrinal requirements imposed on individual church members. That was the toleration Charles Chauncy had endorsed in his 1739 sermon (and, to a similar extent, Jonathan Dickinson and his Presbyterian allies had a few years earlier). But colonial Americans had never before confronted the range of spiritual alternatives that the Awakening presented. Many "Old Light" ministers, who frowned on the New Lights' emotionalism, came to regard the itinerants, even those of their own denomination, with the same hostility once reserved for "sectarians." The Reverend Nathanael Eells noted that, in the past, he successfully "guard[ed]" his congregants against "Men of corrupt Principles," staving off both Baptism and Quakerism, and was not about to permit a prominent revivalist to preach from his pulpit. To their critics, the itinerants' travels were a metaphor for the literal groundlessness of the arguments they advanced. To their adoring audiences, however, their appearance was not unlike the unpredictable, miraculous wanderings of the Holy Spirit.[8]

The preacher whom Reverend Eells refused to admit to his pulpit was the charismatic revivalist George Whitefield. In 1739 Whitefield arrived on the shores of colonial America for his celebrated first tour. No itinerant minister drew more attention than the man that contemporaries referred to as the Grand Itinerant. Crowds as big as armies sometimes gathered to hear this animated Methodist (at a time when Methodism was still just a movement within the Anglican church) preach the joys of the New Birth. Whitefield urged his listeners to prepare their hearts to receive the grace bestowed by their omnipotent creator, to turn their lustful, world-burdened thoughts toward the perils of divine justice and the inimitable bliss that accompanied divine mercy. People of every conceivable church joined the throngs of worshipers. Whitefield welcomed them all. During a conversation with a fellow minister, Whitefield observed that he "saw regenerate souls among the Baptists, among the Presbyterians, among the Independents, and among the Church folks,—all children of God, and yet all born again in a different way of worship," and asked, "who can tell which is the most evangelical?" Whitefield prided himself on being as inclusive in his criticism as he was in his theology.

"As I love all who love the Lord Jesus, of what communion soever," he noted at the conclusion of a well-attended sermon, "so I reprove all whether Dissenters, or not Dissenters, who take His word into their mouths, but never felt Him dwelling in their hearts."[9]

The Grand Itinerant frequently preached out-of-doors, in the streets and in the fields. His words were simple, direct, and well honed through repetition. In those open spaces where Whitefield spoke, his audience could freely weep, gasp, or swoon at his graphic depictions of redemption and sin, heaven and hell. They could succumb to the feverish tremors that seemed to take hold of their bodies. The emotional response, particularly the alleged "bodily effects," Whitefield and his fellow itinerants generated conformed to what learned individuals knew about those possessed of strange or heretical beliefs, or those under the influence of malicious forces. When the popular itinerant James Davenport's infamously tossed his clothing into a bonfire, it only reinforced the connection that some made between evangelism and heresy. But those antirevivalists were in the minority. For the mass of laypeople, and for a growing number of colonial preachers, sincere belief was increasingly signified by the outward signs that it induced: the uncontrollable, unconscious movements of a body freed from its dependence on the prudential calculations and excessive formality of the instructed mind.[10]

What irked contemporary critics almost as much as Whitefield's emotional brand of preaching was the mutability, as well as the multiplicity, of his attachments. To some observers, Whitefield was damningly promiscuous. A Boston broadside, *Mr. W—D's Soliloquy, or a Serious Debate with Himself what Course He Shall Take*, sarcastically represented the choices—both of affiliation and place—that Whitefield confronted:

> Swarms of *Moravians* would have done,
> Had Brother *Tennant* held his Tongue.
> Should I go back to the Church Party,
> They never would receive me hearty:
> The *Quakers* won't admit me now,
> Since I am charg'd with breach of Vow;
> Who, tho' like me they do not pray, Pay Rev'rence
>   to a *Yea* and *Nay*.
> The *Separatists* yet are few,
> Tho' they alone, of all, are true

One Anglican minister deplored Whitefield's "Practice . . . of itinerating over all Parts of the British Dominions," as well as his readiness "to preach the Gospel to any Sect, Party, or Faction, that shew Willingness or Desire to hear

[him]." In addition to the "corrupt principles" he advanced, the "enthusiasm" he displayed in preaching, and the passions that he tended to incite in his listeners, Whitefield's supposed infidelity warranted his exclusion from at least one church. The Congregationalist Nathaniel Henchman prohibited the Grand Itinerant from preaching in his pulpit on account of Whitefield's "frequent changing Sides (In one Country he is a true Son of the Church of England, in a second, a stanch [sic] Presbyterian, and in a third, a strong Congregationalist)." A Pennsylvanian Presbyterian expressed the widely held sentiment that Whitefield proved "inconsistent with himself."[11]

It was not only the multiple attachments but the persuasive authority that Whitefield exercised over his audience—especially the observed physical influence on his female auditors, some of whom experienced "strange unusual Bodily Motions"—that earned him a reputation for promiscuity. The mere fact that so many women found Whitefield's message appealing was a sure sign of mischief. It was well known that wives had been filling their husbands heads with bad opinions ever since Eve passed on advice from the serpent. A pamphlet signed "A Number of Laymen" portrayed Whitefield as an unlearned seducer, referring to him as "the Rev. Batchelor of Arts." The criticism aimed at Whitefield was not new. Dissenting sects had long been accused of committing the most aberrant of sexual acts. Likewise, anticlerical polemics had long accused ministers of abusing the affection of their female worshipers. But Whitefield's charismatic form of preaching was so compelling and the opportunities for inclusive spiritual communion suddenly so much more evident that a collective blush seemed to fall over the whole countenance of American religious life. With so many available alternatives and so few legal restrictions on religious affiliation, there was no telling what theological indecencies might result.[12]

The late 1730s and early 1740s witnessed other potential sources of social disruption, including the appearance of uneducated lay preachers and the increased participation of both free and enslaved African Americans. Such dramatic social developments convinced some skeptics that the New Lights were less interested in revival than revolution. To contain the more unsettling aspects of the Awakening, the Connecticut Assembly passed "An Act for regulating Abuses and correcting Disorders in Ecclesiastical Affairs" in 1742. The Assembly also ordered Hartford's sheriff to "arrest the bodies" of Davenport and another itinerant. Davenport—whose propensity for book and clothes burning, rash judging, and general disdain for established religious authority was renowned—was judged to be "disturb'd in the rational faculties of his mind" and ordered back to Long Island. The New York legislature passed a similar legislation in 1744 that prohibited unlicensed "vagrant Teachers,

Moravians, and disguised Papists" from preaching or teaching "in public or private." In Virginia, Governor William Gooch complained that his colony, which had been "hitherto remarkable for uniformity in worship" was recently marred by "certain *false teachers* that are lately crept into this government . . . without orders or licenses, or producing any testimonial of their education or sect, professing themselves ministers under the pretended influence of *new light, extraordinary impulse,* and *such like* fanatical and enthusiastical knowledge." He promised to use the law to reduce these "seducers" to "silence."[13]

Concerns about the impact of evangelism on orthodox faith and good social order cropped up in Virginia a few years later than it did in the north, when the revivalistic spirit took belated hold in that colony. There, the Anglican Church was established by law, and dissent was sharply curtailed with fines, arrests, and public whippings. There, an admirer of George Whitefield, the Presbyterian Samuel Davies, drew the ire of local and imperial authorities for "disturb[ing]" consciences among the colony's recently settled peoples. A letter from the bishop of London to one of Davies's correspondents suggested that Davies and his fellow Presbyterians were claiming "a natural right to propagate their opinions in religion," something for which the Act of Toleration surely did not provide. According to the bishop, the Act of Toleration was intended to "ease" dissenting consciences, the very consciences Davies was now "disturb[ing]." He accused Davies (as Whitefield had been accused before him) of traveling vast distances to proselytize members of the bishop's own legally established church, in a land where there were almost no dissenters just a few years before. The charges were not without merit. Defending his right to preach unlicensed in multiple parishes, Davies insisted that ministers were entitled to preach outside of their *"particular* Places" if the *"general"* good required it. Davies professed a desire to evangelize without consideration for denominational identities and noted that he would rather have seen "a *pious* [Anglican] than a *graceless Presbyterian.*" Such conciliatory sentiments failed to move Anglican authorities—though the provisions of the English Toleration Act did, and Davies was eventually granted the extraordinary right to preach in five counties.[14]

Whenever it appeared and whatever the status of the established church there, evangelical religion presented many of the same problems for religious authorities. Although New Light faith struck later in Virginia than in Pennsylvania or Massachusetts, its impact proved longer lasting and even more pronounced. Recounting the disturbances raised by one dissenting evangelical, a Virginia Anglican noted that his sermons were delivered with passion and "in a more authoritative, and yet affectionate familiar manner, than the people had ever heard before, and they were proportionably [sic], more affected."[15] Those inspired by evangelical preaching demanded something more than toleration for a few, isolated dissenters. Their movement threatened to con-fuse, divide, and perhaps even destroy the churches that standing ministers had labored so long to build. Opponents of the revivals worried that all pros-pects for religious unity would dissolve in an ocean of itinerant ministers and enthusiastic believers. Their fears had some foundation in reality. In many places where the spirit of revival struck, the number of different churches and ministers increased rapidly. And the number of (sometimes contradictory) private judgments seemed to expand exponentially. Who, one had to wonder, could judge between them?

Partial Judgments

In June 1745, after a friend brought him yet another stack of polemical literature (all of it hostile toward George Whitefield), the Reverend Ebenezer Parkman noted ruefully in his diary: "the world much divided." It certainly must have seemed so to this middle-aged pastor from the eastern Massachusetts town of Westborough. For the past several years, Parkman had found himself embroiled in countless disputes over theological doctrine, differing states of grace, and the relative merits of itinerant preachers. Meanwhile, the local presses had churned out religious treatise after religious treatise and newspaper editors—who had once filled their paper's pages with secondhand accounts of foreign wars and trade news for merchants—now highlighted the activities of controversial reli-gious figures. Like many of his contemporaries, Parkman had initially hoped that the Awakening would unite his congregation and enhance his standing among the laity. But the divisions persisted and his authority continued to deteriorate. In November 1747, Parkman sat on a committee appointed by the local association of ministers to discuss the recent theological turmoil and to reach some consensus regarding their approach to it. By the end of their first and only meeting, the committee "could go no further than to mark and minute the principal Heads without drawing up any report."[16]

There was not much that a small-town minister, especially one of such humble capacities, could do. So Parkman, who had never been terribly inde-cisive in the past, struggled to maintain a critical distance from the polemical debates surrounding the Awakening. On more than one occasion he offered an ostensibly detached account of events. In 1742, for instance, Parkman made the following entry regarding the controversial evangelist, Samuel Buell, who trod dangerously close to his own congregation: "The world full of Mr Buels preaching at Concord. In the Judgements of some great success: In the Judgements of others great Confusion." No further comment followed. Likewise, in a December 1741 letter to Jonathan Edwards, Parkman expressed his desire "that the Evils on both Hands might be avoided, tepidity and Enthusiasm, and that unanswerable rash judging which both sides run into." Again it seemed imprudent for this long-established minister to take sides.[17]

When not playing the role of a detached observer of truth, Parkman sometimes retreated to a feeble religious subjectivism. In late 1742, an irreverent parishioner named Stephen Fay confronted Parkman and revealed his concern for both their souls. The layman suggested that if his minister "had a true sight of Eternal Things he thought [Parkman] should be more Zealous and fervent." Parkman conceded his "Dulness" but "spake of the different Tempers of men; the Diversitys of Gifts." Parkman's "Dulness," or lack of fervor, represented the immediate problem, but the larger question centered on his "sight of Eternal Things," his access to the true and the good. Fay's comment illustrated the extent to which the revivals provided alternative standards against which the conduct and vision of a minister like Parkman could be measured. Parkman's response illustrated the extent to which a hierarchy of knowledge had become difficult to maintain and suggested that true faith might manifest itself in a variety of ways. In Westborough, as in other parts of America, the venerable right of private judgment was taking on some disquieting implications.[18]

Reverend Parkman now occupied an unenviable position. During the midcentury revivals, he would be constantly reminded of his partiality and, at the same time, increasingly asked to exercise impartiality in his judgments. Addressing the congregation in the religiously divided town of Rutland in 1740, Parkman preached the same sermon he had offered to another troubled congregation five years earlier—that is, before the revival had burned through his area. Enjoining his listeners to seek "The Peace of Jerusalem," the reverend communicated the traditional conviction that true faith and right beliefs made communal harmony possible. But something had changed this time. At the conclusion of the discourse, Parkman tacked on an addendum in which he claimed that he was "speaking both to the pastor and to the Flock without partiality or unrighteous regard to one or another." Thus, almost imperceptibly, this small-town minister had slipped out of the role of Jeremiah, reproaching the sinful masses for their differences, and into the role of neutral umpire, arbitrating between competing positions.[19]

Up and down the Atlantic coastline, the revivals generated similar challenges for those who typically rendered authoritative judgments. An anonymous Charleston, South Carolina, minister professed difficulties almost identical to

Ebenezer Parkman's. There was such "a Diversity of Opinions," regarding George Whitefield's character, he noted in a letter published by the *South-Carolina Gazette*, that he had decided to "suspend my Judgment," until he met the Grand Itinerant himself. The plight of men represented by this piece illustrates the problems that ordinary ministers faced as they grappled with the social and theological impact of the Great Awakening.[20] The divisions created by the revivals could make all judgments seem partial. An article in a Boston newspaper observed that what looked like devout piety to some "appear[ed] in a quite different and contrary Aspect" to others.[21] With so many opinions being tendered, with so many alternatives proposed, there appeared to be no single position from which incontestable judgments could be rendered. As traditional religious authorities were challenged by irreverent laypeople like Stephen Fay and fiery itinerants like Samuel Buell, it could seem that all authority was suspect, that every fervent expression of faith was genuine. But who was invested with the authority to judge between conflicting private judgments? Was anyone? Dozens of churches separated during the Great Awakening because they could not settle this question.

The problem extended beyond individual congregations to include whole bodies of clergy. In May of 1743, it appeared that the ministers of Massachusetts had finally reached a determinative judgment on the revival. After convening in Boston, a group claiming to represent the colony's clergymen published its conclusions in *The Testimony of the pastors of the churches in the province of the Massachusetts-Bay, in New-England, at their annual convention in Boston*. The pamphlet condemned itinerant ministers, lay preaching, church separations, and "rash judging." (The assembled pastors also quoted from the published advice of several late seventeenth-century ministers who had warned New England that their "*Unthankfulness*" would provoke God to "send the *Plague of an unlearned Ministry* upon poor NEW-ENGLAND.") The reading public soon learned, however, that the *Testimony of the Pastors* represented the opinions of only a small portion of Massachusetts' pastors—and barely half of those who attended the May meeting. Several of the attendees objected to the negative assessment of the revivals. One of them called for another meeting in July. This time one hundred eleven ministers met and ninety of them endorsed a favorable judgment of the revival. In an obvious rebuke to the May convention, they titled the account of their proceedings *The Testimony and Advice of an Assembly of Churches in New England . . . Occasion'd by the late happy Revival of Religion in many parts of the Land.*[22]

It must have been unnerving for New Englanders to encounter two distinct interpretations of the revival, both professing to be the authoritative testimony of the region's standing churches. Such divisions may have emboldened laypeople, including the few who published their own *Testimony and Advice of a Number of Laymen respecting Religion, and the Teachers of it*. The title's irreverence carried into the text itself. The Laymen claimed to publish "as disinterested Persons, which Ministers are not," and excoriated the provincial clergy for having brought on the present chaos themselves by first welcoming New Light preachers and then warning them off. Praising "freedom [of] Inquiry" and the use of reason in religious matters, the Laymen advised the clergy to avoid emotionalism, to strive for theological coherence, and to stop pretending that the church's pulpit was theirs to share if and when they pleased. It is hard to imagine laypeople airing such a critical judgment of established clergymen during the first three decades of the eighteenth century. Although they had occasionally bickered with their congregants over salary issues, and an occasional layperson had openly challenged their views, the region's standing ministers enjoyed virtually unrivaled authority and prestige. Nonetheless, by the early 1740s, areas touched by revivalistic fervor enjoyed (or suffered—depending on your perspective) an abundance of private judgments. It suddenly seemed that everyone had his own opinion.[23]

More troubling still was the fact that everyone seemed willing to voice his opinions of others. As we have seen, the right of private judgment was already too sacred to be questioned. Instead, antirevivalists bemoaned the fact that thousands of enthusiastic converts presumed to judge other people's faith, and to do so publicly. They singled out George Whitefield as a particularly censorious judge—one who seemed intent upon castigating his fellow ministers publicly. Among those who listened to Whitefield, Charles Chauncy wrote, "there was raised such a Spirit of bitter, censorious, uncharitable judging, as was not know [sic] before; and is, wherever it reigns, a Scandal to all who call themselves Christians." After the Grand Itinerant leveled some disparaging remarks upon Harvard's faculty, Edward Wigglesworth asked "what good" Whitefield hoped to achieve by "calumniating us thus *publickly, in your Journal,* without ever hearing what we had to say for ourselves." According to the Laymen, people were once able to "bear with each other in Charity" and had not always "pretend[ed] to know and judge the Hearts of their Neighbours." The Awakening had changed all of that. With the arrival of the Grand Itinerant, whose followers "pronounc'd this, that and the other Minister, *Unconverted, Pharisee, Dead, dry Bones,*" few displayed forbearance toward those whose faith manifested itself differently. It may have been forgivable to harbor those judgments in one's mind, perhaps even share them with friends through private correspondence. The real offense lay in the public expression of uncharitable sentiments about other people's faith. Moderate and conservative antirevivalists alike contended that the New Lights were attempting to expose the secrets to which only God was rightfully privy. Although we might judge an individual's stated opinion to be false, they implored, no further judgments were warranted.[24]

If New Englanders held George Whitefield largely responsible for the outbreak of rash judging in their midst, Middle Colonists accused the Irish-born Presbyterian Gilbert Tennent. Tennent was among the graduates of his father's one-room college (though he later earned a degree from Yale College) who began to preach in other ministers' churches as early as 1737. Throughout New Jersey and eastern Pennsylvania, these young itinerants harangued clergymen who seemed more interested in inculcating doctrine than converting souls. Their critique culminated with Tennent's infamous *The Dangers of an Unconverted Ministry* (1740), which excoriated the "Pharisees" of the modern world, the "Hypocrites" who dwelled all too comfortably in their professed spiritual accomplishments. Tennent defended the right of the laity to pursue spiritual satisfaction wherever they could find it. He also defended the right of those who had experienced God's saving grace, to cast judgment on other souls. "Tho' he cannot know the States of subtil [sic] Hypocrites infallibly," Tennent wrote, the sanctified individual was entitled to venture "a near Guess." Hypocrites opposed "all Knowing of others, and Judging," he observed, "in order to hide their own Filthiness." Tennent urged individuals to bind themselves to one another by means of that faith which could hardly be spoken. Groups joined by something other than their sincere love for God would resemble "the Unity of the Devils." So, Tennent and his fellows demanded a form of association that would separate the true believers from the false.[25]

It is perhaps indicative of both the prevalence of religious criticism and the increasing animus against it that prominent New Lights eventually began to condemn rash judgment themselves. The New England clergy who assembled to vindicate the revivals in 1743, for instance, stressed at the outset of their published testimony that they intended to proceed "without judging or censuring such of our Brethren as cannot at present see Things in the same Light with us." Even those who were regarded as the source of this alleged outbreak of rash judging were compelled to acknowledge that they had been uncharitable. By the middle of 1742, none other than Gilbert Tennent had disavowed the separate meetings, the excessive "enthusiasm," and the rash judging that accompanied the revivals. By 1744, George Whitefield had issued a *mea culpa* for his attack on Harvard. In the 1756 edition of his published journal, the Grand Itinerant included a footnote that characterized those earlier comments about the college as "rash and uncharitable." This was quite an admission and a testament to the reaction against "rash judgments" that the Great Awakening had inspired.[26]

The New Lights also came under fire for their notion that the saints should seek one another out and for the belief that only they (the saints) had the capacity to identify other faithful souls. On the Old Light view, the revivalists were substituting loud outbursts and zealous mimicry for authentic private judgments. "Let not such powerful arguments as *I think, I am afraid, I believe*, and *I verily believe*," John Caldwell entreated his audience, "hinder us from thinking and believing for our selves." The challenge, he continued, was to avoid letting "such common Place Talk as will prove all Doctrines equally good, have any Influence upon our Minds." By sanctioning rash judgments and by conferring so much authority on individual expressions of belief, Caldwell suggested, the evangelical movement had actually diminished the autonomy provided by the liberal right of private judgment.[27]

Things looked much different from the revivalists' perspective. As they saw it, the right of private judgment included the right to openly describe one's own sincerely felt convictions and to determine who else shared them—as well as the concomitant right to move across parish boundaries freely and attend ministers of one's choosing. No one articulated the logic behind such behavior more powerfully and subtly than Jonathan Edwards. The renowned theologian provoked some of the very earliest stirrings of the Great Awakening in his Connecticut River town of Northampton, Massachusetts. There, in 1734 and 1735, he observed his congregants hearkening to the spiritual tasks he set before them. *His Some Thoughts Concerning the Revival in New-England* appeared almost a decade later, at a time of growing hostility toward the alleged excesses of the revival. In this lengthy treatise, Edwards dwelt on the insufficiency of language in describing the soul's condition. The individual experience of grace was as unpredictable, as resistant to external characterization, as were God's intentions. According to Edwards, the individual perceived saving grace within much as someone would the blowing of the wind. In both cases, shared experience represented the only means of demonstrating what could be indisputably felt but imperfectly communicated. Moreover, Edwards argued, the practice of "Censuring others" was not the altogether unexpected outcome of a period in which many had undergone a profound conversion experience.[28]

Whether New Lights such as Tennent and Whitefield were actually guilty of being "uncharitable," the entire discussion of rash judging marked a dramatic turning point in the way Americans talked about their religious differences. Both traditional Calvinists and liberal rationalists maintained that believers must confine their evaluation of other human beings to their speech and behavior. For them, the only legitimate judgments were outward ones. Therefore, the judgments being rendered by the New Light counterparts, ostensibly based on powerful intuitions, were misguided, if not downright sinful. Among the truly strange and unsettling things about the judgments being rendered by upstart ministers and fervent laypeople were how certain they seemed. For the moment at least, the surest assertions of truth and the most confident invocations of religious authority were not being made by the authorities.

For conventional religious figures this development presented some daunting problems. When religious experience was cast in such forcibly subjective terms, men like Ebenezer Parkman lacked the words to justify their own religious judgments. The surfeit of passionately defended opinions left him nearly speechless. To Parkman, New Light criticism of conventional religion appeared not only rash but "unanswerable." His hopes ultimately resided in the possibility that religious authorities could lay claim to impartiality. Similarly, Jonathan Dickinson asked his audience whether their "dividing Practices" would "stand the Tryal of indifferent Judges," and if not, then perhaps they would consider their practices in light of the account that would be taken on Judgment Day. Impartial judgments were particularly necessary at this moment, John Caldwell noted, when so much "Diversity of Sentiments about Religious Principles Prevail." In addition, the way "Men of contrary Principles equally pretend[ed] to the Direction of the Spirit," and how they were "equally censorious and uncharitable to such as differ from 'em" made an "Impartial Trial" absolutely necessary. Samuel Davies replied to the Virginia publication of Caldwell's tract with his own *The Impartial Trial, impartially Tried, and convicted of Partiality* (1748).[29]

The ideal of impartiality or objectivity appealed to ministers beset by what seemed a thousand different opinions as it would public speakers and newspaper editors throughout the remainder of the century. Frustrated by the first great "Infest[ation]" of New Light preachers in the Carolina backcountry, the Anglican Charles Woodmason proposed that "a Comparison [be drawn] between them and Us" and that "an Impartial Judge determine where *Offence* may cheifly [sic] be taken, At our Solemn, Grave, and Serious Sett [sic] Forms, or their Wild Extempore Jargon, nauseaus [sic] to any Chaste or refin'd Ear." Whatever faith they placed in impartial judgments, few established clergymen could have taken much comfort in the notion that they, the pillars of their communities, now required the services of an outside, impartial judge to justify their authority. According to the historian of science and mathematics, Theodore Porter, "a community founded on objectivity is a weak or endangered community, one without sharp borders on the outside, and one without an effortless shared understanding—in short, a very modern kind of community." Objectivity was indeed a thin reed for a preacher of the Word to stand upon. But in an age when parish lines had withered, when conventional religious judgments were suspect, and traditional religious commitments had lost much of their compulsive force, the ordinary colonial minister did not have much choice.[30]

Of course, established ministers and colonial magistrates in places such as Massachusetts, New York, Connecticut, and Virginia could still resort to the assertion of massive, official authority. As we have seen, they sometimes did so—prosecuting itinerants for vagrancy and treating some New Light worshipers with the severity usually reserved for outspoken heretics. For the most part, however, the antirevivalists had to rely upon less coercive instruments. The most systematic retort to New Light practices issued from the pen of Charles Chauncy. Chauncy's lengthy response to Edwards's *Some Thoughts* called upon the same assumptions that justified the use of state authority against unruly itinerants. In his *Seasonable Thoughts on the State of Religion in New-England* (1743), Chauncy neglected the traditional opening apology and concluded with the signatures of several hundred New England dignitaries, including the governors of Massachusetts, Connecticut, and Rhode Island and Providence Plantations. This was no mere rhetorical thrust. The whole weight of civil and religious power was being mustered to suppress the growing contagion. Here was a judgment that surely even the most irreverent New Light could not contest.

Chauncy prefaced his unfavorable account of the revivals with an extended comparison of the New Light outbreak to the disease that Anne Hutchinson and her fellow Antinomians had spread in defiance of New England's Puritan founders. During the early years of Puritan settlement, Chauncy maintained, these "Opinionists" carried their errors from England to America. The Antinomian "infection" was disseminated effectively, in part, because its proponents successfully acquainted themselves with so many people. Like many of his contemporaries, Chauncy associated New Light preaching with seduction, citing the biblical passages that indicated that in "the last days" there would appear those who "creep into Houses, and lead captive silly Women laden with sins; led away with divers lusts; Ever learning, and never able to come to the knowledge of the truth." Significantly, Chauncy's unapologetic invocation of authority drew upon the libertarian principles that he had invoked just four years earlier. As with Jonathan Dickinson's conservative Lockean attack on Samuel Hemphill in 1735, Chauncy summoned the right of private judgment to challenge the liberties that the New Lights were taking. He insisted that individuals must independently inquire into religious matters, taking nothing on trust either from "single Persons, or public Bodies." Nor should civil magistrates play a role in the determination of religious matters. But here Chauncy's position diverged from the modern liberal defense of free expression that Benjamin Franklin advocated and the New Lights implicitly endorsed. For Chauncy insisted that private judgment be protected to the point of recommending that civil magistrates "restrain some Men's *Tongues* with *Bit* and *Bridle*." In Chauncy's complex synthesis of rationalism, liberalism, and traditional authority, it might be possible to make out the faint echo of the Philadelphia Synod's dispute with Franklin eight years before. As had been the case on that occasion, a committed proponent of the liberal right of private judgment proved amenable to quieting dissent. For the Congregationalist Chauncy, as for the Presbyterian Jonathan Dickinson, the right to privately judge still entailed the obligation to judge in private—and, of course, in one's designated place.[31]

Chauncy's *Seasonable Thoughts* was designed to serve as "a great Preservative against the Errors and Disorders," to which contemporary zealots had succumbed, that it might "not only . . . guard those who are not as yet infected, but [also] to check the Growth of our Difficulties." As it turned out, most of the reading public appears to have been no more impressed by his alleged antidote than they were by the vaccines offered as cures for smallpox. It is hardly surprising that the pamphlet proved difficult to sell. Where religious claims were as hotly contested as they were in mid-eighteenth-century New England, the pretense of speaking univocally on behalf of the general public could not help but fail. Chauncy shared the increasingly unpopular Old Light conviction belief that to be persuaded was to quietly and voluntarily embrace the truths that God (by way of the established clergy and their writings) had made available to everyone. He rejected the notion that a religious society should continually have to justify its existence before its critics. Of course, repeated acts of persuasion were precisely what the rashly judging New Lights were demanding.[32]

While Chauncy's religious liberalism had been put to conservative uses in this instance, his principles remained largely consistent. Among other things, he maintained the important distinction between the mind (which could only be moved by persuasion) and the body (which could be coerced). According to opponents of the revival, like Charles Chauncy, the tremors of the enthusiastic believer, the physically seductive quality of New Light preaching, and the transience of the evangelical preacher were all clear manifestations of how bodily necessity had trespassed upon the autonomy of the individual mind. During the Awakening, religious societies found themselves besieged by dissenters who refused to stay where they were, and refused to remain silent if they did. To the legal toleration that religious dissent generally enjoyed, the midcentury religious revivals added the sanction that individuals demanded for their own subjective experience. The question then arose: Could a community be forged from such notoriously incongruous materials? Could so many private judgments be reconciled? Could those who disagreed so passionately still walk together?[33]

The Divided Church

In the early 1740s, as arguments within the churches sometimes turned bitter enough to precipitate schisms, it seemed that the direst prophecies might come to pass. Perhaps, as Catholic polemicists had long predicted, Protestantism had been overcome by its insistence upon the right of private judgment. After all, what was a voluntary church to do when no one could agree, when everyone's opinion seemed legitimate and yet partial? What was it to do when the authority of traditional institutions had been discredited? How were decisions to be made when everyone's opinion had to be accounted for?

Church separations occurred throughout the northern colonies during the 1740s and 1750s, yet once again the limits of dissent and the right of societies to make decisions for their individual members were tested most visibly in the Presbyterian Synod of Philadelphia. The controversy over the eccentric young Irish preacher Samuel Hemphill had barely ended when disagreements over the examination of ministerial candidates split that body in two. Supporters and opponents of the revival—later referred to as "New Siders" and "Old Siders" respectively—edged toward a showdown in 1738 when the Synod passed two divisive acts, mandating ministerial examinations for those educated in nontraditional colleges and restricting itinerant preaching. Soon after, the New Siders began preaching, uninvited, within the parish bounds of the regularly ordained clergy. Then, the evangelical New Brunswick Presbytery rebuffed the Synod's demand to exclude from its pulpits the Log College graduate who refused to undergo synodical examination. Gilbert Tennent's *The Danger of an Unconverted Ministry* crystallized New Side grievances with the Old Siders. Fed up with the New Side's censoriousness, their itinerant preaching, their resistance to synodical authority, and their emotional brand of piety, the Old Siders presented a formal protest to the entire Synod when it assembled in May 1741.[34]

In certain respects, this latest controversy within the Synod represented a continuation of the disputes in the 1720s and 1730s over the right of ministers to dissent from the church's creed, the Westminster Confession of Faith. But in important ways, the dispute over the Old Side protest demonstrated how the Great Awakening presented a new strain of challenges to both religious authority and church unity. The New Sides were not, according to their own understanding, quibbling over a few points of doctrine. Instead, they were protecting the rights that the newly converted had to voice their sincerely held opinions and to share their newfound love of godly things. For their part, the Old Sides decried the preaching of allegedly "unlearned" ministers to legions of even less learned souls, and they lamented that no authoritative judgment— at least none of *their* judgments—went uncontested. They felt their own obligation to preserve what remained of true doctrines and right practices. To both sides, the fate of Christianity hung in the balance.

While the details are murky, we do know that the New Siders withdrew from the Synod on June 1, 1741, the same day that the Old Siders read their protest aloud before that body. The offending document connected the division within the Synod to the larger problems that the Awakening posed for conventional ministers. In addition to defending the authority of the Westminster Confession within the Synod and the Synod's authority within its territorial jurisdiction, these Old Lights denounced the revivalists' "heterodox and anarchical principles," as well as their "unwearied, unscriptural, anti-presbyterial, uncharitable, divisive practices." The New Light's "rash judging" came in for special condemnation. According to the Old Side protest, men such as Gilbert Tennent and Samuel Blair had persuaded gullible listeners that conversion was measured by "some invisible motions and workings of the Spirit, which none can be conscious or sensible of but the person himself," then "judge[d]" those same listeners' "ministers to be graceless." For the Old Siders, the attack on the Synod's authority, the antinomian approach to conversion, and the outbreak of rash judging were all symptoms of the same malady. Given the vast differences between them, the Old Siders thought continued union would be fruitless. "For how can two walk together, except they be agreed?"[35]

The way the Old Sides handled these events, and subsequently recorded them, reveals a great deal about the main issues involved. One does not have to spend much time with the Synod's official minutes to discover that they were generally written in the same unflappable, passive voice that characterizes this humble genre. That is, until June 1, 1741, the day the Old Light protest was read. The minutes for that day include the following note: "A protestation was brought in by Mr. Cross, read, and signed by several members. . . . Upon this it was canvassed by the former protesting brethren, whether they or we are to be looked upon as the Synod." At that point, the first-person pronoun "we" made a second startling appearance: "*We* maintained that they had no right to sit whether they were the major or minor number" (emphasis added). According to this official account, the New Sides then called for a vote. The text reads: "They were found to be the minor party, and upon this they withdrew. After this the Synod proceeded to business." These few perfunctory lines suggest that the New Sides had hoped to declare themselves the Synod—though they later disavowed any such intention. Nor did the New Sides necessarily depart as abruptly as the minutes suggest. Instead, they claimed to have remained at the session through the conclusion of the final prayer.[36]

The next few years would show that even some of those who sympathized with the Old Lights objected to the continued exclusion of their fellow ministers. For the moment, however, the Old Sides had assumed the voice of the whole Synod (the "We" of the minutes), effectively nullifying dissenting opinion and giving formal substance to the belief that (their) knowledge was certain and their church unified. For the moment, it was as though no true Presbyterian had ever itinerated in another Presbyterian's parish, been awarded a degree from an unrecognized college, or condemned his fellow ministers for a lack of fervency. When traditional judgments were discredited, ostensibly impartial knowledge proved impotent, and established authority subverted, separation allowed for that rarest of pearls: the rapture of complete solidarity. It surely did not last. Yet the prospect of joining a single judgment with seamless unity must have been hard to resist in 1741 when it did seem to Old Light types that few could walk together.[37]

This schism in the Synod of Philadelphia serves as a conspicuous example of the divisions inspired by the Awakening, the disturbances wrought by evangelical itinerants, and the backlash against "rash judging." It also, as the historian Patricia Bonomi has perceptively noted, represents the first occasion in American history—and perhaps in Western history—that a doctrine of minority rights was maintained. The argument emerged as the New Sides contested the notion that the major part of the Synod (the Old Sides) had the right to pass acts to which the New Lights could not fully assent. Just as significant and just as original, however, was the New Side insistence that the Synod's policy *merely* expressed the will of the "majority." To make this claim, according to Old Sider John Thomson, was to presuppose a division that could not exist. When an individual consented to determine a particular measure by means of a vote, Thomson argued, that person both exercised his "Christian Liberty" and bound himself to the determinations of the greater number. There was to be no quibbling about the results for, in the end, there was no distinguishing the so-called majority from the whole.[38]

For Thomson, the New Sides' talk of majorities and minorities was little more than a way of skirting the implicit obligations made when a vote was taken. Nonetheless, as he noted, there seemed to be something extraordinarily compelling, even magical, about this new language. "It appears," he wrote, "that the Words MAJORITY and MINORITY are of exceeding great Use and Esteem with them [the New Sides] in this Debate, as if they had something of a Spell or Charm in them invisibly to bear down all Things against which they are brought." Such novel incantations only betrayed how illusory their claims were. The New Siders, Thomson argued, were demanding a form of government founded on the notoriously unstable foundation of private judgment. As he saw it, such an institution would remain a hostage to the fickle opinions of its members, always changing, ever learning, and never bringing its members to the knowledge of the truth. Reaching agreement among so many self-righteous judges demanded the charms of the religious seducer and demoted the "whole" to the "majority." Religious societies built on such a ground could neither judge, educate, nor bind. Exactly what sort of church were the New Sides imagining they were a part of?[39]

To the Old Sides, the very idea of minority rights was founded on the absurd proposition that knowledge and authority might be partial. This was the ridiculous extreme to which the New Light's logic—the insistence that private judgment could not be curtailed, disciplined, nor directed—took them. Yet pressed, Thomson implicitly conceded the point by invoking the virtue of objectivity. "And now we also leave it to the impartial Reader to judge," Thomson wrote:

> Whether a Separation had not been made, in Effect, by our Brethren. . . . But the Misery is, our Readers, partial or impartial, will judge as they see Cause, without asking our or their Leave: For have not our Party-Readers as good a Right to proclaim themselves impartial Judges, as we to call ourselves impartial Contenders? Let every one therefore contend and judge, as those that shall be judged by a Supream Judge.

The modest and somewhat convoluted language here conveys the discomfort that Thomson must have felt in making this argument. How could a religious authority be "impartial" in important matters of faith? How could he defer judgment to his readers? These were troubling questions for a defender of creeds and a guardian of collective authority who thought that substantive differences had no permanent place within a community of the faithful.[40]

Ultimately, the difficulties nagging the Old Siders boiled down to one urgent question: To what extent could private judgments be compromised in order to maintain a church? The Synod's evangelical faction echoed revivalists in other parts of the colonies who insisted that religious harmony only came with common spiritual experiences, with the spontaneous, uncoerced movement of individual souls toward the same sanctified ends. They shared with the New Lights of New England, in particular, the conviction that ecclesiastical decisions required the explicit consent of all of those effected. Anything short of that might require the division of the church so that unanimity could be maintained. This separatist argument was most famously articulated by the Connecticut Congregationalist Elisha Williams, whose *The essential rights and liberties of Protestants* (1744) became a foundational text in eighteenth-century writing soon after its publication. The immediate occasion for Williams's treatise was the Connecticut Assembly's anti-itinerancy act, which resembled the Philadelphia Synod's policy. Williams, a former minister and law student, began his defense of private judgment with a discourse on natural rights drawn largely from the writing of John Locke. Williams then constructed a lengthy case for both the autonomy of the individual believer within the individual church and the autonomy of the individual church within the community of churches. On his view, social contracts imposed very few obligations on those who agreed to them. Williams maintained that each individual retained the right not only to read, but to interpret, to determine the "*Sense* and *Meaning*" of Scripture for himself. He suggested that the attempt to impose beliefs on the mind was no less "ridiculous" and cruel than the attempt to shape human bodies "'till they are brought to one *Size*, and one *Way of Thinking and Practice*." The mind, like the body, would not be easily "distort[ed]."[41]

Williams insisted that no "Determination" could be made when there was any disagreement over the "*several Modes . . .* of instituted Worship." Even if there was only one mode to choose, no decision could be made unless everyone could agree to it. The right of a society to make decisions for itself should not be privileged above either the individual's right to choose for himself, or the right that a part of the church had to separate and form another. For Williams, religious societies represented entirely conditional bodies from which hardly anyone could be excluded and to which no one could be bound. The decisions of the "Majority" were not to be "considered as the Act of the whole," as they might in a civil matter. In matters "where Conscience and Men's eternal Interests are concerned," individuals could not "transfer their Power to the Community." The fact that the majority represented the whole in a civil society, but not in a religious society, related to the fact that it was possible for individuals or groups to opt out of a religious society, but not out of civil society. The entrance to Williams's ideal church was wide; the exit was wider still.[42]

Williams's *Seasonable Plea* quickly became a classic of American religious thought. It represented one among only a handful of early eighteenth-century

American texts that other colonials would regard as worthy of citation. There are good reasons for it to have received the attention it did. Williams's appeal for liberty of conscience and minority rights in defense of itinerancy, religious separatists, and dissenters from established churches represented the first systematic justification of the physical dislocating, socially disruptive effects that the Awakening generated. He sanctioned what Chauncy—who shared Williams's sincere commitment to the right of private judgment—could barely countenance. Chauncy's argument for liberty of conscience presumed a stability of religious experiences, and a certain residency of bodies, so that "Persuasion" would represent little more than the autonomous choice of an autonomous mind among a few reasonable alternatives within the same physical space. Rational persuasion moved the mind, not the body. By contrast, Williams's argument presumed that perfectly legitimate religious experiences could be radically different and, as a result, that a sincere believer might feel himself bound to repeatedly depart one church for another or repeatedly recreate the one in which he already resided. Williams appears to have been comfortable with the idea that the church would continually need to be made and remade, perhaps as often as an especially persuasive itinerant traveled through town. His vision for religious communities was just what the Pennsylvania Old Siders had feared. There were few imperatives here and even fewer restraints. There was only the right that each individual had to judge for himself or herself, and to act upon that judgment.[43]

Like the Hemphill dispute of the 1730s, the Awakening-era conflict between revivalists and antirevivalists usually played out within a liberal framework. Mutual recriminations and denials made use of the same words. According to Chauncy's use of liberal principles, the right of private judgment was inalienable. However, as quickly became clear during the Great Awakening, Chauncy's definition of religious autonomy only possessed meaning within a particular community. In New England that meant the town or parish. As the revivals gained strength and those traditional boundaries lost their relevance, the standing order closed ranks and Chauncy's rational liberalism became virtually indistinguishable from Thomson's doctrinal orthodoxy. The movement of so many believers across town boundaries, the division of so many church parishes, and the virulent criticism directed against ministers like them did not fit any traditional understandings of the conditions for religious toleration. Yet for Williams and Tennent (and probably for those laymen and laywomen who followed them), the right to move about freely in search of religious fulfillment, across geographical boundaries, in and out of churches, and to point out hypocrisy wherever they discovered it was the very essence of private judgment.

In the end, as we know, the argument for majority rights did quite well in America. Even separatist groups found that they could not do without majoritarianism as an organizing principle—at least not if they wished to remain a unified body. Indeed, when the New Sides established their own Synod in New York in 1745 they agreed that the whole organization would be bound to the decisions of the majority (though only on "essential" matters) and that those members who could not conscientiously agree would have to withdraw. But by its very nature, the argument for the authority of the majority implied a division that religious traditionalists had never wanted to concede. Like the individual minister who invoked the principle of impartiality to defend his judgments, the groups that invoked majoritarianism to defend their decisions had already given up a great deal. In both cases, the legitimacy of differences was already established and acts of compromise, negotiation, and egalitarian gestures of persuasion already under way. In such a context, religious differences would always have their place.[44]

Mortal Visions

Was there any hope then for religious unity? As the revivals came and went, the possibility seemed quite remote. To some it appeared that the painful ruptures inspired by the Awakening could only be healed in death, the end of human criticism and the irrefutable seal of the Lord's Judgment—as would be the case in the coming millennium that so many now predicted. For at least one prominent minister, Jonathan Edwards, the Awakening concluded with visions of dead bodies, motionless, and yet on the brink of an eternity wherein their differences might be healed. Here, just as there was no need for earthly authorities, the authority of God's ministers might be affirmed.[45]

Sixteen years after Edwards set western New England aflame with his ominous warnings of damnation for the unconverted, the great theologian was dismissed from his Northampton congregation (1751). Conceding that he and his parishioners possessed irreconcilable differences, a council of nine churches ruled that Edwards should be separated from his congregation. In his farewell sermon, Edwards dolefully noted that debates between ministers and their parishioners were seldom of any avail. Though they might gather "to hear the Reasons that may be offered on one Side and the other," they often ended with little improvement on the part of those who erred. But, he continued, when they all met on Judgment Day, "there shall no longer be any Debate, or difference of Opinions; the Evidence of the Truth shall appear beyond all Dispute, and all Controversies shall be finally and forever decided." On that day, the Lord shall appear "in his most immediate and visible Presence." On that day, "the Secrets of every heart," which were otherwise inaccessible, "shall be made manifest." On that day, the minister's sincerity and faithfulness shall be evident; on that day, all censoriousness shall be at an end.[46]

In reading the clerical publications of this period, it becomes clear that many of America's ministers were experiencing a similar sense of exasperation, of despair at ever rebuilding the walls of Jerusalem in this world. It may be that we are witnessing the tired concessions of aging men, grown weary of dispute. The Awakening, after all, was largely a movement for the young, by the young. But by the late 1740s, some of America's most prominent clergymen appear to have recognized that they had done all they could to make the church as one, that they would die in a world divided with itself. They seemed increasingly aware that their church was no longer *the* Church, that their word would no longer be seen as *the* Word, and that neither would be again. In Edwards's millennialism we can detect a yearning for a final judgment that would at once sanctify the good and damn the evil, that would do so upon the grounds of a judgment that was just, omniscient, and determinative. Edwards's vision of deathly reconciliation represented a clearing away of irreconcilable differences. Only when living flesh had been transformed into dry bones would the truth be revealed. Whether it was the oft-made suggestion that individuals judge impartially (remembering that they would end up before the absolutely impartial tribunal of heaven), or Edwards's fantasy of deathly omniscience, the appeal of indisputable, objectified truth was apparent throughout the later years of the Awakening. The point often made against scientific rationality by its postmodernist critics—that the dream of objectivity is the dream of disembodied knowledge—possesses some resonance when applied to America's first Great Awakening.[47]

Indeed, only when the most obstinate opponents of evangelism, those defenders of conventional preaching styles and traditional parish lines, had passed from the scene would it become possible to imagine a society in which different beliefs successfully coexisted within the same community. The birth of a pluralistic culture required their death, or at least the death of that self-assured confidence they had once had in their own judgments. Accordingly, when the Synod of New York proposed a reunion with their Philadelphia brethren in 1749, they proposed that "all our former differences be buried in perpetual oblivion." A decade later, Francis Allison expressed his optimism that the reunion of the Philadelphia Synod would be successful because so "[f]ew of those who heretofore differ'd are now alive."[48]

In the end, as the older members of the ministerial class must have realized, the dry bones of reconciliation were their own. The authority of the late eighteenth-century minister and the cohesion of the late eighteenth-century community presumed that everyone's knowledge was in fact partial (not just the dissenter's knowledge) and that the bonds between believers would therefore always be conditional. This, at least, was the understanding carried by those young pastors who had been schooled in the writings of the European Enlightenment and inspired by the religious upheaval of the mid-century revivals. The ministers who came of age during and after the Great Awakening would have many opportunities to lament divisions and deal with separatists as they grew old, but never with the same degree of certainty of those born before them. For they would inherit the tenuous rhetoric of impartiality and the crippled authority that it buttressed. They would confront religious differences from a much less exalted position. In this respect, the story of religious pluralism in America was a gloomy tale for many professional ministers.[49]

The Significance of the Great Awakening

A historian would be hard-pressed to find a prominent American writer of the 1740s and 1750s who was not committed to the right of private judgment and the principle of forbearance. Nonetheless, the age of the great revivals was as much a time of church separation, spiritual segmentation, and virulent criticism as it was a time of individual autonomy and religious tolerance. New England alone witnessed scores of church separations during the 1740s. While disheartening to some, such divisions delighted others. New churches must have represented welcome asylums to those who regarded themselves as unwilling parts of a corrupt body. These churches did for eighteenth-century dissenters what Britain's American colonies did during the seventeenth century. To the theoretical right of choosing one's affiliation, the Great Awakening added the concrete possibility of having a choice; to the quiet dissent of the mind, it added the boisterous movement of the body. Above all, it allowed people to get away from the neighbors they could no longer tolerate.[50]

The liberating effects of the religious revival are thus fairly obvious. But their implications go well beyond the deference now paid to each person's right to their own beliefs. Indeed, those converted during the revivals were less harshly reprimanded for the independent exercise of their judgment than they were for their tendency to judge others rashly. One could argue that it was not then the principle of private judgment, but the alleged practice of rash judging that made the mid-century revivals as disruptive as they were. Those who participated in the Awakening looked beyond their own souls, into the souls of others. In doing so, they demanded a conformity of an utterly new kind; they demanded to see in others what they felt in themselves, a confirmation by fellow saints of their own internal assurance. Meanwhile, those who explicitly condemned rash judgments helped secure the individual conscience from the demands of external authorities. These individuals—many of whom were no more than nominal partisans of the principle of private judgment—insisted that the interior states of believing Christians were inaccessible to all but the believers themselves. So while condemnations of censorious speech and writing evoked old injunctions against lay impudence and clerical dissent, they also anticipated an emergent set of social rules that recognized an essential equality between believers.[51]

The Great Awakening also encouraged a more charitable approach to religious differences by blurring the distinction between true faith and sectarian delusion. The "errors" and "enthusiasm" of the revivalists proved much more widespread and provoked much less demonic behavior than an orthodox clergyman might have anticipated. Of course, the rash judging, the uninvited preaching, and the physical contortions of the converted were lamentable offenses against good order and respectable worship. But New Light preachers always insisted upon their own commitment to the essentials of Protestant (usually Calvinist) doctrine, and the converted exhibited an admirable—if often excessive—fear of God. If this was heresy, it took some unexpected forms. A large segment of the laity and the clergy (a contemporary dubbed them "Regular Lights") simply could not decide whether the revivals constituted the work of God or the devil. Ebenezer Parkman was among those caught in the middle. Convinced of the inviolability of private judgment, increasingly unsure about the authority of their own judgments, and moved themselves by the evangelical message, orthodox ministers had no choice but to tolerate an unprecedented degree of dissent. They accused the lay revivalists of being swayed to and fro like children. But what the Old Lights and Regular Lights experienced proved much more debilitating to the long-range prospects for religious uniformity. If their reticence to judge was the mark of a tolerant society, it was also the mark of a faith that would never again speak with the same assurance.[52]

In the end, the same conspicuous assertion of differences that revealed the contingency of religious authority made intolerance seem less tolerable. Movement across parish boundaries prompted a radical rethinking of the grounds for religious commitment, as well as generating the sometimes mean-spirited comparisons that went by the name of "rash judging." The same cultural context that produced the first grievances against majority rule granted recognition to the religious autonomy of pious laypeople. The same logic that condemned decisions made without the endorsement of the minority condemned those judgments made without the consent of the believer whose beliefs were being judged. Even more than the individual conscience that liberal philosophers and theologians championed, evangelical faith could not be described in anything but the believer's own words. For many mideighteenth-century Americans, divided churches—particularly those divided by those converts who were most certain of their beliefs—stood as visible reminders of how frustratingly partial were the judgments that believers made of one another. These were lessons well learned because, in the coming decades, provincial Americans would increasingly inhabit communities that contained people who arrived at very different kinds of judgments.[53]

3

Open to All Parties

The Ordeal of Religious Integration

Nevertheless, whereto we have already attained, let us walk by the same rule, let us mind the same thing.

—Philippians 3:16

Nothing appears to me, more Beautiful and Glorious, than *Peace* and *Love*, and *Union* among the Professors of the RELIGION, of the *Meek* and *Humble* JESUS.

And therefore I am griev'd in my Heart, for the narrow Notions, of some Pious, and in other respects valuable Men; who are fondly desiring, or vainly attempting, to promote the *good* of the *Church* of CHRIST, either by multiplying, or continuing her unhappy, dishonourable, and dangerous *Divisions!*

—Gilbert Tennent, *Irenicum Ecclesiasticum* (1749)

Throughout the seventeenth and eighteenth centuries, groups migrated from their ancestral homes in Europe to the remote shores of Massachusetts, Pennsylvania, Virginia, and South Carolina with the intention of achieving some degree of material comfort and some semblance of religious autonomy. Those who came for religious reasons usually sought freedom from outside interference and church practices that they abhorred. Probably none moved because they wanted to live in a diverse community. And surely no religious group traveled three thousand miles in the hope of working together with other groups to forge state policies, fight continental wars, or build a nonsectarian college.[1] But that is precisely what happened to them. Although the abundance of cheap land always held out the promise of greater purity in the next town or state, isolation would seldom be achieved. Religious integration was a consequence of the self-determination that drew so many different kinds of believers.[2]

Until the mid-eighteenth century, however, religious integration remained limited, and religious diversity still served as an epithet to describe outsiders. Only during the second half of the eighteenth century did British Americans begin to discover diversity within their own religious communities. It may have happened because those communities became, in a real sense, larger. Immigrants poured in from Ireland, Scotland, and Germany, transportation improved, commerce grew, and the print trade flourished. As a result, the events that people believed they could affect, the range of their sympathies, the extent of the attachments they felt, all expanded dramatically. At the same time, many of the social institutions that made up their world—such as their newspapers, colleges, and fraternal societies—opened to white men of every persuasion. It is probably no coincidence that the phrase "Open to All Parties, But Influenced By None" appeared on several newspaper mastheads. Ecumenism—the promotion of religious unity through greater cooperation or improved understanding—was often preached and sometimes even practiced during this period.[3]

If diversity was expected after midcentury, unity was ever more longingly sought after, its breadth offset by its relative superficiality. In a remarkable number of instances during the second half of the eighteenth century, Americans convinced themselves that they shared the same fundamental religious beliefs. In turn, they dismissed the differences that had once seemed insurmountable as mere "circumstantials." The emphasis on shared doctrines and practices was necessary if the integration of American society was to continue peacefully. Of course, mobilizing disparate religious groups to undertake common actions—from a transatlantic prayer to wartime mobilization—or even just persuading them to get along, proved no easy task. If evangelical preachers turned their variously denominated listeners into "Christians," ambitious politicians turned their diverse constituents into "Protestants." The act of cultivating unity among a wide range of believers demanded prodigious acts of forgetting. Such an achievement entailed talking about shared beliefs and resting content with the vacuous generalization that resulted. It required that leaders who otherwise competed fiercely for church converts, political power, and administrative control of colleges build coalitions of diverse groups and employ ecumenical religious language. Within this context, oft-cited biblical passages such as "be of one mind" (2 Cor. 13:11) and "Can two walk together, except they be agreed?" (Amos 3:3) took on a new meaning. Once injunctions to uniformity, these phrases now constituted an appeal for mere agreement. If believers were now secure in their right to private judgment, they were ever more stridently called upon to agree however agreement might be achieved.[4]

The Rise of Ecumenism

In 1747, three years before he was dismissed from his Northampton, Massachusetts, congregation, Jonathan Edwards endorsed an ambitious plan to unite those separated by both geography and denominational lines. He announced that an anonymous group of Scottish Presbyterians had laid the groundwork for an Atlantic-wide "concert of prayer." This project would enlist believers across the world to pray at exactly the same time. Edwards praised the effort to synchronize distinctive forms of faith. Temporal unity, the great theologian suggested, would more than compensate for theological differences. The concert of prayer would cultivate "mutual Affection and Endearment"; its participants would be united "with one Heart and Voice." Edwards excused the organizers for declining to attach their names to the appeal. With excessive humility perhaps, they had avoided taking credit for this endeavor, as "the first Projectors and Movers of something extraordinary, that they desire should become general, and that God's People in various distant Parts of the World should agree in." And thus, Edwards continued, they insisted that it was "a Thing already set on Foot." To Edwards, the concert of prayer represented a plan already put in motion by an unnamed source; its first movers remained hopelessly unknowable; the plan itself unremitting, predetermined, and universal. His vision dissolved religious particularity in a simultaneous chorus of pious souls, bound together in one Atlantic-wide community.[5]

Though notable for its scale, the plan Edwards endorsed was emblematic of the unprecedented ecumenism that prevailed at midcentury. By the late 1740s such appeals for Christian union were considerably more respectable and widespread than they had been earlier that decade. Many of the revivalists who crisscrossed British North America at the height of the Great Awakening in the late 1730s and early 1740s had promoted interdenominational agreement and cooperation as well. But they usually created more rifts than they healed. The New Light revivalists had the peculiar effect of drawing together people of different churches, while dividing those of the same church. Evangelicals among the Anglicans found common cause with like-minded Congregationalists, Presbyterians, and Dutch Reformed. At the same time, anti–New Light Presbyterians forged alliances with anti–New Light Anglicans, Dutch Reformed, and Congregationalists. George Whitefield was only one of several Great Awakening preachers who possessed a knack for stimulating church separations as he marketed ecumenical principles among his listeners. Dozens of mainline churches split in the wake of the revivalist tide. Some of the smaller denominations were shaken as well.

In the more tranquil era that followed the Great Awakening, the divisions within denominations came to seem less insuperable, and the same forbearance that prevailed between churches was applied within them. "Rash judging" was condemned and charitable language espoused in every quarter. With the passage of years, contemporaries remembered the revivals to be less divisive than they had seemed at the time. By the late 1740s, even the incendiary Gilbert Tennent was calling for the reunion of the Philadelphia Synod that he had done much to divide. Repentant of his earlier sectarian rhetoric, Tennent now insisted that differences of all sorts should be borne with charity. He condemned the inclination to treat subjective convictions as burning truths and lamented the "evil Surmisings, severe Censurings, and rash Judgings of each other" that had severed the Synod in half. We are too fallible, too prone to religious errors, Tennent contended, to be forcing our opinions on others. In a conciliatory 1749 sermon, he declared that he intended to "offend no one" among either the New Lights or Old Lights and to instead consider various avenues of compromise. After all, men often employed a great "Diversity" of means toward the same godly end. The problem was that they allowed their trivial differences to obscure their many points of agreement.[6]

Gilbert Tennent's rhetorical evolution suggests that the New Lights' longing to purify the community by separating the church's wheat from its chaff had given way to the evangelical longing to unite sincere belivers, however different they might seem. Like other major cultural changes, this transformation proceeded by fits and starts. Love for the genuinely faithful was still often of a piece with disdain for those whose hearts seemed cold. Yet with growing frequency, evangelicals such as Tennent and George Whitefield imagined a religious community connected by a common experience of the New Birth, rather than a shared animosity toward those who lacked saving faith. This imagined community was notably *Christian* both in its ecumenical incorporation of all Protestant believers in Christ and in its attention to the person of Christ, whose suffering redeemed all humanity. "Nothing appears to me, more Beautiful and Glorious," Tennent wrote, "than *Peace* and *Love*, and *Union* among the Professors of the RELIGION, of the *Meek* and *Humble* Jesus."[7]

But there was more to the ecumenical atmosphere that developed at the end of the Great Awakening than a higher regard for the meek and humble

Jesus. Above all, perhaps, a tacit agreement to unite around a few, vaguely defined, fundamental principles offered both a resolution to the divisions that the Great Awakening had caused and an explanation for the peculiar unions it had generated. Those anxious to heal divisions, like Gilbert Tennent, insisted that there had never really been a disagreement about the things that mattered. At least one itinerant evangelical now proposed that the inter-denominational alignments brought about by the Great Awakening were the result of a happy coincidence in essential principles. Samuel Davies defended the informal alliance Whitefield and Tennent had forged earlier in the decade. "[T]hey look'd upon an *Agreement* in *essential Points* a sufficient Ground for *walking together as far as they were agreed*," he argued, "notwithstanding a *Diversity* of Sentiments in *extra-essential Matters*."[8]

By midcentury, the notion that bitter strife would give way to blessed unity when essential doctrines and practices were privileged over nonessentials became exceedingly fashionable. Such a resolution appealed to the evangelicals who possessed little patience for theological quarreling, as well as the more liberal minded among their opponents, who had always expressed impatience with the creedal impositions of established churches (and, more recently, with the "rash judgments" of an enthusiastic laity). Essentials, or fundamentals, were those basic premises that all members of a denomination—or all Protestants, or all Christians—allegedly agreed upon. At a minimum, they referred to such things as belief in the veracity of Holy Scripture, the atoning power of Christ's death, a final judgment, and a future state of rewards and penalties. Evangelicals tended to stress the fundamental importance of sincere faith. Liberal rationalists tended to stress the fundamental importance of moderate piety. In either case, midcentury writers asserted with increasing urgency and increasing frequency that a wide range of *non*essential doctrines and beliefs should be tolerated. Most religious and civic leaders had already seen their share of theological quibbling. Most understood that the broader the essential principles they articulated and the less specific they remained, the larger the church, or the coalition, they could build. Most also recognized that their own religious communities had become much more diverse, and that they had no choice but to forbear what they could no longer freely condemn.[9]

By the early 1760s, plans were even laid to bring together the colonies' non-Anglican denominations into a loosely associated, Christian union on just such broad principles. The most ambitious effort was organized by the Rhode Island Congregationalist, Ezra Stiles. In 1761, Stiles published his best-selling *Discourse on the Christian Union*. Encouraging reconciliation between non-Anglicans, he dismissed the notion that any substantive issues had divided revivalists and antirevivalists during the Great Awakening. A "different manner and phraseology in explaining the same principles appears to me to be their chief difference," Stiles wrote. Indeed, he professed himself ignorant of "any very essential or general alteration of the public sentiment on what we all agree to be the fundamental principles of revelation." When the object was to make good men, it was of no consequence whether the "means are diversified." Stiles thought that the American "experiment," which mixed different, mutually hostile denominations together until they formed a cohesive union, could be completed within a century.[10]

To many contemporaries, an emphasis on fundamental points of agreement and tolerance for particular points of difference represented a panacea for this religiously divided world. When Philadelphia's Presbyterian Synod finally reunited in 1758, Francis Alison preached an appropriately conciliatory sermon titled *Peace and Union Recommended*. Alison opened his discourse with a citation from Paul's Second Letter to the Corinthians "Be of one Mind, live in Peace, and the God of Peace shall be with you" (2 Cor. 13). "[I]n a church like ours in America," Alison counseled, "collected from different churches of CHRIST in Europe, who have followed different modes and ways of obeying the 'great and general commands of the gospel,'" members were under an obligation to demonstrate forbearance. Praising Gilbert Tennent's efforts to bring together the two sides, Alison gently reminded his fellow Presbyterians of the fundamental doctrines they held in common, as well as the particular doctrines for which they should display forbearance—all in the name of "the LORD JESUS CHRIST." Fortunately, according to Alison, "no denomination of christians, are more unanimously agreed in the essentials of religion." One could only arrive at this conclusion by forgetting a great number of harsh words and some serious differences. And that was precisely what the Synods of Philadelphia and New York aimed to do. They intended, as one Old Side report put it, to "forgive and forget," and "unite as two contiguous bodies of Christians agreed in principles as though they never had been concerned with one another before, nor had any differences."[11]

Ecumenist impulses came from abroad too. Having been harried out of Germany, the Pietist group known as Moravians planned to reconcile all Americans—Reformed and Lutheran, white and Indian—on essential principles. The Moravians were led by the forceful and ambitious Count Nicholas von Zinzendorf, who arrived in the port of New York in the late fall of 1741, whereupon he set out for eastern Pennsylvania. This land, so free of state authority, so riven by denominational divisions, and so full of German immigrants seemed like an excellent place to begin the task of uniting believers in the Spirit of God. An ordained Lutheran pastor, Zinzendorf immediately began to assemble a transdenominational collection of like-minded Christians in the region. The count did not wish to abolish the denominations. Instead, he treated each as a unique source of religious knowledge with a valuable contribution to make to Christian faith. Zinzendorf enjoined his followers to remember the following triad of values: "in essentials unity, in nonessentials diversity, in all things charity." To that end, the Moravians organized a series of interchurch synods from 1742 through 1745 and gladly ordained both Reformed and Lutheran bishops. The Moravians displayed the same inclusive inclinations as they proselytized Native Americans. Zinzendorf pledged, for instance, that his missionaries would remain among the Indians of the Susquehanna River valley until they had "mutually learned each other's peculiarities." The Moravians even extended the bounds of Christian union to include enslaved African Americans during the first few decades of their American missionary efforts, although economic interest and racial prejudice would eventually combine to undermine that exceptional form of unity.[12]

The mid-eighteenth-century injunction to give priority to points of fundamental agreement over points of circumstantial difference was far from original. The *irenic* tradition, as it usually called, goes at least as far back as the great Dutch humanist Erasmus who lived at the turn of the sixteenth century. During the seventeenth century, liberal-minded Anglicans and Reformed dissenters in England associated "nonessential" ceremonies and doctrines with mere opinion, with that which could not be determined with any certainty— and therefore, that which could not be justly imposed. These English latitudinarians advanced the notion that human knowledge was irreparably partial and that good men were likely to differ somewhat in their interpretation of particular passages in scripture. To various degrees, other groups throughout the Atlantic world developed a similar approach. Even the Puritans of seventeenth-century Massachusetts, whom no one would accuse of taking doctrine too lightly, chastised each other for making too much of the nonessentials of faith. And even they would occasionally sanction small differences as long as the offending believers kept their erroneous notions to themselves.[13]

The same latitudinarian principles were employed in mid-eighteenth-century America with new implications. The novelty of the approach did not reside in the distinction between fundamentals and circumstantials, or the meaning of those words. They were entirely conventional. Instead, it was the frequency of their appearance, as well as the wide extent and novel context of their application that suggests a break with earlier ways of thinking about the problem of religious differences. At midcentury, every religious controversy seemed to have just one such solution: adherence to the fundamentals of Protestant, or Christian, faith. Beginning in at least the early 1750s, orthodox Congregationalists, German Pietists, nonresisting (pacifist) Quakers,

New Light Presbyterians, established Anglicans, and dissenting Baptists invoked the notion that essential beliefs would unite Christians of all types if the particular nonessentials that divided them were ignored or forgotten—and the essentials themselves were left sufficiently vague and capacious. Moreover, these essentials and fundamentals were being championed in an environment where toleration was always expected and religious liberty sometimes protected, and where, as we shall see, a substantial degree of religious mixing was occurring. When dissenters from church establishments were routinely exiled, jailed, and fined for their beliefs; when they were excluded from mainstream institutions, ecumenical rhetoric that extolled the virtues of Christian unity rang hollow. Now the same latitudinarian principles had begun to mean a great deal more.[14]

Contemporary social and political developments gave mid-eighteenth-century Americans several good reasons to minimize the differences among themselves. Perhaps most important, Protestants in England and America were engaged in a common struggle against a shared Catholic enemy. The idea of Protestant unity assumed a particular poignancy during the British Empire's nearly unrelenting wars with France and Spain. To a greater extent than during any of the previous conflicts, the Seven Years' conflict (1756–1763) mobilized and forced cooperation among people of nearly every Protestant denomination. Given the "common Danger" posed by the French and their "*Romish*" religion, Thomas Barton exhorted "PROTESTANT DISSENTERS *of all Denominations*" to be of "*the same Mind, and the same Judgment.*" During the war, colonial soldiers were marched to places neither they nor their families had ever visited. There, they fought alongside men with very different religious backgrounds. Still stranger encounters originated from afar. A surge in immigration after 1730 brought hundreds of thousands of migrants to the colonies, many of them German Lutherans, Irish Catholics, and Scotch and Scots-Irish Presbyterians. Every year from 1748 to 1754, between two thousand and sixteen thousand made their way from Germany alone. The middle decades of the eighteenth century also witnessed a rapid growth in commerce—accelerating after 1740—which drew provincial Americans into commercial fellowship with distant souls. Colonial merchants competed for overseas trade, peddlers crowded provincial roads, and American consumers purchased an unprecedented array of imported manufactured goods. The colonial publishing industry underwent a related, and comparable, expansion, which, like the increase in migration and trade, brought colonial Americans into imaginative contact with many different groups. In 1704, there was only one newspaper in colonial America. By 1765, there were twenty-six, and the number was rising rapidly.[15]

It was not just wars and trade that brought about the change, of course. English theology continued to evolve in more latitudinarian ways and as it did, it gained popularity in the colonies. And then there was that small but influential coterie of religious iconoclasts who embraced something known as natural religion, or deism, which captivated those more persuaded by the idea of a distant, benevolent creator. In its most extreme forms, natural religion seemed to make too much of man's reasoning abilities and too little of God's power. Yet this spare brand of faith also lent the concept of Christian essentials a less sectarian and less exclusivist cast. After all, it made little sense to debate the intricacies of revelation when it was obvious that God operated from a considerable distance and left our rational faculties free to discern the truths he embedded in nature. On the opposite end of the theological spectrum, evangelicals like Gilbert Tennent, who envisioned a much less distant and much more active deity, were taken with the idea that true Christians might disagree on many details of doctrine and practice and still enjoy the same new birth in Christ.[16]

The main reason that the reduction of complex, highly differentiated systems to fundamental principles suddenly appealed to so many may have simply been the diversity generated by the Great Awakening. For a time, it had seemed that there might be no end to the differences that the revivals precipitated. At midcentury, one question recurred again and again: If God's intentions were as perspicuous as the rationalists claimed—or, as the New Lights would have it, if only sincere faith mattered—then how was so much disagreement possible? The answer seemed to sit squarely with the compulsion to make too much of too little. A focus on the essentials promised to diminish the petty disputes over particulars that divided Christians from one another. Midcentury Americans of many persuasions took solace in the possibility that something important joined them to otherwise very different members of their own, expanding communities.

The Integration of Colonial Institutions

If midcentury ministers were now more willing to accommodate different religious beliefs and practices, so were the colonists' secular institutions. In fact, during the two decades prior to the American Revolution, several colonial American newspapers declared themselves "Open to All Parties." The prevailing belief was that the press was obliged to present the public with both sides of every important social, religious, and political issue. No reasonable argument could be rightfully excluded from debate. This doctrine did not lead,

Robert W. T. Martin notes, to an argument for a system of "partisan presses, each representing a leading faction." Instead, inclusivity—which often meant religious inclusivity—was the ideal. Even the famed concept of liberty of the press, historian Stephen Botein pointed out, generally connoted "equal access." One colonial New Yorker defined press liberty as "a Liberty for every Man to communicate his Sentiments freely to the Publick, upon Political or Religious Points." The range of acceptable opinions in midcentury America was growing even faster than the number of presses. And colonial editors— men who served relatively small and religiously heterogeneous markets—were expected to make their pages available to them.[17]

Printers were not alone in incorporating substantive disagreements into their institutions. A significant number of midcentury fraternal societies, colonial legislatures, and provincial colleges made similar gestures. In each case, the bounds of inclusion extended most conspicuously along religious lines. In each case, religious ecumenism slowly became a badge of ethical distinction rather than a symptom of theological degradation. Few writers could identify any redeeming value in religious disagreements themselves. But by minimizing their content or maintaining that they were inconsequential, colonial Americans began to build surprisingly cooperative relationships with those of quite different faiths.

One midcentury institution that boasted considerable religious diversity was the nondenominational fraternal society. As colonial towns grew larger and individual relationships became more attenuated during the latter part of the eighteenth century, these organizations began to supplement the church as sources of community life and identity. Whether their members debated philosophy or planned benevolent activities, they usually welcomed individuals from a host of different religious backgrounds. Fraternal societies would really blossom across the United States after the Revolutionary War, but they had their origins in the mid-eighteenth century. In Georgia, for instance, a charitable organization known as the Union Society was established in 1750. Among its five founders were a Roman Catholic, a Jew, and an Episcopalian. In the late 1740s, a group of aspiring New Yorkers founded the interdenominational Society for Useful Knowledge.[18]

No fraternal society was more prominent—and none better embodied the tendency to reduce Christian beliefs to a few fundamental principles—than the budding organization known as the Freemasons. The Masons claimed an ancient heritage, dating back to the construction of Solomon's Temple. For centuries, stonemasons had gathered together to pass on professional knowledge, share occupational folklore, and enact elaborate rituals. By the seventeenth century, they were joined by nonstonemasons. Gradually, more formal and less specialized organizations came into existence. In 1717, London's Masons formed the first grand lodge, which would be led by noncraftsmen and would claim dominion over individual lodges on both sides of the Atlantic. According to the historian Stephen Bullock, Philadelphia, Savannah, Boston, New York, Charleston, and Cape Fear, North Carolina, all hosted Masonic lodges by 1738.[19]

The Masons played a visible role in the cultural and social life of the colonies from the middle of the eighteenth century onward. One gets a sense of their public prominence from a 1755 issue of the *Pennsylvania Gazette*, which recounted the sight of a parade that had recently threaded its way across the city. Nearly one hundred thirty Masons, the paper noted, bedecked in "aprons, white Gloves and Stockings" marched from the lodge to the pews of Christ Church. Once the group had found its seats in the Anglican chapel, William Smith, who had just been named provost of the newly chartered College of Philadelphia, called upon his Masonic and non-Masonic listeners alike to "Love the Brotherhood, fear God, honour the King." Smith proceeded to demonstrate, according to the *Gazette*, that "these three Grand Duties" were "not only the Foundation of the ancient Society of Free Masons, but of Societies of every Kind," and deduced from some "undeniable principles." Acknowledging that his audience might differ in "things of inferior Moment," Smith noted that he had confined the content of his sermon to those fundamental tenets required to make his point. Nonetheless, he hoped that "the whole Essentials of our Common Christianity would have received the hearty Assent of his Audience, mixt as it was." Invoking the "undeniable principles" of societies as well as "the whole Essentials of our Common Christianity" without actually specifying them must have seemed the best way to address a "mixt Assembly."[20]

It was certainly the Masonic way. The Masons promoted the same ecumenical ideals, and embodied the same tensions, that characterized the theological writing of the period.[21] Formally nonsectarian, the Masons welcomed virtuous men of all creeds. A few lodges even counted Jews and Catholics among their members.[22] Moreover, the Masons, like a growing number of their contemporaries, were conscious of the diversity within their audience. Arthur Browne began his typically Masonic discussion of "universal benevolence" with the following caveat: "As it is highly probable, that I am upon this occasion, to discourse to persons of several denominations, I have pitched upon a subject equally interesting and obligatory upon all." Unlike other groups, Thomas Pollen wrote, the Society "opens wide its arms to every nation under heaven, and offers to take in both *Jews and Greeks*, both *Cretes and Arabians*; following the steps of their master Christ." The increasingly popular language of unbounded Christian fellowship also appeared in some Masonic writings. Browne envisioned the "blood of CHRIST cementing all mankind together." Christ's death, he observed, made universal love imaginable, as well as obligatory. It joined men "merely as Men."[23]

While the Masons opened their doors to individuals of nearly every denomination, they placed a premium on unanimity. No one could be admitted to the privileges of the lodge, for instance, without the consent of every member. And once admitted, the lodge discouraged members from talking about their particular beliefs. "Freedom of Opinion thus indulged, but its points never discussed," was, according to Charles Brockwell, "the happy influence under which the unity of this truly *Ancient and Honourable Society* has been preserved, from time immemorial." The "religion of the *ever blessed* JESUS," Arthur Browne wrote, was "too sacred a subject to be made the topick of common conversation." It was enough, Brockwell insisted, for members to be pious in their faith and upright in their characters. Although there might be "some points or rather modes of worship [wherein] we may differ or dissent from each other," the lodge would "reconcile" them. The lodge brought together men who "might have otherwise remained at perpetual distance," joined them in "conversation," "intermingl[ed]" their "interests." Within its walls, principles were "harmonized" and particularities were ignored; there could be no substantive disagreement. Nor were moral irregularities permitted. Every member was "under the strictest obligation to be a good man, a true Christian ... however distinguished by different opinions in the circumstantials of Religion."[24]

The Masons thus presented the intriguing spectacle of an organization committed to both open discussion and unanimity. Candid conversation among those of different denominations was repeatedly encouraged, but fraternal love, it appears, could only be enacted in the silence of virtuous behavior or the quiet of selfless assent. The Society possessed "a silent universal language of [its] own," which any member, wherever he originated, could recognize. Silence was not its dark secret. Rather, it represented an explicitly stated mode of fellowship, the necessary prerequisite to its commitment to inclusivity. Like so many churches around the same time, the Masons minimized the content of their disagreement by suggesting that the only relevant, legitimately expressed doctrines were those that were fundamental or essential. Such doctrines were common to men rather than just to Christians. Odd as they sometimes seemed, the Masons offered a valuable lesson to provincial Americans. As their lives became more religiously integrated and their awareness of religious differences increased, they would find that living in a diverse society meant living with the things that could not be said and the judgments that could not be rendered.[25]

The Integration of Colonial Politics

In the mid-Atlantic colonies of Pennsylvania and New York and, to a lesser extent, elsewhere, the provincial assemblies trod a path similar to the one that the Masons had brazenly gone down. During the 1760s Pennsylvanians and elite New Yorkers got their first taste of the interdenominational negotiating that would remain a staple of American civic life for many years to come. Consider the journal entry made by the German Lutheran Henry Melchior Muhlenberg following the 1764 assembly elections in Pennsylvania: "[t]he English and German Quakers, the Herrnhuters, Mennonites, and Schwenkfelders formed one party, and the English of the High Church and the Presbyterian Church, the German Lutheran, and German Reformed joined the other party and gained the upper hand." Such coalition building, Muhlenberg continued, was "a thing heretofore unheard of." In New York City and Philadelphia, interdenominational cooperation now constituted an electoral necessity. As a broadside posted in the 1760s boasted: "Our ticket is composed of honest men of various denominations."[26]

The introduction of religious considerations into politics was not a simple matter in eighteenth-century America. Literate colonists lived with half-remembered nightmares of civil wars between Catholics and Protestants and between different Protestant sects. It was not long ago, after all, that Scottish Presbyterians had joined with their Independent English brethren to overthrow an Anglican king, that a Protestant uprising against Hapsburg Catholic rule sparked a thirty-year war, or that French Protestants were massacred by Catholics in the streets of Paris. The colonists had been told again and again that violence often resulted when religious groups competed for state power. So it was probably with some trepidation that midcentury Americans contemplated the politicization of the many religious groups that lived within their bounds. Only in hindsight, three decades hence, could an unassuming Virginian named James Madison console his readers with the thought that a society had nothing to fear from politically active religious groups—as long as there were enough of them. They would, Madison maintained in his famous Federalist Number Ten, act as a mutual check upon one another. As influential as it would later become, Madison's approach to religious and political differences does not seem to have represented the general opinion in the 1760s, and perhaps not even at the end of the 1780s. At midcentury, colonial Americans still had trouble seeing factions, particularly religious factions, as anything but dangerous to the health and well-being of their societies. They took their lead from English writers such as John Trenchard, Thomas

Gordon, and Lord Bolingbroke, who condemned parties of all kinds. And they understood that inviting different religious groups into the same political and social institutions increased the possibility that interdenominational disputes would upset whatever harmony existed within them. Given this possibility, cooperation, equal representation, and a focus on the essentials of faith could seem like the best means of securing peace—and, of course, electoral success. In this realm, as in the divided Synod of Philadelphia and the religious variety of the fraternal meeting, old points of contention would have to be forgotten as old conflicts were buried.[27]

Religious diversity first became conspicuous in Pennsylvania politics during the middle decades of the eighteenth century. By the 1740s, Presbyterians and Anglicans had begun to make their electoral presence felt on the colony's Quaker-dominated political scene. Contemporaries also observed a newfound political consciousness among the smaller sects, especially those of German background. Addressing an English audience anonymously in 1754, William Smith—the same gentleman who would address the Freemasons in the following year—contended that Pennsylvania's various smaller denominations, which had once been "employed only in establishing themselves," were beginning to "turn their Thoughts to the Public." Particularly troubling was the fact that the colony's Quakers enjoyed so much success in soliciting the support of these newly politicized sects. Lamenting the Quakers' ability to influence Pennsylvania's German voters, Smith expressed his hopes that the Anglican-Presbyterian Proprietary Party would be able to construct a "*Coalition*" with these same groups. Until that happened, he added, the imperatives of military security demanded that the Germans should be deprived of their suffrage and loyalty oaths administered to their political allies who sat in the Assembly (that is, to the Quakers who refused to supply war material).[28]

It is possible to view William Smith's warning as a precursor to James Madison's conflict-based pluralism. However, it might be more profitable to see it as a begrudging acknowledgment of how pressing it now seemed to accommodate multiple religious groups. If the minister's worried review of Pennsylvania's affairs points to the extent of interethnic and interdenominational conflict midcentury Americans experienced, it also suggests how appealing interethnic and interdenominational coalitions had become. It was not long before the coalition that Smith envisioned actually came to fruition. As William Allen noted in a private account of the 1764 election, the Proprietary faction received "great help from the Lutherans, and Calvinist among the Dutch[;] from their other Sects we had great opposition: we had about half of the Church of England, and the Presbyterians to a man." While not averse to using intimidation if it might keep German Mennonites at home, another

Proprietary stalwart recommended that the party "run" a "popular Lutheran or Calvinist [Reformed]" for election in the following year. By the late 1750s, not even Pennsylvania's Quakers could forge a political majority from their own numbers. As historians such as Alan Tully and Patricia Bonomi have demonstrated, Middle Colony politics now featured a jumble of competing factions, often motivated by deep-seated religious convictions. Success required a policy platform that accommodated a wide range of interests and a rhetorical style that was at once sensitive to the differences between groups and purposely forgetful of those differences that could simply not be reconciled.[29]

For a time, the Quakers managed to keep a powerful interdenominational coalition together in Pennsylvania. As the unofficial war with France became official in 1756, the pacifist Quakers looked to lose much of their sway within the legislature they had long dominated. Their loyalty to the empire, their fitness for public service, even their commitment to their non-Quaker neighbors all came into question. A large faction simply declined to run for an office they could not faithfully serve. Had the so-called Quaker Party sponsored only Quaker candidates for election in 1756, its prospects would have been dismal. But its leaders did something entirely unorthodox that year: running like-minded Anglicans, Presbyterians, Dutch Reformed, and Swiss-Mennonites in the place of those Quakers who chose not to run. The strategy worked. Even as the deep divisions among Quakers persisted, and even as the number of Friends in the Assembly declined from twenty-seven before June 1756 to just twelve by October of that same year, the Quaker Party managed to maintain its political muscle. From this point onward, it was represented in the Assembly by men of several denominations.[30]

Like the newspaper editors who claimed that they opened their pages to all parties, and the evangelicals who welcomed pious men and women of all denominations, Pennsylvania politicians expressed a newfound consciousness of the religious diversity within their community. An act of the Pennsylvania legislature on the eve of the French and Indian War explicitly acknowledged that it would be as unjust to demand religious service of pacifist Quakers as it would be to deny it to the colony's nonpacifists and recognized that the colony's libertarian religious laws had attracted multitudes of non-Quakers to their land. The point of the legislation was to make it possible for nonpacifists to form themselves into militia companies. Given that their body "represent[ed] all the People of the Province, and [was] composed of Members of different religious Perswasions," the legislation read, it was only right that members of every group be permitted to carry out what they "Judge[d]" to be their "Duty." The prospect of imminent defeat at the hands of the French and their Indian allies heightened an already growing consciousness of diversity and reinforced the tendency to make ecumenical gestures amid Pennsylvania's mixed multitude.[31]

At the same time that they drew attention to the colony's internal diversity, the imperial wars with France and Spain elicited demands for religious unanimity and the suppression of particular articles of faith that might undermine the larger effort against the common Catholic enemy. In the early days of another war in 1740, Philadelphia's governor lamented that his effort to treat the whole body of the Assembly "as Protestants" without "distinguish[ing] the particular religious Perswasion of every Member" (noting only that they were not of that "bloody Religion of *France* and *Spain*") had failed. Instead of preparing for battle, as he had hoped, they insisted upon that peculiar principle of pacifism. Likewise, when a provincial fast was declared in 1756, some proportion of the Quaker population abstained. To the dismay of their fellow Pennsylvanians, the pacifist Quakers ignored the call directed at " 'all his Majesty's loving subjects . . . of whatever Denomination'." *An Address to Those Quakers Who perversely refused to pay any Regard to the late provincial FAST* bemoaned their failure to comply. According to the anonymous author(s) of the tract, the Quakers had spoiled an opportunity to repent unanimously, thereby thwarting the wishes of "a great Majority." "[W]hat a glorious Prospect it would have been," the author lamented, "to have beheld two or three Provinces, without one dissenting Voice." Though extreme in its implications, this dream of a voluntary agreement "without one dissenting Voice" could have been embraced by mid-eighteenth-century New Lights and Freemasons.[32]

A pattern of interdenominational consciousness and ecumenical rhetoric emerged in New York at roughly the same time that it did in Pennsylvania. Two broad and unwieldy coalitions of religious groups would compete for control of New York's Assembly during the 1760s and early 1770s. New York City's major political parties, one led by the Anglican DeLancey family and the other by the Presbyterian Livingston clan, each depended upon interdenominational alliances. The DeLanceys maintained a comfortable majority because they could rely with some assurance upon the votes of six Dutch Reformed representatives and the Livingstons just five. The situation changed, however, when the Livingstons made a concerted effort to obtain relief from the laws that forbade some dissenting churches from owning property and required others to pay for the support of the Anglican Church. Once the Assembly votes were held on these matters, friendly Dutch Reformed representatives broke ranks with their Anglican allies and sided with the Livingstons.[33]

The debate over the New York Assembly election of 1769 illustrates the significance of religious coalitions to contemporary politics in the region. A group of non-Anglican New York politicians, led by William Livingston, first proposed that Anglicans and non-Anglicans divide the four contested Assembly seats between them. Their proposal rebuffed, the Livingston faction attempted to capitalize on anti-Anglican sentiment in the heated election campaign that ensued. In doing so, they vainly hoped to win over the province's Dutch Reformed population. Promoting the interdenominational sensitivity of the city's "Churchmen," an author replied that the loosely Anglican, popular party, had been "honoured with the Voices of every Denomination" at the last election. "Nothing could be more distant from their Thoughts," he continued, "than to serve one Denomination, at the Expence of the Rest." By contrast, DeLancey's Anglican party maintained, their Presbyterian opponents seemed intent on bestowing their patronage upon fellow Calvinists, which would leave the members of other sects in the cold. The DeLanceys backed up their polemics with a religiously diverse election ticket, featuring two Anglicans, one Presbyterian, and one Dutch Reformed.[34]

The Anglican faction made an equally meaningful gesture toward religious diversity by encouraging non-Anglicans to believe that religious belief was irrelevant to political worth. While brandishing their own ecumenical credentials, the DeLancey faction called upon New York's voters to look beyond their particular denominational affiliation to those virtuous qualities that united good men of all churches. Their contention was that "*Party* Attachments" should not be "made the *Test* of Merit." "The Question, my Friends," an anonymous author wrote, "ought not to be . . . to what CHURCH or Meeting a Candidate belongs; but whether he be worthy of a Seat in your House of Representatives." "Independent L-wy-rs," one DeLanceyite wrote, were attempting to acquire influence in the city by "endeavour[ing] to interest Men's Consciences in the Quarrels they excite." Their main objects were the Dutch Reformed, who were "to be converted into a political Ladder" for electoral success.[35]

While this denomination-conscious, ecumenical style of politics undoubtedly made religious traditionalists uneasy, it also ensured that a wide array of religious groups would be compelled to work together toward common goals and use language that was acceptable to all of them. In this environment, there was simply no alternative to extending public recognition to other sects. New York City and Philadelphia witnessed their share of denominational competition during the middle of the eighteenth century. But the end result was not a free market of religious competition as might be assumed today. On the contrary, where religious diversity was most evident and where competition between sects was most intense, we can see the emergence of interdenominational cooperation and significant efforts to reach out to men of very different religious backgrounds. In the legislative halls as in the fraternal meetings of midcentury America and the outdoor performances of evangelical preachers, a keen new consciousness of religious diversity was emerging, and a new ecumenical rhetoric was transcending it. In each sphere, colonial Americans were being asked to remember their fundamental points of agreement and forget that their religious differences mattered.

The Opening of American Colleges

Religious integration was also taking place in American colleges during the middle of the eighteenth century. The same commercial growth that attracted new migrants to the colonies and brought those of very different religious and ethnic backgrounds together also made possible the level of material comfort that usually leads communities to establish colleges. By the 1750s, colonial America had entered upon the early stages of a broad expansion in higher education. The population was exploding and so was the demand for literate ministers. At midcentury, control of a college still seemed vital for any denomination that wished to fill its pulpits with an educated ministry, keep up with the growing competition from other churches, and extend its provincial sway. Seven new colleges were established between the 1740s and the 1770s, and several more were planned. The forms that these schools took, the conflict over their composition and their administration, and the rhetoric that justified their existence all point, once again, to an incipient consciousness of religious diversity and a growing commitment to ecumenism.[36]

The midcentury transformation of colonial college life speaks volumes about the changes taking place in American culture because universities had long functioned as extensions of the church, at once theological centers and ministerial training grounds. America's own institutions of higher learning remained religiously exclusive until the middle of the eighteenth century. The three earliest colonial colleges—Harvard, Yale, and William and Mary—were all instruments of a single denomination. They began with a mandate to educate pastors for service in particular churches. In the north, aspiring Congregationalist ministers attended Yale and Harvard. In the south, aspiring Anglican preachers attended William and Mary. Reflecting a broad culture preference for uniformity, these early colleges were expected to serve as bastions of orthodox faith. A statute enacted in 1727 required the president of William and Mary to give a theological lecture every year, explicating scripture or railing "against hereticks." At Yale, students were forbidden to attend any religious service not "appointed by Public Authority or Approved by the President," and both Yale and Harvard expelled New Lights during the Great Awakening.[37]

Although most of the colleges established during the middle decades of the eighteenth century were designed for the customary purpose of training ministers for specific denominational duties, a growing number began to profess themselves open to all parties. From the 1740s onward, as the cultural climate changed and as an increasingly diverse body of wealthy parents demanded educational opportunities for their students, the major institutions became religiously integrated. The College of New Jersey (later Princeton University) was emblematic of the change taking place. Like all of its predecessors, Princeton was chartered in 1746 as a seminary of learning for a particular group of Protestants: the New Light Presbyterians. But in announcing a nonsectarian admissions policy, which granted liberty of conscience to every student, the college's founding marked the onset of a new educational regime. By the 1750s, males of all Protestant denominations would be welcome to matriculate at colonial colleges. The new schools in Rhode Island (the College of Rhode Island, later Brown University), New Jersey (including Queen's College, later Rutgers University), New Hampshire (Dartmouth College), and Pennsylvania (the College of Philadelphia, later the University of Pennsylvania) all formally rejected religious tests for students. As a consequence, some of these academies became quite mixed in their religious composition. The College of Philadelphia, for instance, would soon boast a student population drawn from nine different colonies and five different denominations.[38]

Rhetoric changed along with policy. At the College of Philadelphia's 1767 graduation ceremony, Provost William Smith proudly announced that Philadelphia's "happy Experiment" had demonstrated "that Men of various & different Persuasions may share Power, & live peaceably together." Addressing an audience of potential Anglican patrons in the West Indies, the College of New Jersey's John Witherspoon maintained that none of its students had ever complained of "uneasiness or disrespect" with regard to their various religious affiliations. He added that religious controversy was so carefully avoided at his college that he was not even aware of which church some of his graduates had attended during their schooling (those names, those *mere* names—as was the case with the organizers of the Concert of Prayer and the particular denominational affiliations of the Masons—had apparently been forgotten). New York City's Anglicans took offense at what they understood to be Witherspoon's implicit aspersions upon their own college, but not because they objected to its ecumenical premises. In fact, one aggrieved author insisted that religious profession "was never any Impediment" to faculty hiring at their college and that no problems ever resulted "from their Diversity of religious Sentiments." Another offended Anglican made a point of noting that the College of Philadelphia's trustees and faculty members came from "a Variety of Denominations." He contrasted the situation there with the College of New Jersey, where the small number of non-Presbyterians would certainly struggle to maintain their faith in such a hostile and religiously homogenous environment.[39]

Surely, as some historians have pointed out, an increasingly competitive market for students at midcentury helps explain the inclusive college environment. But market competition is only part of the story, and the need to appeal to religiously diverse audiences both inside and outside legislative meeting halls cannot be dismissed. Indeed, the governors and assemblymen who approved college charters stipulated that their trustees be selected on the same inclusive principles that justified inclusive admissions policies. The provincial colleges created at midcentury were overseen by interdenominational governing boards (always excluding Catholics and usually maintaining the colony's most powerful denomination in the majority). For example, the man appointed the first provost of the College of Philadelphia, William Smith, was an Anglican, while the man appointed the first vice-provost, Francis Alison, was a Presbyterian. The Baptist-dominated Rhode Island Assembly mandated that a fixed proportion of Quakers, Congregationalists, and Anglicans be appointed as trustees to the Baptist-dominated college it established. The modifications made to his original plan disappointed Ezra Stiles who tried to establish another college in Newport where college offices would have actually rotated among the denominations. New Jersey politicians demanded Anglican and Quaker representation on their college's board. New England Anglicans appealed for the same on Harvard's board of overseers. In response, an apologist for Harvard College maintained that the school was open to "Protestants of all Persuasions." When religious particularism was so strongly frowned upon, a college could ill afford a reputation for sectarianism.[40]

There were limits to the pluralism embodied in midcentury schooling. Indeed, the new educational inclusiveness was almost exclusively aimed at Protestants—and mainly white, male Protestants. No one expected white women or African Americans to apply for admission to Harvard or the College of Philadelphia. Nor is it likely that white women or African Americans would have been accepted if they had applied. White colonists could barely countenance letting enslaved blacks read, let alone attend college. Native Americans were a different matter. For much of the eighteenth century, colonial elites viewed young Indian men as fit subjects for proselytization. And they thought that English schooling might transform these poor souls (like the Germans of Pennsylvania and, later, the Irish Catholics of New York) into loyal subjects and respectable Protestants. For instance, Dartmouth College, which guaranteed liberty of conscience to students of every Protestant denomination, was also obliged by its charter to cultivate the "learning which shall appear necessary and expedient for civilizing and Christianizing children of pagans." The college grew out of the vision of Eleazar Wheelock, a Connecticut New Light minister, who had earlier founded a charity school for Native Americans. Having failed to convert more than a few of his pupils, Wheelock established Dartmouth College as a missionary school for *both* young Indian and white men, though it would primarily educate just the latter. The full scope of the college's religious commitments is worth reflecting upon given the larger changes taking place in American education. The founders of eighteenth-century colleges generally abjured proselytization, and they repeatedly promised to instruct their students in nothing but the fundamentals of faith. Yet as broadly as the fundamentals were defined, they were always Christian, and usually Protestant. For adherents of Native American faiths, those simply designated "pagans," there was little to distinguish college "learning"—even broadly based and tolerant Christian learning—from missionary activity. That great irony was lost on almost all eighteenth-century religious commentators, even the most ecumenical among them.[41]

Nor did everyone welcome the religious diversification that did occur in American colleges. Exclusionary academic policies could be defended on the same Lockean liberal grounds that vindicated exclusionary church policies during the Great Awakening. Such was the position taken by Yale's embattled president, Thomas Clap. Clap contended that his school's status as a voluntary society endowed it with the right of "self-preservation." Accordingly, Clap insisted that he and the fellows of Yale College had resolved that the students were not "to be instructed in any different Principles or Doctrines" than those prescribed by the Founders. Clap forbade his students from attending churches off campus, which meant that they could only worship with the Congregational minister on campus. He subjected the faith of every official to a test of orthodoxy and refused to accept a Baptist merchant's gift of books to the school. In a manner resembling that of Philadelphia's Presbyterian Old Siders during the 1730s, Clap argued that Yale was a sovereign religious society with the power to make and enforce its own standards of membership. Every man was at liberty to found his own college and set up laws according to the dictates of his conscience. However, no parent had the right to enroll his child in a religious society, such as Yale, and then expect the young scholar to disobey the college's rules. Nor was it appropriate for a college to institute policies that were "mathematically proportioned" to represent the religious interests of those whose tax money and personal donations helped fund the college. Institutions designed for the public good simply could not accommodate every dissenting opinion.[42]

The times, however, were clearly against Clap and his stated preference for a religiously exclusive college establishment. Open admissions policies and mathematically proportioned boards of trustees would soon prevail nearly everywhere. Clap himself felt compelled to note that Yale had "always freely admitted, Protestants, of all Denominations"—as long, of course, as they conformed to "our Way of Worship; while they are there." Many an Anglican minister had been educated within the confines of his college, he noted. Indeed Yale had begun to graduate a substantial number of minority confessors during the decades following the infamous Yale Apostasy of 1722. In that year, four young men had announced their defection to the Church of England (apparently, they had been corrupted by reading several volumes of recently donated Anglican latitudinarian writing). Thereafter, approximately ten percent of the college's graduating classes went on to seek ordination in the Church of England. The college would remain firmly Congregationalist for the next several decades. But the changes that were taking place in the wider culture could not be ignored. Within the ecumenical religious environment of the mid-eighteenth century, Clap's days were numbered. After enduring tutor desertions, vocal legislative enmity, and an assault on his home by an angry throng, the curmudgeonly Dr. Clap resigned the presidency.[43]

The debate over King's College, later to become Columbia University, demonstrates how the principle of ecumenism coexisted uneasily within the colony's increasingly competitive religious and political environment. Mid-century Anglicans resented the creation of a Presbyterian-controlled college at Princeton and laid plans to found one of their own in New York City. At the outset, it appeared that they would get their way. Their own Trinity Church had donated the land for building and seven of the ten men appointed to serve as the college's original trustees were Anglicans. So it is understandable that local Anglicans assumed they would exercise nearly exclusive authority over the "intended college." After all, they already maintained a limited establishment and occupied most of the major provincial offices in a city whose Anglican inhabitants made up no more than one-tenth of the total population.[44]

Proponents of Anglican control, however, had badly misjudged the cultural and political climate. Like so many other issues during the second half of the eighteenth century, the struggle to shape the religious identity of King's College quickly moved from personal conversations, committee meetings, and legislative deliberation to local newspapers and pamphlets, where it was debated before the reading public. Questions that might have easily gone without public comment twenty years before were now vaulted to the forefront of the city's consciousness. The fierce controversy that erupted over the composition of King's College owed something to the increasing prevalence of religious competition, the increasing importance of religious ecumenism, and the explosion of printed materials from the 1720s onward—and to the work of one publisher in particular.

Among the college's three non-Anglican trustees was the brash Presbyterian lawyer, William Livingston. In 1752, Livingston assumed the editorship of a new journal called *The Independent Reflector*. Following a controversial defense of the unpopular Moravians, Livingston instigated what an early chronicler referred to as a "paper war" in which "persons of all degrees, of all denominations, of all religions, and almost of all ages" eventually participated. Over the ensuing years, the *Reflector* contested every Anglican attempt to gain control over the college. The *Reflector's* paper war represents one of the few sustained debates over how an actual institution would accommodate multiple religious groups. What role would such groups play in a public college? How would their differences be addressed? Could believers from different churches live and learn together?[45]

To the *Reflector*, it was obvious that the Anglicans should be prevented from acquiring administrative command over New York's intended college. Episcopal control, William Livingston argued, would turn a "public" institution into a "Party" dominated institution. Even the admission of students from other denominations was insufficient compensation for such an arrangement. The *Reflector* objected to the notion that students from "dissenting" denominations would be merely tolerated, that the Anglicans would rule the college like an established church ruled the state. "[W]here none but the Principles of one Persuasion are taught, and all others depressed and discountenanced," the *Reflector* warned, students would be "fetter[ed]" with "Prejudices." The *Reflector* worried that if exclusive practices dominated the college, they would soon dominate the rest of the province.[46]

Livingston's ecumenical proposals seemed patently absurd to his Anglican opponents. How could a college possibly integrate several different faiths into the content of its teaching, discipline, and worship services? How could a college *not* be affiliated with one particular church? Writers for the Anglican-dominated *New-York Mercury* suggested that Livingston's plans would leave the college "neither Christian nor Infidel, neither Popish nor Protestant, Episcopalian nor Presbyterian, *English* nor *Dutch*, Independent nor Quaker, Old-Light nor New-Light, *nor yet Moravian*." Instead, it was "*to be both, all, and none of these at the same time*." Accordingly, the *Mercury's* writers ridiculed the nonsectarian prayer Livingston proposed for the college. One apologist for the Church accused the *Reflector* of having "spliced together" something that hardly resembled a prayer. "Who would establish a College upon such a Bottom?" it was asked. Another confessed his befuddlement that the *Reflector* endorsed public worship, but of "no *particular Method* whatsoever."[47]

In truth, Livingston advanced a conception of Christianity that was virtually devoid of theological content. One of the *Reflector*'s essays especially galled the Anglicans: "No. 31: *Primitive* Christianity *short and intelligible, modern* Christianity *voluminous and incomprehensible.*" Here, the *Reflector* reduced the requirements of Christian faith to a mere two points: (1) the belief "that *Christ* was the promised *Messiah*," and (2) adherence to "its moral Directions," which he noted might be "contained in a Sheet of Paper." While most contemporary writers distinguished between essentials and nonessentials, hardly anyone was brazen enough to go as far as Livingston. Here was a latitudinarianism that even the most liberal clergymen could not countenance. Here was a doctrinal bottom that could barely support itself, his opponents concluded, let alone an entire college.[48]

King's College finally began offering classes in the summer of 1754. Despite Livingston's efforts, it was clear from the beginning that the Church of England would exercise a firm grip. New York's Anglican clerics had succeeded in ensuring that the president would be Anglican and the Church's liturgy would be employed during daily worship services. But the charter otherwise followed the College of New Jersey's inclusive framework. Historian David C. Humphrey notes that "[t]he Anglican clerics readily conceded that 'all protestant Youths should be admitted on a perfect Parity' with full toleration of their religious beliefs." Moreover, by nominating the Anglican Samuel Johnson for the presidency, William Livingston made it impossible for his Anglican counterparts to oppose the man he nominated for Johnson's assistant: the Congregational minister Chauncey Whittelsey.[49]

At the same time, Johnson—who had fought vigorously to keep the institution in Anglican hands—demonstrated his church's newfound mastery over the language of religious inclusion. Johnson's announcement of the college's opening assured New York's diverse religious population that "the college would not 'impose on the scholars, the peculiar tenets of any particular sect of Christians,' and would instead 'inculcate upon their minds, the great principles of Christianity and morality in which true Christians of each denomination are generally agreed.'" Inclusive words were accompanied by inclusive practices. Each of the city's Protestant denominations was granted a seat on the board of governors and, although Sunday church observance was mandatory, students were free to attend their own houses of worship. At midcentury, even men as devoted to their church's success as Johnson were capable of recognizing the measures that an ecumenical culture demanded and the logic that an ecumenical language entailed.[50]

The conflict over King's College was waged in the vast open columns of the city's newspapers, but it could only be resolved in the halls of the colonial assembly. There, opposition to Anglican control was led by none other than

William Livingston. The competition focused—as it would for the next two decades—on the Dutch Reformed assemblymen who held the swing votes in that body. The fight for King's College generated the same denominational negotiations that characterized Middle Colony politics generally. Livingston's Anglican opponents argued that his attempts to open up the administration of the college were designed so that the Presbyterians, with the unwitting assistance of the Dutch Reformed—whom they were apparently attempting to "cajol[e]... into a Coalition"—might seize control. Livingston's Anglican opponents viewed the *Reflector*'s efforts at coalition building as a symptom of his utter indifference to particular religious practices and beliefs. But the Anglicans had their allies as well. In fact, they ultimately succeeded in enlisting support from the city's Dutch Reformed churches.[51]

These Anglican successes aside, Livingston's ecumenism does seem to have been effective. Opposition to exclusive Anglican control over King's College extended beyond the confines of New York City's clergymen to include a broad segment of the public. Although one polemicist derisively noted that a large proportion of Livingston's supporters were "Cobblers and Irish Taylors," the Anglicans could not ignore the fact that Livingston had succeeded in culling support from a wide range of New Yorkers. Whether that support was based upon simple anti-Anglican prejudice or a more idealistic commitment to nonsectarian education, or some combination of the two, it was clear that there was significant opposition to the Anglican plan. In the following decade, that inchoate resistance would coalesce as part of a colony-wide, interdenominational union against the introduction of Anglican bishops to America. For the moment, it stood as a symbol of the notable changes that ecumenical rhetoric could produce.[52]

Religious Identity in an Ecumenical Environment: Denominationalism

The bitter invective directed against Livingston sometimes suggested that he was a tool of the Presbyterians and sometimes a religious dilettante. Livingston fancied himself—as did an increasing number of his contemporaries—a sincere believer, unfettered by prejudice, and endowed with the right to associate with whomever he pleased. Whatever the case, Livingston and his fellow travelers do seem to have operated under the assumption that church identity represented a mere coincidence, a potentially irrational choice amid a host of reasonable alternatives. In fact, two of the *Reflector*'s three essayists, Livingston and John Morin Scott, had recently moved from the Dutch and French

Reformed churches, respectively, to the Presbyterian Church. There was less of the convert's zeal in their opposition to Anglicanism than an abiding skepticism toward anyone who strove to monopolize public discussion and compel individuals to abide by other people's beliefs. Those who did not share their religious skepticism might still share their opposition to constraints on religious affiliation. For instance, the minister who led the campaign against Massachusetts' religious establishment—the evangelical Baptist, Isaac Backus— would later quote John Locke's argument against the notion that faith should simply pass from parents to children. Thinkers as dissimilar as Locke, Backus, and Livingston objected to the notion that religious identity should constitute a perpetual burden on the conscience, like the debts that sometimes passed from fathers to their sons. Instead, they conceived of church institutions as banks for spiritual capital, invested for as long as the soul received adequate dividends.[53]

A few of Livingston's neighbors suggested that a child's first religious identity should not be considered his last. A New York official, Archibald Kennedy, did so as he urged the provincial legislature to avoid embroilment in the King's College morass. Religious disputes were particularly vituperative and long lasting, Kennedy contended, because "BIGOT[s]," which he defined as those "foolishly obstinate, and perversely wedded to an Opinion," always took the leading role in them. Kennedy then hypothesized a conversation with a son about to set off for college. Stressing the fortuitous nature of all religious attachments, Kennedy remarked that his family turned "Dissenters" when the local church was renovated, moving the family's pew further from the altar. Kennedy then lectured his audience directly: "I believe few of you can give a better Reason, for your Professions, Persuasions or Religion, call it which you will." Accordingly, he and his wife had merely instructed their college-bound son in his duty to God and neighbor, "without attempting to enter [him] into any formed System." They had taught him piety and decency, without inculcating a particular form of worship.[54]

During these same years, the Pennsylvanian Hermon Husbands articulated the conviction that religious identities could be made and unmade. Husbands began his personal account of denomination hopping by recalling how a fellow Quaker asked him, "by what Accident" he had come to join the Friends. According to his own "impartial" narrative, Husbands had grown up in the Anglican church, but was influenced by the visits of a Presbyterian minister. Later, after hearing the revival preaching of George Whitefield, he had gravitated toward the New Light Presbyterians. Moved by Whitefield's sympathy for the Friends, Husbands became convinced that there were at most minor differences between the evangelical Presbyterians and the

Quakers. Thereafter, he found himself defending Quaker doctrines and practices. Eventually, Husbands was introduced to some canonical Quaker texts, which purportedly convinced him to become a Friend himself. Like his contemporary, William Livingston, Husbands encountered a variety of different religious groups during his lifetime and these meetings may account for the ease with which he discounted their apparent "ceremonial Difference[s]." His migration from Anglicanism to New Light Presbyterianism and finally to Quakerism, Husbands suggested, was facilitated by the body of fundamental tenets and practices that these different denominations held in common. Indeed, he claimed, these denominations even shared many of the same theological particulars. They were only distinguished by their relative degrees of piety.[55]

The disdain shown toward church boundaries during the middle decades of the century left the old church partisans in an increasingly untenable position. When eighteen Presbyterian New Lights endorsed a letter on behalf of a former Presbyterian applying for a position as an Anglican rector, the Old Lights were appalled. The New Lights had stressed the mutual respect with which both Presbyterians and Anglicans held "Fundamental Doctrines" and insisted "that no Difference in lesser Matters, nor any selfish Attachment to a Party" could change that. When the missive's contents were revealed, an angry Old Light tract asked whether there were any limits to their brethren's theological forbearance, or any hope for denominational cohesion. "If the Church of England be possess'd of the Truth," another pamphlet protested, "we are possessed of Error." If the eighteen ministers were correct in their assessment, then "All our Scruples of Conscience are answered at once, by resolving them into nothing else but a selfish Attachment to a Party." If their fundamental beliefs were undistinguished and their circumstantial doctrines insignificant, then they might as well pledge their obedience to Anglican bishops. If all disagreements between Presbyterians (and perhaps all Protestants, even all Christians) were just expressions of petty dispositions, then what ground was there for the many different churches that made up the provincial landscape? And what reasons could be given for maintaining confessions of faith, those ostensible embodiments of particular denomination's essential doctrines?[56]

Pennsylvania's Old Light Presbyterians were not alone in confronting the dilemmas resulting from the ecumenical language of midcentury believers. Connecticut Congregationalists ran into a similar bundle of problems as they defended their colony's rules for Congregational and Presbyterian churches, known as the Saybrook Platform. They discovered, as had Thomas Clap, that an argument premised upon the value of orthodoxy would no longer persuade many people, even those whose own beliefs were "orthodox." And so apologists for the Platform mounted a defense more appropriate to the spirit of the times. Instead of framing their confession of faith as a universal standard, they portrayed it as an instrument of group identity. Thomas Fitch contended that confessions of faith constituted the means by which a church or individual "explain[ed] themselves, to those with whom they are about to join in fellowship." It demarcated the "sentiments, principles or opinions of particular men," providing them with "credible evidence" of their agreement. The anonymous author *Catholicus* suggested that such creeds were best regarded as faithful representations of a church's beliefs. They demonstrated "how far [the world's various churches] are agreed, and wherein they differ." Another anonymous author asserted that religious tests were only legitimate if employed as "public declarations of the religious opinions of christian communities."[57]

Dissenting opponents of creeds had always regarded such institutions as secular perversions of sacred words. Now, even their supporters seemed willing to concede their contingent quality. Once a formidable instrument of conformity, the creed—like the denomination itself—appeared on its way to becoming a marker of difference and a relatively modest means of collective self-definition. These were precisely the qualities that would make it useful in an egalitarian and pluralistic society where tradition was suspect and uniformity was scorned. In an age when religious coercion was on the wane, when individuals could move freely from one church to another, when religious identity could seem like an accident, when denominations divided and then reunited, a statement of principle was still something more than a mission statement, but also something less than a final statement of truth. Amid the increasingly cosmopolitan, increasingly integrated public world in which mid-eighteenth-century Americans discussed their differences, church boundaries were becoming less a sign of permanent, disfiguring, and irreconcilable divisions than a reminder of the fallibility of human knowledge and the minor variations that would always exist between reasonable creatures of differently named groups of Christians, called denominations.

The ecumenical language of this period, together with the emergence of interdenominational fraternal societies, politics, and colleges, all weighed against the particular sectarian identities that believers had long maintained. It is probably no coincidence that the Moravians' entrance into the colonies coincided with the beginnings of Freemasonry. Yet it is important to remember that the ambition to unite disparate denominations failed. In this regard, the Moravian example is especially instructive. For their great dream of interdenominational love and cooperation ultimately ended in the creation of yet another denomination. Likewise, as the historian Jon Butler notes, the "nondenominational" churches formed by followers of George Whitefield's did not survive much past the preacher's death in 1770. The fate of Philadelphia's New Building is worth considering as well. Constructed in the early years of the Awakening to host revival preachers, this Moravian-inspired house of worship was originally intended, in Benjamin Franklin's words, "expressly for the Use of any Preacher of any religious Persuasion . . . , the Design in building not being to accommodate any particular Sect . . . so that even if the Mufti of Constantinople were to send a Missionary to preach Mahometanism to us, he would find a Pulpit at his Service." It did not take long, however, before the building was appropriated by Gilbert Tennent on behalf of the city's New Light Presbyterians. Both Tennent and Whitefield agreed that the structure should remain a gathering ground for evangelicals and not become, as they put it, a "Bable [sic] of confusion." In other words, they thought it should host New Lights, not Moravians. But in 1749, under Franklin's guidance, a new group of trustees seized New Building from Tennent and established it as the home of Philadelphia's nonsectarian Academy and Charity School. A few years later, New Building was remade again as the home of the nonsectarian College of Philadelphia.[58]

The tumultuous early history of New Building suggests that interchurch cooperation worked best when it took place in such secular institutions, where traditional religious practices would not necessarily be sacrificed to ecumenical ideals.[59] The idea of a church (or even a church building) without a distinct identity seemed preposterous to most. Even the dissident New Light Samuel Davies, who badgered Virginia's established church by asking "whether the laws of England forbade men to change their opinions, and act according to them when changed," objected to the way they had lumped him "promiscuously with the methodists, as though [he] were of their party." Denominational identities may have been repeatedly condemned as narrow, constantly transcended through ecumenical rhetoric, and repeatedly exchanged by the spiritually adventuresome, but they held up better than the parish lines that itinerant preachers, colonial printers, and Atlantic merchants blurred to the point of indistinction. They held up in part because an increasingly equal, open, and diverse society still required some means of differentiation and some well-anchored source of identity.[60]

It is no coincidence that when historians of American religion discuss the kind of intellectual and cultural developments that others just refer to as pluralism, they often employ the term "denominationalism." Whereas the term "sect" implies that a group has seceded from a legitimate, established church, "denomination" implies peaceful coexistence among various, equally privileged, mutually respectful groups of believers. For more than two centuries now, American Christians have generally treated their fellow churchgoers as differently named believers. Though they may have always reserved a good deal of private disdain, perhaps even hatred, for other faiths, and while they have generally seen their churches as better than the rest, Americans have long been compelled to treat their neighbors' beliefs with some measure of civility.[61]

It is even tempting to see the eighteenth-century denomination as the cultural equivalent of the racial and ethnic groupings we use today. As ethnic affiliation now occupies a central place in identity formation and in discussions of "difference," so did denominational affiliation in the eighteenth century. As ethnic self-definition is often the preeminent marker of identity today, so was denominational identity in the eighteenth century. The denomination operated as a mode of self-definition that would be recognized everywhere, as a standard unit of public discussion. To a greater extent than perhaps any other moment in American history, eighteenth-century Americans conceived of their identity and their differences in denominational terms. Midcentury Americans spent so much time and effort trying to persuade their audiences that such distinctions did not matter because they did. Your church had a history and many of the people you knew belonged to it. It supplied you with words to describe daily events, rituals to organize your time, and meaning to understand your life. From this point onward, denominationalism would remain the measure of early American pluralism—always more malleable than racial categories and usually less acrimonious than politics.

Ben Franklin Revisited

One of the best means of understanding a cultural and ideological shift is to consider the reaction it engenders. By the 1760s, the boundaries of religious identity seemed to have become so evidently constructed and ecumenical sentiment so stiflingly pervasive that a very modest rebellion resulted. This rebellion, called Sandemanianism, was the exception that proved the ecumenical rule. Robert Sandeman, an elder in a Scottish Presbyterian splinter group known as the Glasites, established several churches in New England during the 1760s. The Sandemanians eschewed a paid ministry, and were probably best known for the kisses with which they greeted one another and the communal dinners they held, called "love feasts." Although the group had its origins across the Atlantic, it was in post-Awakening America that its leaders hoped to make the most significant inroads. Like the Masons, the Sandemanians espoused "unanimity" and "*Brotherly Love.*"[62]

But theirs was no vague devotion to points on which every rational being could agree. Unlike the Masons, the Sandemanians understood the obligation to "walk by the same Rule, and mind the same Thing" as a substantive commitment to embrace the same beliefs. According to Samuel Pike, the Sandemanians did not distinguish between essential and circumstantial matters. They considered every passage of scripture "*sacred* and *indispensable*." Every member was free to exercise his own private judgment, but the church would expel those who persisted in their dissent. A central and controversial tenet of the Sandemanians was the principle of "non-forbearance." Abjuring tolerance toward dissenting opinions seems to have required a kind of conversion experience. This, as much as anything, indicates how radical a transformation Sandemanianism demanded. Indeed, Pike evoked the angst of the repentant sinner, striving to turn toward God and away from his own worldliness, when he wrote:

> [T]his doctrine of unanimity and non-forbearance has come with great weight upon my mind, time after time, and even while I professed and preached the sinful forbearance, my own conscience would often recriminate; by some of the most plain and simple reasonings imaginable, such as these, if Christ forbids any thing, must we not think he would have it avoided? if he requires any thing, must we not suppose he would have it punctually perform'd?

To subscribe to a principle of "non-forbearance" in 1766 was indeed to adopt a radical stance toward the world. Moreover, to refer to the principle itself as "non-forbearance," rather than merely as "unanimity," was to consciously invert the reigning cultural conventions. With the Sandemanians, there would be no illusion of a preexisting consensus. They would demand explicit evidence of agreement. And they would exorcise all of those who differed, even in circumstantial matters, rather than forbearing the particularities that so many other believers were now urging one another to ignore.[63]

The future surely did not lie with these non-forbearing Christians. The Sandemanians could boast of only six churches in 1775. The years between the First Great Awakening and the imperial conflict that preceded the Revolutionary War witnessed the blossoming of ecumenical thought in America. The process began in Pennsylvania and New York. But, as we shall see, it was about to take hold in New England and Virginia as well. Everywhere, provincial Americans were coming to see themselves united—literally in fundamental ways—with other Protestants, other Christians, and even people of non-Christian faiths. In some cases, as in the flood of European migrants making their way to the colonies, they had no choice in the matter. But in many other cases, such as Edwards's Concert of Prayer, the meetings of Freemasons, or the interdenominational "Society for Useful Knowledge" that Livingston and his fellow *Reflectors* established in the late 1740s, midcentury Americans made deliberate choices to interact with those of other religious persuasions. Thus, for one reason or another, they found their fate bound up with those of very different beliefs and practices. To achieve the unity after which they so desperately strove, provincial Americans sometimes posited an instrument of spiritual unanimity—piety, love, essential doctrines, prayer, thanksgiving fasts, or just silence—through which differences had always already been resolved. More frequently than in the past, their imagined agreements were not of the sort that required the individual's spoken assent to a body of doctrine, just some generally understood and undeniable principles. They would often require merely an inclination to do good for others and to sustain the faith, to love and to believe.

Few believers would have conceded that they could only love more when they believed less. Nonetheless, like their Old World contemporaries, American writers evinced a growing hostility toward the religious "BIGOT," the person "perversely wedded to an Opinion." A changed mind was no longer necessarily a corrupt mind. Indeed, it was become increasingly difficult (though it was certainly still possible) to associate any particular faith with corruption, heresy, or disease. To acknowledge the contingency of religious identity was also, in some ways, to concede the legitimacy of believing differently. Here was the ground upon which every religiously inclusive society was built. The cohesion of the interdenominational college, fraternity, and provincial assembly rested upon the conviction that a variety of religious faiths could coexist within the same society as long as individuals were willing to privilege the beliefs they held in common and to keep their group's particular beliefs to themselves. Such a perspective seems commonsensical today because we live in a world that takes the virtue of inclusion for granted.

Within this context, Benjamin Franklin was no longer an apostate. Moreover, Franklin's ecumenical approach to religion—which had seemed outrageously unconventional during the Samuel Hemphill dispute of 1734 and 1735—was making increasing sense to midcentury Americans. It made especially good sense in Pennsylvania where the range of beliefs seemed to expand by the day. A shift in American culture, rather than any change in Franklin himself, rendered the man we take to be an exemplar of eighteenth-century American life, exemplary. Raised in a family of Massachusetts Congregationalists, young Benjamin had transported himself to the religious melting pot known as Philadelphia in 1723. There he patronized various churches, some of which he found excessively dogmatic. A local minister's sermons, for instance, struck the young Franklin as "dry, uninteresting, and unedifying," mainly because they did not convey "a single moral Principle." "[T]heir aim," he continued, "seeming to be rather to make us Presbyterians than good Citizens." Nevertheless, Franklin was always careful to avoid the dreaded charge of unbelief. Recalling his first years in the city, he maintained that he had always possessed "some religious principles," those "Essentials of every Religion." He was sometimes a caustic skeptic and always a latitudinarian, but never a professed atheist.[64]

In religion, as in other areas of life, Franklin strove to steer clear of controversy and avoid giving offense. There was more at stake in the printer's preference for religious civility, however, than a commitment to good manners. Because "all the Religions we had in our Country" embraced fundamental doctrines, Franklin wrote, they all deserved "Respect." For Franklin, demonstrating respect to all meant striving "to avoid all Discourse that might tend to lessen the good Opinion another might have of his own Religion" and donating money toward a number of different church building projects. It meant founding nonsectarian schools such as the Academy of Philadelphia and the College of Philadelphia. This is not to say that Franklin was immune to religious bigotry of his own. In fact, he worked hard to make sure that both the Academy and the College had an Anglican, and not a Presbyterian, at their head (the candidate he settled upon for provost was his Freemason lodge brother, William Smith). Nonetheless, deference toward any form of genuine piety was a principle Franklin articulated in both public and private. The critical premises of an emergent pluralism were all here: civil speech, a due regard for the "essentials" of faith, and charity that knew few distinctions between churches. Franklin's virtues would never serve as the foundation for a church, but they would be critical to the successful integration of a religiously diverse society. And now other influential figures were openly embracing them.[65]

One group of believers that did not yet enjoy the fruits of this Protestant ecumenism were, unsurprisingly, Catholics. In fact, the religious unity that Americans espoused was often premised on opposition to Catholicism and Catholic powers. Anti-Catholic rhetoric remained rife and anti-Catholic laws remained common at midcentury. In times of peace, "Papists" and their "heathenish" Indian allies were treated with simple disdain. When those groups presented themselves in the shape of a tangible military threat, however, the gloves came off. Amid the frontier hostilities that preceded the Seven Years' War, an anonymous writer named *Philanthropos* warned his fellow Pennsylvanians of the dangers presented by French and Indian forces. If nothing was done, he predicted, the western settlements would be disbanded and the people of Pennsylvania confronted with the choice of dying a cruel death at the hands of the Indians or submitting, like slaves, to the French king. So far the alternatives were not attractive. But it made the prospect even more terrifying, *Philanthropos* contended, to "consider the Affair in a religious View." A French victory would mean that all their Protestant liberties, all the work of their ancestors, would come to naught. Their children would be laid at the mercy of "bigoted Priests" who would banish or execute those "such as they call Hereticks." It was just such a prospect that imbued anti-Catholic rhetoric with its sharp edge, and Protestant unity with some of its growing appeal.[66]

Still, for many of those who lived in the middle of the eighteenth century, the world had truly become bigger and more diverse—and it required new virtues. Nor was it only the cosmopolitans of the great towns that understood this. At some level, men like the humble Massachusetts minister Ebenezer Parkman did so also. In a sermon delivered to his Westborough congregation in 1751, Parkman prescribed a new set of standards for speech and conduct. Explicating the biblical phrase "the Peace of Jerusalem," which he had once associated with theological uniformity, Parkman now pointed out that it was not especially difficult to abide "those whose interests are blended with ours." The challenge for the believer was to live peaceably among those who have much "different" interests, those of "different *Nation*[s]," "*different Opinions*," and "*different Religions*." If this lesson was being learned in Westborough, so much the more in Philadelphia and New York, in New Haven and in Princeton. It is likely that every time a coalition was formed, every time a joint venture was undertaken, every time a meetinghouse was shared, every time people had to transact business with those of another faith—every time Americans did indeed interact with those of "different Nation[s]," "different Opinions," and "different Religions"—the abrasive language of the past became a bit gentler. As the doors of American institutions were opened to men of all faiths, religious civility would become a prerequisite of public life. At the same time, agreement would be forged on ever fewer and ever more inclusive principles.[67]

4

"None Are Tolerated"

The Rise of Religious Liberty

Therefore is the name of it called Babel; because the LORD did there confound the language of all the earth: and from thence did the LORD scatter them abroad upon the face of all the earth.

—Genesis 11:9

Religious Liberty does not therefore consist in the settlement of Points which never can be settled, at least to the Satisfaction of both Parties; but religious Liberty consists in this, that they who maintain Bishops to be of Apostolical Institution shall have their Bishop, and they who maintain the Presbytery to be of Apostolical Institution shall have their Presbytery.

John Camm
—"To the Reverend Mr. Thomas Gwatkin, on his Defence of the Protest" in Purdie and Dixon's Virginia Gazette (15 August 1771)

Yet no one who is properly sensible of the important Blessing [civil and religious liberty] can help being alarmed at the Attempts lately made by many of the Episcopal clergy and some of their Laity to introduce Bishops into America. . . . Should such be the Event, *how terrifying the prospect!* We should be obliged to bid farewell to that religious Liberty, in which Christ has set us free.

—Draft of a Letter from The Society of Dissenters (21 March 1769)[1]

By Religious Liberty we mean a free, uncontroled liberty of thinking, worshipping and acting in all religious matters as we please, provided thereby, we are not prejudicial to the state.

—Barnabas Binney, An Oration . . . at Rhode-Island
College (Boston, 1774)

Toleration came as a great blessing to early modern Europe and America. It brought an end to decades of religious slaughter. It helped bring peace to Germany, prosperity to the Netherlands, and migrants to New York. Nonconformists benefited most. Toleration secured their church property, liberated their ministers, and relieved them from the constant dread of persecution. In colonial America, toleration moved dissenters toward a rough legal equality with their established counterparts. And yet, by the 1760s, a growing chorus of essayists and petitioners derided toleration as little more than the condescending gesture of state-supported clerics and oppressive rulers. As the Revolution approached, fewer and fewer proved willing to defend that once revered principle. Instead, they demanded full religious equality.

The causes of toleration's decline were manifold, but the expansion of an open print trade, the disruption of parish boundaries, and the opening of institutions to men of almost all Christian persuasions certainly made it difficult to assert that any group was merely tolerated. The end of exclusive church establishments would make it nearly impossible. As the ideal of toleration faded, so did much of the cultural apparatus surrounding it. Toleration's demise undermined the traditional vocabulary of religious differences. It was no longer suitable, for instance, to speak of "dissent" or "dissenters"— at least in public. The change was not unlike that which Pierre Bourdieu ascribed to the opening of communication between members of different classes and ethnic groups. In that case, Bourdieu wrote, "there are no longer any innocent words." By the beginning of the Revolutionary War in 1775, "toleration" and "dissent" were among those words that had lost their innocence. By the time peace returned in 1783, they had lost their relevance.[2]

The disestablishment of state churches and the eclipse of toleration did not, as we have been led to expect, lead directly to the triumph of a transcendent principle called "religious freedom." Instead, the growing appeal of something called "religious liberty" proceeded unevenly. In its common usage, religious liberty denoted an individual's right to worship as he or she pleased. But it could mean more than that too. When it was invoked from the 1760s onward, religious liberty often implied a high degree of reciprocity and a sizable measure of equal recognition. In many cases, the arguments for religious liberty centered less on the individual right to be free of government interference (or what the twentieth-century political philosopher Ira Berlin referred to as *negative liberty*) and more on the right that each group had to the fullest public expression of its beliefs and modes of worship (that is, on *positive* forms of liberty). Between these two ideals—one compatible with the old dogma of toleration, the other with the new demand for equality—much of the religious confusion and many of the religious conflicts of the period would arise.[3]

The shift from toleration to religious liberty, together with the public way in which the shift itself was discussed, brought newfound attention to the diversity of meanings that different people imposed upon the same terms. The challenge of establishing the common meaning of words and phrases is acute in integrated societies and even more acute when one form of public language gives way to another. In their prolonged and widespread discussion of religious rights during the revolutionary period (roughly 1763 to 1783), Americans demonstrated a new sensitivity to harsh words, especially religious ones. The opening of provincial institutions to an increasing diversity of believers provided the occasion for new insults to be recognized. In this integrated religious setting, misrepresentation became a kind of violence and prejudice verged on persecution. With a much larger range of groups participating freely in the discussion of public problems, the scope of injury was widened to include the intangible slights that once would have gone unnoticed. Intolerance had been found in places no one had ever expected to find it.

Religious Competition in New England: The Missionary Controversy

In October 1761 an elegant new Anglican church was constructed in Cambridge, Massachusetts. Not far away, a large home, built in the fashionable Palladian style, neared completion. The house belonged to the new church's rector, the Reverend East Apthorp. The size and elegance of Apthorp's house quickly earned it the label "Bishop's Palace." No bishop lived there of course—the Anglicans had never been permitted one in North America—but the appellation bespoke the towering ambition that the Church's opponents were coming to expect. Apthorp's handsome home was distinguished by an immense portico and two stories of pilaster, by intricate carvings around the front door, and mahogany furniture inside. Both church and house made conspicuous additions to the landscape of this traditionally Puritan town. Many of the surrounding buildings now appeared quaint, if not crude. Reverend Apthorp cut an impressive figure himself. Just twenty-eight years old when his immense home was finished, he was regarded as a young man of great prospects.

Apthorp had declined Samuel Johnson's offer of the King's College vice presidency so that he could assume this prestigious position on the vanguard of Anglican expansion. English-educated, liberal-minded, and exceptionally wealthy, he was the very embodiment of the eighteenth-century Church.[4]

From Harvard Yard, the academic stronghold of New England Congregationalism, one could watch Christ Church being raised. Among those who looked upon the construction with foreboding was an alumnus of the college named Jonathan Mayhew, a local Congregationalist minister. It was Mayhew who dubbed Apthorp's disquietingly expensive home the "Bishop's Palace." The youngest son of a modest family, Mayhew had attended Harvard on scholarship. Through the 1750s and into the 1760s, he oversaw Boston's affluent West Church. In an age of increasing politeness, especially among the clergy, Mayhew was something of an anomaly. His biographer described him as "impetuous." A more apt term might have been petulant. Mayhew had no more patience with the hidebound views of New England Calvinists than he did with the emotionalism of their New Light challengers. Shunned by the congregational establishment, Mayhew became known for his unorthodox views at an early age. He even challenged an "essential" tenet of mainstream Christianity—the doctrine of the trinity. In the end, however, Mayhew's quarrels with Calvinism would be forgotten. One does not have to look far for an explanation. In the early 1760s, Mayhew emerged as the leading opponent of East Apthorp, the Church of England, and the proposed colonial bishop that so many of his colleagues dreaded. In contemporary New England, there was no more popular cause and perhaps no more popular minister.[5]

Relations between New England's Congregationalists and Anglicans had never been particularly congenial. But as the Seven Years' War concluded, competition between them had reached a new level of intensity. To this point in their history, the people of Massachusetts had simply not experienced the religious diversity that their counterparts in Rhode Island, New York, and Pennsylvania had encountered. The Great Awakening had momentarily altered that. Yet two decades after it began, New Light separatism seemed contained. Thousands of dissenters inhabited the province, but they posed no imminent threat to the Congregationalists' dominance in politics or cultural life. At midcentury, the Massachusetts Standing Order appeared relatively secure. Then, gradually at first, and with increasing momentum thereafter, the Anglican threat emerged. Whether thirteen thousand Anglicans now inhabited New England, as the Reverend Ezra Stiles claimed, their membership was a far cry from the mere "handful" that had once populated the region. For anyone who dared to take note of the trend, the Church's growing influence in provincial affairs was unmistakable.[6]

Devoted Congregationalists feared the worst from their Anglican counterparts who had long denounced the power these "dissenters" wielded within the king's own provinces. Yet if they listened carefully enough to what Anglican leaders said, Massachusetts' Congregationalists might have discerned a notable change in rhetoric. When East Apthorp delivered a sermon honoring the newly opened Christ Church in 1762, his style was far from bellicose. After making some brief, critical remarks about Calvinist predestinarianism, Apthorp invoked the same ecumenical principles that had grown so popular on both sides of the Atlantic. Extolling forbearance, moderation, and a focus on the shared fundamentals of Christianity, Apthorp rejected the notion that communion outside the Church of England condemned a believer to hell. Just as important, Apthorp observed that the church's construction proceeded "on truly *christian* principles, with views of adding to the extent and stability of our common faith, uninfluenced by party, bigotry, or intolerance." The following year, Apthorp reiterated this same extraordinary ideal. "A Protestant Country, in such a Climate as ours," he wrote, "cannot well be overstocked with Churches, and resident Ministers." "The different persuasions," Apthorp continued, "need not interfere with each other." They might even "cöoperate" in the achievement of their common ends. As the young missionary portrayed it, the Church's relationship to colonial religious life was additive. For Apthorp, the Church of England would add its own religious particularities to the expanding range of institutions that constituted American Christianity. This was no zero sum game.[7]

Ecumenical sentiments such as these might have been acceptable to New England's Congregationalists. But Apthorp hadn't stopped there. In fact, he also suggested that the object of SPG proselytizing, the means of advancing Christ's empire, would not be the Native Americans, but—as New England clergymen had long suspected—colonial "dissenters." Apthorp's 1763 pamphlet announced ceremoniously that the conversion of Native Americans was secondary to the Society's "principal most excellent and comprehensive object, that of giving *all* the British subjects on this vast continent the means of public Religion." Although they expected their Anglican counterparts to treat them with contempt, New England's Congregationalists were nonetheless appalled. They were, after all, under the impression that they enjoyed a respectable religious life.[8]

The Congregationalists' reaction would, as everyone expected, come from the pen of Jonathan Mayhew. New Englanders had awaited Mayhew's response with great anticipation. The minister from West Church was already well known as a foil for Anglicanism and a defender of New England's liberties when Apthorp's first pamphlet appeared. Boston's faithful would not be

disappointed. Mayhew produced 180 pages of audacious prose, a frontal assault on Apthorp's claims and the Church's ambitions. In this tract, Mayhew
assured his Anglican counterparts that there was no need to evangelize those
who already enjoyed the benefits of a legitimate Protestant church. He suggested that the SPG should instead focus its efforts among the appropriate
objects of "charity," "the Negroes and Indians," who were so evidently in
need of the gospel. Mayhew also reminded them that their church was not
established in New England, nor its ministers exclusively "*Orthodox.*" (In a
subsequent pamphlet he would contend that the "airs of superiority" maintained by the Episcopalians resulted from their assumption that the other
churches were merely tolerated, that its members were "their *dissenting parishioners.*") The obvious corollary was that New England's non-Anglican denominations did not require the indulgence of the Church of England.[9]

Months of vitriolic controversy followed. The vast majority of the invective
issued from aggrieved Congregationalists who could not countenance the
notion that they were merely tolerated. New England's Calvinists had always
been especially sensitive to suggestions that they—who maintained their own
establishment in everything but name—were dissenters from another church.
What distinguished this moment in the controversy from those that preceded
it was the context in which it had reemerged. Apthorp represented an Anglican church that was at once more aggressive in its proselytizing, and yet
considerably more cognizant of religious diversity within the empire and
significantly more ecumenical in its treatment of other faiths. Mayhew represented the region's Congregational churches who were themselves beset
by a large number of separates, ever more inclined to cooperate with like-
minded Protestants, and ever less inclined to castigate those who differed
from them. Men such as Apthorp and Mayhew had largely resigned themselves to living in a world where their church would be just one of several
churches. They stressed the importance of private judgment, knew how to
write respectfully of other faiths (and how to complain when someone did not
write respectfully of theirs), and continually demonstrated the efficacy of
emphasizing shared, fundamental principles. Yet neither could fully concede
the rights claimed by the other. For no matter what they said, neither had
relinquished the assumptions of toleration.

The missionary controversy came to an end when the archbishop of
Canterbury himself, Thomas Secker, published a conciliatory response to
Mayhew's tracts. Anglican missionaries, Secker observed, were instructed to
preach nothing but the duties of adhering to "*the great fundamental Principles
of Christianity*" and the practice of piety. In a remark that would have gone
over better in Old England, Secker observed that the Act of Toleration was

held in unqualified esteem by his fellow countrymen. The critical concession came near the conclusion of Secker's tract where the archbishop endorsed Mayhew's proposal to conduct missionary activity among Native Americans and African Americans. Secker pledged to redirect the SPG in its ends, prohibiting missionaries from proselytizing among other denominations, so that it could devote more attention "to the dark Corners of the Colonies." Long employed as a justification for intrusions upon Native American lands and the enslavement of non-Christian people, the object of converting Indians and slaves was one that individuals of all denominations could endorse. Compared to the spiritual chasm that separated them from non-Christians, Anglicans and non-Anglicans seemed to share a great deal in common.[10]

Secker's concession to the sensibilities of his American audience highlights the evolving contours of religious discussion in late eighteenth-century America. While biological racism was still in its infancy, and discussions of racial differences virtually unknown, the egalitarian treatment of white Protestants was already woven into public discourse. Pleasing to some, abhorrent to others, the diversity of American Protestants was gradually becoming a daily experience for anyone who read the papers, attended college, sat in the Assembly, or went to the market—even in Massachusetts. The great published religious debates of the 1760s and 1770s reflected this reality. And the ensuing years would demonstrate just how sensitive and how inclusive colonial language had become. There would be little room for toleration here.[11]

The Bishop Controversy and the End of Toleration

The publication of Mayhew's attacks on Anglican missionary activity was front-page news in prerevolutionary Boston, and it soon drew attention elsewhere. Newspapers as far away as London eventually carried details of the dispute. Yet the controversy would pale next to the religious controversy that followed. Mayhew died an early death in 1766. In the months before his passing, he had begun organizing opposition to an institution that New Englanders feared almost as much as plague, fire, or Indian raids: a colonial Anglican bishop. Seldom presenting itself as more than a rumor in the past, the very idea of a resident prelate was about to receive a full public hearing. Over the course of this Atlantic-wide controversy, toleration would lose its privileged status and a new principle, called "religious liberty," would begin to take its place.[12]

The bishop controversy occurred at an inauspicious moment in British-colonial relations. In April of 1764, Parliament passed the Molasses Act. The

hated Stamp Act followed. Throughout the ensuing years of political controversy, colonial writers argued that they were being taxed without their consent.
When Parliament's defenders responded that the colonists were "virtually
Represented" within its halls, colonial writers replied that every true representative of the people must be actually chosen by the people he was said to
represent. The colonists argued, furthermore, that every true representative
must inhabit the same local community. The outcry generated by the proposed bishopric spread almost as widely as the uproar over stamp collectors
and customs commissioners. It even proceeded along the same lines of communication, through the port cities of Boston, New York, and Philadelphia.
Eventually it made its way to the south. In each place, many of the same ideals
were at stake. Whether the debate was civil or religious (or some combination
of the two), whether the issue was imperial taxation or a colonial bishop, there
was a new attentiveness to the meaning of rights and the value of equality.[13]

Unfortunately for its proponents, non-Anglicans viewed the possibility of
an Anglican bishop on this side of the Atlantic as a grave danger to both their
free institutions and their individual liberties. Despite the protests of moderate Anglicans, years of reading and listening had hardwired the connection
between political tyranny and imperious bishops into dissenting thought. The
seeming complementarity between parliamentary assertiveness and Anglican
arrogance only reinforced what many colonists already believed. Colonial
writers were quite certain that the introduction of a bishop to North America
would serve as but a prelude to civil despotism. Of course, the Anglicans were
as much to blame for the ensuing acrimony as their dissenting counterparts.
Probably every educated colonist was familiar with the old Church of England
dictum that the monarch was unsafe without his prelates: No Bishop, No
King. Conservative Anglicans still liked to invoke that memorable phrase—as
did their opponents who liked to arouse the suspicion of colonial dissenters.
These circumstances would make it next to impossible to persuade colonial
Presbyterians and Congregationalists to accept a colonial bishop. Eager colo-
nial churchmen were nonetheless prepared to try.

The unenviable job of presenting the proposal for an American bishop fell
to the Reverend Thomas Bradbury Chandler. Now the pastor to an Anglican
congregation in Elizabeth Town, New Jersey, Chandler had grown up in
Congregationalist Connecticut and attended Yale College shortly after the
Great Awakening peaked. Chandler was a veteran of the King's College debate,
a dear friend of the latitudinarian, Anglican partisan, Samuel Johnson, and
generally well schooled in the constraints imposed by an integrated religious
context. Colonial Anglicans had chosen well when they appointed him to
vindicate the proposal for a colonial bishop. Though convinced that the British

Constitution and the ecclesiastical structure of the Church of England were mutually dependent, Chandler was willing to couch his goals in the alluring rhetoric of mutual charity and equal liberty. Again and again, he displayed a sophisticated understanding of contemporary religious culture.[14]

Chandler's *An Appeal to the Public, in Behalf of the Church of England in America* (1767) set the tone for the ensuing battle over a colonial bishop by emphasizing the Church of England's vulnerability. The minister insisted that "Every Opposition" to the plan for an American episcopate, "has the Nature of Persecution, and deserves the Name. For to punish us for our religious Principles, when no Reasons of State require it, is Persecution in its strictest and properest Sense." While use of the word "persecution" was traditionally reserved for impositions of state power, Chandler thought that the dissenting opposition to the proposal was just as bad. He also appealed to the sympathy of his largely dissenting audience, which would have readily condemned religious persecution, by asking if they had to "suffer" the same hardships, they would not also feel aggrieved. (Like his fellow American-born Anglican ministers, Chandler had endured the long voyage to England in order to receive ordination from a bishop. That was the suffering of which they usually wrote.) After all, "[w]e have the same Feelings, the same Sensibility with other Persons, and are equally affected by any Sufferings." Chandler praised the "liberal Turn" that many American "dissenters" had taken in their "Sentiments and Manners." However, "an intolerant persecuting Disposition" still seemed to prevail among some.[15]

Chandler's effort to portray opposition to the proposal as an attack on religious liberty itself was an argument framed in terms that he could have expected his American audience to appreciate. Rather than taking the conventional tack of emphasizing the church's legal preeminence within the empire, he appealed for an understanding of the particularities of Episcopal worship. The Episcopalians were not, according to Chandler, demanding "superiority" in colonial affairs (though, he noted, they deserved it). They were only requesting "the Liberty of enjoying the Institutions of our Church, and thereby of being put upon an equal Footing with our Neighbours." This was no slip of the pen, for the same sentiment had appeared in recent Anglican missionary controversy tracts and would be reiterated on several other occasions during this dispute. In Chandler's hands, religious liberty was something more than the freedom from physical or material punishment. It entailed a set of positive obligations on the part of the non-Anglican denominations. "The Principles of religious Liberty professed by the Dissenters," he argued, "must not only restrain them from opposing an American Episcopate, as now settled and explained, but oblige them, if they would act consistently, even to *befriend* it." For to suffer persecution one need only be denied that which made one's church complete—in this case, a bishop. "[E]very Good we are deprived of," he insisted, "is equivalent to an Evil inflicted."[16]

Chandler's invocation of religious liberty prefigured a larger change in Anglican rhetoric. While they still sometimes hinted at the presumption that their church, the established church in England, deserved privileged treatment, the leading Episcopalians more often directed attention away from the Church's persecutory past, and toward its present handicapped condition in the colonies. Anglicans merely sought, in one minister's words, "only...the like privileges for themselves, and an exemption from their insults." In doing so, they deferred to the notion that all churches were equally distinctive. Thomas Chandler noted that even the Moravians were permitted their own colonial bishops. Why then should the Church of England be denied its particular modes of worship—those essential to its own liberty and unrelated to anyone else's?[17]

The Anglicans' positive conception of religious liberty was supported by a surprisingly relativistic and egalitarian approach to religious truth. In his defense of the *Appeal*, Chandler reiterated his subjectivist argument. "[W]e maintain," he contended, "that the Validity of our Plea for *American* Bishops depends not upon the absolute Truth, but upon our Belief of the Truth, of those Principles." The object of the appeal, he noted, was "to set before the Public, the Necessity and Importance of Episcopacy, *in the Opinion of Episcopalians*, and to shew the wretched Condition of the Church of England in America for Want of Bishops." Likewise, Chandler argued that English dissenters had never argued for toleration "on the absolute Truth and Certainty of their respective Tenets." They too had only maintained their right to worship in whatever manner best suited them.[18]

Here one can make out the new shape of public discourse. Like his dissenting opponents who would soon open up a full-scale assault on the plan, Thomas Chandler suggested that persecution might be as much a disposition as a disability, as much a characteristic of polemical writing as a legal punishment visited upon the body. His novel language stretched the meaning of religious liberty. The rights asserted in his pamphlets were collective and grounded in the expectation of mutual, public recognition. On this logic, one did not have to be fined, whipped, beaten, or even just excluded from office to be persecuted. Persecution could be much more subtle and its effects much less tangible. It might result from uncharitable published sentiments or—in what amounted to the same thing—opposition to a church community's plans for itself. In either case, Chandler's concept of religious liberty went well beyond the right of private judgment, or even public

preaching. It presumed the legitimacy of other religious opinions and demanded respect for his own. It asserted the increasingly widespread equiva-
lence of feelings, beliefs, and institutions, which were making charges of
intangible harm seem plausible. In short, it came strikingly close to a profession of religious equality. More important, as we shall see, Chandler was
not alone in articulating it.

Contemporary Anglican pleas for religious liberty, or even toleration, are
especially striking when they came from Virginia where the Anglicans had
long maintained an uncontested establishment. What could religious liberty
mean for an already established church? To the conservative John Camm, as
for Thomas Chandler, religious liberty entailed "that they who maintain
Bishops to be of Apostolical Institution shall have their Bishop, and they who
maintain the Presbytery to be of Apostolical Institution shall have their
Presbytery." "[O]ur American Episcopate," he wrote, "is no Attack on either
civil or religious Liberty, but has its Foundation in both." One would have
thought that religious liberty was something that an Anglican in Virginia
already enjoyed and toleration not something he would have required. But the
Episcopal controversy had introduced a truly new dynamic into American
religious culture. Like other Anglicans at the time, Camm was writing as if his
church were not the established one and as if his audience consisted of men
with different, even dissenting, beliefs. He was writing, moreover, as if religious liberty entailed public recognition and interdenominational cooperation.
To conceive of religious liberty this way was to think of it as something more
than an indulgence of the state or even an independent right to worship
autonomously. No wonder his dissenting opponents insisted that they could
not understand him.[19]

The Anglican's equation of religious liberty with the establishment of a
colonial bishopric was largely wasted upon hostile Congregationalists and
Presbyterians who saw only the superficial reweaving of the Church's wolfish
fur into the sheep's wool of mutual toleration. In their eyes, the Church's
apologists were to be pitied on the grounds that they were not established—
and these were hardly adequate grounds for sympathy of any sort. The anti-
Anglican essayists, the "Centinel," simply mocked Chandler's appeal for
sympathy. Charles Chauncy sarcastically remarked that "[i]f the church of
England cannot be FULLY TOLERATED in the Colonies, unless it is suffered
to EXIST IN ALL ITS PARTS," then the Church could not be tolerated without
being established. The conviction expressed by one commencement orator,
that where there was "a *full* toleration there can be no establishment," seems
to have captured the general sentiment: the logic of full, or equal toleration,
entailed an end to establishments. The Church's demand for toleration of its

particular establishment perverted the notion that "full toleration" emerged from the establishment of none.[20]

During the ensuing five years of controversy, both Anglicans and non-Anglicans would continue to accuse their opponents of appealing for the privilege of toleration while secretly desiring the power of persecution. It was still hard for many to conceive of religious liberty as something more than mere toleration and something distinguishable from domination. An anonymous broadside, which called for a "union and coalition" among non-Anglicans in Philadelphia, suggested that the Anglicans "[n]ot content here with toleration . . . aim at a superiority." The same arguments were advanced against non-Anglicans by Anglicans. The Presbyterians, one Anglican wrote, were "not content with Toleration," but strove after "Dominion and Power." Each side suspected the other of abusing the ordinary meaning of words, employing plaintive demands for toleration to advance their secret desires for dominance. On the surface, there was more comedy than tragedy here, more facile acts of misunderstanding than disastrous failures of judgment. Underneath it all, however, a seismic cultural shift was underway.[21]

From a certain perspective, there was nothing unusual about this controversy over the meaning of toleration and religious liberty. One can find examples of semantic disputation in nearly every heated print debate. But there was more to these accusations of misrepresentation than the usual churlishness would have produced. The problem of connecting words with their correct meanings seems to have had a special resonance for those who debated the Episcopal question. Indeed, contemporaries returned to the problem of linguistic indeterminacy again and again throughout the 1760s and early 1770s. As late as 1772, Thomas Chandler remarked sarcastically that it might be helpful for his anti-Episcopal adversary to "publish a *Glossary*, wherein the Singularities of his Phraseology" would be "carefully explained." Similarly, the Virginia COUNTRY MAN urged his anti-Episcopal adversary to read English grammar books, including those of English dissenters, to discern the proper use of a certain term in their dispute.[22]

Rhetorical bewilderment seems to have afflicted the opponents of the proposal for a colonial bishop as well. At the opening of one of their many anti-episcopal essays, the authors of the Centinel recalled that Anglicans had always proved particularly adept at exploiting the "the varying and unsettled meaning of Names and Terms." They were once again abusing the shared public language to justify their otherwise outrageous proposals. Non-Anglicans claimed to be especially confused by Thomas Chandler's vocabulary. "The 'Church,' the 'American Church,' 'the church of England in America,' are the names which he affects to distinguish that denomination of Christians, to which he belongs," the authors of the Centinel wrote. "I wish," they continued, "the Doctor would please to define his terms, and tell us what he means, by Church, and why that name should be applied to English Episcopalians only." Equally suspect was the Anglican practice of referring to other denominations as "dissenters." To offended Presbyterians and Congregationalists, the Anglican distortion of language constituted something far worse than a semantic error. The very term "dissenter" contained an implicit threat, a presumptuous reminder of the toleration that could be withdrawn at any moment.[23]

The alleged distance between what was intended and what was ostensibly read, between different interpretations of the same words, remained vast as the bishopric controversy continued into the 1770s. To the perceived problem of lexical misuse was joined the perceived problem of public misrepresentation. The opponents of an American bishop, like the opponents of parliamentary taxation of the colonies, insisted that the views and interests of colonial Americans were inadequately represented in English institutions. Drawing on the language employed against the Stamp Act, which distinguished between the ideal of direct representation and the English Parliament's claim to virtually represent the entire empire, the Centinel predicted that once the Church of England had successfully allied itself with the colonial governments, "all *Dissenters* [would] be considered as *virtual* Churchmen, and made liable to Censures accordingly." The authors pointed out the absurdity of assuming the agreement of colonial Anglicans. By Chandler's reasoning, they contended, "every Episcopalian, as a true son of the *Church*, must . . . be at least a *virtual* Supplicant on this important Occasion."[24]

Anglican writers had their own charges of unfair representation to lodge. They repeatedly claimed that their words had been detached from their intended meanings, and thus "misrepresented." Thomas Chandler's defense of his *Appeal* asserted that the dissenters had misconstrued the objects of his defense. Far from arguing for the supereminence of an Anglican bishop, he really was arguing for the mere toleration of a denominational peculiarity. "[T]he Episcopate of my Opponents," Chandler wrote, "is not the Episcopate of the *Appeal*." He had been misrepresented; his intended meaning distorted. "[H]owever we may be misrepresented," the Anglican "Freeholder" argued, "our Conduct has evinced the most liberal Sentiments towards every Denomination of Christians."[25]

For both the authors of the Centinel and their opponents, what most needed explaining was the meaning of toleration and religious liberty. Neither would, nor could, grant the definition that their opponents were advancing. And yet both were closer than either realized. The trouble was related to the vast differences over the political impact of a colonial episcopacy. But there was a good deal more going on here. Standing amid this linguistic morass was an embarrassing fact—neither side could frame their arguments in the traditional language of toleration, nor yet fully concede to their opponents the religious liberty that they desired themselves.

The tangled rhetoric of the Episcopal debate was itself emblematic of an evolving, post-toleration understanding of religious rights. If both sides in the Episcopal debate were convinced that the other side had abused the common meaning of words, each was also convinced that the other had engaged in "violent" acts of misrepresentation. As outlandish as such claims might seem, when religious liberty depended upon public recognition and when it was merely a hostile disposition that constituted persecution, malicious words *were* threatening. The Episcopal controversy invested social niceties with the gravity of an ethical obligation and transformed injunctions to religious forbearance into injunctions against violence. It demonstrated that with the decline of toleration and the rise of religious liberty, there might be no more innocent words.[26]

The Appeal of Numbers

If words no longer retained their innocence in the pluralistic context of the late eighteenth century, the same could not be said for numbers. During the 1760s, the invocation of numbers—especially those related to demography and representation—emerged as an appealing alternative for those who had something to say about religious differences in this society. Certainly a statistical fact could not infringe upon any believer's religious liberty. Certainly a number could not cause anyone harm. In a culture that increasingly shied away from qualitative descriptions of religious differences, even rudimentary quantitative descriptions must have been attractive to those embroiled in a contest for public opinion. Numbers supplied an efficient and ostensibly neutral means of talking about religious differences.

Perhaps the best known religious calculation in colonial America appeared in Ezra Stiles's famous *Discourse on Christian Union* (1761). Stiles, the pastor of a Rhode Island church, served as a conduit between Presbyterians to the south and his fellow Congregationalists to the north and was among the most influential ministers of his day. He was also among the most compulsive measurers. Stiles measured everything, from the height of his children to the surface area of the local wharf. His *Discourse* reads like so many sermons of the day as it invokes the usual assortment of biblical and historical evidence to make its case for a union of non-Anglican denominations. But two-thirds of the way through, Stiles's appeal for Christian union takes an unexpected turn. At that point, Stiles tabulated the estimated number of Anglicans, Quakers, Baptists, and Congregationalists in New England in 1760 and the projected figures for the next century.

A.D.	Episcopalians	Friends	Baptists	Congregationalists
1760	12,600	16,000	22,000	440,000
1785	23,200	32,000	44,000	880,000
1810	46,4000	64,000	88,000	1,760,000
1835	92,800	128,000	176,000	3,520,000
1860	185,600	256,000	352,000	7 Millions

Stiles was not the first American provincial to engage in such demographic speculation. A decade before, his friend Benjamin Franklin had predicted that the colonial population would continue to double every twenty-five years. Franklin had concluded his internationally renowned work on demographic growth by lamenting the low proportion of Anglo-Saxons among the world's differently hued peoples, observing that "the Number of purely white People in the World is proportionably [sic] very small." Stiles's innovation lay in the application of the tools of demography to religious faith.[27]

Religious numbers mattered deeply to Stiles. Like most of his contemporaries, he was considerably more concerned about denominational competition than he was about racial or ethnic calculations. It was only the degree of commitment that distinguished him. Stiles may have discovered the social significance of religious demography in the early 1760s when he drew up a college charter proposal for the consideration of the Rhode Island Assembly. The religious quota system he proposed gave each major denomination a prescribed number of delegates on Brown University's board of trustees. After Stiles held a spinning contest at his home in support of the anti-imperial boycott movement, he noted that among the spinners "were two Quakers, six Baptists, [and] twenty-nine of my own Society." Religious cooperation, like religious competition, could be measured in numbers.[28]

Stiles's appeal to demography in *The Christian Union* was the first of many employed by both pro- and anti-Episcopal writers in the decade and a half leading up to the Declaration of Independence. In a religiously diverse land, where authoritative judgments were increasingly difficult to make and individual judgments were increasingly immune to criticism, numbers seemed to offer a desperately needed form of rhetorical currency. As language failed to produce agreement and the value of words diminished, numbers provided a common and seemingly objective medium of persuasion. Religious counting had been used during the Great Awakening to measure the outpouring of grace and the efficacy of evangelical preaching. The vast crowds that gathered to hear itinerant ministers had prompted observers to take careful note of their size— ten thousand were said to have gathered in one city, fifteen thousand in another. By the 1760s, religious numbers were being used with some frequency to measure such things as political influence and denominational appeal. During the Episcopal controversy, for example, one bone of contention centered on the large proportion of Anglicans occupying colonial offices. A newspaper essayist implored his readers to "Look around...and then tell me what post or what office is not engrossed by them!" "Could all this happen by chance," he asked, "in a province where they constitute so small a minority?" Another essayist responded that the number of Anglican officeholders, few as they were, could be "easily computed." Nor, he noted, were there more than two Anglican candidates in the present election.[29]

Religious demography could also be used in making the case for disestablishment. That is precisely what the Charlestown, South Carolina, Presbyterian William Tennent did when he argued that:

> inequality of the religious burden, is the more evident, when you
> consider, that the number of the established Churches in this
> State is only twenty and many of them very small, whereas the num-
> ber of formed dissenting congregations, the generality of which are
> much larger than those of the establishment, is at least seventy-nine,
> as appears from a schedule now in my hand.

This call for religious "equality" was novel both in content and in form. We do not see here the plaintive cries of a persecuted sect for toleration, but the concrete empirical assertion ("from a schedule now in my hand") of injustice by an emboldened majority. The shape of colonial discourse had certainly changed.[30]

Comparable demographic concerns emerged from Anglican writers. "We are not seldom tauntingly told that the dissenters are daily increasing," Jonathan Boucher lamented in his 1771 apology for an American Episcopate. "[A]lthough thirty years ago there was not in the whole colony a single dissenting congregation," this one-time Virginian observed, "there are now... not less than eleven dissenting ministers regularly settled, who have each from two to four congregations under their care." In the ecumenical, but highly competitive environment that prevailed in America's Middle Colonies during the 1760s and 1770s, Anglicans, like their dissenting counterparts, eagerly sought to bolster their membership rolls, especially in the contested frontier areas. "If Numbers were to be counted here," the bitter Anglican itinerant, Charles Woodmason, noted in his journal, "the Church People would have the Majority." Woodmason did count, carefully documenting the numbers of auditors and communicants at each of his stops through the many thousands of miles he traveled in the Carolina backcountry. Anywhere between one and three hundred would attend his sermon, out of which Woodmason could usually count several Anglican communicants.[31]

It turned out, however, that the invocation of numbers was not as safe as it might have appeared. Even such alleged facts were subject to dispute, to the misrepresentations of malicious pens. Thomas Chandler came in for ridicule when he grandly estimated that one million Anglicans resided in the colonies—a number that included southern slaves. His opponents, especially the authors of the Centinel, treated Chandler's calculations with contempt. The Centinel's attack on Chandler's math formed part of a larger assault on Anglican demography. By contrast, the Centinel referred reverently to the population accounting of the "inquisitive and accurate Dr. Stiles, of *Rhode-Island.*" Drawing on Stiles's statistics, the authors dismissed the notion that there were anywhere near a million Anglicans in the colonies. Even if the demographic facts were challenged, however, they still weighed heavily in this controversy. Although Charles Chauncy denied Chandler's implicit claim of numerical superiority, he expressed concern that the introduction of Anglican bishops would produce a rash of conversions, thereby inverting the demographic status quo, so that "Episcopalians would quickly exceed the other denominations of Christians, as much as they now exceed them."[32]

According to the opponents of a colonial bishopric, religious arithmetic of this kind revealed precisely how unrepresentative its supporters were. The Centinel found Chandler's assumption that the *slaves* of his "virtual Episcopalians" could be counted among the ranks of Episcopal partisans particularly galling. Here, the misplaced presumption of virtual representation, the distortion of religious demography, and the arrogance of an English church seemed to converge. The Centinel suggested that Chandler was again assuming the assent of those whose speech was either ignored or disregarded. Disputing his calculation of colonial Anglicans, they asked: "Where then did the Dr. get above 500,000 of his *Churchmen?*" The reply to their rhetorical question was: "Only among the Negroes, those *virtual* Episcopalians, who chiefly belong to Episcopal Owners." The force of the Centinel's argument traded on the slaves' complete exclusion from colonial social life. But it also pointed toward the Anglo-Episcopal capacity for counting on more support than they rightfully should have, and for deriving consent from nothing more than silence.[33]

In the bishop controversy, as in the ongoing imperial controversy, the dispute over representation strongly favored the colonials. Advocates for a colonial bishop never stood much of a chance on these grounds. One example seemed especially poignant to the dissenting opposition. In April 1771, supporters of an episcopate in Virginia announced an upcoming convention of their fellow Anglican ministers. Apparently the organizers failed to attract more than a few participants, so they called for another meeting in June. Rhetorical misunderstanding was at issue right from the start. The second advertisement noted ruefully that the first notice "was not taken in the Sense I designed it should have been, and therefore has not produced the Effect intended." To avoid another misunderstanding, the Anglican Commissary explicitly noted that the subject under consideration was an Anglican bishop. More linguistic precision yielded similarly disappointing results. This time, only twelve of the colony's one hundred Anglican clergyman attended.[34]

A protest, authored by two clergymen professors, soon appeared in print. Samuel Henley and Thomas Gwatkin, both Anglican clergymen and both professors at the College of William and Mary (the latter, a mathematician), began their remonstrance by lodging an objection against the convention's assertion that it could act on behalf of the colony's clergy. "[A]s the number of the Clergy in this colony is at least a Hundred," they wrote, "we cannot conceive that twelve clergymen are a sufficient representation of so large a body." "The Clergy of this Province must have been egregiously injured" by these transactions, Henley later noted, "unless they are mere Ciphers, on the left Hand of a Sum."[35]

Virginia's advocates for episcopacy seemed to understand the importance of religious representation, as well as its potential for persuasion in contemporary rhetoric. And they attempted, in a much less effective and much less consistent way, to employ it themselves. John Camm, who led the public campaign for a bishop in Virginia, tendered an immediate reply on the issue. At the very beginning of an extended letter, Camm insisted that the ministers who attended the convention "did not meet to do any Business in the Way of *Representation*." Another reply came in response to the House of Burgesses' anti-episcopal resolution. An anonymous "Gentleman of Virginia" estimated that "more than nine-tenths" of the measure's supporters in the Assembly (and at another point, "more than nine tenths of the whole Assembly") "are in reality sincere and hearty friends to episcopacy, and were not aware that they did it an injury, or gave its enemies an advantage over it." A third Anglican, who styled himself "An American," tried to harness the rhetorical force of numbers as well. How was it possible, this writer asked, that Professor Henley could "represent the Sense of the People," when he himself would "not allow several Clergymen to represent the Feelings and Sentiments of the Clergy."[36]

Such pious attention to representation in particular and numbers generally, marked the onset of a heated competition between America's Protestant denominations (and between factions within denominations) for influence in the court of public opinion and for control of institutions that were increasingly open to all. Where authority was determined by vote and individuals mixed with those of many different persuasions, demography promised the certainty that religiously diverse societies did not otherwise provide. When words repeatedly missed their intended targets, when the meaning of terms such as "toleration" and "religious liberty" were so malleable and accusations of misrepresentation so rife, the invocation of demography may have constituted an attractive rhetorical tool. In our own age, we tend to view the use of mathematical calculations as telltale signs of secularization. While there might be some truth to this assumption, we should also understand such instruments as powerful new means of measuring success in an ecumenical *and* competitive religious environment. Large numbers of converts were the end of missionary efforts. Numbers were also the means by which members of the same community communicated problems and solutions and the means by which members of different communities addressed one another. And, given the unstable quality of language and the intensity of competition among the denominations, numbers must have seemed an indispensable tool of persuasion. Their frequent use during this period was perhaps the most conspicuous demonstration of the polite, ostensibly impartial, rhetoric that would be required as toleration ended.

The End of Toleration in Virginia

In Virginia, the last major strand of the Episcopal debate concluded in February of 1772. Then, on March 26, just a little over a month after the final episcopal essay was published in the Virginia papers, a bill sponsored in the House of Burgesses appeared on the front page of Rind's *Virginia Gazette*. "*A Bill for extending the Benefit of the several Acts of Toleration to his Majesty's Protestant Subjects, in this Colony, dissenting from the Church of England*" began with the provision that all Protestant dissenters in the colony "shall have and enjoy the full and free Exercise of their Religion, without Molestation or Danger of incurring any Penalty whatsoever." But this generous gesture was followed by a number of conditions forbidding dissenters from congregating at night, locking their doors, or worshiping alongside slaves. Compared to the penalties imposed on those who extended their faith to African slaves, however, fines imposed on those white ministers who preached at night or behind locked doors were relatively inconsequential. Any minister (or "pretended" minister) who encouraged slaves to disobey their masters "under Pretence of religious Worship" or offered the sacrament of baptism or church membership to them, without the owner's permission, would go to jail for a year. No bail could be posted, no leave tendered.[37]

To read this piece of legislation is to be thrown back in time, to briefly lose sight of the fact that Virginia's leading Anglicans had just spent the last year attempting to convince the reading public that they only wished for the same religious liberty that every other denomination enjoyed. To read it is to confront the inertia of religious laws and the persistence of establishment ideals. To read it is to witness the growing divide between the religious equality that would soon be conferred upon all white Protestants and the utter subordination of the enslaved African Americans who made up forty percent of the colony's population. As with so much of the liberal legislation passed during this era, only *freemen* would benefit from it. Early Americans simply did not conceive of religious liberty as something that applied to enslaved people. The Baptist elder John Leland represented one of the few exceptions. In the history of religion in Virginia he published nearly two decades later, Leland insisted that "Liberty of conscience, in matters of religion, is the right of slaves beyond contradiction; and yet," he continued, "many masters and overseers will whip and torture the poor creatures for going to meeting, even at night, when the Labor of the day is over."[38]

Virginia's 1772 toleration bill did represent a small improvement from the white dissenter's point of view. It was meant to address the ambiguity that had existed in colonial law since the English Act of Toleration passed in 1689. Political authorities and religious spokesmen alike had long worked under the assumption that dissenting groups were tolerated in the colony, yet existing legislation provided no sure guarantee. When dissenting clergymen had largely confined their activities to the distant western territories, the tenuous legal status of toleration in the colony provoked no widespread discontent. That changed, however, in the late 1760s and early 1770s. With dissenting converts becoming more conspicuous, their religious oppression becoming more evident, and petitions for religious relief now flooding their docket, the House of Burgesses was compelled to act. The challenge its members faced was to adapt the language of their traditional religious laws to the more diverse and tolerant social environment. This process had actually begun three years earlier when the House had instructed the Committee for Religion to draw up a bill exempting Protestant dissenters in May 1769. Just a few months later, the same committee was issued new instructions. This time they were ordered to grant full toleration, rather than a mere exemption from the existing laws against nonconformity. The Burgesses' attention then hastily shifted to the troubled vestry system and toleration legislation was shelved until the Assembly readjourned in February 1772. Still under mounting pressure for a better defined policy, the House of Burgesses produced the 1772 bill.[39]

It never passed. In fact, no general toleration bill ever gained the approval the House of Burgesses. There were simply too many objections. There was also too little time, for this Assembly's life was nearly used up. Called into session and then just as quickly dismissed several times between 1772 and 1775, the colonial legislature had become a victim of imperial politics. With the demise of the old regime, toleration was quickly becoming a byword. Its day had also passed. Pleas for toleration were rapidly giving way to assertions of religious equality. By this time, events in Virginia had incited both the growing number of evangelical dissenters and the growing number of moderate and liberal Anglicans. Those groups led the opposition to the 1772 toleration bill. Those groups also objected to the continued whipping and jailing of the dissenters who refused to apply for licenses. To evangelical believers and moderate Anglicans alike, toleration was no longer a sufficient end.[40]

The pace of change accelerated during the next few years. By the time the state constitution was adopted in June 1776, a rhetorical shift as abrupt as any in American history had taken place. George Mason's proposal that the state provide "the fullest toleration in the exercise of religion" would have seemed generous a few years earlier. Yet to a twenty-five-year-old representative named James Madison, even the fullest toleration implied that there was only one legitimate form of religious faith and that dissent from it was a regrettable mistake. Madison proposed to replace the phrase "fullest toleration" with the "free exercise of religion." In the end, the Virginia Bill of Rights provided that religion could "be directed only by reason and conviction . . . and therefore all men are equally entitled to the free exercise of religion, according to the dictates of conscience." At last there was a degree of clarity. The first important step had been taken toward resolving the conflicts that characterized the Episcopal controversy. Although the Church of England continued to enjoy a privileged place in Virginian life for the next several years, its establishment—together with the toleration that the church purported to extend to dissenters—had effectively ended. Dissent from Anglicanism would no longer be defined as a crime, and the exemptions granted to acknowledged "dissenters" would be renewed annually. By 1786, there would be nothing to exempt Presbyterians, Baptists, and Quakers from. They would no longer be dissenters.[41]

The rapid progress of disestablishment and the rapid collapse of toleration in Virginia coincided with the conspicuous ascent of the colony's dissenting population. Indeed, Thomas Jefferson justified the exemption of non-Anglicans from ecclesiastical taxes partly on the grounds that "there are within this commonwealth *great numbers of dissenters*" (emphasis added). There is little doubt that the state's officially stated policy would not have changed so swiftly had it not been for the growing power and public prominence of the Presbyterians and the Baptists. Until the early 1770s, the colony's religious dissenters were weak and isolated and their campaign for toleration heavily segregated. There was no equivalent to Britain's Dissenting Interest, no cohesive group of lobbyists and petitioners for religious liberty. In colonial Virginia, the journey to toleration by the state had been a lonely one. Each denomination petitioned for toleration on its own behalf. Each church petitioned for its own right to hold services. Each minister applied for his own license to preach. And those who would not took an even lonelier path to jail.[42]

By the mid-1770s, these patterns had begun to shift. Both the Episcopal controversy and the imperial crisis had brought together dissenters and moderate Anglicans against the church-state establishment. Accordingly, the newly established General Assembly began to receive petitions from groups denominating themselves "Dissenters in General" or from "Dissenters in Albemarle, Amherst and Buckingham." One extraordinarily popular petition may have included ten thousand signatures. As the supporters of religious equality in Virginia coordinated their efforts, so did they adopt a more universalistic language. Exemption from certain state-imposed penalties grew into calls for full religious toleration, and then for full religious rights. In the process, the groveling language of indulgence gave way to the emboldened language of liberty and equality. Petitions from the Dissenters in General called for the end of the Anglican establishment so that "every religious denomination" would be placed "on a level, animosities may cease, and Christian forbearance, love, and charity, practiced towards each other, while the Legislature interferes only to support them in their just rights and equal privileges."[43]

The transformation of public rhetoric was also evident in the printed debate surrounding the various proposals for toleration and religious liberty. As the Assembly's Committee on Religion considered the flood of petitions submitted to it, newspaper essayists took up the question of a religious establishment in earnest. Some of the language bore the marks of Virginia's cantankerous religious culture where dogmatic New Light Baptists and Presbyterians were still fighting dogmatic Anglicans in battles spawned by an extended Great Awakening. Few had ever been charitable to the other, and many refused to begin now. One evangelical professed that he could no longer restrain his anger: "Let those *dumb dogs* be displaced," he wrote, "and the faithful servants of the Lord enjoy their places." Nonetheless, a substantial portion of the newspaper print was more civil than in the past and most of the sentiments expressed in the papers and the petitions to the legislature kept with the ecumenical tone of the Episcopal debate. At the very least, they acknowledged that they were part of a common, interdenominational conversation and that they addressed a diverse audience. "A Friend to Equal Liberty" noted at the outset of his proposal for the reform of the church that he meant not "to vilify any profession different from our own." Some of the newspaper essays from the period convey the same sentiment that emerges in the petitions to the legislature—that the intangible benefits of equal treatment and mutual recognition mattered as much to the dissenters as tax relief or disestablishment.[44]

A collection of militiamen and freeholders from Augusta framed the issue more revealingly as they made the case that "all religious denominations" in the state should enjoy "equal liberty, without preference or pre-eminence . . . and that no religious sect whatever be established in this commonwealth." The conjunction "and" here is significant. Again and again, Virginia's advocates for religious liberty demanded that the Church of England cede its "pre-eminent" position within this society. In no other instances, however, did they distinguish so pointedly between the institutional mechanism of establishment and the formal esteem accorded to the established church. These white men from Augusta meant it when they called for *equal* liberty. They demanded these rights not "as the pittance of courtesy" but as their rightful "patrimony." They were, like those who participated in the Episcopal debates, putting a strikingly egalitarian spin on their argument for religious liberty. The liberty they sought went well beyond any legal reforms that may have been enacted. Instead, it represented an attack on the whole superstructure of hierarchical assumptions and demeaning religious rhetoric that had so long prevailed in the colony. It did this all, at least, for white believers.[45]

Religious liberty and white social equality maintained an intimate connection in the following years as Virginians debated the fate of the Anglican church establishment. It took another decade after passage of the state's Bill of Rights for Virginia to reach a resolution on the vexed question of religious establishment. No one did more to shape the final settlement than James Madison. Brought up an Anglican, Madison was already on an unconventional trajectory by the age of seventeen. Rather than enrolling him at nearby William and Mary, which was then in some disarray, Madison's parents sent their promising scholar to the College of New Jersey (Princeton). Since its inception two decades earlier, the College of New Jersey had admitted loyal

Protestants of all denominations and guaranteed them liberty of conscience. At Princeton, Madison would study alongside young men drawn from different regions and religious backgrounds throughout the colonies, though the majority were probably New Light Presbyterians. By the time Madison matriculated, the College of New Jersey was under the direction of its eminent, Scottish-born president, John Witherspoon. At Princeton, Madison encountered the liberal, empirically grounded philosophy of the Scottish Enlightenment. There too, he probably read widely in William Livingston's *Independent Reflector*. It wasn't the education that a teenage boy would have experienced in many other places in the world. It certainly was not one that Madison's father or grandfather would have enjoyed. Yet the College of New Jersey exemplified the novel form of education that an aspiring leader might acquire in pre-revolutionary America.[46]

Perhaps influenced by the secularist bent of his education at Princeton, Madison decided against the career path that so many thoughtful men of his day took. He decided to become something other than a clergyman. Yet even as the Revolution drew James Madison into the political service that would constitute his life's calling, he was burdened with religious concerns. Madison worried, in particular, about the five or six evangelical preachers who now sat in a local jail for the mere act of "publishing their religious Sentiments." He worried, in general, about the persistence of an oppressive religious establishment in Virginia. He thought that Pennsylvania might provide a good model of church-state relations and requested, in December of 1773, that his Philadelphia friend, William Bradford Jr., advise him as to "the extent of your religious Toleration." The use of the term "Toleration" suggests that even the far-sighted Madison had difficulty conceiving of religious differences outside the traditional categories of establishment and dissent. Less than three years later, we know, Madison successfully argued that the Virginia Constitutional Convention should substitute "the free exercise of religion" for the "fullest toleration." By that point, he could draw the distinction between religious liberty and toleration as adeptly as anyone. The latter implied subordination of some groups to others, the former implied an equality between them—at least that is what people were beginning to say.[47]

Madison's views on church-state relations emerge most fully in his widely read 1785 plea against religious establishments, the "Memorial and Remonstrance against Religious Assessments." There, Madison maintained that toleration was only one degree removed from outright religious persecution. It represented the final "step . . . in the career of intolerance." "It degrades from the equal rank of citizens," he wrote, "all those whose opinions in religion do not bend to those of the legislative authority." Madison offered other reasons for disestablishment as well—persecution discouraged migrants, corrupted faith, and infringed upon the individual's sacred relationship with his Creator. Yet the argument repeatedly came back to equality. Madison objected to the imposition of "peculiar burdens" and the grant of "peculiar exemptions," the subordination of some believers and the "pre-eminence" of others. "Equal and complete liberty" was the only "remedy" for the "disease" of religious establishment.[48]

The debate over church and state in America certainly did not end in 1785, nor with the First Amendment that Madison would see to passage during the first federal Congress of 1789. Yet Madison's "Memorial and Remonstrance" exhibited an ideological precision that had been missing from the last decade and a half of debate. The conflict between the toleration maintained by Anglican authorities and the religious liberty they demanded—and later between the free exercise granted by the state's Bill of Rights and the remnants of a church establishment that persisted in the state—had finally been resolved. The tract, Jefferson noted, was "extensively signed by the people of every Religious denomination." Perhaps because of the consensus that it did so much to advance, we are too quick to remember Madison's case against establishment as a brief for individual liberty. In doing so we neglect the peculiar quality of the debates that preceded it, the assertions of positive rights that sometimes characterized it, and the looming presence of religious diversity that frequently overshadowed everything else. In the "Memorial and Remonstrance," Madison hearkened back to an overlooked phrase in the state's Bill of Rights, which specifically enjoined the "mutual duty of all to practise Christian forbearance, love, and charity toward each other." As they traded toleration for religious liberty, James Madison and his fellow Virginians were thinking about more than the preservation of their private rights of worship. Like their counterparts in other parts of the country, they were acutely sensitive to social slights, acutely aware of public misrepresentation, and acutely concerned with the task of managing their differences. There was reason for concern. From this point onward, the uniformity that church establishments enforced and the social isolation that toleration presumed would no longer protect Virginia's believers from one another.[49]

Religious Liberty in Massachusetts

If one takes the arguments of leading Massachusetts' ministers seriously, their state did not maintain a religious establishment in the 1770s. This idea seemed curious to the non-Congregationalists who recalled that Congregational churches had, for a century and a half, enjoyed privileges notably similar to established churches elsewhere. While there was no official connection between the government and the churches, nor any required creed, Congregationalists enjoyed the tax support of their own towns and a monopoly on the main sources of institutional power in the colony. To many of those at the time and for most of us today, this arrangement had all the trappings of an establishment. The obvious implication was that the colony's Baptists, Quakers, and Anglicans, who could apply for exemptions from taxation, were merely tolerated under the law. But if apologists for the Congregational establishment had never had much use for the term "establishment," they had never had much use for the term "toleration" either. It smacked of the establishment that they denied maintaining. More than defenders of church privileges elsewhere, they had always preferred to think of their land as a bastion of liberty—even when it meant the "liberty" for dissenters to stay away or the "liberty" of conforming to strict Calvinist doctrine. Nonetheless, toleration was the policy they practiced (at least after the British government forced them to in the late 1720s) and the conventional grammar of establishment and dissent still shaped public rhetoric well into the eighteenth century.[50]

After midcentury, however, that rhetoric began to change. Like their Anglican counterparts in the colonies, New England's Congregationalists no longer guarded their establishment from the ramparts of an imposing orthodoxy or with the sword of unquestioning faith. Instead, they cast their domination in the disarming platitudes of enlightened piety and superior learning.[51] The region's liberal rationalist elite that Whitefield and his admirers attacked during the Great Awakening had grown still more liberal and rationalistic by the time of the American Revolution. Charles Chauncy remained its leading spokesman. Refined modes of worship, restrained expressions of piety, a diluted Calvinist theology, and a broadening latitudinarianism were ever more its defining characteristics. A revealing assumption shared by at least some of these rationalist liberals was that important questions should be considered from many angles. There was nothing implicitly wrong, these genteel clergymen insisted, with suspending judgment until a number of different possibilities had been considered.[52] Reflective thought did not make you as a child tossed to and fro, and carried about with every wind of doctrine. Accordingly, when the Massachusetts Constitutional Convention concluded its work in the 1780s, the delegates recalled proudly that "the debates were managed by persons of various denominations" and espoused the virtues of having "a Variety of Sentiments offered to public Examination concerning it."[53] They added the additional counsel that "wise Men are not apt to be obstinately tenacious of their own Opinions: They will always pay a due Regard to those of other Men and keep their minds open to Conviction."[54]

Upon such ostensibly pluralistic assumptions, a New England clergymen could build a case that religious liberty truly manifested itself when the believer considered a problem from different perspectives. In his *Religious Liberty an Invaluable Blessing* (1768), Amos Adams did just that. The minister insisted that no aspect of Christianity would "suffer, by the freest and fullest enquiry." Adams was typical in that he rejected the very notion of civil rulers "punish[ing] heretics," yet he was perfectly comfortable seeing those dissenters "supporting *schools* and *colleges* for training up our youth for the work of the ministry; and ... giving due encouragement for men of ability to undertake the sacred employment." The notion of religious liberty advanced by Adams was perfectly compatible with Massachusetts' religious establishments. Adams made no mention of the growing chorus of dissenting voices in the colony who did not find such subtle distinctions plausible.[55]

For New England's Baptists and New Light Separates, Adams's reasoning remained as hollow and abstract as Charles Chauncy's had to evangelicals in the early 1740s. What was religious liberty if you could not physically move your body from one church to another or choose your own minister without being subject to persecution? What was religious liberty if one's beliefs always had to be certified by the state? These were precisely the questions posed by the Baptist preacher, Isaac Backus. During the second half of the eighteenth century there was no more prolific an advocate of disestablishment. Backus's career exemplifies both the continuing challenge that evangelism posed to colonial religious establishments and the egalitarian convictions that drove the assault. At the height of New England's Great Awakening, this young Connecticut farmer underwent a radical conversion experience. Shortly after the Old Light majority in his Norwich church vetoed the proposal to demand a "public relation of their experience," Backus and a group of sympathizers bolted. Like other New Lights separatists at the time, Backus was disgusted by the moral and religious laxity of his fellow congregants. He also engaged, as contemporary critics of the Awakening would have put it, in "rash judging." By 1742, Backus and his fellow Separates had founded their own church, which adhered to the traditional Puritan practice of requiring candidates for church membership to deliver oral testimony of their own conversion. Among the other measures to which the new church committed itself was lay ordination of ministers. Soon after he was so ordained, Backus began preaching itinerantly across New England.[56]

In 1748 Backus became the minister of his own New Light church in Middleborough, Massachusetts. There, his life-long resistance to compulsory taxation began. As members of a Separate church, the New Lights were not entitled to the exemptions granted to the established Quakers, Anglicans, and Baptists. Consequently, they paid to support both their own Separate church and those of their neighboring Congregationalists. The subsequent imprisonment of Backus's brother and mother for their refusal to pay taxes in his old parish reaffirmed the preacher's grievances. Over the next several years, Backus gravitated toward the Baptists, ultimately dissolving his church to form another one organized on his newly adopted principles. From this point onward, Backus played a leading role in the campaign against the Massachusetts church establishment, which required Baptists to obtain certificates if they wished to avoid supporting the local standing church—and seized the livestock, tools, and even foodstuffs of those who refused to comply. Probably never far from Backus's mind was the indignity that anyone known as a "certificate man" endured as his most sacred rituals were ridiculed, his children teased, his efforts to buy land frustrated (where Baptists moved, property values often fell), and his attempts to simply obtain proper certification impeded.[57]

In developing his argument against the establishment, Backus was fond of citing the liberal political philosopher, John Locke, but his arguments for religious liberty were largely premised upon the strict Calvinist commitment to making the true church visible. This true, or visible, church became "manifest" in the authentic description each individual offered regarding their faith, in expressions of their *"gracious* sincerity." According to Backus, Congregational ministers had alienated their parishioners by substituting *"written* accounts which have often been framed by somebody else" for the personal testimony of the individual believers themselves. As Backus saw it, an individual could no more allow someone else to articulate his or her reasons for joining a church, than they could be subjected to the discipline of a church through the accident of their birth. While expressing his regret for the rash judgments he had leveled upon those who differed with him in the past, Backus continued to insist that only the saints could recognize authentic faith in one other.[58]

In Backus's mind, to possess religious liberty was not merely to have the right to think for oneself. True religious liberty entailed the right to articulate one's own faith on one's own terms, to choose a minister who suited it, and to live freely in a community that sustained it. It entailed that both a man's words and his deeds follow the injunctions of his soul. Massachusetts authorities seemed to be under the impression that they already indulged such liberties by demanding that dissenting individuals only be conformists in their own way, fully adhering to their particular, tolerated system. After all, didn't its certificate policy allow religious minorities to obtain tax relief merely by registering themselves with their towns as sober, churchgoing dissenters? As Backus saw things, however, the state was still depriving dissenters of their liberty by defining them in a predetermined way. It even stuck them with an unwelcome title: Anabaptists (which, Backus pointed out, meant "re-baptizers"). Like the ministers who substituted written confessions for the spontaneous confessions of aspiring church members, the state supplied the description through which legitimate dissent was to be articulated. It effec-tively restricted them "to one circumstantial mode."[59]

For Backus, religious liberty also implied that neither his church, nor any individual within it, should be treated with less respect or accorded fewer privileges than another. Backus's concept of religious liberty entailed both equal recognition and the right of self-definition. Those who could not act on their own sincerely held beliefs were treated with no more reverence than a child or a servant, those compelled to "yield a silent consent." "[L]iberty of conscience" was universally admired, Backus wrote, but poorly understood. It resided in expressions of "our sentiments and the grounds of them." The trouble was that so many would "go a step further, and judge for others as well as our selves," and lavish "contempt or abuse" on those who disagreed. Was not the real issue, Backus wrote, "that common people claim as good a right to judge and act for themselves in matters of religion, as civil rulers or the learned clergy?" The case for religious liberty had rarely, if ever, been posed in such a starkly democratic form.[60]

Backus's egalitarian arguments against the Massachusetts religious es-tablishment carried on the peculiar New Light commitment to both spiritual and physical autonomy that George Whitefield and his followers had inspired, and Elisha Williams had articulated. For Backus, as for these earlier propo-nents of religious liberty, a person's body was directly implicated in matters affecting his or her soul. "One is not to act as unconcerned *spectators*," Backus wrote, "but as persons really engaged to *practice* what they know." So much then for the liberal Congregationalist position that religious liberty entailed the right to entertain a variety of perspectives. Backus distinguished between the persecution that had long prevailed in England and Massachu-setts and what he called "modern" persecution. The persecutors of old had demanded conformity of both mind and body. The persecutors of his own day only required that the body conform, that the "outward man" obtain his license or pay his fees. Their utter indifference to the dissenter's conscience was symptomatic of their indifference to otherworldly matters generally. Their ancestors had often been brutal, but at least they possessed the virtue of consistency. Similarly, Backus complained that the state's ecclesiastical laws embodied "partiality" that was rooted in their unwillingness to live under the same conditions as the dissenters. The equal protection of the laws, Backus suggested, entailed that this possibility always remain open. But in Massachusetts, the lawgivers rested securely in the knowledge that they would not have to exchange places. In other words, they rested securely in their privileged social and political position, just as they rested securely in their spiritual inertia. What they called impartiality, he called indifference. What they called liberty, he called persecution.[61]

Isaac Backus was no ecumenist. He was far from the Protestant pluralism of a William Livingston or even an Ezra Stiles. He probably deserved the charges of rash judgment that were leveled against him. Nor were Backus and his fellow dissenting clergymen necessarily opposed to compulsory religious taxation as long as it was equally collected and its proceeds equally distributed. It was every man's duty to support his church, and if the state had to compel people to carry out that duty, so be it. Ultimately, Backus articulated the strident evangelism that would broker no compromise on matters of conscience, that would permit no man to represent another's soul, that would demand equal recognition for the humblest group of believers. His failure to end the colony's system of compulsory taxation was due, in part, to the fact that he was never able to link his particular Baptist cause to the cause of dissenters generally. That failure, in turn, owed something to the fact that the dissenting population in Massachusetts was small and relatively homogenous. Unlike Virginia, his state neither attracted large numbers of religious outsiders nor produced an alienated, liberal elite who would challenge the establishment. Add to this the fact that the Congregationalist clergy had repeatedly demonstrated its republican credentials during the war (in contrast to their Anglican counterparts to the south) and the continued vitality of the state's religious establishment becomes considerably less mysterious. As a new state constitution was discussed between 1778 and 1780, Backus must have eventually realized that the chances for significant change were not good.[62]

The constitution that emerged out of the Massachusetts constitutional convention in March of 1780 realized Backus's fears. The proposed charter included two separate religious clauses. Part One, Article Two guaranteed that no harm would come to any worshiper of "the SUPREME BEING" in the province. To this measure, there was little opposition. The next, however, generated vociferous resistance both within the convention hall itself and among the larger public. It may never in fact have gained the necessary two-thirds majority to become part of the constitution. Nonetheless, it was ratified along with the remainder of the document. Part One, Article Three required that each town or parish make provision "for the support and maintenance of public Protestant teachers of piety, religion, and morality." In practice, this meant that the majority (in most cases, the Congregationalists) would maintain the bulk of their privileges, while the dissenting Baptists, Quakers, and Anglicans would have to keep applying for exemptions. The only significant difference was that all of the incorporated minority sects in a town or parish could now apply their tax monies directly to their ministers. Nearly everyone would be compelled to pay to support their *own* church. Other states seriously contemplated a multiple establishment of this kind, but few actually implemented anything like it.[63]

Examining the practical implications of Article Three, one might sensibly conclude that the religious climate in contemporary Massachusetts differed little from the religious climate of half a century earlier. But if the legal shape of the new system did not appear much different from the one that had been in place since the late 1720s, the cultural context had certainly changed, and so had the justifications offered for this system. In 1780, no one would demand that the dissenters shut their mouths. No new legislation would pass regulating the conduct of itinerants. No claim of orthodoxy was made by the Congregationalists who would enjoy establishment-like privileges in most townships. In fact, neither "Congregationalist" nor "orthodox" appeared in the document. Nor did advocates assert that religion was synonymous with Congregationalism. In fact, they denied the charge of conflating the two concepts when opponents made it. Instead, the measure was justified as a means "to promote [the people's] happiness and to secure the good order and preservation of their government," and concluded with the assurance that "no subordination of any one sect or denomination to another shall ever be established by law."[64]

Suddenly, Massachusetts' Congregational elite seemed unable to offer a religious reason for a religious establishment. Their particular form of religion was, like that of their establishment counterparts in Virginia, no longer self-legitimating. Isaac Backus was right when he wrote: "A little while ago it was for religion . . . but now 'tis to maintain civility." The process began even before Article Three made it into the constitution. Backus recalled that "in order to obtain the vote, it was asserted that there never was any persecution in this land; but that what had been so called were only just punishments upon disorderly persons, and disturbers of the peace." Apparently it was not enough simply to deny the existence of an establishment. Proponents of government support for religion had to deny a long history of persecution and the existence of dissenters as well. It is emblematic of public rhetoric in the late eighteenth century that a measure intended for the support of religion could not be justified on religious grounds, even in a state where one denomination (the

Congregationalists) still made up eighty percent of the population. Backus and his allies might have taken small comfort from such knowledge. However, it does reveal a dramatic alteration in public sensibilities.[65]

It is also emblematic of late eighteenth-century rhetoric that the religious establishment guaranteed in Article Three formed part of the constitution's Declaration of Rights. Somehow religious establishment had been transmuted into a form of religious liberty. During the printed discussion of the article, the conflation of compulsory tax support with religious liberty remained largely implicit. Only the brazen "Irenaeus" (Samuel West) dared to fully draw out the logic. Opponents of Article Three, he argued, were an "enemy to the religious liberty of the people of this state." One might dismiss Irenaeus's claim as a rhetorical flourish if the point had not been made on at least three separate occasions. It boggles the modern reader's mind as much as it did Irenaeus's opponents' to understand how an article mandating religious liberty could be considered not only consistent with, but even dependent upon, an article that would impose fines on nonconformists. Nonetheless, there is nothing here that John Camm in Virginia and Thomas Chandler in New York might not have said. As with those embattled Anglicans, Irenaeus's unusual arguments testify to both the compelling cultural imperative of religious liberty and the remarkably diverse connotations attached to that concept. They also testify to the rhetorical uncertainty that (along with the assertions of rhetorical abuse and misrepresentation) gave so many of these public conversations their peculiar character.[66]

In the accompanying newspaper debate, as in the constitutional provisions for religion, there was a strong correspondence to earlier controversies. Congregational polemicists were once again obliged to deny that an establishment had ever existed in their colony—at the same time that they defended an institution that very much resembled one. But the state's extended public conversations about Article Three and the religious differences at stake also assumed a notably nonjudgmental and egalitarian tone. The newspapers included respectful treatments of other faiths, at least by the standards of the past. Early in the long debate on the subject, the conservative "Hieronymous" contended that "all protestants are . . . in the view of our laws, *equally orthodox*; and no men are deemed hereticks, *except Papists and Atheists*." Later on in the controversy, Irenaeus was careful to point out that "honest" Baptists and Quakers were not opposed to compulsory taxation. The latter, he supposed, only wished "that others should enjoy the same liberty of conscience which they themselves possess." While evangelicals such as Isaac Backus probably appreciated such ecumenical gestures in the abstract, they regarded these particular statements as clever machinations to fortify Congregational hegemony. Disingenuous they may have been. Either way, there was no denying that the shape of public rhetoric had changed considerably. New imperatives, new constraints, and new opportunities had emerged. In the end, Massachusetts' Congregationalists proved no more exempt from them than New England Baptists or Southern Anglicans had. In revolutionary Massachusetts, as in the other united states, everyone felt the need to write (and probably to speak) more charitably on religious matters.[67]

The central elements of the Massachusetts establishment survived for several more decades afterward and, alongside it, the widespread profession of both religious equality and ecumenism. Too many committed and semi-committed Congregationalists enjoyed the tax advantages of the system for the existing system to be scrapped. Yet, in this once great outpost of Calvinist purity, terms such as "Orthodox" and "Toleration" had been transformed or even abandoned, and terms such as "piety" and "religion" had been problematized. While there was a great deal of disagreement over what constituted equal religious liberty, the principle was as well ensconced as the right of private judgment and toleration had once been. The skeletal remains of an inequitable tax system—which no proponent dared call by its true name—were now all that survived of a once vigorous establishment culture. An establishment that openly shared orthodox status with other Protestant churches, that appealed for compassion instead of castigating dissenters, and posited inter-denominational sympathy instead of lamenting diversity would not prove to be much of an establishment.[68]

Pennsylvania Pacifism and the Limits of Religious Liberty

Pennsylvania had never experienced toleration. There had never been an establishment and there had never been dissenters. The colony's reputation as the home of equal religious liberty and a haven for every variety of Protestant church was deep-rooted by the 1760s. William Penn's 1682 Frame of Government had guaranteed that no believers in God, who were "obliged in conscience to live peaceably and justly in civil society," would be "molested or prejudiced for their religious persuasion or practice . . . nor . . . compelled . . . to frequent or maintain any religious worship, place or ministry whatever." The prospect of unencumbered worship and cheap land first drew English Quakers, then Scots-Irish Presbyterians and German Lutherans, and nearly every other sect that northern Europe produced. From the Palatinate to Scotland, from Charleston to Boston, Pennsylvania's generous provisions for believers were admired by libertarians of many creeds. Partisans of religious liberty portrayed it as an idyllic model of individual autonomy and inter-denominational harmony. Their opponents viewed it as a portent of sectarian conflict and theological chaos.[69]

Whatever people thought of Pennsylvania's experiment, the concept of religious liberty was well anchored in the colony's international identity. Its meaning for those who lived in the colony, however, was far from fixed. Beginning in the 1750s and continuing through the early 1780s, an uncon-ventional belief held by Quakers, Mennonites, Moravians, and a few smaller sects—nonresistance, or what we know as pacifism—served as a continuing source of public dispute and presented a continuing challenge to the tradi-tional meaning of religious liberty. To these "peace churches," the principle of nonresistance was fundamental to their system of worship and an essential element of their religious liberty. To their opponents, it was a strange pecu-liarity, a convenient doctrine, or an "alleged scruple," and required an in-dulgence from the state that went far beyond the liberty guaranteed in the colonial constitution. Even those we would define as latitudinarians, who stressed the essentials that united Protestants and deemphasized the cir-cumstantials that separated them, could not reconcile themselves to nonre-sistance. The conventional logic of ecumenism failed here. In cases such as this one, there was no easy way of reconciling the "fundamental" require-ments of liberal government with the "fundamental" doctrines of the sect in question.[70]

In what became the United States, the extent of the dilemma posed by religious pacifism would never go away, but neither would it ever again reach this level of importance. The problem was that as the scope and scale of warfare became larger during the eighteenth century, bigger and more ex-pensive armies were required. And as the call for complete mobilization grew, Pennsylvanians confronted a deeply troubling fact: a large proportion of Pennsylvania's religious groups, including its most powerful denomination, the Quakers, refused to bear arms. In the 1750s, Quaker leaders had suc-cessfully parsed the pacifist military obligations by ambiguously agreeing to contribute funds for "the King's Use." The justification had always been unequivocally biblical—Caesar should be given his due. This explana-tion sufficed as long as the Proprietors still exercised great authority, as long as militia service remained limited and voluntary, and as long as the imperial wars remained distant. But as the Assembly's powers increased, the Quakers who dominated that body found themselves in the awkward position of ac-tually being Caesar, responsible for preserving its citizens' lives and property. And when Catholic France and its Indian allies ravaged frontier communities across western Pennsylvania, the need for a large, ready army was no longer just a hypothetical possibility. The compromise carefully orchestrated by Pennsylvania's Quakers over many decades had come apart.[71]

The Seven Years' War represented a turning point in the official treatment and public discussion of nonresistance. Pacifist assemblymen managed to defeat the first militia law proposed by the governor and his allies in 1755. But unsettling news that the French had constructed several fortresses in the Ohio River Valley, shocking accounts of western villages reduced to smoldering ruins, and the disheartening report of General Braddock's defeat at Fort Duquesne convinced many Pennsylvanians that nothing short of full mobilization for war could stave off impending disaster. If that did not do it, the "Waggon-Load of . . . scalped and mangled bodies" that a group of German settlers drove to the Philadelphia State House may have. In this environment, pacifism seemed like a theological indulgence, if not a civic heresy.[72]

As the violence on the frontier escalated, public sentiment and militia laws became less forgiving and a brutal, decade-long critique of pacifist doctrines and Quaker politics began. The New Side Presbyterian, Samuel Finley, led off the blistering assault on the Quakers and their allies by referring to them as "NEUTERS" in the midst of a war that "admits of no Neutrality." Finley, who had argued against the imposition of a rigid Calvinist creed on his own churches, now claimed that the Quakers' appeal to conscience could not justify them in their dissent. "How sad," he lamented, that their "religious *Principles* are their *Crime!*" The duties of a Christian could not possibly be incompatible with the duties that all men shared in common. No Christian could be without the instinct for "*Self-Preservation.*" And no particular belief could "*cancel* our *Obligations* to our *King,* and our *Country*" "[T]heir very fundamental Principles of Non-Resistance" were perfectly acceptable as religious principles, professed and believed, but surely they should disqualify Quakers from civil leadership in times of war, *Philopatrius* later argued. While nonpacifist denominations had never been particularly sympathetic to the arguments the Quakers made for their peculiar aversion to war, they had generally tolerated them. But at a time when the entire colony was imperiled by merciless Frenchmen and Indian "savages," some argued that the Quakers who persisted in this dangerously particular belief would have to cede their political privileges. Even Old and New Side Presbyterians found common cause in their opposition to pacifism. Few could countenance this doctrinal peculiarity in a time of urgent military necessity.[73]

The official end of the war in 1763 did nothing to dilute the growing hostility toward Pennsylvania's pacifists. That was because the conflict on the frontier between white settlers and their Indian neighbors continued unabated. Backcountry whites blamed the Quakers who lived comfortably in eastern

Pennsylvania and dominated the colony's politics. Their resentment grew as settler town after settler town was burned and no legislative aid arrived. The Quaker-dominated Assembly could not bring itself to authorize funds for explicitly military purposes. And still the killing on the frontier continued. The cycle of raids and counterraids culminated on December 14, 1763, when a group of several dozen Scots-Irish men set upon a small Indian village at Conestoga with guns, knives, and axes. Three men, two women, and a young boy were shot, stabbed, and hacked to death. Seeking to protect the remainder of the villagers, Pennsylvania officials moved some neighboring Indians to Philadelphia County for protection, and the governor, John Penn, issued a proclamation calling for the apprehension of the murderers. He also forbade anymore harm from coming to local Indians. But he could do nothing about the depredations that persisted in the west. Two weeks after the initial assault, the so-called Paxton Boys ambushed another contingent of unarmed Indians in the Lancaster workhouse, this time taking the lives of fourteen Conestoga.[74]

As western pleas for assistance went unheeded, an explanation was ready at hand. Thanks to their success in building an interdenominational coalition, their capacity for intradenominational consensus, and some long-held privileges, the predominantly Quaker counties of eastern Pennsylvania held onto a disproportionate number of seats in Pennsylvania's Assembly. Presbyterian grievances were often directed at this Quaker Party, which repeatedly vetoed appropriations for defense, and accommodated the western Indians. Unsurprisingly then, the controversy surrounding the actions of the Paxton Boys featured some of the most vitriolic religious writing of the colonial period. A debate that began with vague disparaging references quickly descended into a printed brawl featuring specific vituperative references to "the CHRISTIAN WHITE SAVAGES of *Peckstang* and *Donegall!*" (by none other than Benjamin Franklin) and then to denominationally specific attacks on Presbyterians and Quakers. In the ensuing debate, the battle lines corresponded with church lines. Whole denominations were implicated in the actions and words of individual members. The western Scots-Irish Presbyterians, for instance, were often identified simply as Presbyterians. An angry Quaker writer argued that an opponent's tract had been written with a "truly Pious Lying *Presby—n* Spirit." To one Quaker, the source of the colonies woes was self-evident: "the *Presbyterians* have been the Authors, and Abettors, of all the Mischief, that's happened to us, as a People." To an opposing Presbyterian, the source was also equally clear—though altogether different: "Quaker politicks, and a Quaker faction," he argued, were responsible for all of the province's woes. For his part, an Anglican invoked the old metaphor of religious disease, referring to "the Infection of *Quaker Non-Resistance.*"[75]

If the bitter language of this dispute was more reminiscent of 1723 than 1763, there were also signs of the rhetorical changes that were emerging in other contexts. As with the Episcopal controversy, public expressions of malice mattered to the people engaged in the pacifism debates, and probably to their audience as well. Titles such as *The Conduct of the Paxton-men, Impartially Represented* indicate the importance of public respect and sincere self-definition. *Philopatrius* claimed to respect every man's write to "profess his Belief"—as long of course as they "adher[e] strictly to what they Profess." Likewise, both Presbyterians and Quakers took offense at the belligerent rhetoric aimed at them during this vociferous dispute and both groups acknowledged the importance of depicting other churches fairly. One disputant agreed with his opponent that "to talk against Presbyterians as such, is the effect either of party-spirit, malice or nonsense." But he added, it was "equally" uncharitable to "talk against Quakers" that way.[76]

As the Revolutionary War began, Pennsylvania's pacifists once again sought protection within the colony's venerable Frame of Government. This forced the opponents of pacifism to argue that an apparently obvious violation of Quaker faith and worship was something else. They would have to maintain that no religious persuasion was involved, only universal and irrefutable civil obligations—that no theological error was being condemned, just a political sin. "We know of no Distinctions of *Sects*, when we meet our Fellow Citizens on Matters of public Concern," the officers of Philadelphia's military association noted. The Quakers were being asked for financial contributions "not because of their *religious Persuasion*, but because the general Defence of the Province demands it." This group appealed, like *Philopatrius* during the Seven Years' War, to the transcendent principles of civil society. In fact, given the current crisis, they were "of Opinion that speculative Disputes should not now be gone into." Whether pacifism was fundamental to the churches that maintained it or not, the Redcoats were approaching.[77]

Significantly, the Associators did not seem to have thought their arguments for civil obligation entirely sufficient. For they also made the case that if wealthy Quakers did not have to contribute funds, "it will in some Degree be an Invasion of our Liberty of Conscience by denying us the Means of... making a warlike Opposition against our Oppressors, which cannot be done without Money." The military association must have felt a bit awkward about this argument. The qualification "in some Degree" suggests as much. Yet they were not alone in advancing the proposition that the rights of nonpacifists were being violated when a religious peculiarity of the pacifists was indulged. The legislature's 1755 militia bill (later vetoed by British authorities) had maintained an "Equal Right to Liberty of Conscience" for those who wished to fight.[78]

During the bleak years of 1777 and 1778, as British troops chased the Continental Army out of New York, through New Jersey, and into eastern Pennsylvania, the nonresistant sects found little sympathy among the general public. A message delivered to the Pennsylvania Council of Safety petitioned for the exile of those who expressed the intention of actively resisting the revolutionary government. Yet even at this most desperate of moments, the petitioners "profess[ed] liberality of sentiment to all men" and adherence to "the pure doctrine of universal liberty of conscience." "[W]e undertake not to judge of the religious rectitude of tenets, but leave the whole matter to Him who made [us]." In fact, whenever possible, the opponents of pacifism made the issue a civil matter. The Philadelphia Whig Society claimed to know only "FRIENDS" and "ENEMIES" to the revolutionary cause. In their patriotic calculus, no "peculiarity" of religious "sentiment" mattered.[79]

In the end, there would be no triumph for either the pacifists or their nonpacifist brethren either in Pennsylvania or the country as a whole. On this as on many other occasions, Pennsylvanians demonstrated that the absence of a religious establishment did not guarantee religious harmony. The mutual recriminations, outright acts of distortion, and impassioned charges of misrepresentation that characterized the Episcopal debate appeared here as well. Pennsylvania's pacifist controversy had engendered the most belligerent denominational conflict of the day. And yet, as elsewhere, the punishments inflicted upon the "dissenting" pacifists were comparatively mild. As Peter Brock, the leading historian of American pacifism, wrote, the "main hardship endured by Quakers during the Revolutionary War was neither loss of life nor harsh physical treatment for imprisonment on the scale of the early 'heroic' period of Quakerism of the third quarter of the seventeenth century." Instead, Brock continues, Quakers and other pacifist sects suffered mainly financial penalties. As painful as such property loss surely was, it was probably preferable to the corporal punishment meted out to religious heretics in the past, and political dissidents at the time.[80]

The payment of money in lieu of militia service represented the compromise to which much of the nation would cling for many years afterward. This resolution helped bridge the conspicuous gap between the demands of military security and equal civil obligations, on the one hand, and the nation's libertarian commitments and ecumenical ideals, on the other. A few states, in fact, included a provision in their original constitutions that exempted the "conscientiously scrupulous" from "bearing arms" as long as they paid an "equivalent." And yet explicit provisions for pacifism were excised from the original proposals for the Second Amendment. Neither fish nor foul, neither treasonous behavior nor religious liberty, pacifism would be permitted as a religious peculiarity, not enshrined as a fundamental right.[81]

The nation's ambivalent approach to pacifism in the statute books also characterized its public rhetoric. Responding to a missive from the Quaker Yearly Meeting, which begged indulgence for their commitment to pacifism, President George Washington went so far as to say that there was "no denomination among us, who are more exemplary and useful citizens"— excepting their commitment to pacifism, of course. He assured them "that in my opinion the conscientious scruples of all men should be treated with great delicacy and tenderness" and expressed the wish "that the laws may always be as extensively accommodated to them, as a due regard to the protection and essential interests of the nation may justify and permit." Washington's response here emblematized America's ambivalence toward pacifism. Like those who came before him, the president showed himself willing to indulge "conscientious scruples." However, he made no mention of religious liberty or the essentials of Quaker belief. In fact, the only essentials mentioned were the "essential interests of the nation."[82]

No legal reforms were adopted nor wartime indulgences promised by the president. Washington offered nothing more than an expression of affection for a beleaguered denomination. His reply may not have been exactly the endorsement for which the Yearly Meeting had hoped, but they were satisfied enough to publish the exchange as a broadside in 1789. The former general had gone as far as any respectable public figure was likely to go at the time. In Washington's letter, as in the nation at large, pacifism occupied an uncertain legal and rhetorical position. The doctrine remained mired in the space between tolerated dissent and full religious liberty. It never escaped from the taint of political subversion that dissent implied and religious liberty denied. Like the prerevolutionary proposal for colonial Anglican bishops and post-revolutionary Catholicism, pacifism always seemed to pose a threat to civil society. In the language of the time, it remained a "scruple of conscience." It remained something to be indulged rather than honored. Seldom, if ever, was it portrayed as an instance of religious liberty. As a religious liberty, protected by state and federal constitutions, pacifism would have required more legal recognition than Americans were willing to extend to it. In a sense, this denominational peculiarity, this notion that there was no freedom in killing, has survived since that time as a cultural relic, an artifact from an age before churches and states were separate, before most Christian doctrines were accorded respect, and when toleration was still something for which a dissenter might strive.[83]

Toleration's Fall

For Englishmen and Englishwomen, there was nothing new about the practice of allowing believers to maintain their dissenting faiths as long as they paid their taxes, refrained from criticizing the government, and made no attempt to blow up Parliament. Toleration triumphed during the seventeenth and eighteenth centuries as European states permitted nonconformists the right to worship privately and eased the penalties placed upon them. It nonetheless proved perfectly compatible with the exclusive privileges that established churches continued to enjoy and the public contempt that dissenting sects continued to endure. Thus there was something truly novel about the growing presumption of religious equality and the widespread commitment to the concept that people called "religious liberty." Eighteenth-century Americans were not the first people to institute toleration. But they just may have been the first to permanently abolish it.

The demise of toleration and the emergence of religious liberty in the 1760s and 1770s had a direct parallel in the legal and political changes of the period. In 1763, there were still seven exclusive establishments of religion in the American colonies. By 1785, there were only three—and those three considerably weakened.[84] Before the imperial crisis of the 1760s, it was common to write of religious relationships in terms of dissent and toleration. By the end of the American Revolution, as exclusive establishments of religion were eliminated, and multiple establishments debated, the language of toleration and dissent lost its prominent position in public life. Of course, terms such as "sectaries" had been around too long to simply disappear. And it was probably as difficult to convince Congregational or Anglican grandparents to stop using terms such as "enthusiasts" as it is to get white grandparents to stop saying "coloreds" today. Former dissenters had their own reasons for keeping the old terminology around, if only to argue against it. That language evoked painful memories of persecution and inequality that no one could afford to defend—and it made Episcopalians squirm.

Nonetheless, by the last quarter of the eighteenth century, the ideological foundations of exclusive establishment had been undermined along with the establishments themselves. At the very least, it would now be difficult to equate toleration with religious liberty. Even the addition of adjectives such as "Full" or "Universal"—as in "Full Toleration" or "Universal Toleration"—failed to satisfy the growing legions of advocates for unqualified equality. "The very term of *toleration* is exploded," the Catholic Charles Plowden wrote in 1791, "because it imports a power in one predominant sect, to indulge that religious liberty to others, which all claim as an inherent right."[85] The Universalists of Gloucester, Massachusetts, contended that under the state's constitution, "the idea of toleration is inadmissible."[86] "The very idea of toleration," the Virginia Baptist John Leland remarked in 1790, "is despicable."[87] Finally, an anonymous booster (probably Tench Coxe) informed potential immigrants that, in the newly formed United States, "None are tolerated."[88]

For revolutionary-era Americans, the religious liberty that replaced toleration often entailed both freedom from state control *and* favorable public recognition. "*By* Religious Liberty," the young Baptist graduate Barnabas Binney declared in 1774, "*we mean a free, uncontroled [sic] liberty of thinking, worshipping and acting in all religious matters as we please,* provided *thereby, we are not prejudicial to the state.*" Whereas "the right of private judgment" (a phrase sometimes used interchangeably with "religious liberty," along with "liberty of conscience") had once been a matter of securing the individual conscience against the encroachments of a solitary, unified force of government power and Church doctrine, Binney suggested that it now entailed something else. "[I]f superior *power* cannot justify any man, or men in dictating what shall be the faith of their fellow creatures," Binney wrote, "neither can superior *learning* or *knowledge.*" In this sentiment, Binney echoed the arguments of his contemporaries. The animus toward church establishments emerged as much from the imperative to acknowledge doctrinal equality and extend mutual respect as it did from an inclination toward individual autonomy. For late eighteenth-century Americans, religious liberty often meant not having to recognize anyone else's convictions as better than their own.[89]

In places as different as Virginia and Massachusetts, the distinction between toleration and religious liberty was clearly drawn during the 1770s and 1780s. The ambiguity that had infused the bishop controversy passed—along with the royal governments that had reinforced that ambiguity. The same unequivocal distinctions were made elsewhere. By 1776 the prominent New York essayist and assemblyman William Livingston was elected the first state governor of New Jersey. Like Benjamin Franklin, this religious iconoclast and radical ecumenist had gradually risen to the highest echelons of American political life. In an essay published two years into his term, Livingston belittled England's policy of "toleration." There was, he maintained, no confusing it with true religious liberty. According to Livingston, the British government "punish[ed]" dissenters "for not embracing the religion of others." At the same time, Livingston praised his adopted state's new constitution, which "renounce[d] all discrimination between men, on account of their sentiments about the various modes of church government, or the different articles of their faith!" Distinguishing between toleration and religious liberty, between the country that treated members of small denominations as second-class citizens from the one that conferred dignity and equality upon all (at least, all those that were white and Protestant), had become one more way of distinguishing this new republic from its recent adversary.[90]

There is, perhaps, no better example of the way in which the legal and ideological edifice of religious toleration had been eroded in America than the case of the Anglican church. During the bishop controversy, a religious society that considered itself to be a pillar of British government was effectively reduced to an exclusively religious denomination, with no special civil or spiritual privileges. When Thomas Chandler wrote that the episcopate represented by his dissenting opponents was not the episcopate that he had proposed, he captured the intrinsic significance of this controversy. Putting aside the charge of misrepresentation, Reverend Chandler appears to have been making an explicit attempt to reconceive the Anglican church as just one among many. On this occasion as well as others, elite Anglicans (especially northern Anglicans) wrote themselves out of any claim to supremacy and into the country's emerging denominational system. If, as Chandler put it, they were merely attempting to secure, "the full Enjoyment of their respective Forms of Ecclesiastical Government and Discipline"—if they were only attempting to secure religious liberty, religious equality, or even just toleration—they had effectively ceded their claim to establishment status and the privilege of extending toleration. They were certainly not alone in doing so.

As we have seen, the transition from toleration to religious liberty was fraught with venomous slanders and angry retorts. Like all revolutionary eras, this one was marked by a semantic shift as old meanings failed to attach themselves to their traditional objects. What made this shift particularly volatile was the newfound importance of words themselves. In an era when American religious groups approached one another more openly and pointedly, in which equal recognition was demanded, fair representation expected, and full accommodation for the particular beliefs of each group considered, words seemed to take on an even greater significance. Charges of misrepresentation had probably been around as long as printed polemic itself. They abounded during the Great Awakening and they would appear whenever printed controversies heated up. But they may have never played as important a role in religious discourse as they did during the 1760s. As with the emphasis on fundamentals and essentials that had emerged at midcentury, or the charges of rash judgment issued before that, it was not so much the novelty of the language of misrepresentation as its widespread usage.

Again and again, disputants in the missionary, bishop, establishment, and pacifist controversies demonstrated an acute consciousness of the way that public statements could distort, sully, or even injure the believer and his church. That is what people do in times of significant change. And, to a lesser degree, that is what people do in integrated, liberal societies all the time. The opening of American life to an increasing variety of churches, the diversification of both audiences and institutions, provided the occasion for new slights to be perceived and new injuries to be recognized. Yet it also permitted religiously diverse coalitions to be built upon "fundamental" principles. During and after the revolution, when the exigencies of war and the founding of a new political system transformed heavenly dreams of spiritual harmony into the worldly fact of political union, Americans would build the largest and most diverse religious coalitions the world had ever seen. Each and every one centered on an expansive, and generally shared, definition of religious liberty.

5

"Equality or Nothing!"

Religious Pluralism in the Founding
of the Republic

Behold, how good and how pleasant it is for brethren to dwell
together in unity!

—Psalm 133:1

[L]et us agree to differ.

—Nathaniel Whitaker, *A Brief History of the*
Settlement of the Third Church in Salem,
in 1769: And also of the Usurpation and
Tyranny of An Ecclesiastical Council

In 1784, Hannah Adams published her innocently titled *Alphabetical*
compendium of the various sects which have appeared in the world from
the beginning of the Christian era to the present day. The book's 220
pages contained brief descriptions of a dizzying array of groups.
Adams began with the Abrahamites and the Artotyrites, made her
way through the Hattemists and the Keithians, and concluded with
the Servetians and the Zwinglians. Her encyclopedic account testifies
to the extent to which late eighteenth-century Americans were cognizant of religious diversity, both within their community and without, in their own time and in the distant past. Just as significantly, the
compendium was preceded by an "Advertisement" that articulated
a series of extraordinary aspirations for the tract. Among its professed aims were: "To avoid giving the least preference of one denomination above another," "To give a few of the arguments of the

principal sects, from their own authors," and finally "To take the utmost care not to misrepresent the ideas." The Advertisement's promise of an unbiased account, which reproduced the voice of each sect—to the point of allowing each to describe itself in its own words—exhibited the profound change American culture had undergone over the last several decades.[1]

The sentiments expressed in Adams's Advertisement were tempered by the cautionary tone of the preface. There, her editor, Thomas Prentiss remarked:

> It is truly astonishing that so great a variety of faith and practice
> should be derived with equal confidence of their different abet-
> tors, from one and the same revelation from heaven: but while we
> have the lively oracles, we are not to adopt any of the numerous
> schemes of religion, further than they have a manifest foundation
> in the sacred pages. To the law and to the testimony; if they speak
> not according to this word, however specious their systems may ap-
> pear, "there is no light in them."

Prentiss's comments reveal some of the tensions that characterized religious thought in the latter half of the eighteenth century. The "variety of faith and practice" to which so many people confidently committed themselves pre-sented an astonishing, even unsettling, prospect. Prentiss's familiar gesture toward the reliable compass of scripture was entirely in keeping with late eighteenth-century conceptions of how different opinions might be sorted out. There was no controversy so strident, no difference so stark, that the Bible, the final measure, could not resolve it. But whereas the good book's specific meaning once seemed certain, it now functioned as a vast, undefined referent. In the absence of a creed to prescribe particular tenets and state power to enforce it, mere adherence to fundamental scriptural principles had become an inclusive standard from which, contemporaries believed, only a very small minority could dissent. To the extent that Hannah Adams's brand of pluralism prevailed in late eighteenth-century America, it would be mitigated by her editor's assumption that all legitimate faiths shared the same essential Prot-estant, or at least Christian, elements.[2]

During the founding period that began with the Declaration of Indepen-dence in 1776 and continued through the ratification of the new Federal Con-stitution in 1788, many hoped that the country's republican principles would play the same role in politics that the Bible did in religion. Devotion to Christian scripture and the fundamentals derived from it were matched by professions of loyalty to the newly drawn up constitutions and the essential liberties (especially the religious liberties) those documents were designed to preserve. A fervent zeal to maintain individual rights, together with a forceful commitment to equality, formed the crux of an American identity more compelling than their English identity had ever been, and at least as compelling as many of their particular religious identities. Accordingly, the Pennsylvania Assembly's designs for a military association included the provision that "All National Distinctions in Dress or Name . . . be avoided, it being proper that we should now be united . . . for defending our Liberties and Properties, under the sole Denomination of *Americans*." After the Revolution, a shared dedication to republican government and equal liberty would come to represent the essential tenets of this peculiar "Denomination." They represented the fundamental principles that were, like the fundamentals of religion, somehow always already agreed upon. Never had a people made such expansive provisions for dissent, nor extended recognition so widely and so equally. But neither, perhaps, had any people recently presumed so much agreement among themselves.[3]

Fundamentals

In 1779, for the first time, a non-Congregationalist was invited to preach the annual Election Sermon before the Massachusetts General Court. Samuel Stillman, a Baptist minister, took this occasion to deliver an impassioned plea for religious equality. Stillman expressed his desire that the Commonwealth enact a bill of rights that would "contain its fundamental principles." Apparently taken with the phrase, he suggested that such "fundamental principles" were "perfectly agreeable to a fundamental principle of government," that of popular sovereignty. A few pages later, Stillman noted that "if the magistrate destroys the equality of the subjects of the state on account of religion, he violates a fundamental principle of a free government." Here were universals built upon universals. Individual rights, popular sovereignty, and legal equality all somehow managed to be "fundamental principles" in this sermon. Unsystematic as it may have been, Stillman's redundancy conveys something of the need his culture felt to establish irrefutable foundations, self-evident positions, from which there could be no dissent, some essential principle of union upon which a pluralistic society—in which there would be nothing *but* dissent—could be constructed.[4]

By the end of the Revolutionary War, there was general support for the notion that if the nation could not be exclusively Calvinist, then at least it might be Protestant, and if it could not be exclusively Protestant, then at least it might be Christian, and if it could not be exclusively Christian, then at least it might be religious. Eighteenth-century Americans made the transition from the seventeenth-century conviction that established religion preserves order to the nineteenth-century conviction that religion, in and of itself, preserves order. In the absence of private religious faith, public duties would suffer. Many subscribed to the notion that if civil authorities disregarded religion, then the average citizen would no longer have a reason to behave well, there would be "no handle by which we can take hold of him; no principle by which we can bind him." Without religion there would be no morality, no honesty, and no trust.[5]

To those of the founding era, republican government required the essential principles that animated every legitimate religious faith. Too much regard for the particulars of faith, however, would fray the bonds of union. Every good citizen required a church, every good citizen needed to believe a few essential things, but nothing would substitute for patriotism. Appropriately, New England's Baptists may have earned Stillman's invitation to deliver his election sermon because of their declaration of support for the revolutionary cause in 1775. When President George Washington wrote to Virginia's United Baptist Churches fourteen years later, he recalled having "often expressed my sentiments, that every man, conducting himself as a good citizen, and being accountable to God alone for his religious opinions, ought to be protected in worshipping the Deity according to the dictates of his own conscience." Neither the tone nor the content varied much when Washington replied to the well-wishers of other denominations. Whether he was addressing Jews, Quakers, Episcopalians, or German Reformed, he remained on message. In almost every instance, Washington explicitly tied religious faith to civil loyalty or upright moral character. The essentials of Christian faith, he repeatedly remarked, contributed to the health of republican societies. Most of his contemporaries seemed to agree.[6]

Amid the flush of patriotic fervor that accompanied the Revolution, America's public figures were persuaded that their republican governments would complement their own religious institutions. Men of all persuasions embraced what Robert Bellah identified over three decades ago as a "civil religion," encompassing a commitment to private worship and the enactment of God's will through nonsectarian public policies. There is probably no better example of this conviction than the sermon Samuel Williams published in 1780. Religion, Williams suggested, could be considered as both "a private thing" *and* a "public concern." Religion was a "private thing," in the sense that the magistrate had no right whatsoever to determine its doctrines or modes of worship. It was a "public concern," in the sense that the state had an interest in supporting preachers, who, at the very least, were the "keepers of the morals of the people." As Williams noted, "the religion of Jesus Christ will be found to be well adapted to do the most essential service to Civil Society." The Northwest Ordinance of 1787 captured the agreement on both the fundamental importance of religious liberty and the ill-defined, and absolutely irrefutable, value of "religion." After providing that no "peaceable and orderly" persons in the new territories would "ever be molested on account of his mode of worship, or religious sentiments," the Ordinance stipulated that "Religion, morality and knowledge, being necessary to good government and the happiness of mankind, schools and the means of education shall forever be encouraged." The ordinance could not have been stated more blandly, but neither, perhaps, could it have better expressed the national consensus in 1787.[7]

Dividing religion into its private and public components, between intimate matters of conscience and general considerations of morality, effectively meant drawing the familiar distinction between the nonessential and essential elements of faith. In 1788, the Connecticut theologian and future president of Yale College, Timothy Dwight, proposed an ecumenical scheme of national religious government that would have advanced shared moral principles, while leaving each group "sovereign" in its particular beliefs. In his *Address to the ministers of the gospel of every denomination in the united states*, Dwight suggested that a "convention of christians" be established to which "each sect [would] appoint a representative." Punishing sabbath breakers, limiting alcohol consumption, and stretching out the time between elections was every believer's obligation, he maintained, no matter what his theological peculiarities. "In this business," Dwight wrote, "you are neither catholick nor protestants—churchmen nor dissenters." Dwight's convention of Christians would, however, consider nothing related to the unique convictions of any group. These would instead "be considered as badges of the sovereignty of each particular sect." Nor would Dwight's assembly be empowered to interfere with any group's distinctive mode of faith. Religious diversity was an essential and ineliminable part of the human condition. Christians could not avoid dividing themselves into sects, Dwight pointed out, any more than they could avoid dividing themselves into nations or families. Like so many authors at the time, Reverend Dwight was as opposed to the idea of establishing one church as he was committed to the notion that the fundamental elements of religion (or Christianity, or Protestantism), and the morality derived from them, could be collectively maintained.[8]

Legal developments at the time suggest that such sentiments were not confined to a few high-minded clergymen. During the founding period, exclusive establishments of religion were abolished in most of the states where they had once prevailed. All the southern states disestablished the Anglican Church. In New England, change occurred more gradually. Connecticut's Congregationalists clung stubbornly to the remnants of their establishment.

Massachusetts would still provide financial support for religion, though the apologists for this arrangement continued to deny the existence of an establishment, and the new constitution made it possible for religious minorities to make use of their own tax money. Multiple establishments like the one that existed in Massachusetts were considered throughout the union during the 1780s. Across the republic, debate turned not on the question of whether a single church would be established in any particular state, but on whether the government would support a *multiple* establishment of religion—whereby tax monies would be allocated to at least several churches—or *no* establishment at all. While most states eventually rejected a multiple or "nonpreferential" funding system, the persistent appeal of multiple establishments testifies to both the widespread animus against inequitable religious establishments and the widespread commitment to state-supported religion.

To support religion in general, but not to prescribe particular tenets, was the resolution to which many of the new states first tended. Such a position permitted Americans to persist in what might be called a form of religious reductionism, so that religious meant Christian, Christian meant Protestant, and Protestant often meant Calvinist. This logic was first successfully challenged in Revolutionary Virginia. The process through which a multiple establishment was defeated there reveals how America's nascent republican institutions were adapted to religious pluralism.[9]

As we have seen, the legislative revolution in Virginia began in 1776 when the newly created Assembly passed a declaration of rights, guaranteeing to each individual "the free exercise of religion." Among the measures proposed over the ensuing years was that a prayer acceptable to "all persuasions" be read in the House of Delegates at the beginning of each session. Unsurprisingly, no such thing could be agreed to. A general assessment bill placed before the Assembly in 1779 would have ensured that nearly all monotheists were "freely tolerated." It would have established the "Christian Religion," rather than a particular denomination. It would have endowed most organized religious groups in the state with equal rights. To be "incorporated and esteemed" as a church under the provisions of this act, a group of free men would merely have had to designate a church affiliation and subscribe to four broad articles of faith, including a belief in an eternal god, a future state of rewards and punishments, the idea that the "Christian Religion is the true Religion," and the divine inspiration of both the Old and New Testaments. Groups that did not allow laymen to choose their own pastors or did not require their ministers to teach "from the Scriptures" would have been denied these privileges. Under the bill's provisions, Catholics and Quakers might have been excluded from the benefits of assessment, and Jews certainly would have been. This first general assessment was voted down in 1779. But so, interestingly, was Thomas Jefferson's bill "for Establishing Religious Freedom," which would have ruled out any establishment, even the most mild system of general assessment. On the question of church and state, Virginia remained in limbo through the middle of the following decade.[10]

Then, in 1784, another, less exclusive general assessment plan began to make its way through the Virginia House of Delegates. Shortly afterward, James Madison returned to the house floor, where he orchestrated resistance to the proposed measure. Never known for his oratory, Madison could distill important issues to their essence and best his rivals in the process. He proved particularly adept at dissecting the language that sustained inequality. As Madison took up his legislative responsibilities once again, however, he faced a daunting task. The latest assessment bill appeared to be almost as popular as its chief sponsor, Patrick Henry. The proposal, titled "Establishing a Provision for Teachers of the Christian Religion," looked bound for approval. For the most part, Henry's bill struck the right tone. Eschewing the hierarchical language associated with exclusive establishments, it drew upon the egalitarian rhetoric of the post-revolutionary period. "[I]t is judged," the bill's passive voice proclaimed, that a nonpreferential establishment might be introduced without undermining "the liberal principle heretofore adopted and intended to be preserved by abolishing all distinctions or preeminence amongst the different societies or communities of Christians." Henry's bill was framed as an educational measure benefiting "Christian Teachers," rather than an establishment bill. It insisted upon the value of Christian faith to the public good, rather than stipulating tenets of belief. In short, it resembled almost all of the other multiple establishments proposed at the time.[11]

As inclusive as Henry's assessment bill might have appeared, it would not survive the scrutiny of some who subscribed to liberal principles. Almost from the beginning, the Virginia Assembly confronted the difficulty of defining precisely what exactly this thing, "Christianity," was. Madison dwelled upon the subject in an overlooked speech he gave sometime in the fall of 1784. A series of cryptic, handwritten notes provide a glimpse of what he said and the dilemma he posed for the legislature:

3. What is Christianity? Courts of law to Judge
4. What edition, Hebrew, Septuagint, or vulgate? What copy—what translation?
5. What books canonical, what apocryphal? the papists holding to be the former what protestants the latter, the Lutherans the latter what other protestants & papists the former

6. In What light are they to be viewed, as dictated every letter by inspiration, or the essential parts only? or the matter in generally . not the words?

7. What sense the true one, for if some doctrines be essential to Christianity, those who reject these, whatever name they take are no *Christian* Society?

8. Is it Trinitarianism, arianism, Socinianism? Is it salvation by faith or works also—by free grace, or free will—&c &c &c—

9. What clue is to guide Judge thro' this labyrinth? When the question comes before them whether any particular Society is a Christian society?

10. Ends in what is orthodoxy, what heresy?

Once raised, Madison's questions proved impossible to dismiss. He understood that support for Christianity could only be justified on the condition that everyone remained content with vacuous generalities. Madison noted later in a letter to Jefferson the danger of substituting the word "christian" for the word "Religion." The peril he identified did not reside, as his ancestors may have believed, in the expression of an insidious theological principle. Instead, it became evident in inclusive, egalitarian cultures, where the public meaning of words held special import. By laying out a series of questions, rather than a list of doctrines, Madison essentially reversed the sequence of reductions that his contemporaries had been falling back upon. He helped to convince them that religion might be something more than Christianity, Christianity more than Protestantism, and Protestantism more than Calvinism. Madison designated Protestantism as a species of Christianity and Christianity as a species of religion. Ultimately, he asked his fellow Virginians to expand the meaning of each—in other words, to practice the "liberal" principles they espoused.[12]

For a fleeting moment, Virginia's assemblymen adapted an inclusive compromise proposal that would have extended the benefits of assessment to all *religious* groups. But the proponents of an establishment lost no time, in Madison's words, "reinstating discrimination"—that is, in once again making the general assessment bill a Christian bill. In the end, a flood of hostile petitions, as well as Madison's widely popular "Memorial and Remonstrance" shifted the tide decisively against general assessment. "Who," Madison asked, "does not see that the same authority which can establish Christianity in exclusion of all other religions may establish with the same ease any particular sect of Christians in exclusion of all other sects?" Apparently very few now. By the fall of 1785, Madison's fellow assemblymen had been persuaded that the state should not legislate religious belief, even for the seemingly benign purpose of supporting the pious in their worship. Having been buried at the end of the previous year's session, Henry's bill for the support of Christian teachers would never again, in Thomas E. Buckley's wry phrase, be "resurrected."[13]

Virginia's decision becomes all the more notable in light of how Massachusetts handled the same types of questions. There, the Congregationalist elite had yet to learn Madison's lesson when their constitution was drafted in 1779. Eventually they paid the price. There were warning signs along the way. After copies of the proposed constitution were circulated throughout the Commonwealth, several towns complained that Article Three, which contained the provisions of the multiple establishment, was simply too "ambiguous." A delegation from Raynham, Massachusetts, recommended that the language be made "more Explicit so that it may be Easily under stoot [sic] by all men." Another (from Isaac Backus's hometown) complained that "it means any thing, or Every thing: or Really intends Nothing." The law was not made more explicit and reasonable men quickly disagreed over its meaning. Particularly troubling divisions occurred when the opposing sides in this dispute began talking about the meaning of "piety" and "religion." As with the Episcopal controversy, seemingly innocuous words revealed deep divisions. The New Light Congregationalist, "Philanthropos," asserted, like James Madison, that the definition of words mattered, especially when they were employed to buttress a rigid system of tax support. He posed the matter in surprisingly cosmopolitan terms. What if, he asked, his opponent were in Turkey and overheard a discussion of religion? Could he not safely assume that they were talking about Islam? If he overheard Jews discussing religion, could he not safely assume that they were talking about Judaism? And (inverting the logic) if the delegates at the Massachusetts constitutional convention spoke and wrote "about *protestant teachers of religion*, may we not be sure that they mean thereby *christianity*?"[14]

Philanthropos understood, like Madison, that the meaning of terms such as "religion" and "piety" depended upon their context. They were understood differently by people who lived in different places and even by those who lived in the same place. Their ambiguity made it possible for everyone to praise them. But as Philanthropos had already discerned, any state that applied such terms always did so with a particular meaning in mind. That was the source of oppression. Given the provisions of the state's constitution, the right to define piety entailed the right to require a certain form of it. And a Congregationalist-dominated state, Philanthropos suggested, was no more justified in imposing its particular brand of faith than was an Islamic state. The advocates of church establishment in Massachusetts came around to Madison's view only in the third decade of the next century—after many of their churches had been seized by Unitarians and their privileged status in the Commonwealth relinquished. Virginia's churches were saved this misfortune because of Madison's realization that religion could be neither adequately nor fairly defined in a religiously diverse society.[15]

The experiences in Massachusetts and Virginia were similar in the breadth and intensity of the controversy that occurred in each state. But on the question of establishment, the Old Dominion better epitomized the changed national culture. George Washington was himself exemplary of the transformation taking place. Commenting on Madison's Memorial and Remonstrance, Washington told George Mason that he had not originally been "alarmed at the thoughts of making people pay towards the support of that which they profess" if they were Christians, and relief was provided to professing non-Christians, such as Jews and Muslims. But after having observed the commotion that Henry's general assessment bill raised, he now opposed the measure. Always in step with his time, Washington's newfound opposition to an establishment existed next to a firm conviction that the nation's civic health was intimately bound up with its religious vitality.[16]

Long regarded as a bastion of intolerance, Washington's Virginia suddenly found itself a model for liberal-minded folks everywhere. Instead of a general assessment bill, the Virginia Assembly passed a revised version of Thomas Jefferson's proposal "for Establishing Religious Freedom" in 1786. Like some other prominent Virginians, including James Madison and George Washington, Jefferson had never proved more than a nominal Anglican. Like some of his fellow founding fathers, including John Adams and Benjamin Franklin, he subscribed to beliefs that brought him perilously close to deism. Jefferson laid out his views on the relationship between government and religion in his *Notes on the State of Virginia* (1781–1782). There, the slaveholding sage described, with no apparent sense of irony, Virginia's system of "religious slavery." Turning the traditional rhetoric of disease and dissent on its head, Jefferson suggested that while civil restrictions on religious beliefs might confirm a man "in his errors," they could "not cure them." The idea "seems not sufficiently eradicated," he wrote, "that the operations of the mind, as well as the acts of the body, are subject to the coercion of the laws." It was no better, Jefferson continued, for our rulers to prescribe beliefs for our minds than it was for them "to prescribe . . . medicine and diet" for our bodies.[17]

Though it proclaimed God to be "Lord both of body and mind," Jefferson's Act for Establishing Religious Freedom focused most of its attention on the mind. The statute condemned the practice of conferring religious decisions upon civil authorities. No one but the believer was entitled to judge his religious beliefs or practices. Each man's religious *opinions*, the preamble asserted, were his own to maintain privately or promote publicly. Jefferson's argument recommended itself most strongly to theological rationalists and pious evangelicals. Yet there was also something here for the moderate Anglican and the devout Presbyterian who worried about the proliferation of religious differences, worried that Protestantism and Christianity might not be the same thing, worried—as Jefferson put it in the *Notes*—that there might indeed be a "thousand different systems of religion" and theirs "but one of that thousand." These more conventional believers may have instead been convinced by Jefferson's insistence on the vigor of truth and the virtue of open debate. Where men were free to speak their minds and persuade their neighbors, Jefferson assured them, truth would always triumph over error. Those certain of their beliefs had nothing to fear. In place of the comforting conviction that their own religion was the only true form, Jefferson offered the consolation that it would undoubtedly be proved so. In place of the essential religious beliefs that were supposed to support republican governments, Jefferson offered another foundation: "the natural rights of mankind."[18]

A year after the Virginia Assembly endorsed Jefferson's bill for establishing religious freedom, these liberal principles made their way into the U.S. Constitution. Late in the Philadelphia convention, Charles Pinckney of South Carolina moved to have the following words inserted: "no religious Test shall ever be required as a Qualification to any Office or public Trust under the United States." In an age when European governments and the American states (with the new, notable exceptions of Rhode Island and Virginia) still prescribed religious qualifications for government officers, what became Article Six, Section Three of the Constitution remained an uncontroversial proposal in Philadelphia. If there were opponents they mostly kept their objections to themselves. Connecticut's Roger Sherman objected, but only on the grounds that the prohibition on religious tests was entirely gratuitous given the nation's "prevailing liberality." Affirming that the measure had received support from "a great majority of the convention, and without much debate," Luther Martin of Maryland noted that there had been some "*so unfashionable* as to think . . . that in a Christian country, it would be *at least decent* to hold out some distinction between the professors of Christianity and downright infidelity or paganism." Luther's opinion was, in our terms, politically incorrect. Among those who attended that great meeting in Independence Hall, it was indeed passé to employ the power of the state on behalf of even the broadest conceptions of religion.[19]

A Faith in Faith

Unfashionable as he may have been within the Philadelphia Convention, Luther Martin voiced a widespread concern among the larger public. In fact,
many contemporary commentators took the rejection of Virginia's multiple
establishment law and federal prohibition of religions tests as evidence that
this fragile young nation was decaying into infidelity. From Philadelphia, John
Swanwick observed Virginia's move toward disestablishment with dismay.
Swanwick thought Virginia's Statute for Establishing Religious Freedom
worth his notice, as well as the notice of the *"Clergy of all Christian denominations in the City of Philadelphia, and to the Public Friends of the respectable
Society called Quakers."* For the contagion of irreligion appeared likely to
spread. "[C]onsidering the tolerating spirit prevailing all over America," the
bill seemed entirely gratuitous. Its enactment could undermine the religious
foundations of the republic, substituting the amorality of unbelief for the
verities of the Bible. Under its unaccountably generous provisions, anyone,
even an atheist or Muslim, could serve in the legislature, however hostile or
indifferent he might be to the fate of republican government. Indeed, Virginia's commitment to disestablishment of any particular religion, Swanwick
argued, constituted a commitment to subverting all religion, indeed all of
American society. "[W]hat is the religion which Virginia calls 'our religion'?"
he wondered. "Is it that no man is compelled to frequent or support any
religious worship, place or minister whatsoever?" For Swanwick, the stakes
were enormous: liberty was founded upon true faith, and true faith could not
subsist in the absence of the state's commitment to support at least one particular variety of it.[20]

Opposition to Article Six of the Constitution revealed a similar set of
worries. Critics expressed their fear that Catholics, Jews, pagans, deists, even
Muslims, could now wield power in this traditionally Protestant land. Would
Americans allow the pope to be president? Would they permit Jews to command their armies? Would they be satisfied with the loyalty of atheists? Even
Isaac Backus, that strident proponent of equal privileges for Baptists, was
opposed to the mere possibility of Catholics holding public office. Most
contemporary constitutions ensured that none of these awful possibilities
would be realized. At the time, almost all of the states restricted such positions
to trinitarian Christians, some just to Protestants. Maryland required officeholders "to declare their loyalty to the state *and* their belief in the Christian
religion." Pennsylvania required its legislators to swear to a belief in one God
("rewarder to the good and punisher of the wicked") and the divine inspiration

of both the Old and New Testaments. In the wake of Article Six's passage, however, a significant easing of those restrictions began.[21]

The concern about irreligion may have also been due to the fact that the atheist, who appeared to many in the guise of the deist, no longer seemed to represent the remote possibility that he once had. According to William Tennent of South Carolina, "Infidelity" had "infected not only our recluse Philosophers, but every Rank and Profession." Of course, with the exception of a handful of brave souls, no one publicly professed to embrace deism. This did not prevent the suspicious from seeing them everywhere. Deists began with the perfectly acceptable premise that the universe had a divine creator, that it operated according to general and predictable laws, and that moral principles were either embedded within us or easily discoverable from nature. The trouble (as contemporaries saw it) was that they seldom ventured beyond this point. Their minimalist theology left little room for revelation or miraculous interventions and treated churches and creeds as accidental inventions. It reduced the fundamentals of faith to a degree that left most aghast. Within the intellectual framework of the time, to attack a particular form of revealed religion was uncharitable, perhaps even unpatriotic. But to implicitly denigrate the whole of revealed religion, as the deists did, was to threaten the very underpinnings of society—it was a public offense that placed the whole republican endeavor in jeopardy. For contemporaries, deism was less an erroneous theological system than the negation of them all. Deism, according to one Presbyterian minister, could "be described only by negatives." While Catholics at least formed a society of believers, sharing articles of faith, the deists were distinguished only by what they did not do and did not believe. Deists could not ever constitute a legitimate religious society because they "cannot agree in fundamentals."[22]

If deism seemed dangerous to late eighteenth-century souls, so was the indiscriminate doctrine of universal salvation. The Universalists took eighteenth-century ecumenism to its logical extreme. Their schemes granted salvation to every believer, no matter which church they belonged to, or which doctrines they embraced—though they generally held that the wicked would have to spend time in hell before they too ascended to heaven. The animus toward this doctrine was so severe that the leading Boston Congregationalist Charles Chauncy felt compelled to keep his Universalist musings to himself until after the Revolutionary War. For many years, those who knew about Chauncy's convictions secretly referred to his potentially scandalous universalist writing as "the pudding." The treatment of theological eccentrics greatly improved by the last quarter of the eighteenth century, but the Reverend John Murray might be forgiven for having failed to notice. When he announced his

commitment to Universalism in the coastal Massachusetts town of Gloucester, his fellow townspeople reacted angrily. Murray "was arrested for vagrancy, cursed and stoned by angry crowds, and threatened with deportation."
He also suffered accusations of both Loyalism and Catholicism. Nor was he
alone. A South Carolina Baptist complained of being harangued in the streets
for espousing the doctrine of the Universal Restoration. As most viewed the
matter, granting salvation to everyone would, like the denial of God itself,
destroy the entire system of rewards and punishments upon which civil society rested. No omniscient deity or pious mob could look favorably upon such
a development.[23]

To contemporaries, Universalism and deism appeared as symptoms of an
equally troubling, if less conspicuous, disease afflicting the country: religious
indifference. To those who had witnessed the coercion exercised by Europe's
established churches, however, such indifference seemed a blessing. Detailing
how these provincials were being transformed into the curious people that
they were, the famous French immigrant J. Hector Saint John Crèvecoeur
noted that American religion was becoming as "mixed," as wonderfully diluted, as Euro-American blood was becoming. In fact, intermarriage and the
subsequent production of an amalgamated race of people, he suggested, represented the quickest means to the dissolution of the country's religious
differences. "A very perceptible indifference, even in the first generation,"
Crèvecoeur wrote, "will become apparent; and it may happen that the daughter
of the Catholic will marry the son of the seceder, and settle by themselves at a
distance from their parents." What religious conflicts the mixing of bloods did
not dispel, the vast American landscape surely would. In America, Crèvecoeur
suggested, religious conflict "evaporates in the great distance it has to travel . . .
it burns away in the open air, and consumes without effect." The residue of this
benign mixture of various faiths and open space would be a harmless "indifference" regarding the religious differences that seemed to matter so terribly in
Europe.[24]

There was enough sentiment, contemporaries sometimes called it "liberality," to lend credence to Crèvecoeur's claims. By the last decades of the
eighteenth century, elite Americans adopted the fashionable preference for
cosmopolitan open-mindedness, with its complementary hostility toward
narrow-minded bigotry. The capacity to consider an issue from multiple
perspectives was the ideal to which those who considered themselves liberal
aspired. Not coincidentally, these were the same principles that the Freemasons, whose popularity and influence continued to grow during the late
eighteenth century, constantly reiterated. On this liberal view, the bigot slav-
ishly clung to his particular interpretation of scripture and his peculiar

practices without considering the validity of the alternatives. The comments of contemporary Europeans suggest the extent to which such liberality had penetrated American culture. A French transplant to the New World, Jacob Duché said in regard to Philadelphia that "there is less religious bigotry here, than in any place I have yet visited." Other European observers, less sanguine about the prospect of such indifference, were no less convinced of its existence.[25]

The renowned Congregationalist, Ezra Stiles, saw the same promiscuous sentiment lurking in the growing hostility toward the compulsory support of religion. Everywhere, Stiles lamented, people were tearing down even their most "liberal and generous establishments." Civil magistrates were discouraged from having anything to do with religion, other than to keep the peace between "contending sects." As a consequence, he wrote, "it begins to be a growing idea that it is mighty indifferent...whether a man be of this or the other religious sect...and that truly deists, and men of indifferentism to all religion are the most suitable persons for civil office." In fact, Stiles huffed, the conviction was taking hold that to ensure impartial government and prevent religious resentment, government should be turned over to "those who...have no religion at all." With disestablishment looming, Stiles feared for America the very thing that Crèvecoeur thought would make it great. He feared that the admirable ecumenism of its institutions would encourage a soulless neutrality among its citizens. The concern was less that people would adhere to unorthodox religious beliefs, as had been the case in the past, but that—as Stiles feared—they would adhere to no religious beliefs.[26]

Thus, by several accounts, late eighteenth-century America certainly witnessed an upsurge of indifference. But indifference toward the particular forms that religion took should not be confused with indifference toward religion generally. The historian Nathan Hatch has noted that a defining characteristic of early republican religion was the way Americans repeatedly moved from one church to another. A contemporary noted that the phenomenon of ever-changing religious affiliations was "the versatile season with *America.*" A "change of religious profession has become almost as common, and as little noted," he continued, "as the variation of the weather in this most changeable climate." Even when they did not change affiliations, laypeople could be found visiting several different churches and listening to a variety of preachers, especially during the revivals that periodically swept through early America. The diary kept by Mary Cooper of Oyster Bay, New York, from 1768 to 1773 records numerous outings to Anglican, Baptist, Quaker, and New Light churches. Sometimes Cooper attended two different churches in the same day. Yet her journal hardly smacks of indifference to religion, or even to

the distinction between churches. Cooper's ownership of a pamphlet challenging the traditional practice of infant baptism suggests that she was at-
tuned to doctrinal issues, as well as the immediate condition of her soul.
Lengthy discussion of religious matters kept her up late at night and sometimes occupied entire days. The entry for July 7, 1772, indicates that Cooper's
sister and a friend had stopped by and that the three were engaged in "[m]uch
talk about churches." For ordinary Americans such as Mary Cooper, the
practice of attending many different places of worship may have represented
the sincerest form of piety.[27]

On the nation's frontier, the perception of indifference may have actually
resulted from the *absence* of choice. Someone who visited the "backcountry"
was as likely to find a paucity of permanent church communities as he was
likely to encounter a large number of semiattached believers. The English-
born Anglican Charles Woodmason bemoaned the fact that the families he
encountered in the South Carolina Piedmont were beset "by Itinerant
Teachers, Preachers, and Imposters from New England and Pennsylvania—
Baptists, New Lights, Presbyterians, Independants, [sic] and an hundred other
Sects—So that one day You might hear this System of Doctrine—the next day
another—next day another, retrograde to both.... And among the Various
Plans of Religion, they are at a Loss which to adapt, and consequently are
without any Religion at all." In the sparsely populated western regions of
Pennsylvania, New York, Virginia, or the Carolinas, where church buildings
were in short supply, individuals often listened to any preacher who traipsed
through town. The general shortage of ministers throughout the nation's
frontier regions meant that those who wished to worship often had no choice
of church or pastor. In other words, what European critics saw as indifference
may have represented a general need, as well as a general willingness, to try
out the country's many religious alternatives.[28]

To some critics, it was impossible to distinguish between wholesale indifference to religion and the polite ecumenism that prevailed among elites.
These scrupulous souls were offended by the rise of theological liberalism and
the indiscriminate pluralism that seemed to follow from it. The most eloquent
spokesman for doctrinal rigor was Timothy Dwight. A native of Northampton,
Connecticut, Dwight spent much of his early life trying to match the achievements of his maternal grandfather, Jonathan Edwards. Despite severe physical
limitations, Dwight developed into an influential theologian, an accomplished
poet, a leading Federalist, and the president of Yale College. As an adminis-
trator and a teacher, Dwight would propel the university into national prominence and inspire some of the nineteenth century's most influential religious
figures. Temporal success never dimmed Dwight's devotion to Edwardsian

theology and, throughout his career, he ranked among the most inveterate opponents of deists, Universalists, and so-called infidels. His poem, "The Triumph of Infidelity," represented a learned critique of both religious skepticism and the Universalism that Charles Chauncy (Jonathan Edwards's former rival) had recently endorsed. There was, for Dwight, no separating the stiff mortar of Reformed Calvinism from the moral edifice of republican government. Dilute the former and the latter would surely crumble. As we have seen, Dwight was capable of considerable ecumenism when it came to relations between the nation's Protestant churches. Yet he drew a sharp line between the cooperation that a common Christianity might make possible and the polite liberalism that invested too much faith in human judgment. In an anonymous newspaper essay, a playful Dwight mocked his age's excessive concern for religious politeness. Recalling the admonitions of the British mannerist, Lord Chesterfield, Dwight offered the following tongue-in-cheek advice: "We ought never, wound an innocent man's feelings in company, especially with regard to his religious sentiments." Someone who really cared about their manners, who was sincerely concerned about other's feelings, would not dare speak of faith! Dwight's satire suggested that the nation needed *more*, not less theological quarreling. In his view, too many Americans were sacrificing their well-founded theological systems for empty expressions of piety and neighborly expressions of respect. The mass of humanity didn't deserve such a high degree of religious deference. They were simply not that good.[29]

Although it is difficult to gauge, the theological scrupulosity of someone like Timothy Dwight appears to have placed him in the minority, both in the general population at the time and among his fellow clergymen. Even at this early date, Americans manifested what one mid-twentieth-century commentator called a "faith in faith." Protestant, Christian, or even trinitarian belief had come to be regarded as sufficient in itself. The prominent Baptist minister John Leland made just that point. Leland, who is perhaps best known for offering the gift of a giant cheese to President Thomas Jefferson on New Year's Day, 1802, wrote that it was better "*to learn* how *to believe, than to learn* what *to believe.*" Hannah Adams, the religious encyclopedist, would probably have agreed. At the conclusion of the Revolutionary War, she resumed research on her history of the world's religions by slogging through works of theological controversy. Adams later remembered that wading through these dense tomes had induced "the most painful nervous complaints," by burdening her mind with contradiction and unsettling her most cherished opinions. She added that females were educated through light fictional works, rather than the hefty treatises that imparted firmness to an individual's judgments. Though surely too modest about her own capacity for careful reading, Adams's recollections hint at the culture's growing intolerance for the intricacies of theological disputation. By contrast, the diligent effort she made to represent the views of each religious faith (however different from her own) in her alphabetical compendium suggests a growing respect for the many forms that piety took. Religious adherence continued its rise in the years leading up to Timothy Dwight's death in 1817, as theological quibbling fell into further disfavor and the evangelical denominations began to displace the old-line churches. Where faith itself was so important, those who insisted upon doctrinal rigor were likely to be dismissed as cranks, or worse yet, bigots.[30]

This widespread faith in faith infused late eighteenth-century religious life and probably accounts for much of the indifference that contemporary critics identified. So does the Revolutionary War, which disrupted the nation's churches by shattering some congregations, pulling ministers away for extended military service, and keeping many believers at home on Sunday. In their own peculiar way, Americans of the founding era professed their commitment to sustaining faith, continually reminded themselves of its importance to the success of their experiment in republican government, and yet also disavowed religious exclusion. To get a sense of how strained this reasoning could become, one need only consider Tennessee's constitution of 1796. There, as the historian Edwin Gaustad points out, the founding charter included a provision forbidding religious tests for state offices, yet "in the very same document at the very same time (and almost in the very same breath) . . . stated 'that no person who denies the being of God, or a future state of rewards and punishments, shall hold any office in the civil department of this State.'" For the moment, this ramshackle logic would suffice. It served—like the nation's passing commitment to multiple establishments—to reconcile a deeply ingrained habit of associating faith with communal prosperity and an ever-growing awareness of the religious differences around them. If this solution smacked of religious indifference to some, it appeared to many others as the only way of squaring the faith they had long experienced, the equality they now embraced, and the diversity they could not escape.[31]

Equal Recognition

Something had indeed changed in America. In the generally expressed preference for piety over theology, in the generally expressed disdain for restrictive creeds, in the easy mixing of America's sects in voluntary societies and constitutional conventions, Crèvecoeur's claim that America was growing in-different to the particular forms that its religion took rang true. While few could blithely countenance a nation of semicommitted believers, increasingly, to be an American was to be indifferent about the specifics of your neighbor's faith. The obligations upon the national government and public discourse were somewhat greater. As we have seen in the case of the Episcopal and Pacifist debates of the 1760s, an ideology was emerging that equated religious liberty with the full expression of each group's religious identity. The Associate Re-formed Synod of Philadelphia may have put the matter best. When a gov-ernment like that of the United States had been "established by a combination of different denominations of Christians, who are so intermixed . . . that sep-arate governments, would be impracticable," it asserted, the government is obligated to safeguard each group's "peculiarities." The language was some-what convoluted yet the message clear. An integrated, heterogeneous group of denominations had combined to form one government, which could only fulfill its mandate by protecting the elements of faith and worship that dis-tinguished each denomination from all the others. Here was a strikingly pluralistic take on religious differences in the United States. Even more striking is how unexceptional these sentiments were.[32]

On the whole, the Revolutionary War reinforced the connection between public civility and religious liberty that had emerged in recent years. Changes underway for a long time accelerated during the prolonged conflict with Great Britain. To begin, the war hastened the religious integration of American society. Reflecting upon the makeup of the Continental Army, John Adams wrote that it included Catholics, Episcopalians, Presbyterians, Methodists, Moravians, Baptists, Lutherans, Calvinists, Universalists, Congregationalists, and nearly every other conceivable religious group (as well as unbelievers). The perceived need for interdenominational harmony during the conflict and political unanimity afterward placed an even higher premium on the re-spectful treatment of other citizens' beliefs. When the Reverend John Car-michael told a Pennsylvania militia company to "[l]et every denomination of Christians treat each other with love and respect, as brethren engaged in, and struggling for the one and same common cause," he articulated both a mil-itary necessity and an emerging cultural principle. Those who ignored this injunction could find themselves in hot water. At the beginning of the revo-lutionary conflict, a Pennsylvanian by the name of Thomas Smith was sum-moned before a patriotic committee where he was compelled to express contrition "for having uttered expressions, derogatory to the Continental Congress, invidious to a particular denomination of Christians, and tending to impede the opposition of my countrymen to ministerial oppression."

Whatever words Smith had used, the charges against him suggest a powerful connection between charitable religious speech and patriotism. Truly something extraordinary had occurred when religious bigotry, rather than religious dissent, could be associated with political subversion.[33]

In 1787, that scourge of colonial bishops and opponent of indifferentism, the venerable New England Congregationalist Ezra Stiles, articulated a similarly ecumenical notion. European observers had studied America, Stiles noted, in hopes of imitating the "friendly cohabitation of all sects" that it maintained. To the astonishment of the world, this country had demonstrated "that men may be good members of civil society, and yet differ in religion." More interesting, however, was Stiles's commitment to permitting every church to "complete" itself according to its own particular specifications. "The united states will embosom all the religious sects or denominations in Christendom," Stiles predicted. "Here they may all enjoy their whole respective systems of worship and church government, complete." That included the former Church of England, which would occupy a "distinguished and principal" position in the new nation *and*, Stiles noted with no apparent anguish, would soon "furnish themselves with a bishop" or two. Stiles then offered a detailed and quite deferential description of particular ecclesiastical structures here. That is notable. And so is the fact that the man who had once led the opposition to a colonial episcopate now insisted that even the Episcopal church in America was entitled to maintain its full complement of bishops. According to Stiles, all the churches possessed the right to enjoy their own particular institutions in all their peculiar variety. We are now a long way from the mere right of private judgment espoused by the generation that came before Stiles.[34]

The defensive tone of Samuel Macclintock's provocatively titled *The Artifices of Deceivers Detected and Christians Warned Against Them* (1770) testifies to the pervasiveness of this sentiment that now connected religious liberty to equal recognition. Macclintock railed at the restrictions placed upon those who only wished to protect their readers and listeners from heretical doctrines. Other people's religious "principles," he insisted, may be "censure[d] and condemn[ed]" "without infringing their liberty, condemning their state, or setting up his own opinions as a standard of orthodoxy for others." Macclintock's angry denial indicates the widespread currency of the conviction that an individual's or group's liberty was in fact infringed when their principles were censured or condemned. Such admonitions against excessive liberality were clearly not heeded. Americans continued to grow more charitable in the religious language they used and more sensitive in the slights they perceived. Take the Benevolent Congregational Society. When this group appealed for incorporated status in Rhode Island, they demonstrated an extraordinary diffidence toward those who believed differently. In case anyone suspected that their attempt to create a legally recognized religious society was meant to cause offense, the Benevolent Congregationalists assured the public that they were by no means designing "to give one denomination of Christians a superiority over another." Likewise, in his 1794 memoir, the Virginia clergyman, Devereux Jarratt, took care to note that he did not regard Anglicanism as "better than Presbyterian[ism]," which he had converted from, "but equally as good." (Jarratt also estimated that he had possessed "a truly catholic spirit" since at least the early 1760s.)[35]

The same deferential imperative extended to individuals as well as groups. The Reverend Dan Foster articulated this form of religious egalitarianism when he wrote that to be excommunicated by a church society in 1780 was to be "treat[ed] ... injuriously," to be denied "the right of private judgment." "Withdrawing communion, in America," Foster argued, "signifies the same thing with dragooning, beheading, or burning in popish countries; is practiced upon the same principles, and to be justified by the same reasons." Similar sentiments were expressed by the Reverend John Tucker. "[I]f such exclusion sets a brand upon them as men of bad principles," Tucker wrote, "if it hurts their reputation in the world and subjects them to other inconveniences and hardships;—and deprives them of privileges," then this unofficial action was no different than the legal penalties once prescribed by states for nonconformity. Cognizant of the distance that separated their "persecution" from that experienced by people in times and places, Foster and Tucker defined what it meant to experience injury in late eighteenth-century America. To be excluded, to be de-recognized, to lose reputation, to be associated with violence, subversion, or intolerance, to be misrepresented; these were injuries to religious minorities and individual believers, these were violations of religious liberty, that would only be acknowledged in a pluralistic culture.[36]

The subjective character of contemporary claims for religious equality is perhaps best revealed in the repeated insistence that groups had the right, indeed the obligation, to call themselves by their own names. The astonishing variety of religious groups in the new nation was matched only by the variety of names those same groups gave themselves. Prior to the Revolution, few believers were willing to allow others to define their own group's identity. Afterward, such an act would have presented an affront to American religious liberty. To cede the prerogative of fully defining one's faith was to cede the equal recognition that the eighteenth century gradually afforded to nearly every Christian believer, the claim on which Americans of all persuasions now prided themselves. Perhaps no one made a stronger connection between religious freedom, equal recognition, and self-definition than the spokesmen for a group of Gloucester Universalists. In their 1785 *Appeal to the Impartial Publick*, these Christian Independents—as they called themselves—insisted that the meaning of Article Three in the Commonwealth of Massachusetts' new constitution, which permitted the members of each denomination to apply their tax money toward the support of their own churches, depended upon the elusive "meaning of the word Sect." There, the term unjustly "include[d] and describe[d] those persons who dissent from legal establishments which are instituted for religious purposes." The Christian Independents recommended that the term "sect" remain ambiguous, and that it be left open to future descriptions. It was bigoted to suppose that it could be "confined in its meaning to the Sects only which existed at that time." Fixing the meaning of the term would stifle religious liberty. On this and countless other occasions, late eighteenth-century Americans insisted that their various religious appellations did not matter, that they were all equally worthy—or, alternatively, that each group had an inalienable right to determine its own. In either case, self-definition had become both a right and a virtue. Individual believers and churches alike now expected to describe themselves on their own terms. In public as in private, they would be called by their own names.[37]

The same sensitivity to the wide range of faiths and the same unwillingness to declare for any one of them revealed itself in the post-revolutionary restructuring of provincial colleges. Following the Revolution, King's College acquired a new, more republican-sounding name: Columbia College. New Yorkers demonstrated a new awareness of religious diversity too as they reconstructed Columbia. Unlike its predecessor, the college was given a distinctly nonsectarian mandate. In addition to forbidding preferential treatment for any particular sect and religious tests for professors, the New York legislature permitted "any religious body or society of men" to establish a "professorship . . . for the promotion of their particular religious tenets, or for any other purpose" consistent "with religion, morality and the laws of this State." Similarly, a 1779 act of the Pennsylvania Assembly mandated "that the leading clergymen of the principal denominations" should serve on its college's board. Long a bastion of Anglican orthodoxy, William and Mary came around as well. In a letter to Ezra Stiles (now president of Yale College), the president of the College, James Madison (a distant relative of the more famous James Madison), explained why the professorship of divinity had been eliminated. The position was "formerly instituted for the Purpose of the Church of England," he wrote, "but it is now thought that Establishments in Favr [sic] of any particular Sect are incompatible with the Freedom of a Republic." Madison then remarked that the college was "open to all." Major colleges, like the state governments that directed them, were now even more inclined to trumpet their inclusiveness and spread religious recognition widely.[38]

The debate over a religious establishment in Maryland offered an especially revealing example of how religious discourse had changed during the eighteenth century. For two and a half months during the late winter and early spring of 1785, a newspaper debate raged in the pages of the *Maryland Journal and Baltimore Advertiser*.[39] Every contributor, it seemed, made an appeal to Christians of all denominations. Writers took pains to bestow kind words upon the once benighted Methodists, Baptists, and Catholics. Defenders of the plan took pains to emphasize the "religious equality" embodied in the legislation. They appealed for a full understanding of marginal Christian doctrines and minimized the differences between all Christians. Some cognizance was even taken of Jews, Muslims, and "Infidels." Authors in the Maryland debate repeatedly demonstrated their awareness of religious diversity within the state. Essays written by both supporters and opponents of the multiple establishment bill posited the inviolability of private judgment and the importance of interdenominational cooperation. They assumed that their audience consisted of men from many different churches and that the society they inhabited was integrated. Defending their proposal for a new state college amid the larger debate over establishment, the Maryland Assembly proudly noted that plans for the school had been "drawn up by three clergymen of known abilities and different religious persuasions"—a prominent Catholic, a prominent Episcopalian, and a prominent Presbyterian.[40]

The polite tone of the Maryland debate did not mean, of course, that no aspersions were cast upon Presbyterians, Methodists, Episcopalians, or Catholics. In fact, several disparaging allegations appeared in the contemporary papers. Yet these charges were subdued by historical standards and usually involved an accusation of intolerance, rather than an indictment of a particular creed. Moreover, they were always countered by another writer. "A Marylander" offered some of the most ecumenical gestures in this generally ecumenical debate. Of the state's "Papists," he wrote with a conviction that required capital letters: "AMERICA CONTAINS NOT BETTER MEN." The state's Baptists and Presbyterians, he added, had shown themselves equally patriotic during the Revolutionary War and scrupulous practitioners of both "piety and morality." On one occasion, "Marylander" took "A Protestant" to task for casting sly aspersions upon Catholics. For his part, "Protestant" had maintained that "[t]here is abundant room in the *American* States for ministers of every denomination; they have all equal rights to preach and pray; and to do all the good in their power."[41]

The heightened sensitivity displayed in controversies such as this one irritated earnest thinkers like Timothy Dwight. And indeed, serious theological controversy may have been sacrificed when individuals expressed as much concern about the injury inflicted upon religious groups as they did about the distinction between grace and works. Yet many more late eighteenth-century authors—and many more late eighteenth-century ministers—made broad ecumenical gestures and condemned uncharitable judgments than complained about the absence of doctrinal rigor. New standards of public discussion gave almost everyone an incentive to deal respectfully with those of other faiths. The question is: How wide did the circle of equal recognition extend?[42]

The Expanding Limits of Equal Recognition: Catholics and Other Outsiders

Next to the absence of religious faith, Catholicism represented one of the few popular forms of belief that late eighteenth-century Protestants could still treat with open disdain. Hatred of Catholics ran wide and deep through the landscape of American culture. Protestants bemoaned its devotion to tradition, symbols, and alleged superstitions. Most frightening, however, was the Church's affiliation with foreign powers. Contemporaries worried about the attachments that Roman Catholicism purportedly forged between its adherents and Vatican-controlled European monarchs. In the minds of many Americans, Catholicism threatened the independence of the nation as a whole, and the independence of every citizen individually. Laypersons and clergy alike associated all forms of religious and civil tyranny with Catholicism. The British Parliament's passage of the Quebec Act in 1774, which limited representative government and accorded special privileges to Roman Catholics in Canada, confirmed the suspicion that there was an Anglo-Catholic conspiracy to displace both Protestantism and republicanism in the New World. A torrent of anti-Catholic invective flowed from the presses. And, during the early years of the Revolution, many a patriot went off to fight with the intention of combating both "King" *and* "Popery."[43]

Late eighteenth-century New Englanders were especially well schooled in the subtleties of anti-Catholicism. This peculiarly Calvinist form of education generally began in childhood, but training was also available in college. Every four years, in fact, Harvard undergraduates gathered in the school's chapel to learn just how erroneous and just how dangerous Roman Catholicism was. A Massachusetts judge named Paul Dudley had endowed a four-part lecture series for the college at which student attendance was mandatory. Depending on the year, prominent local ministers explained either the virtues of natural religion, divine revelation, congregational ordination, or the errors of Popery. Speakers were asked to employ the latter occasion "for the detecting, and convicting, and exposing the idolatry of the Romish church; their tyranny, usurpations, damnable heresies, fatal errors, abominable superstitions, and other crying wickednesses in their high places; and finally to prove that the church of Rome is that mystical Babylon, that man of sin, that apostate church, spoken of in the New-Testament." As he began his own Dudleian lecture in 1793, John Lathrop recalled that much important ground had already been covered. His predecessors had documented the Roman Catholic Church's idolatry, falsehood, sinful tendencies, and "persecuting spirit." Lathrop decided to place his own emphasis on the its usurpation of Christ's authority.[44]

The continued existence of the Dudleian lecture series illustrates the extent to which anti-Catholicism remained an acceptable prejudice well into the founding period. Nonetheless, Roman Catholicism clearly benefited from late eighteenth-century inclination to discount religious particulars in relation to essentials. It also benefited from the growing imperatives of religious civility. Reverend Lathrop's sermon highlighted the shift. In his address to this impressionable group of young men, the minister was careful to distinguish between the historical sins of the Catholic Church and its present state and membership. In fact, he referred to Roman Catholics as "Our Catholic brethren" and noted that "we highly esteem [them] for their learning and piety." And he hoped that they would not be "offended" by his critique. Lathrop's qualifications testified to the gradual change that had been occurring over the last thirty years.[45]

The Revolutionary period witnessed a pronounced transformation in public discourse on Catholicism. We do not have to search very long to locate short-term causes. The war itself played an important role. Roman Catholics were among those who fought and died for the patriot cause—against mainly Protestant enemies. Just as important, noncombatant Catholics demonstrated their loyalty throughout the war—in stark contrast to the behavior of many Anglicans. A second likely reason for the sudden diminution of anti-Catholicism was that revolutionary America desperately required the assistance of Catholic France. Among the strange alignments formed during the Revolution, none was stranger than the military alliance eventually established between the Continental Congress and the French government. Despite the reservations that many must have had, the compact was forged and yet another publicly spoken prejudice yielded to the demands of an interfaith coalition. The Franco-American alliance, together with the effort to gain the assistance of Catholic Quebecois, placed Americans in the position of extending gestures of respect to a people and a religion they had long identified with the antichrist. As awkward as the diplomatic experience may have been, the cultural ramifications were momentous.[46]

Anti-Catholicism also began to disappear from American laws during the founding period. At the beginning of the Revolution, many of the newly adopted state constitutions still retained Protestant privileges. Some banned Catholics from serving in public office. Others granted public support to Protestant ministers, but not Catholics. Yet, over the ensuing years, as the last remnants of the old church establishments were dismantled, religious tests for state officeholding were eliminated, and religious equality was mandated at the federal level, the legal distinctions between Catholics and Protestants started to dissolve. In 1789, Benjamin Rush let potential migrants to the United States know that America offered an "equal share of power ... to men of every religious sect" and observed that three Catholics had already been elected to the U.S. Congress. The changes were sometimes less immediate in their impact and more nuanced in their justification. The framers of the Massachusetts Constitution of 1780, for instance, were careful to note that they had not intended to exclude all Catholics from office, just those "who will not disclaim those Principles of Spiritual Jurisdiction which Roman Catholics *in some Countries* have held, and which are subversive of a free Government established by the People." The anti-Catholic prejudice so long ensconced in colonial law and culture did not disappear all at once, but it would now have to justify itself in a public sphere that expected at least a veneer of religious equality.[47]

For some unlucky Continental troops, the new religious environment meant that they would not be able to enjoy their traditionally raucous Pope's Day celebration. Once a year over the previous century, New Englanders had merrily commemorated the discovery of a Catholic plot to blow up Parliament, all its members, and the king on November 5, 1605. Parades featuring effigies of the Pope were accompanied by fireworks and the lighting of bonfires. Keeping with their tradition of idiosyncratic irreverence, eighteenth-century Bostonians sponsored a "mock combat" between the Pope of the North End and the Pope of the South End until John Hancock persuaded them to sponsor a single effigy as a symbol of their anti-British solidarity. The Revolution, however, brought a halt to the tradition. When General George Washington learned that soldiers in the Continental Army were planning to enjoy their traditional festivities, he forbade it. Washington wondered how his troops could be so grossly impolitic. "[T]o be insulting their Religion" at this moment, he wrote, was "so monstrous, as not to be suffered or excused."

Though hardly a ringing endorsement of Catholicism, Washington's scolding was a signal that standards of religious propriety could and did shift in radically pluralistic ways by the late eighteenth century.[48]

George Washington's friendly gestures toward Catholics were not unique. The passing of rabid anti-Catholicism took powerful symbolic forms during the founding era. Early in the war, for example, members of the Continental Congress went so far as to attend a Mass where they paid their respects to a recently deceased Spanish agent. Following his defection to the British side, Benedict Arnold openly wondered whether his patriot counterparts knew that their Congress had committed such a transgression. Could they imagine the horror with which their pious ancestors would have beheld such a spectacle? Undoubtedly, some were sufficiently horrified themselves. Yet even the most devout Protestants were now sometimes forced to concede that Roman Catholicism represented a species of Christianity. Many an idolatrous superstition and many a pagan ceremony had been appended to it, but the core remained. Furthermore, its limited presence was certainly preferable to the oppressive rule of British ministers and their Anglican vicegerents.[49]

If there was a Catholic counterpart to George Washington, he was Father John Carroll. When Hannah Adams wished to learn more about Catholicism, he was the one she consulted. Raised in Maryland and educated in France and England, Carroll returned to America on the eve of the Revolution. In 1776, the Continental Congress asked him to go to Canada and seek the support of Catholics there. The mission ended in failure, but on almost every future occasion Carroll succeeded at squaring Roman Catholicism with the nation's republican institutions. Like Washington, Carroll proved a quick study when it came to the constraints of the nation's religious discourse. In a 1784 letter to a friend in Rome, Carroll stressed the importance of understanding that "in these United States our religious system has undergone a revolution, if possible, more extraordinary than our political one." Because of the religious rights granted by the states, American Catholics were obliged to demonstrate their unqualified commitment to republic government. That meant that the Holy See should permit American Catholics as much autonomy as possible. "[P]rudence" dictated that they function independently of outside influence— or at least appear to function independently. Otherwise, they were sure to invite suspicion and perhaps even open hostility, as the doleful experience of the Church of England had demonstrated.[50]

Following the war, Carroll engaged in a series of printed debates with Protestant authors that established Catholicism as a faith suitable for extended public discussion. This was no small achievement. From the beginning, America's presses had treated Roman Catholicism as an object of derision and rhetorical hyperbole, never giving it serious consideration on its own terms. Change became evident in 1784 when Charles Henry Wharton, a former Catholic clergyman who had converted to Protestantism, published his reasons for leaving the church. For the most part, Wharton adhered to the standards of traditional anti-Catholicism, contending that the doctrines of transubstantiation and penance were both scripturally unfounded and that the Catholic Church was uniquely intolerant. Yet Wharton also employed the popular late eighteenth-century rhetoric of equal recognition, assuring his former Catholic brethren that his intention was to apologize "for *my own* conduct, not to throw the most distant reflection upon yours." In addition, Wharton remarked that he was "proud to see them [Roman Catholics] elevated to that equal respectability, to which, as zealous supporters of their country's freedom and as a christian society, they are essentially entitled."[51]

John Carroll used similarly ecumenical rhetoric in his response. Professing an inclination "to do justice to the humanity of protestants," Carroll noted that he was happy (rephrasing Wharton) *"to live in habits of intimacy and friendship with many valuable protestants"*—he just happened to think that Roman Catholics were more open-minded than Wharton made them out to be. Father Carroll also employed the language that proponents of an Anglican Episcopacy had used during the 1760s. Making note of the way Catholic doctrines were distorted, as well as the particular way Wharton had "misinformed," he indicated how "painful" it was to have to vindicate his Church's doctrines. Carroll stressed the importance of making sure his faith was properly understood. Before the church could liberate itself from public prejudices, Carroll claimed, it had to first liberate itself from "common misrepresentations," especially the notion that it still held to the doctrine " 'that out of HER COMMUNION no salvation can be obtained.' " In other words, he wanted to ensure that Catholicism was not unfairly represented as an intolerant faith.[52]

It is indicative of the changed religious climate that no contemporary Protestants bothered to weigh in on behalf of Wharton and against Carroll. That did not mean that Roman Catholics would enjoy a free ride. Their church's compatibility with republican government was still in question. John Carroll confronted the issue directly when a front-page article in the *Gazette of the United States*, signed "E.C.," asserted that Protestant faith should be awarded "every possible distinguishing mark of pre-eminence and respect, not repugnant to the true spirit of Toleration." Carroll opened his retort by again invoking the shared "pain" that "[e]very friend to the rights of conscience, equal liberty and diffusive happiness must have felt" when they read E.C.'s article. But this was no mere appeal to public sympathy or the subjectivity of faith. Carroll forcefully challenged the notion that the United

States was exclusively colonized on behalf of Protestantism. Nor, he contended, had one particular form of religion been responsible for erecting this new nation. Instead, its celebrated rise reflected the combined effort of the whole citizenry. Carroll made no mention of the toleration that E.C. assumed, referring instead to "equal liberty," "religious freedom," and "a free participation of equal rights." With Carroll's explicit rejection of Protestant preeminence, and his implicit rejection of toleration, the dispute abruptly ended.[53]

In 1790, John Carroll became America's first Roman Catholic bishop. Never before in the history of these former colonies had the church's spiritual hierarchy been complete. Now, as the fundamentals of civic faith became more inclusive, all the "peculiarities" of the Church's worship were in place. Here were tangible manifestations of the equal recognition that public discourse now extended. The change could be seen in Catholic rhetoric too. Well before most Catholics were willing to concede that they were just another denomination, Bishop Carroll had taught them to write, speak, and act as if they were. Although he was not comfortable with the popular Protestant notion that religion could be divided into essentials and nonessentials, Carroll did insist that Catholics and Protestants shared the most important doctrines in common. Carroll was a friend to both republican government and liberal principles. In a characteristic act that was both pragmatic and ecumenical, Carroll worked successfully to remove the phrase *exterminare Haereticos* from the list of tasks expected of American bishops. And he insisted, in discussing plans for the school that would eventually become Georgetown University, that an academy would have the advantage over a seminary because of its more inclusive character. "Being admitted to equal toleration, must we not," he asked, "concur in public measures, & avoid separating ourselves from the Community?" A proposal for the academy conspicuously stated that it would "be open to Students of *Every Religious Profession.*" In addition, matriculants would be allowed to attend their own places of worship. Only their "moral Conduct" would "be subject to general and uniform Discipline."[54]

At the same time that he was making such congenial gestures toward his Protestant brethren, Father Carroll insisted upon the preservation of both Catholic dignity and the distinctive elements of his church's traditions. He rejected the very possibility that loyal Catholic citizens and soldiers would endure "the degrading mark of distrust, or the galling yoke of inferiority." And when a gentleman who styled himself "Liberal" objected to the use of the title, "JOHN, BISHOP OF BALTIMORE" (which suggested that the city was an exclusive Roman Catholic domain) Carroll avowed that the writer had misconstrued the meaning of the term "Liberal," and in doing so, had twisted the substance of the nation's religious pluralism. "To be *liberal,* in the modern use of the term," Carroll admonished his critic, is to exercise the liberty "of professing doctrines, following the usages, and speaking the language of our respective Churches." Here, as on so many other occasions, Carroll articulated the religious pluralism that predominated in late eighteenth-century America, and persisted even amid the resurgence of anti-Catholic bigotry in the next.[55]

Catholics were not the only group to experience a dramatic improvement in treatment during the founding period. Within the new, post-revolutionary cultural climate, a group that had suffered centuries of persecution in Europe eventually managed to obtain equal rights in most of America, as well as an impressive measure of recognition. As late as 1800 there were probably less than three thousand Jews in the United States. Partly because they possessed no official ties to foreign powers, refrained from proselytizing, and confined themselves to small, respectable communities, America's Jews never attracted the animus that Catholics and some evangelical groups encountered in eighteenth-century America. Nonetheless, when state constitutions were drawn up in the 1770s and early 1780s, these documents maintained the European tradition of discrimination against Jews. If civil offices and tax support were not exclusively reserved for Protestants, then they were limited to those who accepted the authority of the New Testament. Yet the arguments that justified equal treatment for marginal Protestants and Roman Catholics would increasingly be applied to non-Christians. A 1783 petition, requesting that Jews be admitted to Pennsylvania's General Assembly on the same terms as their Christian counterparts characterized the state's current policy as "a stigma upon their nation and their religion." Contemporary Christians would have a difficult time countering such objections. In a religious culture that was already so integrated, egalitarian, and committed to free religious expression, charges of inequality possessed an undeniable appeal. Following passage of Virginia's Statute for Religious Freedom in 1786, one state after another removed the restrictions on Jewish religious liberties and Jewish officeholding. Article Six of the Constitution, which forbade religious tests for offices, as well as the ordinances applied to new territories in the 1780s and 1790s, made no religious distinctions whatsoever.[56]

Not everything changed at once. In fact, the "stigma" of inferiority remained with America's Jews for many years. Even in otherwise liberal states such as Rhode Island and Maryland, full legal equality was still decades away. Yet, with the changes made in U.S. law during the 1780s, Jews enjoyed more rights under the federal government than they did under any other national government in the world. At the same time, Christians were beginning to use respectful language and sometimes even extend kind gestures towards their

Jewish neighbors. George Washington's open letters to the Jewish congregations of Charleston, Savannah, Newport, Philadelphia, Richmond, and New York invoked the same universal rights and evinced the same degree of religious civility to which other marginal religious groups were becoming accustomed. It appears that some less conspicuous citizens acted upon similarly liberal principles. When Philadelphia's Jews required funds to help pay off their congregation's debts, historian Jonathan D. Sarna notes, several prominent Christians stepped forward with contributions. And when New York's Shearith Israel congregation required immediate assistance in order to spare its cemetery from collapse, local Christian merchants subscribed liberally. In their public behavior as in their laws, early Americans were beginning to acknowledge that Protestantism, and even Christianity, represented just one species of respectable faith.[57]

Some Protestant Christian groups also operated on the margins of religious pluralism during the founding period. America's Anglicans found themselves in an especially unfortunate position after the war. With Cornwallis's surrender at Yorktown, all pretense to their constituting a national establishment disappeared. Nonetheless, the Church's allegiance now seemed to lie outside the United States. Many Anglicans were tainted with the suspicion of loyalism. It would be a hard road back for the beleaguered Church—not least because it would be outcompeted by the various evangelical denominations in the decades following the Revolution. But in contrast to the traditional pariah status of Roman Catholicism, Anglicanism's Protestant origins automatically guaranteed it some degree of respect. Nor did it hurt that prominent Anglicans such as George Washington and Patrick Henry had played a leading role in the patriot cause. Such considerations ensured that the Church would regain some rhetorical equality with their Protestant counterparts before long. In a 1790 pamphlet, Samuel Seabury noted that "the prejudices of the Presbyterians and Independents in America" against the church were "much abated." Anti-Episcopal prejudices may have also abated because of a general willingness among church members to relinquish their pre-war privileges, forgo any pretensions to political authority, and finally assume the status of one denomination among many others. In the wake of the American Revolution the Church of England even took on a different name—the Protestant Episcopal Church—that reinforced its humble new American identity.[58]

Despite the new appellation, anti-Episcopal suspicions remained. At least a few Episcopalians grasped the problem immediately and proposed concrete acts of conciliation. Above all, the Church urgently needed to sever its association with England, antirepublican politics, and the social arrogance that established churches too often displayed. In 1782, William White offered a modest plan, "a frame of government," that self-consciously appealed to American sensibilities. First noting apologetically that Episcopalians "entertain a preference for their own communion," White contended that it would be "Inconsistent" with the patriotic allegiance they displayed during the war for the members of this church to be subject "to any spiritual jurisdiction, connected with the temporal authority of a foreign state." "Such a dependence," the author continued, "is contrary to the fundamental principles of civil society." This dependence seemed especially ill-suited to the fundamental principles of American society, in which churches were expected to buttress the nation's republican institutions. In the same spirit, White concluded that religious societies should refrain from group political activity. Otherwise "they will be suspected by all others, as aiming at the exclusive government of the country." White saw the writing on the wall, and his appeal may have served as a warning to the country's more aggressive Episcopalians. The republic would tolerate religious preferences of all sorts, but would not take kindly to foreign attachments, the retention of old privileges, or concerted assertions of religious power.[59]

Not everyone got the message. In several states, the Church of England attempted to maintain at least a portion of its former privileges. The subsequent reaction, however, suggests that extent to which the language of equal recognition now prevailed. In Maryland, for instance, the Church's efforts in this regard occasioned resistance to the principle of establishment, rather than the Church's own "peculiar" principles. A public debate broke out there in 1783 when the Episcopal clergy (with the aim of retaining the Church of England's property) sought the state's permission to alter their liturgy and organizational structure. Summarizing the opposition's stance, the Presbyterian minister Patrick Allison argued that the debate itself "neither is nor can be properly called religious." Of course, Allison noted, he had no qualms with the Anglican church itself. "Certainly not a syllable has dropt from my pen reflecting on the articles, the discipline or devotion of any Christian society throughout the State," Allison declared, "nor the least endeavour used to diminish their importance on a religious score." There were various reasons for adhering to a particular communion, not all of which were compatible with one another, or with salvation for that matter: "One persuasion may admire the venerable order and beautiful form of their worship—another may admire the elegant simplicity and evangelical purity of theirs—a third, the spiritual, extatic [sic], heavenly raptures of theirs." In keeping with the ecumenical rhetoric of the period, Allison made no effort to draw qualitative distinctions between different modes of worship. Yet he also affirmed the general conviction there was no cause for preferential religious establish-ments of any sort. No church, Allison argued, had the right to the state's "particular countenance, distinction and protection." "All possible descrip-tions of Christians are equally entitled to the countenance and favour of gov-ernment," he maintained, as long as they posed no danger to the state or its citizens.[60]

Considered merely as one denomination among others, the former Church of England benefited from the public esteem granted to most main-stream churches in the pluralistic religious climate of the late eighteenth century. Some less fortunate denominations did not receive the same re-spectful treatment. New groups, or groups who adhered to unorthodox beliefs and practices, often still had to endure excoriation. A flourishing evangelical movement in the south, for instance, continued to draw sharp volleys from the old-line clergy. During the early part of 1774, Philip Vickers Fithian re-ported that a Virginia minister delivered a series of sermons portraying Baptist faith as "whimsical Fancies or at most Religion grown to Wildness & Enthusiasm!" Then again, the Episcopal hostility toward evangelicals was hardly unprovoked. Southern Methodists and Separate Baptists continually badgered Anglican clergymen and laypeople with unwelcome evaluations of their spiritual states and their (alleged) moral laxity.[61]

The bad blood between southern Episcopalians and their evangelical ri-vals was largely unique in late eighteenth-century America. But it was cer-tainly not new. Its beginnings can be traced to the migration of New Light Presbyterians to Virginia and the conflict that almost immediately ensued. Since the Great Awakening arrived in Hanover County during the late 1740s, the salient issues had changed little. The Episcopalians continued to stress the virtues of patient devotion, constant piety, ordered ritual, and a minister's fidelity to his own parish. And they displayed unqualified disgust for the way the "enthusiasts" (as they still liked to call evangelicals) violated social deco-rum, railed at traditional hierarchies, and—perhaps worst of all—cultivated the affections of enslaved African Americans. The evangelicals offered a well-developed critique of their own. They portrayed Episcopal clergymen as enfeebled spiritual leaders, corrupted by their rationalistic faith and their comfortable, state-supported livings. They also emphasized the desperate urgency of conversion and wondered how Anglicans could remain compla-cent while the pits of hell yawned beneath them and the devil beckoned their listless souls. In most of the thirteen colonies, the conflict between Old and New Lights reduced to a slow simmer from the mid-1740s onward. But in the south it still boiled, fueled by the long-standing privileges of the established churches and the terrifying fear of slave uprisings.[62]

In the north, a tiny religious sect known as the Shakers generated concern for the same reasons its more prominent Catholic and Episcopal counterparts did—less for its theology than its reputed foreign-bred threat to republican government. The church's origins were quite recent. In 1772, an English admirer of George Whitefield named Ann Lee received a vision, instructing her to establish a new kind of church in New England. Witnessing the early death of every one of her four children had persuaded Lee that sexual intercourse was the original sin. Once in America, she and her followers developed their enigmatic theology that drew upon New Light Calvinism, but also sanctioned female preaching and held out the possibility of perfection here on earth. When their commitment to pacifism during the Revolutionary conflict was added to their prophetic claims, their celibacy, their emphasis on perfectionism, their evangelism, and their English origins, the dangers they posed to the republic became unmistakable. In July 1780, the local militia arrested six church members and the Continental Army seized Shaker property. Several members were mobbed, and on one occasion, even whipped, for alleged "collaboration with traitors" in the Massachusetts town of Harvard. Mother Ann herself spent that fall in prison.[63]

In contrast to so many of their sectarian counterparts, the Shakers resided outside the realm of respectable religious discourse. Consequently, material punishments were soon followed by public indictments. A Shaker apostate named Amos Taylor assumed responsibility for alerting the country to the menace of Shakerism in his *Narrative of the Strange Principles, Conduct, and Character of the People Known by the Name of Shakers*. According to Taylor, "these Errors" had already "spread in several Parts of North-America." Taylor expressed concern, given the "infant state of civil power in America." Here, he argued, "every infringement on the natural rights of humanity, every effort to undermine our original constitution, either in civil or ecclesiastical order, saps the foundation of Independency." Such a state of affairs rendered the nation dangerously susceptible to subversion. Distant, unscrupulous forces appeared to be at work. "To see a body of more than two thousand people, having no will of their own, but governed by a few Europeans conquering their adherents into the most unreserved subjection," Taylor noted, "argues some infatuating power; some deep, very deep design at bottom."[64]

What does Taylor's uncharitable rhetoric tell us about late eighteenth-century religious culture? Had nothing really changed? Indeed, Taylor's alarmism harkens back to an old model of religious difference, within which errors spread like a plague. But if these old terms of intolerance were being trotted out again, their meaning can only be understood in their post-revolutionary context. It must be remembered that, to some late eighteenth-century writers, a republic so new and so fragile was as vulnerable to the subversion of political nonconformity and as inclined to alternative objects of allegiance as the godly community once had been. Shakerism demanded such a rigorous internal conformity that it seemed to subordinate the common principles and practices that bound the larger society together. Like Catholicism and Episcopalianism, Shakerism appeared to cultivate loyalties beyond the bounds of the nation within which all forms of patriotic dissent were supposed to be legitimate. Shakers conscientiously avoided the mainstream institutions that would, they believed, corrupt both the faith and the faithful. In these early years of the nation's history, few things were more suspect than a group whose demands radically exceeded the fundamentals of Christian faith and, by extension, paid scant attention to the essentials of good citizenship. The other problem was that the Shakers were simply new.[65]

Two particularly grievous denominational sins of the post-revolutionary era were excessive privacy and perceived intolerance. The odd group known as the Sandemanians were taken to task on both counts. Why, John Huntington asked, did the members of this group not show their faces at commencements or elections? Why did the Sandemanians refuse to converse with the members of other churches? Why did they not visit with them? In a fashion reminiscent of the way evangelical separates had been criticized for at least three decades, Huntington disparaged the Sandemanians for their lack of charity toward other churches, for their stiff admission standards, and for their "schismatical spirit."[66]

If late eighteenth-century discourse invested individuals and groups with the right to describe themselves on their own terms, they grew anxious when such descriptions remained private, when groups avoided civic occasions and social intercourse, and when they dwelled upon the errors of other groups. Nineteenth-century Americans would condemn Catholics and Mormons on these same grounds. Interestingly, during the late 1780s and early 1790s, several marginal sects took the liberty of publishing their particular group's articles of faith and forms of discipline. The Sandemanians, who seem to have been able to both preach and practice nonforbearance, thus trespassed against the civil religion by isolating themselves from public contact. Their uncivil hostility to the allegedly friendly entreaties of the larger Christian community rendered their group unacceptably private. Their secretive practices constituted a malignant opacity within a culture that championed the civic-minded, well-mannered private life. Their reclusive intolerance represented an affront to the liberal sociability upon which the wider culture prided itself. In the reaction to religious practices such as these, the limits of early American pluralism were partly drawn.[67]

Fractious Majorities and Unanimous Wholes

The widespread commitment to religious pluralism in late eighteenth-century America had significant implications for the shape that religious authority would take in the new nation. Since the Great Awakening of the 1740s, the rising demands for equal recognition and the continual expansion of dissenting voices had placed traditional religious authority on tenuous grounds. We have seen how theological creeds lost their status as expressions of universal truths and standing ministers their status as infallible interpreters of God's Word. We have seen how a Synod was shattered by the demand for minority rights and how powerful churches conceded their exclusive power to make civil law. The opening of provincial institutions, the broadening of religious equality, and the tremendous weight now given to direct representation posed some deeply troubling questions. How could decisions be made by people with diverse opinions? Who could make the final, determinative judgment?

For some, there was no debating the matter: the will of the majority should take precedence. Philadelphia's recently formed Associate Reformed Synod was unambiguous when framing its proposal for a new system of church government in 1787. Acknowledging that not everyone observed the traditional Christian Sabbath, the Synod insisted that "those who are of another opinion" should "be compelled so to behave as to give no disturbance to the great majority who profess to believe it should be religiously observed." As popular and unequivocal as contemporary assertions of majoritarianism were then—and remain today—they begged important questions. In an oft-cited 1776 letter to James Sullivan, John Adams asked: "How then does the Right arise in the Majority to govern the Minority, against their Will?... Whence arises the Right of the Majority to govern, and the Obligation of the Minority to obey?" These were just some of the dilemmas that the revolutionary upheaval of the 1760s and early 1770s had produced. The leaders of a country at war are seldom satisfied when the cause is supported by only a small majority. They demand unanimity. Ironically, so did many marginal religious groups at the time. After all, they asked, what gives the numerically superior portion of the community the right to speak on behalf of all believers? In the end, is a religious majority—the arithmetic of believers—any better than state-enforced conformity? Do not both systems deprive the individual of his absolute right to private judgment and self-definition? The disestablishment of colonial churches, like the overthrow of imperial government, made such questions suddenly and urgently relevant.[68]

This tendency to privilege unanimity over majoritarianism culminated in that most famous of all conjurings—"We the People"—that opened the Constitution. The invocation of unanimity, however, was not just a savvy rhetorical gesture. The founders seemed to have actually believed in its efficacy. On July 7, 1787, as the Constitutional Convention wound down, an aged Benjamin Franklin advised the delegates that they strive for "unanimity" and avoid any pretension to their own "infallibility." People, like "sects in Religion," he observed, were reluctant to relinquish the notion that they were impervious to error. The author of *The Autobiography* then invoked his own life as an example:

> For having lived long, I have experienced many instances of being obliged by better information or fuller consideration, to change opinions even on important subjects, which I once thought right, but found to be otherwise. It is therefore that the older I grow, the more apt I am to doubt my own judgment, and to pay more respect to the judgment of others.

In this spirit, Franklin urged those assembled to refrain from criticizing the document in its final instantiation. They should compromise, he suggested, rather than stubbornly adhering to their own private judgments. This was not the spontaneous, affectionate union that many later imagined. Instead, it emerged from a willingness to recognize a great variety of opinions, to engage those differences with respectful gestures, and to accept agreements based on shared, essential principles.[69]

In religion as in politics, the call for unanimity was never more insistent than it was during the American Revolution, as distinctions once made between Churchmen and Dissenters gave way to distinctions between Whigs and Tories, Patriots and Loyalists. For the first time in the eighteenth century, colonial Americans found themselves fighting a full-scale war against a non-Catholic enemy. A transcolonial political affiliation now subsumed all regional affinities and religious identities. Despite the compromises that accompanied every assertion of unanimity, the Revolution mobilized people into bodies that repeatedly claimed to speak for all Americans. Broadsides proclaimed the indivisibility of public opinion, the union of the whole people. The Sons of Liberty ferreted out, tarred, feathered, and generally silenced political dissenters. Americans marveled at their own capacity for unanimity. A sermon preached on the eve of the war noted the "surprising agreement in opinion, that has prevailed in persons at a great distance from each other," their letters containing "nearly the same proposals to each other, as though the inspiration of the Most High gave them the like understanding."

A graduation oration by Timothy Dwight expressed gratitude that "this continent [was] inhabited by a people, who have the same religion, the same manners, the same interests, the same language, and the same essential forms and principles of civil government. . . . That a vast continent, containing near three thousand millions of acres of valuable land, should be inhabited by a people, in all respects one, is indeed a novelty on earth."[70]

But when did a large majority of the people become "one" people? When did many similar opinions become a single principle? A Thanksgiving sermon preached before encamped troops in Massachusetts captured the prevailing sentiment:

> It has been universally admitted, that the greater part of a community should govern the minority in all matters of public concern. When nine or eight tenths of that community unite in any matter, commonly speaking, they are not divided; their voice is in every sense the voice of the whole. That the continent is as much united, if not more perfectly, cannot be denied.

When a community appeared as imperiled as this one did, a large majority was near enough to "the voice of the whole" to be treated as though it were. A republic premised on equal recognition had to be sure that more than a mere majority agreed on its fundamental aims. And the need for unanimity was far too great to allow a few inconvenient facts to get in the way.[71]

For some, the rule of the religious majority could not be conceived as a distant cousin of unanimity. Instead, it appeared to be a close relation to the oppression of the traditional establishments. That, at least, was how dissenters from the Massachusetts religious establishment saw the matter. Massachusetts' system of awarding tax revenues to the minister chosen by the majority in each town drew repeated criticism from those like the anonymous author who thought "LORD MAJORITY" at least as oppressive as "LORD DIOCESAN." Article Three of the Massachusetts Constitution was criticized for compelling the minority in each town to cede its rights of conscience to the majority. In response to such criticism, Isaac Backus's newspaper adversary Hieronymous contended that it was "incident to a state of society, that the majority should govern the whole." "To insist upon an unanimous vote for the choice of a minister," he argued, would deprive countless churches of the preachers they desperately required. Hieronymous interpreted Backus's position as an unwillingness to abide by one of the fundamental rules of society—majoritarianism—and instead, to wait for that unanimity which could never be attained here on earth.[72]

The spirit that favored voluntary unanimity was continually reinvigorated by the shared belief that rational, autonomous, and equal individuals could and must consent to every collective act. Unanimous agreements were especially attractive within America's democratic, egalitarian cultural environment because they seemed to offer a basis for unity that was independent of even the mildest coercion. The desire that discordant opinions might be transmuted into a single, inclusive expression of them all was at least as popular in religious speculation as it was in political thought. Yet there was also, in the diverse, post-establishment America, a discernible conviction that the majority could really represent the true convictions of the whole—or if not, then it was the only practical means of approximating it. After all, even the minority New Lights who withdrew from the Old Light majority in the Synod of Philadelphia had bestowed substantial power upon the majority when they established their own body. Most denominations found that they were unable to abandon the principle of majoritarianism. Unanimity was a fine principle. It was, perhaps, the only one fully consistent with religious pluralism. But you could not easily run a church or a nation with it.[73]

In the end, neither majoritarianism nor unanimity triumphed in the nation's religious culture. The practice of majoritarianism and the ideal of unanimity would maintain an uneasy truce throughout American history. Majoritarianism would be buttressed by the profound deference shown to democratic governance and the ideal of unanimity by the incessant demands for equal recognition. Over the ensuing years, both would be employed to justify Sabbatarian laws, days of national thanksgiving, and Bible reading in the schools. In religious matters, majoritarianism and unanimity would each stand as testaments to the grasp that uniformity no longer maintained and the diversity of opinion that could never again be ignored. From them, fundamental tenets emerged; through them particular beliefs were reconciled. Or at least that is what has always been claimed.

An American Production

In 1788, a Presbyterian minister from Delaware, Henry Pattillo, articulated the postrevolutionary religious outlook in a well-subscribed book of sermons. Pattillo referred to his compilation as "an *American* production." It surely was. Pattillo condemned deism, recommended harmony between different groups of Christians, and noted his own appreciation of a good Baptist or Methodist sermon (he simply ignored the occasional denominational "peculiarit[y]").

No more surprising, perhaps, was Pattillo's disapproval of the Methodist policy of permitting women to speak and pray with their male brethren. Also, in typical late eighteenth-century American fashion, Pattillo noted that "religious disputations" seemed "*irreligious.*" Pattillo went on to suggest that charity should take precedence over orthodoxy, pious practices over correct doctrines. "One evil word; one wicked action; one harsh censure, as they proceed from the heart, and are the choice of the will," Pattillo intoned, "have infinitely more of evil in them, than a mistaken judgment has." Almost nothing our neighbor believed could do as much harm as our condemnation of his belief. Pattillo invoked the words of John Wesley, the Englishman who founded the Methodist movement: " 'We think, and *let* think: We agree to *disagree.*' "[74]

To think and let think. To agree to disagree. Here were the core assumptions, contradictory as they might seem, of late eighteenth-century religious pluralism. Over the succeeding decades, America's leaders would rarely call for conformity, nor uniformity, so far as the innocuous "circumstantials" of faith or politics went. But they rarely hesitated to invoke the essential, unifying principles contained in the Bible or the Constitution as they dismissed the many, seemingly trivial differences between them. For those who endorsed or defended the nation's religious pluralism, there still had to be some bottom, some preexisting foundation, some unquestioned agreement—begotten, not made.[75]

"Our government makes no sense," President Dwight D. Eisenhower remarked in 1952, "unless it is founded in a deeply felt religious faith—and I don't care what it is." For late eighteenth-century Americans, as for Dwight Eisenhower in the mid-twentieth century, religion was the essential handmaiden of good government and a harmonious social order. It did not matter exactly what Protestant, Christian, or even monotheistic tradition you belonged to, as long as you believed. No republican government was sustainable in the absence of a rigorous civic religion that embodied the essentials of faith. Indeed, the most effective remaining justification for religious establishments was that they maintained the moral vigor necessary for republican government. Gradually losing the prerogative to publicly denigrate any particular Protestant (or Christian, or even religious) belief as false or dangerous, late eighteenth-century Americans were more worried that there would be no belief than that there would be erroneous beliefs.[76]

Agreement on the menace of atheism (or anything resembling it) left nonbelievers and skeptics in an unenviable position. Even into our own time, men and women with reservations about organized religion have usually found it best to keep their contrarian sentiments to themselves. If a white man's particular brand of faith no longer proved a legal barrier to most public offices by 1787, unbelief almost always did. That fact became apparent in the 1800 campaign for the presidency when Thomas Jefferson found himself beset by charges of atheism. Federalists accused the Sage of Monticello of harboring the same bloody intentions as the violent French secularists known as Jacobites. Could you put your faith in a man that did not put his faith in God, they asked? Could you invest great responsibility in a person so hostile to your own convictions? "Thomas Jefferson differs from you," A Layman wrote, "not merely as Quaker differs from a Calvinist, or Lutheran from Papist, but he differs from you totally inasmuch as he is in no sense, and according to no forms a Christian."[77] Luckily for the Republicans of that day, their candidate may have been too popular to lose. Since then, countless political aspirants have been considerably less fortunate.[78]

Without charity, of course, faith meant less. If belief itself, rather than the institutions and beliefs of a particular church, was now looked upon as the guarantor of a good society, then undue criticism of other people's beliefs, rather than an epidemic of heretical beliefs, now posed one of the most urgent challenges for this religiously diverse society. The Great Awakening had introduced colonial Americans to the pain that "rash judging" could produce. The increasing presence of religious diversity in their daily lives was reflected in a growing sensitivity toward religious diversity in public discourse. Both developments gave Americans a reason for not casting aspersions on those with whom they disagreed. "[W]e are intolerant," one minister wrote, "when, in the common offices of friendly intercourse, we refuse to *have any dealings* with any respectable and worthy men, either as individuals, or in any corporate capacity, merely because they are of a different communion from ourselves."[79] In the late eighteenth-century, charity usually meant equal recognition and George Washington thought that his fellow citizens possessed an abundance of it. In a letter to four Jewish congregations, the president noted that the "liberality of sentiments toward each other which marks every political and religious denomination of men in this country stands unparalleled in the history of nations."[80]

Even as the most durable boundaries of religious exclusion began to crumble, racial lines only hardened. In late eighteenth-century America, Native Americans and African Americans still represented potential objects of evangelization, rather than equally recognized members of civil society. The diverse audience of which public figures were cognizant did not include either group. Into the mid-nineteenth century, those whose beliefs fell out of the major monotheistic traditions were still known simply as "heathens." Nor was there any evidence that Native Americans and enslaved African Americans would make it into the Christian unions envisioned by men like Ezra Stiles.

Charles Woodmason urged white Presbyterians to "live like Brethren in Unity" with non-Presbyterian whites, else they fall victim to Indians or that "*Internal* Enemy Not less than 100 [thousand] *Africans* below us." Despite the novel interest taken in so many obscure forms of belief during the late eighteenth century, Americans seemed generally uninterested in the subtleties of Native American and African faiths. Colonial Americans rarely even recognized their forms of worship as religion.[81]

To almost every one of those who had something to say on the matter, Native Americans and African Americans appeared so radically different in their religious rituals and everyday practices that no accommodation seemed possible. According to East Apthorp's 1762 tract, America's indigenous populations had so far not proved receptive to Christianity because their cultures were so "uncultivated," their "languages so hard to learn, and so little adapted to the doctrines of Religion" and their settlements so transient. Significantly, during the bishop controversy of the 1760s, the ostensibly violent Indian and the disenfranchised status of African Americans served as models of misrepresentation. In an inclusive religious world, prejudice and misrepresentation constituted social and cultural persecution because they were instruments of de-recognition. The outsider status of Indians and blacks thus emblematized the experience of the white folks who objected to having their assent taken for granted, their beliefs censured, and their souls proselytized. Such things mattered when inclusion was expected and self-definition demanded.[82]

There is very little evidence that the prejudices against Native American and African American religions had abated by the end of the eighteenth century. In short, the civility extended to a wider and wider variety of white believers was denied to Indians and blacks. Wherever contemporaries stood on the question of converting non-Europeans, both groups were thought to reside outside the realm of civilized life and both were subject to truly uncivil discourse. That Native Americans and African Americans were neither readers of colonial newspapers, representatives in the legislatures, nor members of the same churches and fraternal societies made their wholesale denigration all the more unsurprising. Even when devout Christian missionaries became acquainted with Indian religious beliefs and practices well, even when they came to love Indians like brothers and sisters, they seldom treated traditional Native American faiths as anything more than pagan ignorance at best, and nefarious devil worship at worst.[83]

The small numbers of African Americans who regularly attended Christian churches confronted a different kind of prejudice. The segregation that they experienced in New York, Boston, and Philadelphia resembled the discrimination that would later prevail in the post-Reconstruction South. Perhaps no one illustrated the distance between religious inclusion and racial exclusion at the end of the eighteenth century than Samuel Stillman, the first Baptist minister to be invited to deliver Massachusetts' annual election sermon. When an African American preacher of his own denomination arrived in town, Stillman reportedly refused to grant him his pulpit, noting that "it was Boston, and that they did not mix colours; or words of that import."[84] In Boston, as in New York, Philadelphia, Baltimore, and Charleston, black Christians sat in the back of the churches, or in the galleries above their white brethren. When neither of those alternatives was available, a wooden partition or a wide central aisle might be used to keep white and black worshipers adequately separated. African Americans were generally denied full church membership, and even when they achieved it, were generally denied leadership positions in the church. Death brought no end to the discrimination. Many churches would not allow the bodies of black congregants to be buried in their cemeteries. In those cases, African American believers would have to find their own plots so that their white brethren would not have to rot alongside them.[85]

The first American blacks to publicly challenge the system of racial segregation in the churches were those who gathered around the Reverend Richard Allen. Allen was born a slave, but managed to purchase his freedom and eventually made his way to Philadelphia, where he served as assistant minister of St. George's Methodist Church. He was helping to formulate plans for a black church in town when that famous and oft-told incident occurred: kneeling black congregants were instructed to get up and move to the back of the meetinghouse. A scuffle ensued and the black congregants departed as a body. Allen concluded his account of these events by dryly remarking that the whites would be "no more plagued with us in the church."[86]

America's earliest black church was completed a few years later. Initially conceived as an inclusive, nondenominational institution, the African Church of Philadelphia became the African Episcopal Church of St. Thomas in 1794. The denominational choice prompted Richard Allen, who was still devoted to the Methodists, to found the Bethel African Methodist Episcopal Church. Similar developments took place in Baltimore, New York, Wilmington, and Boston over the ensuing years. The African American members of Samuel Stillman's Baptist church were among those who established their own religious societies. Racial prejudice was beginning to yield its own denominational fruit.[87]

A little more than two decades after walking out of St. George's, Allen was appointed the bishop of the African Methodist Episcopal Church, which had just—in keeping with an already venerable American religious tradition— formally separated from its fellow Methodist churches. Unlike John Carroll's appointment as a Roman Catholic bishop, however, the office bestowed upon Allen did not so much signify the expanding bounds of religious pluralism as the constricted limits of racial inclusion. The shame that African Americans endured in the Christian churches prompted Allen to complain that black members of the church had been "treated worse than heathens." It would be hard to deny that a powerful element of personal and community dignity was at stake here. Given the enormous gap between the humiliation of racial subordination and the social cache that accrued to church members in American society, it was probably difficult for blacks to resist the lure of in-dependent "African" churches—just as it was difficult for whites to resist leveling charges of excessive pride and ingratitude on those who did so. Whether they were damned because of their culture or their race, the con-sequences were largely the same. Denied basic civil and religious rights, segregated from their white neighbors, nineteenth-century Native Americans and African Americans would be seen as essentially different.[88]

However malicious and however enduring the prejudice that men such as Richard Allen confronted, the religious ideals that white Americans now embraced—the rights of private judgment, collective self-definition, and public recognition—reproduced themselves. Religious pluralism in early America owed a great deal to the rise of reflexive egalitarianism, a development Charles Taylor has called "the politics of universal dignity." Equal recognition could not be denied to any group without threatening the inclusive foundation upon which all claims to recognition were made. The Presbyterian minister William Tennent denounced South Carolina's multiple establishment plan by bluntly insisting upon: "EQUALITY OR NOTHING!" Not coincidentally, over the next several decades, religion would remain the one sphere of American life in which people of both sexes and all races came closest to participating as equals. With the passage of time, Native Americans and African Americans would be denigrated less and less because of their religion, and more and more because of the alleged inferiority of their respective races. For those who lived in the late eighteenth and early nineteenth centuries, race was becoming a better justification for oppression than religion. Where talk of barbarism and hea-thenism had once sufficed—each remedied by "civilization" and Christian conversion—Americans began describing Native Americans and African Americans in the unalterable categories of anatomic difference.[89]

With these sober qualifications in mind, the religious pluralism of late eighteenth-century America stands as a remarkable achievement. Early American culture did more than liberate religious judgments from external constraints. It also freed believers from many of the indignities that external judgments had once imposed. The emergent notion that each group and individual was entitled to its own self-definition carried with it the conviction that the criticism of religious beliefs, institutions, and practices was impermissible. Restraint, once demanded of individuals regarding the seditious, contagious things that might emanate from their corrupt minds, gradually became a mechanism for civility, the foundation of collective action. When Thomas Jefferson wrote that his neighbor's beliefs did no harm to him, he *did not say* that his neighbor should be free to cast aspersions upon other beliefs. When James Madison granted every individual "a freedom to embrace, to profess and to observe the Religion which we believe to be of divine origin" he rejected the implication that such liberty might be invoked to deny "an equal freedom to those whose minds have not yet yielded to the evidence which has convinced us." Three decades later, when a future Roman Catholic bishop of New York arrived on American shores, it was upon those very terms. Twenty-year-old Irish immigrant John Hughes expected that here, "no stigma of inferiority would be impressed on my brow, simply because I professed one creed or another." There was more to Hughes's hope than equal standing before the law. By the early nineteenth century, he, like so many others, was taken with the promise of equal recognition.[90]

Conclusion

"[M]ingle with Us as Americans": Religious
Pluralism after the Founding

Thou shalt have no other gods before me.

—Exodus 20:3

Congress shall make no law respecting an establishment of religion,
or prohibiting the free exercise thereof; or abridging the freedom of
speech, or of the press; or the right of the people peaceably to assemble, and to petition the government for a redress of grievances.

—The First Amendment to the Constitution

On a visit to Newport, Rhode Island, in 1790, George Washington
received the usual assortment of welcome messages—from the local
Protestant clergy, from the local Freemasons, and from the citizens
who assembled at the town meeting. In addition, the town's Hebrew
Congregation wished the president well and praised the federal government, which offered "bigotry . . . no sanction" and "persecution no
assistance." The Jewish population in Newport was small; approximately twenty-five families made their homes there during the Revolution. But they were not ignored. Washington issued a prompt and
characteristically polite reply. After acknowledging the kind sentiments extended to him and expressing his own hopes for the nation's
success, the Founding Father proceeded to make a point regarding the
national government's approach to religious diversity. "It is now no
more that toleration is spoken of," he wrote, "as if it was by the
indulgence of one class of people, that another enjoyed the exercise

of their inherent natural rights." "For happily the Government of the United States, which gives to bigotry no sanction, to persecution no assistance," Washington repeated, "requires only that they who live under its protection should demean themselves as good citizens, in giving it on all occasions their effectual support." The Jews of Newport and the president of the United States agreed: neither persecution nor bigotry would find a home in this land that welcomed all "good citizens" of whatever faith they might be. Persecution was about to be made unconstitutional and bigotry had been rendered culturally unacceptable. It no longer made sense to talk of toleration.[1]

The following year, 1791, the Bill of Rights was ratified. Universally acknowledged as a guarantee of individual religious liberty, the first of these ten amendments to the Constitution can also be seen as a testament of the nation's commitment to religious pluralism. To begin, the First Amendment provided that there would be "no law respecting an establishment of religion." Debate continues as to whether the framers intended this clause to mean that government activities should be free of religious influence or to merely preclude the establishment of a single faith at the national level. The ambiguity of the phrasing provides no easy answer. Nor does the great diversity of late eighteenth-century opinions on the subject. What can be said with assurance is that this amendment prohibited the established conformity that defined early modern European states and the majority of colonial settlements in North America. There would be no establishment, there would be no toleration, there would be no more instances of state-imposed uniformity. As the First Commandment forbade the people of Israel from embracing other forms of faith, this First Amendment forbade the American government from prescribing any.[2]

The Amendment's second clause, which guaranteed the "free exercise" of religion, was equally important. Here was no mere indulgence for "pretended scruples," "dissenting consciences," or even "private judgments." The religious liberty implied by the phrase "free exercise" entailed a freedom to congregate, worship, and cultivate the particular institutions that distinguished the great variety of late eighteenth-century denominations from one another. It is important to note that guarantees for speech, press, and assembly were just a semicolon behind. Religious differences became legitimate in eighteenth-century America in no small part because clergymen were free of most legal restrictions on their speech, the rapidly expanding presses offered a venue for dissenting ideas, and new assemblies of believers sprang up everywhere. No provision was made for religious forbearance and no injunctions were enforced against "rash judgments." None had to be. Americans were expected to avoid religious bigotry on their own.

The First Amendment did at the federal level what so many state governments did within their own jurisdictions. The constitutional provisions made for religious liberty during the last three decades of the century gave worshipers the right to freely incorporate their churches and openly preach their faith. These changes were particularly helpful for religious minorities in places such as Massachusetts and Virginia where church establishments had retained a strong foothold during the eighteenth century. At the time the First Amendment was ratified, the United States ranked among the most religiously diverse areas in the world. Yet the number of churches in America had not even neared its peak. Over the next few decades scores of new religious groups would make their appearance across the continent. The Sandemanians, Shakers, and Methodists would be followed by the Universalists, the Mormons, and the Seventh-Day Adventists. Many of these groups would take root in the vast, thinly settled stretches of land that ran from Lake Erie in the north to the Gulf of Mexico in the south, from the Appalachians to the Rockies. These religious radicals would not be tolerated by the federal government—rather they would be given the opportunity, as Washington put it, to "sit in safety under [their] own vine and figtree."[3]

At the same time, competition to convert the unchurched, the indifferent, and the ignorant only became fiercer in the decades following the Revolution as the nation's established religious denominations rushed headlong across the continent in an often futile attempt to keep up with the sprawling American population. This competition took many forms. In carefully planned debates that could attract a thousand or more listeners for several days at a time, Methodists, Baptists, Catholics, Disciples of Christ, Universalists, Calvinists, and Arminians advanced impressively erudite arguments. The newly incorporated churches of the early nineteenth century also showed that they were prepared to adopt the latest organization and marketing principles in their effort to gain advantage over rivals. Some very pious folks organized carnival-like camp meetings and published sensationalized religious fiction. These novel forms of proselytizing turned out better for some than others. The Baptists and Methodists, who made up an astonishing 70 percent of Protestants by 1850, tended toward the evangelical ecumenism that made unprecedented gains. Their entrepreneurial energy, their disdain for pompous displays of learning, and their willingness to accommodate the interests and sensitivities of ordinary laborers gave them a significant advantage in this aggressive new religious culture.[4]

The proliferation of churches and denominations was accompanied by a number of efforts to forge cooperation between America's white Protestant denominations. Beginning in the early part of the nineteenth century, multidenominational evangelical groups distributed Bibles by the tens of thousands, and short religious tracts by the hundreds of thousands. Missionaries seemed especially inclined to cooperate when the objects of their proselytizing were the non-Christian Indians. President Washington even promised that the newly established federal government would "co-operate, as far as circumstances may conveniently admit, with the disinterested endeavours of" the once-despised Moravians "to civilize and Christianize the savages of the wilderness." The older reformed Protestant denominations, particularly those with strong roots on the East Coast, often found common cause. An early indication of the direction that such common efforts would take appeared in 1790 when William Livingston (the Presbyterian governor of New Jersey), George Clinton (the Dutch Reformed governor of New York), and William Samuel Johnson (the Episcopal president of Columbia College) endorsed a three-volume collection of sermons drawn from "the several most important religious denominations." Almost all of the tracts were composed by ministers of Presbyterian, Episcopal, Congregational, and Dutch Reformed churches. The works of Baptists, Methodists, and Catholics were noticeably excluded. Among other objectives, the editor hoped to "form such a collection of discourses, as may amount to a system of Christian faith and practice" and "direct the present prevailing disposition to liberality in matters of religion into a proper channel; and open the door for Christian communion, upon principles ACKNOWLEDGED and UNDERSTOOD." The capital letters highlighted the ever more desperate effort to cut through the abundance of post-revolutionary faiths to a common, widely recognized system of beliefs and practices.[5]

Nineteenth-century religious cooperation was usually something less than the result of explicit collaboration between the churches or the harmonious union of believers that ecumenical dreamers had always imagined. It evolved haphazardly because of the absence of traditional restrictions on officeholding, the increasing prevalence of commercial exchanges, the rise of interfaith marriages, and the sheer extent of American religious diversity. By the early nineteenth century it had become nearly impossible for most groups to separate themselves from those with whom they differed, even if they had wanted to. The only exceptions were those zealous upstarts who were willing to pack up their belongings and carve out a settlement in remote places such as western New York or Utah's Great Basin.

Most never escaped the religious diversity that had become a hallmark of American society during the late eighteenth century. Even those who moved west were usually compelled to work together. In the thinly populated settlements of the frontier, the Presbyterians simply could not afford to set up a common school without the help of their Baptist and Methodist neighbors. The same was true of many of the small denominational colleges that cropped up throughout the United States during the first decades of the nineteenth century. As committed to one faith as their founders may have been, they often depended on the patronage of a diverse range of believers within their area. Moreover, in some states, even privately chartered colleges were forbidden to discriminate on religious grounds. Meanwhile, the integration of publicly supported state colleges, state and federal legislatures, fraternal societies, and large workplaces continued unabated. A Charleston Jew named Isaac Harby reminded Secretary of State James Monroe of this fact in 1816. Chastising Monroe for recalling a Jewish emissary, Harby insisted that it was "upon the principle, not of *toleration* . . . but upon the principle of equal, inalienable, *constitutional rights*, that we see Jews appointed to offices, that we see them mingling in the honours of their country." They were not tolerated; they were not a *"religious sect."* American Jews made up their own *denomination* that was equal and "in every respect, woven in and compacted with the citizens of the republic," united with "Quakers and Catholics, Episcopalians and Presbyterians, [and] Baptists" as "one great political family."[6]

Many of the smaller and more ambitious denominations were eager to establish institutions of their own during the first half of the nineteenth century. But major public institutions and the large universities remained committed to the nonsectarian path that had been worn in the nation's culture decades earlier. Anglican emigrant John Robert Godley remarked that:

> [i]n public schools, in the halls of the legislature, in national institutions, all religions are placed upon an equality; chaplains are selected indiscriminately from each, as the majority of the day may happen to determine (one year, perhaps, a Roman Catholic, and the next a Unitarian); and the smallest preference of one religion to another . . . would not be admitted for a moment.

Another Englishman, James Dixon, marveled how public officials here seemed "united in the common service of their country indiscriminately, irrespective of their creed or religious connexions." The nonsectarian trend was particularly evident in the newly founded state colleges. In 1841, the University of Michigan's regents proudly declared that, while their board consisted of men drawn from most of the major Christian denominations, their religious differences had never caused strife between them. These men were convinced that the nation's churches shared enough in common to make "co-operation" on a college campus possible. The young nation furnished other examples of such educational ecumenism. In an effort to stave off the "fever of fanaticism,"

Thomas Jefferson proposed that the newly established University of Virginia allow each denomination to establish its own professorship on the campus. The former president hoped that "by bringing the sects together, and mixing them with the mass of other students, we shall soften their asperities, liberalize and neutralize their prejudices, and make the general religion a religion of peace, reason and morality." When it came to religious principles, the man whose adult life had been dedicated to expanding the nation's geographical bounds and averting the dense, corrupting complexity of urban life, thought that integration worked best.[7]

As Jefferson had hoped, asperities were softened and prejudices did diminish during the nineteenth century. There was, however, no large-scale turn to the Unitarianism he embraced. For all of the interdenominational gestures, for all of the disdain expressed for sectarianism, the denominations retained their vibrancy, along with their independence, over the succeeding decades. Denominational publishing initiatives expanded with the same vigor as interdenominational initiatives; theological seminaries were built nearby nonsectarian universities. While the "most inventive sectarians in nineteenth-century America all justified their splinter movements as efforts to restore the one true church," R. Laurence Moore observes, no effort to unite America's Christian churches ever succeeded. The nineteenth-century faithful would make do with a somewhat adulterated version of the denominational concept that historians have ascribed to them. It asks too much of any human being to believe that other churches are as close to the truth as is his own. But in the nineteenth century, as in the late eighteenth, Americans would have to act as if this were the case. Public discourse would continue to be shaped by the recognition of religious diversity and the demands of equal recognition.[8]

The New Anti-Catholicism

Some glaring exceptions to the general rule remained. The most obvious example was the virulent anti-Catholicism that raged across the nation from the late 1830s to the mid-1850s. The extended period of religious civility that prevailed from the 1780s to the early 1820s gave way amid a massive influx of Irish and German immigrants. Its symptoms were ubiquitous and ugly, epitomized by routine denunciation of "Popery," the burning of churches, the mass publication of stories depicting lascivious priests and promiscuous nuns, and the formation of interdenominational anti-Catholic societies with far more commitment than the anti-Anglicans of the 1760s. Nativists warned of Jesuit conspiracies to infiltrate the nation's institutions and undermine its democratic foundations. They portrayed Catholic believers as automatons, unthinking servants of Europe's reactionary regimes. The historian Ray Allen Billington noted that some city bookstores actually devoted themselves entirely to the anti-Catholic genre. By the 1830s, public disdain toward "Romanism" had become socially respectable—and financially lucrative.[9]

There are qualifications to be made to these qualifications. On the one hand, antebellum anti-Catholicism lasted too long and drew too many adherents to be dismissed as a mere aberration, as a misstep in a long, uninterrupted march toward the even wider, more universal pluralism of the late twentieth century. On the other hand, it reflected a peculiar social development. Seven hundred thousand new faces appeared on American shores between 1820 and 1840. More than four million arrived between 1840 and 1860. Because these emigrants were predominantly Irish, the American Catholic church expanded from the tiny minority it represented at the time of the Revolution, to the largest single denomination of Christians by the time of the Civil War. That in itself was a lot for native Protestants to digest. But American anti-Catholicism also owed something to the undemocratic structure of the Catholic Church, which subordinated individual judgment to the authority of custom and clergymen.[10]

Consequently, many of the critiques aimed at American Catholics focused either on the fast-growing, and largely impoverished Irish population, which (as many Protestants saw it) clung mindlessly to its intolerant faith, or the papacy and its Jesuit agents, which (as many Protestants saw it) was working to undermine the nation's republican institutions. Yet even those Protestants who might be suspected of the worst kind of bigotry deferred to the popular injunctions against religious prejudices. The chronicler of the xenophobic American Party, for instance, was careful—as were the "Know-Nothings" generally—to note that there was nothing among their stated principles to sustain the charge of "religious intolerance and proscription." Similarly, the author of a widely republished phamphlet, which defended the use of Protestant texts in the public schools, maintained that the current conflict over educational practices was "not between Protestants and their Roman Catholic fellow-citizens," but instead "between Protestant institutions in this country and the genius of Papacy as it prevails at Rome."[11]

The tensions between the new anti-Catholicism and the already revered tradition of religious pluralism were captured in the seminal anti-Catholic tract published by Lyman Beecher in 1835. Beecher's *A Plea for the West* focused on reputed Catholic machinations in the western territories. Only through a concerted effort to expand Protestant education, the renowned evangelical counseled, could the wicked designs of popish despots and Jesuit missionaries be thwarted. Yet even amid this inflated litany of Catholic dangers to republican government, Beecher invoked the still vibrant grammar of late eighteenth-century pluralism. He professed "no fear of the Catholics, considered simply as a religious denomination, and unallied to the church and state establishments of the European governments hostile to republican institutions." (Though he could not help from hinting that theirs was a "system of religious error.") Nor, Beecher insisted, should Catholics be deprived of their just liberties or be publicly ridiculed. Then, in an extraordinary gesture, he noted that Catholics, "as strangers and a minority," should be permitted a "more aggressive language" than the "protestant majority."[12]

It says a great deal about the contours of religious culture in the early republic that Beecher conditioned the most charitable of his remarks toward Catholics on their willingness to integrate. "Let the Catholics mingle with us as Americans," he wrote, "and come with their children under the full action of our common schools and republican institutions, and we are prepared cheerfully to abide the consequences." The integration for which Beecher appealed contained an important caveat. Catholics would have to "regard themselves only as one of many denominations of Christians," looking after their own business, and excluded from any direct role, as a church, in public affairs. It was clear, moreover, that by asking Catholics to mingle among their fellow Americans, Beecher was asking them to, in his own words, "assimilate." He did not bother to mention any fundamentals or essentials that Catholics and Protestants shared. Moreover, Beecher later warned that Catholics were prepared to manipulate "the vital energies" of the nation's open "institutions," suggesting that he might not be as comfortable with their integration as he had otherwise intimated.[13]

Beecher's ambivalence concerning the integration of Catholics into the nation's public life might be attributed to many factors. Not least was the widespread conviction that Catholic prelates could never bring themselves to regard the church as merely one of many denominations. "Catholics are taught to believe," Beecher wrote, "that their church is the only church of Christ." They were also taught, according to Beecher, that heresy must be punished, free inquiry stifled, and wayward governments brought into conformity with popish dictates. Here, the great preacher exaggerated. Yet neither the Church nor the Catholic monarchs who ruled continental Europe had proved especially friendly toward the rights that Anglo Americans cherished. Beecher quoted from Pope Gregory's 1832 encyclical, which referred to liberty of conscience as that "pestilential error," while decrying that "execrated and detested LIBERTY OF THE PRESS." For the nineteenth-century Catholic who strictly observed his faith, complete liberty of conscience and the press were indeed out of the question. So was a pluralistic perspective on religious differences. All of this provided more than sufficient anti-Catholic fodder for those Protestant evangelists, political demagogues, and inveterate nativists whose only shared goal may have been to prevent Catholics from undermining, or just reshaping, the nation's republican institutions.[14]

Concerns about integrating Roman Catholics into the larger polity were rife at midcentury, and were no better revealed than in the widespread and often vociferous debates that surrounded the nascent common schools. Educational reformers regarded these institutions as absolutely vital to individual success and the health of republican government. The thousands of common schools that cropped up during the first half of the nineteenth century were officially nonsectarian: no creeds were explicitly inculcated, no denomination was accorded formal preferences. Influential men such as the liberal reformer Horace Mann and the popular preacher Alexander Campbell maintained that common school students would be taught nothing but the tenets of their allegedly shared Christian faith. Mann insisted that the Massachusetts school board simply sought to let the Bible *"speak for itself."* The unique and divisive doctrines of each denomination were to be excluded, relegated to the home or Sunday school. Protestant advocates of public schooling explained to legislators and Catholic ministers alike that common school students would learn from reputedly nondenominational texts, the nonsectarian religious instruction of their teachers (drawn from different denominations), and the unadorned King James Bible. Again and again, they pointed out how inclusive the system was. In New York, where the common schools generated the best-publicized controversy, trustees of the Public School Society noted that their body consisted of men of many different faiths. The trustees also argued that their nondenominational system allowed future citizens to "mingle," or "amalgamate together," by "interchanging the same kind and benevolent feelings." Catholics already sent their children to religiously integrated colleges. Why, they asked, not send them to integrated public schools too?[15]

Leading Catholics found these Protestant apologies for nonsectarian education less than reassuring. A letter from the church's clergy to the laity condemned the schools' books that "misrepresent our principles . . ., distort our tenets . . ., vilify our practices and . . . bring contempt upon our Church and its members." Similarly, a petition from the Catholics of New York complained that the word "POPERY" could be found peppered throughout the schools' elementary reading assignments. "This term," the petitioners continued, "was one known and employed as one of insult and contempt towards the Catholic religion, and it passes into the minds of children with the feeling of which it is the outward expression." In the common schools,

Catholic history was distorted and Catholic authors neglected. These have since become familiar pleas in the history of American pluralism, and were taken quite seriously by contemporary apologists for the public school system who repeatedly forswore any animosity toward the Church.[16]

Ultimately, the Protestant-Catholic divide over the common schools proved too wide to bridge. Probably no single person did more to maintain it than New York's Roman Catholic bishop (later archbishop), John Hughes. Hughes was born in Ireland where he had experienced the poverty, the discrimination, and the humiliation that so many of his fellow Catholics there endured. His training for the priesthood was interrupted in 1814 because his family was simply too poor to pay for it. Hughes resumed his education after migrating to the United States, which seemed to offer so much to those of every faith. Working his way through college, Hughes went on to join the priesthood. Later he was appointed bishop, then archbishop. Hughes challenged anti-Catholic bigotry with even more vigor than he fought demands for lay authority. His witty polemics delighted those who packed into Carroll Hall or the basement of St. James's Church to hear him. Their shouts of approval and frequent bouts of laughter were loud enough to bring his speeches to a temporary halt. Yet when it came to the pressing question of Catholic rights in this largely Protestant society, Hughes was deadly serious. He understood the intricacies of American culture, and he knew both the weaknesses and the strengths of his Protestant opponents. He knew that they felt obligated by the national commitment to equal religious rights and the imperative to act charitably toward other faiths. He also knew that they liked to trot out terms such as "equality" and "charity" in defense of an ostensibly nonsectarian yet thoroughly Protestant system.[17]

With the steady support of New York's Protestant governor, William H. Seward, Bishop Hughes led the campaign for the public funding of Catholic schools. Hughes insisted that the common schools were both less religious and more sectarian than their proponents admitted, and he openly sought to keep Catholic children out of them. No matter how many changes New York's Public School Society offered to make, Hughes believed, Catholicism would always be slighted in them. What was the scripture they described, "without note or comment?" Was that not the Protestant Bible? Catholics had their own version of scripture, which the Public School Society would never agree to place in the hands of its youngsters. For Hughes, the issue was fundamentally about Catholic dignity. "Have you not seen the young Catholic," he asked, "whose mind has been filled with these calumnies, half ashamed, when he enters the world, of his Catholic name and his Catholic associates, regarding them often as an inferior, worthless set?" Rather than acceding to that prospect, the bishop pressed for a system of separate Catholic education. In cities across the country, bishops, priests, and laypeople followed his lead.[18]

The discussion surrounding the New York public schools anticipated some of the more vociferous controversies of our own multicultural era. In fact, before negotiations broke off, an official committee of Protestants and Catholics proposed a compromise. This resolution would have required the New York Public School Society to attempt to exclude "every work written with a view to prejudice the mind of the reader against the tenets or practices of the Roman Catholic Church, . . . wound the feelings of Roman Catholic children, or . . . diminish their respect for, the religion of their parents." The committee stipulated, in turn, that Catholic educators refrain from making "any derogatory remarks . . . against the creeds of different denominations." Neither side, however, was willing to make concessions on the central issue of public funding. So from 1842 onward, Hughes and his fellow clergymen committed themselves to the separation that many had sought all along: church-supported, parochial education. They also refused to help as the Public School Society eliminated the textbook material (sometimes by simply blotting out passages or pasting pages together) that offended Catholic sensibilities. Meanwhile, the New York legislature wrested power of the educational system from the Public School Society and invested it in the local wards—and forbade "sectarian" teaching in its schools.[19]

Even as immediate hopes for full educational integration faded, the dream persisted. In 1853, the influential and controversial Congregationalist theologian, Horace Bushnell, made a revealing appeal for Catholic participation in the common school system. Bushnell's sermon reflected an understanding of the obstacles that stood in the way of that goal, as well as the preacher's own ecumenical appreciation for the beliefs held by other churches. It invested Lyman Beecher's plan for interreligious mingling with an appeal that was both more pragmatic and more conciliatory. Bushnell began his discourse with the conventional lament about Catholics demanding special privileges and bemoaned Archbishop Hughes's refusal to assist with the textbook-editing process. He also disparaged those who "exclude[d] themselves" from the these institutions as "not Americans." Nonetheless, Bushnell conceded that the common school system was obliged to make "concessions" and "accommodate" itself to the "peculiar principles" of those whose beliefs forbade them from participating in good conscience, including Catholics. "[M]oderation and impartial respect to the rights and feelings of minorities," he maintained, were essential to the success of the system. Only if the Douay Bible was used alongside the King James Bible could Protestants begin to talk about how tolerant their system was. Bushnell stressed the importance of mutual understanding and maintained that more "Christian truth" could be "communicate[d] . . . to a Catholic and a Protestant boy, seated side by side, in the regulation of their treatment of each other" than catechisms or stale biblical exercises could ever supply. Although it is doubtful that the unconventional Bushnell represented a large swath of public opinion, his musings do suggest the degree to which Protestant pleas for Catholics to "mingle" among them were premised on an actual comprehension of the measures required for such a thing to occur.[20]

Comprehension was one thing, actual compromise was another. Despite some notably ecumenical gestures, and the surprisingly high degree of Protestant-Catholic cooperation that characterized the Great School Wars, the full integration of Catholics into the American public school system was postponed indefinitely. So then was the integration of Catholics into American society. Roman Catholic Bishop John England's insistence in his 1826 address before the U.S. Congress that "we [Catholics and Protestants] shall be more bound together in amity, as we become more intimate" may very well have been true. At least the converse held: less "intimacy" did not lead to more "amity." The formation of parochial schools sustained the religious segregation that prospered into the twentieth century. In Bishop Hughes's time, the religious "mingling" that Protestants lauded was the "mixed education" that Catholics feared. Emboldened by their numbers and chastened by a surge of Protestant bigotry, the Catholic leadership rejected the established formula of religious pluralism in the United States. Full integration would simply have required too many unforgivable concessions. Decades passed before either they or the Protestant majority were fully ready to once again treat Catholicism as just one of many denominations.[21]

The Protestant Problem

Catholics were not alone in challenging the notion of a common (and largely Protestant) Christianity and capitalizing on its divisions. The Church of Jesus Christ of Latter-Day Saints (LDS), better known as the Mormon Church, could be neither fully accommodated nor fully ignored in antebellum America. Mormonism's appeal lay partly in its unique capacity to cut through the tangle of the nation's religious heterogeneity. Today most consider the nearly endless array of religious alternatives in the United States to be a great blessing. But earnest nineteenth-century Protestants faced a potential existential crisis as they contemplated all of them. What made any of these denominations better than the others? What assurance did the individual believer have that he had joined a true church? Who, if anyone, had the authority to judge between them? Those increasingly beloved histories of all religions that Hannah Adams helped to popularize only aggravated the problem. The need to locate acceptable answers was especially pressing in places like New York's Burned-Over District along the Erie Canal, where a powerful series of religious revivals had generated a seemingly endless variety of faiths. There, amid a "war of words and tumult of opinions," a young farmer named Joseph Smith asked himself with painful clarity: "What is to be done? Who of all these parties are right; or, are they all wrong together? If any one of them shall be right, which is it, and how shall I know it." In an astonishing development, Christ himself explained to Smith that the sects were "all wrong" and that he should "join none of them."[22]

Various contemporary movements—collectively known as Christian Primitivism—issued the same injunction, urging Protestants to give up their creeds, cast off their ministers, and return to the uncorrupted Bible. These arguments against "creedalism" or sectarianism must have exerted some influence on Smith's thought. If so, they provided him no assurance. Spiritual relief only came to Smith after he was visited by the angel Moroni, who directed him to dig up several scriptural tablets. Afterward, he kept to Christ's command and abjured the existing churches by forming one of his own. The certainty that came to Smith through the revelations he received and the strict discipline he developed comforted many other souls as well. First dozens, then hundreds, and eventually thousands joined his movement.[23]

The intensity of opposition outside the movement matched the intensity of support within. From the beginning, Smith's translation of the Book of Mormon was vilified by critics. Its publication in 1830 met with boycotts and repeated denunciations. One editor stated that Smith's book "was almost invariably treated as it should have been—with contempt." The abuse did not end there. Over the coming years, Mormon believers were tarred, feathered, and beaten; their houses were looted and their temples burned. Mobs harassed them nearly everywhere they went. The entire church was expelled from Missouri. In 1844, Joseph Smith and his brother were murdered while they sat in an Illinois jail. How, given the nation's purported commitment to religious pluralism, do we explain such intolerance? How do we account for the Missouri governor's order to "exterminate" the group, or for the seventeen Mormons who were shot, stabbed, and hacked to death by his state's militia?[24]

It might seem impossible to square the argument that America had developed a pluralistic culture with the sufferings of the Mormons. Yet there is evidence to suggest that the LDS constitutes something other than a glaring exception to the larger tradition. The literary historian Terry L. Givens, for example, has argued that it proved difficult for nineteenth-century critics to disparage Mormonism on exclusively religious grounds. Keeping with the traditions established during the previous century, LDS opponents felt compelled to portray their hostility in moral, political, and even ethnic terms. And, as it turned out, the sometimes-violent harassment of Mormons could be justified in ways that permitted Americans to uphold their self-image as a religiously tolerant people. Mainstream commentators displayed plenty of contempt for Joseph Smith's newly unearthed scripture and surely many of their attacks were inspired by their own faith. Yet some of the harshest criticism and the most scurrilous ridicule was reserved for the Mormons' anomalous social behavior. By turning over their property to the church, embracing polygamy, recruiting their own militias, and voting en bloc, Mormons provided ammunition for critics. For these reasons and more, Americans could avoid framing their resentment as a criticism of someone else's faith.[25]

There was another important factor at work here: Joseph Smith and his followers believed that they were right and other Christians wrong. Worse, they said so publicly. Like Catholics, Mormons operated with the formal assumption that theirs was the one, true, and universal church. They would not grant their Protestant counterparts the essentials, the "common core of Christianity," which had sustained America's religious pluralism since the end of the colonial era. For nearly a century, Americans had reconciled their religious differences by pretending that those differences were either illusory or inconsequential. In exchange for a rough harmony between the denominations, they had maintained a considerable degree of public insincerity. Contemporary norms confined expressions of certainty to private life—to Sunday school programs, church services, and the home. But the collective assurance of the Mormons and the Catholics, the rocklike conviction that came with either a new dispensation or a conciliar decree, gave them a reason to reject this resolution, and to live independently of their Protestant neighbors. It also gave their Protestant neighbors a reason to exclude and persecute them. Both Mormons and Catholics could say with great confidence that their own faiths were correct. With equal confidence, their Protestant counterparts could insist that anyone who thought so highly of their own customs did not deserve the charity reserved for the publicly circumspect. Separationist inclinations among both Mormons and Catholics abetted popular prejudices against those whose practices were shrouded in secrecy, whose decisions descended down through an earthly hierarchy, or whose tenets emanated from a recent revelation.[26]

In this regard, Bishop Hughes's experiences are once again instructive. Hughes agreed with the self-proclaimed advocates of "nonsectarian" schooling in the sense that he thought "that men should know the rights of conscience of others, and . . . they should learn to respect them." But that was not what was happening in New York City's public schools. Instead, the principle of unbridled liberty of conscience was taught and Roman Catholicism was mocked. To Hughes's critique, a Dutch Reformed minister replied: "Sir, my children are exposed, by mingling with the community, to things which are adverse to their feelings." Their church might be indirectly criticized and their ministers ridiculed, but their attachment to the Dutch Reformed Church did not wane. "They at once say, Those persons don't think as I do; they don't feel as I do. . . . We think we are right and they are wrong, and we let it pass." To weather the religious diversity of the public schools, this Protestant minister suggested, a believer simply needed thick skin and unflappable convictions. Hughes begged to differ. For him, "let[ting] it pass" was not an option. As the bishop saw it, the nonchalance of Protestant Americans, which allowed theological error to go unchallenged, was the first step toward religious indifference in general, and anti-Catholicism in particular.[27]

In November of 1850, as Protestant-Catholic relations approached another low point, Bishop Hughes gave a speech in New York's St. Patrick's Cathedral that Bishop Carroll never would have made in his day. Hughes's infamous discourse, titled *The Decline of Protestantism and Its Causes*, made no pretensions to either civility or charity. Amid a host of inflammatory comments, Hughes affirmed that anti-Catholic allegations of a popish plot to convert the western territories were true. "Everybody should know it," he exclaimed. "Everyone should know that we have for our mission to convert the world, including the inhabitants of the United States, the people of the cities, and the people of the country, the officers of the navy and the marines, commanders of the army, the Legislatures, the Senate, the Cabinet, the President, and all!" By Hughes's accounting, Protestant faith was in deep trouble. Born as a movement on behalf of private judgment and against authority, it could not persuade and it could not bind. It could only divide, and then divide again. There was no stopping the descent into Protestant fanaticism, Hughes suggested. Just look at its latest manifestations: the campaign for woman's rights and "Joe Smith and the Mormons."[28]

As might be expected, Hughes comments sent Protestant activists into a frenzy. The Protestant authors of an article in New York City's *Journal of Commerce* insisted that Hughes was welcome to try to convert the United States to Catholicism. But since America had "opened" itself "to the efforts of Romanism," they asked, should not Catholic Europe extend the same equal treatment to Protestants? Hughes incendiary tract and the resulting controversy suggests that the process that brought religious pluralism to

America—the embrace of individual rights, religious integration, and charitable language—could be reversed. Between the 1830s and the 1850s, many
Protestants and Catholics convinced one another that they shared few, if any,
fundamental beliefs. The failure to locate common ground on principles such
as the right of private judgment or the proper authority of scripture made it
difficult to sustain the religious integration to which Protestants had become
accustomed. The resulting separation, in turn, removed the informal sanc-
tions that had long regulated hostile religious dispute. According to the prominent publicist and Catholic convert, Orestes Brownson, anti-Catholicism,
rather than hostility toward Irish immigrants, accounted for the rise of nativist
sentiments. The source of the problem, he wrote in 1845, was that Catholicism encouraged its believers to congregate close together, around the parish
church, where they could readily partake of its rich sacramental life. Those
peculiar tendencies marked them as "a separate people, incapable even in
their political and social duties of fraternizing . . . with their Protestant fellow-
citizens." If the Irish were Protestants, Brownson speculated, the situation
would be different. That is, "if they could mingle with the native population
and lose themselves in our Protestant Churches," he wrote, "very little opposition would be manifested to their immigration or to their naturalization."
Brownson was no advocate of indiscriminate mixing when he penned these
passages, but he certainly recognized the importance of religious "mingling"
to the United States.[29]

This latest Protestant confrontation with Catholicism highlighted the
delicate balancing act that had been required to justify religious inclusion over
the last several decades. From the mid-eighteenth century onward, the nation's pluralistic approach to religious differences had been buttressed by a
widely shared and comfortably vague reliance on Christian scripture. The very
antiquity of those revelations and the variety of meanings attached to them
justified charitable rhetoric and cooperative endeavors between the different
Protestant denominations. Retiring as head of Massachusetts' board of education in 1848, Horace Mann held up the (King James) Bible as the only
suitable text for the common schools. When used in class, without any accompanying sectarian interpretation, the Bible enabled students of many
different Christian denominations to learn together. Daily scripture reading,
Mann contended, had made Massachusetts' schools Christian without making them sectarian. Likewise, the counsel for New York's Public School Society confidently maintained that, when it came to "moral teaching," "the
Bible contains that in which all sects can agree—from which no sect can
dissent." Catholic critiques of the common school system challenged such
platitudes, prompting one Protestant speaker to ask: "[I]s there no common

principle in which all agree? Is there not a principle to which all religious men refer?" Catholic and Mormon leaders answered in the negative. And Catholic bishops pointed out the absurdity of maintaining that "all religions are alike, as if contradictory propositions could be at the same time true."[30]

Indirectly, at least, some Protestants were also beginning to acknowledge that the Bible could no longer constitute a universal reference point. In his popular account of religion in America, for example, the Presbyterian minister Robert Baird drew a sharp distinction between the nation's (right-thinking) "evangelical" faiths and its "unevangelical" religions. By Baird's reckoning, Presbyterians, Congregationalists, Methodists, Baptists, Moravians, Lutherans, Dutch Reformed, even Quakers and Episcopalians, could be defined as evangelicals for whom the Bible was the basis of all spiritual knowledge and worship. By contrast, Catholics, Mormons, Unitarians, Universalists, Jews, atheists, Socialists, and Fourierists employed some other, clearly inferior, foundations. That did not mean that all of the unevanglicals were equally wrongheaded. But even if they were better than alien subversives, Jews, Catholics, and serious Unitarians did not rank among the "churches whose religion is the Bible, the whole Bible, and nothing but the Bible." There were, in Baird's voluminous work, strong hints that the injunctions of religious pluralism still prevailed. For instance, Baird seems to have been more intent upon counting the numbers of Catholics in the United States than in condemning their doctrines. In addition, he expressed approval of the substantial "intermingl[ing]" that went on between different groups of evangelicals (who were divided only by "non-essential points") across the nation. And he commended the ecumenical character of organizations such as the American Sunday School Union, which published "nothing repugnant to the doctrines of any of the evangelical denominations." He just could not imagine "unevangelical" Catholics, Unitarians, Jews, or Mormons joining them in the same religiously mixed classrooms.[31]

Baird's work illuminates the gap that was beginning to open up between Protestant Biblicism and religious pluralism. If an unreserved endorsement (and literal reading) of the entire King James Bible were required for full recognition and interdenominational mingling, then a lot of nineteenth-century believers were going to be marginalized. The explosive growth in the Catholic population made it difficult for Protestants to promote their vague, religious essentialism—a primary instrument of tolerance during the latter half of the eighteenth century—as a form of inclusion in the 1840s and 1850s. Their continued effort to do so is a testament both to the persistent demands for religious pluralism and the persistent (Protestant) contempt for Roman Catholicism.[32]

When it came to antebellum Catholics and Mormons, the Protestant formula of equal rights for private judgment and social integration largely failed. State and national governments provided the religious liberties that allowed highly committed and distinctive groups to avoid integration. Anonymous living in the increasingly populous cities and the vast expanses of cheap land outside them also helped to make it possible. The hegemony of Protestantism made it attractive. Mainstream Protestants had extended the canopy of ecumenism so broadly that they may have had a hard time understanding why anyone would refuse to take refuge beneath it. What reason could be given for such recalcitrance? When the answer was excessively complex or sufficiently unappealing, Protestants blamed Catholic missionaries and secret Mormon rituals; they blamed the pope and they blamed Joseph Smith. Whenever possible, they refrained from blaming anyone's particular beliefs, just as they refrained from blaming their own.

Religion and American Pluralism

No one should be misled by this study into thinking that the tradition of religious pluralism was an exclusively American phenomenon. In many ways, eighteenth-century American culture was derivative, the offspring of mainly British ideals and British standards of conduct. The oft-cited appeals for toleration made by liberal Englishmen, such as the philosopher John Locke, were all written before 1730. In fact, many solutions posed to the problem of religious difference in eighteenth-century America—the most important of these being the distinction between the essentials and nonessentials of belief— had already been a part of northern European vocabularies for several generations. Toleration was often imposed, or at least encouraged, by London. Much of America's religious diversity was English in origin and so were some of the greatest advocates of ecumenism in the colonies. Unconventional European movements—from John Wesley's Methodists to Ann Lee's Shakers— added to America's religious diversity and challenged prevailing standards of tolerance.

The religious civility evident in late eighteenth-century America also had European parallels. The French philosophe Voltaire said of England what so many Europeans on both sides of the channel said of England's colonies: "This is the land of sects. An Englishman, as a free man, goes to Heaven by whatever route he likes." By itself, one sect might rule tyrannically. Two might ignite a civil war. Luckily, Voltaire wrote, "there are thirty, and they live in peace and happiness." Voltaire lavished special praise on London's Royal

Exchange, where the "Jew, Mohammedan and Christian deal with each other as though they were all of the same faith, and only apply the word infidel to people who go bankrupt." In places such as London, the center of international commercial activity, religious considerations must often have been subordinated to the profits that could be made from tolerance. Social refinement and well-mannered civility were hallmarks of eighteenth-century British culture and central to the way that genteel Europeans defined themselves. So, to some extent, was interdenominational cooperation. In fact, Horace Bushnell's 1853 sermon on the common schools drew upon Dutch and Irish examples of Protestant-Catholic collaboration in the public school system.[33]

To a European, in fact, early Americans could seem entirely *un*civil. Compared to their European counterparts, early Americans were indeed rude and unpolished. Few had received college educations. Most lived in small villages with few cultural amenities outside of their numerous churches. Even their cities were tiny by European standards. Foreign observers would delight in pointing out their barbarous lack of manners. Some still delight in it today. What then made developments in America distinctive? First, the religious civility that developed here emerged amid rapidly expanding guarantees for toleration and religious liberty. Second, it emerged in a society characterized by a high degree of mobility where many parish boundaries proved permeable, ecclesiastical courts were never commissioned, and both state and church authorities were usually distant and very often divided. Third, American religious civility emerged in a culture steeped in the writing of the Protestant Reformation and the early Enlightenment, among a people who would be known at home and abroad for both their knee-jerk egalitarianism and their "liberality," for their uninhibited speech and their open political institutions. Finally, it emerged in an era that saw the ascendance of representative government and the rise of majoritarian ideals.[34]

And whereas their European counterparts continued to treat dissent as a form of political subversion well into the eighteenth century, Americans radically extended the boundaries of religious inclusion. It was one thing to tolerate the dissent of a few respectable minorities. It was another thing to insist, as Americans did by the end of the century, upon equal recognition for many different faiths. Confronted by the sometimes unwelcome fact of religious diversity, as well as the genteel admonitions of contemporary Europeans, eighteenth-century Americans were compelled to learn the habits that a religiously diverse republic requires. Americans were hardly exceptional in their embrace of politeness. But in the extent to which they joined religious rights and religious civility, equal legal treatment and equal public recognition, they certainly were distinctive.[35]

Over time, Americans—as well as foreign observers—would come to associate religious pluralism with the United States itself. Ironically, a toll may have been paid in actual religious diversity, because those who wished to succeed and exercise power would have to consider themselves and their neighbors as members of "the sole Denomination of *Americans.*" The nonsectarian God that pious politicians and patriotic clergyman never ceased to invoke, the deity who ruled the universe and blessed the United States of America, expected nothing less of them. Nevertheless, because Americans have generally proved so ready to conceive of themselves as both ecumenical servants of the republic *and* devotees of particular churches, they have been able to make religious pluralism central to their national identity. It was not simply the "almost endless variety of religious factions" in the United States that annoyed the English-born Frances Trollope in the early 1830s, but the fact that "to be well received in society, it was necessary to declare yourself as belonging to . . . a particular congregation." The Anglican opponents of William Livingston in the early 1750s, who contended that he would turn King's College into something that was "neither Christian nor Infidel, neither Popish nor Protestant, Episcopalian nor Presbyterian, *English* nor *Dutch*, Independent nor Quaker, Old-Light nor New-Light, *nor yet Moravian*," who suggested that he wished it *"to be both, all, and none of at the same time,"* said more than they knew. When it comes to religious matters, Americans have long possessed the capacity to transform their governments, voluntary societies, and schools into institutions that claim to be "both, all, and none of these at the same time." John Carroll understood the practical value of tying one's religious identity to one's American identity and giving both precedence above all others. Facing ethnic divisions within his Boston parish in the years after the Revolutionary War, he urged his fellow American Catholics to "lay aside national distinctions & attachments, & strive to form not Irish, or English, or French Congregations & Churches, but Catholic-American Congregations and Churches."[36]

There is a striking correspondence here to the argument advanced by the political philosopher Michael Walzer in an essay on American ethnic identities. Invoking Henry St. John Crèvecoeur's famous 1782 question, by asking, "What is it to be an American?" Walzer pointed out the inclusive nature of American identity. America, he wrote, "is not a jealous nation." According to Walzer, "[w]e have made our peace with the 'particular characteristics' of all the immigrant groups (though not . . . of all the racial groups) and have come to regard American nationality as an addition rather than a replacement for ethnic consciousness." Walzer's insight was brilliant and aptly describes American thought and culture from the late nineteenth century onward. But as late as the mid-nineteenth century, it was religious identity, rather than ethnic identity, that served as a complement to American nationality. The assimilation that mid-nineteenth-century reformers demanded was almost always cultural or political, and rarely religious. Instead, Catholics were called upon to "mingle" with their fellow Protestants as fellow Americans and to demonstrate their commitment to democratic institutions, civil rights, and a respectable Christian morality. Liberal Catholics and Protestants alike emphasized the political principles they shared with one another (as well as the principles that immigrants should be taught to share), just as they demanded equal recognition for particular churches and particular religious beliefs. When it came to national identity, religious doctrines were considered the lesser points, the circumstantials, the peculiarities, that distinguished people who shared the same fundamental political principles.[37]

Over the course of American history, racial and ethnic identities often did supplant the religious identities that had been so central to early white Americans. Yet as that happened, many of the same patterns emerged. A common template appeared again and again in the public interaction among different groups. In almost every case, the codification of equal rights was followed by social integration and the extension of public recognition. The civil rights movement of the last half century is the best and most prominent example. Building on the suppressed implications of the Fourteenth Amendment, African Americans acquired possession of the legal equality so long denied them. The trend accelerated from the mid-1950s onward as judicial mandates, executive orders, and congressional legislation broke the back of segregation. Once segregation had been outlawed, once formal legal rights had been given force, the painful ordeal of racial integration took place. By the mid-1970s, America's public institutions—its media, military and educational systems, its clubs, charities, and professional organizations—began to resemble the nation's demographic makeup. Like the earlier campaigns for equality in America, this one was premised on more than the achievement of civil rights, or even economic justice. As the judicial majority put it in the decision of *Brown v. Board of Education*, separation on the basis of "race generates a feeling of inferiority" that might never be overcome. Equal recognition was again—as it had been for late eighteenth- and early nineteenth-century commentators on religious differences—at the heart of the matter.[38]

Since the 1950s, we have seen a shift in public language regarding race that was matched only once in American history—by the shift in public language regarding religion that occurred during the eighteenth century. We can be as thankful that terms such as "colored" and "negro" have mostly disappeared from our vocabularies as late eighteenth-century liberals and evangelicals were that terms such as "sectaries" and "heretics" had mostly disappeared from theirs. We decry the racial bigot, just as they decried the religious bigot. In both cases, the principle that weighs against exclusivist and implicitly hierarchical language is equal recognition. In both cases, integration helps to ensure that uncharitable language is confined to private life. The demand for public understanding, subjective assertions of identity, and a heightened sensitivity to prejudice did not originate with ethnic minorities in the 1960s. The tradition of cultural egalitarianism that underlies what we now call "political correctness" has a long, distinguished history in America. No apology will be made for its excesses, yet it might do us some good to pay attention to its surprising lineage.

If the peculiarities of worship were treated with a high degree of multicultural sensitivity by the late eighteenth century, political differences were another matter. The post-revolutionary editor of the *Maryland Journal and Baltimore Advertiser* may have summed up the distinction best when he explained why he had rejected a submission during the heated church establishment debate there. After affirming his commitment to publishing any piece intended for "rectifying the Public Opinion," alerting the community to impending dangers, or criticizing corrupt government officials, the editor noted two exceptions to his open press policy. His paper would reject all pieces that would "create Diffidence between Man and Man, in *private Life*, or ridicule and revile the religious Profession of any Set of Men." He treated political criticism and religious criticism as two distinguishable categories of public discussion. The former was acceptable; the latter was not. Obviously this editor had no qualms about heated debates on the church establishment— after all, that's how he sold newspapers—as long as no aspersions were cast upon particular groups and their particular doctrines. The same protections were not extended to political doctrines or political groups.[39]

By the late eighteenth century, American political discussion took place within the increasingly unrestrained and often harsh field of open discussion that the philosopher Jürgen Habermas has described as a critical "public sphere." Religious discussion, by contrast, took place in what might be called a *non*critical public sphere. Several decades passed following the ratification of the Constitution before political parties had become as palatable as religious denominations. An aversion to factionalism ran deep in Anglo American thought. Like their English counterparts, early Americans had a difficult time conceiving of their opponents as legitimate contenders for power. In addition, while increasing deference was shown toward religious beliefs, political opinions remained vulnerable to accusations of deceit or subversion. Into the nineteenth century, they were still subject to the laws of libel and sedition. Early national opponents of Federalist policies, for instance, were forced to invoke the principle of Federalism—rather than just a natural right of political dissent—in defense of their right to criticize. Liberty of conscience was still an insufficient justification for political dissent. And when the Democratic-Republican and Federalist parties began to take shape during the 1790s, they did so without the blessing of the supremely popular George Washington and against the inclinations of many other important figures. Not until the early 1840s, in fact, did sustained party competition become a fully legitimate part of American culture. Even today in the United States it is usually more acceptable to denounce a neighbor's politics than her religion.[40]

If political opinions received different treatment than religious opinions at the turn of the nineteenth century, those who wrote about political disagreement would have been hard pressed to ignore the lessons learned during a century of religious disagreement. In his first inaugural address (1801), Thomas Jefferson made his famously generous declaration that "every difference of opinion is not a difference of principle. We have called by different names brethren of the same principle." The president proclaimed that Americans should not "countenance a political intolerance as despotic, as wicked, and capable of as bitter and bloody persecutions" as the "religious intolerance" they had already "banished." Jefferson's invocation of a common republican principle thus recast the potentially explosive problem of political criticism into the benign matter of differentially applying the same essential convictions. He made all Federalists into Republicans, while hinting that all Republicans might be Federalists. Furthermore, he suggested that "the essential principles of our Government" might serve as "the creed of our political faith," the measure by which all particular decisions could be tried. Whether Jefferson intended it or not, he had articulated the basic conditions of American party politics: agreement on certain fundamental principles and faith in the constitutional creed that embodied them.[41]

For the man who later claimed that he wanted to be remembered, above all else, for Virginia's Statute for Religious Freedom, the lessons learned in religious matters were readily transferable to politics. In this, Jefferson was like Benjamin Franklin, George Washington, and much of the late eighteenth-century writing public. Indeed, it was in the realm of things spiritual that Americans had learned to value fundamentals above particulars, to change affiliations without condemning the affiliations of others, to speak loudly but censure mildly. Perhaps we should not be surprised that the fundamentals of American politics—the commitment to representative government and certain essential rights—would be more rigidly circumscribed and that political opinions would always be subject to greater criticism. As everyone in the eighteenth century knew, political disagreements would need to be resolved in this world.

Notes

1. Carroll to Charles Plowden, 11 June 1791, *The John Carroll Papers*, ed. Thomas O'Brien Hanley, 2 vols. (Notre Dame, Ind.: University of Notre Dame Press, 1976), 1:505. The experience was not unfamiliar to Carroll. Returning to Baltimore following his consecration, the local newspaper reported that Carroll had been greeted "respectfully . . . by a number of his fellow citizens of various denominations who conducted him to his residence." See *Maryland Journal and Baltimore Advertiser*, 10 December 1790, quoted in Annabelle M. Melville, *John Carroll of Baltimore: Founder of the American Catholic Hierarchy* (New York: Charles Scribner's Sons, 1955), 122. I would like to thank Ray Gadke, Simon Johnson, Paul Lakeland, Tricia T. Pyne, and Kevin Schmiesing for their generous responses to my H-CATHOLIC query regarding what Bishop Carroll might have been wearing at the time. As some of these respondents noted, Carroll would probably have been dressed much like his gentlemen contemporaries as he walked the streets of Boston. The distinctive roman collar and clerical suit were not required for Roman Catholic clergymen in the United States until after the Civil War. Dr. Pyne, who was especially helpful, discovered the following guidelines in the proceedings of the first diocesan synod in 1791, in a section titled "Concerning the Protection of the Morals of the Clergy:" It reads: "All the Clerics in this diocese, according to the decrees of various canons and especially of the council of Trent, *should dress in a manner befitting their state of life.* Let their dress not only be modest, but such as reminds themselves and others of their profession in life. Consequently, we decree that clerics should always wear black clothes, or as close to black as possible" (*John Carroll Papers*, 1: 533).

2. Just as remarkably, the day's events concluded with a banquet at which "a separate table," covered only by kosher foods, was prepared. See Naphtali Phillips, "The Federal Parade of 1788," *American Jewish Archives* 7 (January 1955): 65. An excellent overview of the event appears in Morton Borden, *Jews, Turks and Infidels* (Chapel Hill: University of North Carolina Press, 1984), 4–5.

3. See *Pennsylvania Packet, and Daily Advertiser,* 10 July 1788.

4. [Benjamin Rush],"Observations on the Federal Procession on the Fourth of July, 1788, in the City of Philadelphia; in a Letter from a Gentleman in this City to his Friend in a Neighbouring State," *The American Museum, or Universal Advertiser* 4 (July 1788), 77.

5. For accounts of church-state relations in early America, especially during the late eighteenth and early nineteenth centuries, see Thomas E. Buckley, *Church and State in Revolutionary Virginia, 1776–1787* (Charlottesville: University Press of Virginia, 1977); Thomas J. Curry, *The First Freedoms: Church and State in America to the Passage of the First Amendment* (New York: Oxford University Press, 1986); Derek H. Davis, *Religion and the Continental Congress, 1774–1789: Contributions to Original Intent* (New York: Oxford University Press, 2000); Daniel L. Dreisbach, *Thomas Jefferson and the Wall of Separation between Church and* State (New York: New York University Press, 2002); J. William Frost, *A Perfect Freedom: Religious Liberty in Pennsylvania* (University Park: University of Pennsylvania Press, 1993); Philip A. Hamburger, *Separation of Church and State* (Cambridge, Mass.: Harvard University Press, 2002); Isaac Kramnick and R. Laurence Moore, *The Godless Constitution: The Case against Religious Correctness* (New York: W. W. Norton, 1996); Leonard W. Levy, *The Establishment Clause: Religion and the First* Amendment, 2nd rev. ed. (Chapel Hill: University of North Carolina Press, 1994); Michael W. McConnell, "The Origins and Historical Understanding of Free Exercise of Religion," *Harvard Law Review* 103 (May 1990): 1409–1517; Mark D. McGarvie, *One Nation Under Law: America's Early National Struggles to Separate Church and State* (DeKalb, Ill.: Northern Illinois University Press, 2004); and William G. McLoughlin, *New England Dissent, 1630–1833: The Baptists and the Separation of Church and State,* 2 vols. (Cambridge, Mass.: Harvard University Press, 1971). For an extensive and still vital work that covers all of American history, see Anson Phelps Stokes, *Church and State in the United States,* 3 vols. (New York: Harper & Row, 1950). A dated work that still provides some useful information is Sanford H. Cobb, *The Rise of Religious Liberty in America: A History* (New York: Macmillan, 1902).

6. Here I make a fairly conventional distinction between toleration and pluralism. "Toleration" is generally taken to mean both "the act . . . of tolerating, esp. of what is not actually approved; forbearance" and "allowance, by a government, of the exercise of religions other than the religion officially established or recognized; recognition of the right of private judgment in matters of faith and worship." By contrast, "pluralism" usually implies either the social fact of religious diversity, or peaceful coexistence and expressions of mutual respect. This book will rely upon the latter definition of pluralism, which is discussed in more detail later in this chapter.

NOTES TO PAGES 7–9   229

The definition of toleration appears in *Webster's Unabridged Dictionary of the English Language* (New York: Portland House, 1989), 1491.

7. To this point, three scholarly books on the Middle Colonies of New Jersey, New York, and Pennsylvania have explicitly addressed the subject of colonial religious diversity in colonial America. They are: Douglas Jacobsen, *An Unprov'd Experiment* (Brooklyn, N.Y.: Carlson, 1991); Richard W. Pointer, *Protestant Pluralism and the New York Experience: A Study of Eighteenth-Century Religious Diversity* (Bloomington: Indiana University Press, 1988); and Sally Schwartz, *"A Mixed Multitude": The Struggle for Toleration in Colonial Pennsylvania* (New York: New York University Press, 1988). I have benefited from the research presented in each, especially that of Pointer and Schwartz.

8. Richard J. Hooker, ed., *The Carolina Backcountry on the Eve of the American Revolution: The Journal and Other Writings of Charles Woodmason, Anglican Itinerant* (Chapel Hill: University of North Carolina Press, 1953), 73–74. Church statistics cited in Clinton Rossiter, *Seedtime of the Republic: The Origin of the American Tradition of Political Liberty* (New York: Harcourt Brace, 1953), 38.

9. The historian Jon Butler estimates that in relatively homogenous New England three-quarters of all congregations were Congregationalist in the 1770s (this proportion total would have been higher in the past). In the Middle Colonies, by contrast, there had long been an impressive amount of religious diversity. The largest group in that region, the Presbyterians, made up only one-fifth of the total number of congregations, with German-speaking congregations making up one-third of the Middle Colony total. In the South, where Baptist and Presbyterian preachers made significant inroads during the second half of the century, only about one-third of all congregations were Anglican by the time of the Revolution. See Jon Butler, *Becoming America: The Revolution before 1776* (Cambridge, Mass.: Harvard University Press, 2000), 191–92. On the significance of intradenominational divisions, see Rossiter, ibid. On the nineteenth-century divisions among Baptists and Methodists, see William M. Newman and Peter L. Halvorson, *Atlas of American Religion: The Denominational Era, 1776–1990* (Walnut Creek, Calif.: Alta Mira: 2000), table 2.1, 39.

10. On church membership rates, see Roger Finke and Rodney Stark, *The Churching of America: Winners and Losers in our Religious Economy* (New Brunswick, N.J.: Rutgers University Press, 1992), 24–30. Finke and Stark's work should be read in conjunction with Patricia U. Bonomi and Peter R. Eisenstadt, "Church Adherence in the Eighteenth-Century British American Colonies," *William and Mary Quarterly*, 3rd series, 39 (April 1982): 245–86, which focuses on regular church attendance. On the preference for religious works among southern readers, see Richard Beale Davis, *A Colonial Southern Bookshelf: Reading in the Eighteenth Century* (Athens: University of Georgia Press, 1979), 24, 88–89. For the continuing vitality of religious publication in Connecticut during the eighteenth century, see Christopher Grasso, *A Speaking Aristocracy: Transforming Public Discourse in Eighteenth Century Connecticut* (Chapel Hill: University of North Carolina Press, 1999), appendix: figures 21 and 22. Thomas Tanselle observes that the proportion of

theological titles produced by American presses fell from roughly 35 percent in the period between 1730 and 1750, to roughly 19 percent between 1779 and 1785. Books on politics and history showed a marked rise during this same period. Yet religious titles still formed a decisive plurality of all works published in America as late as the mid-1780s. See Tanselle, "Some Statistics on American Printing, 1764–1783," in *The Press and the American Revolution*, ed. Bernard Bailyn and John B. Hench (Boston: Northeastern University Press, 1981), 327–28, especially table 2A. Tanselle's statistics mainly relate to the number of entries listed in Charles Evans's *American Bibliography: A Chronological Dictionary of All Books, Pamphlets, and Periodical Publications Printed in the United States of America from . . . 1639 down to and Including the Year 1820*, 14 vols. (New York: P. Smith, 1941–1959). These entries include pamphlets, books, broadsides, and almanacs. Newspapers, which often featured more secular material, are not included. Therefore, the proportion of religious reading that eighteenth-century Americans did would almost certainly have to be revised downward from the figures mentioned above. Nonetheless, the predominance of both religious publishing and reading seems incontestable.

11. Charles Taylor, *Philosophical Arguments* (Cambridge, Mass.: Harvard University Press, 1995), 232, 256. For a subtle and relevant distinction between what he calls the "conscience paradigm" and the "equality paradigm" in liberal thought, see Andrew R. Murphy's *Conscience and Community: Revisiting Toleration and Religious Dissent in Early Modern England and America* (University Park: Pennsylvania State University Press, 2001), esp. 278, 293.

12. For examples of Christian missionaries who developed affection and respect for Indian souls, but not their traditional religious faiths, see Gerald R. McDermott, "Jonathan Edwards and American Indians: The Devil Sucks Their Blood," *New England Quarterly* 72 (December 1999): esp. 551; and Richard W. Pointer, " 'Poor Indians' and the 'Poor in spirit': The Indian Impact on David Brainerd," *New England Quarterly* 67 (September 1994), esp. 422. For an insightful overview of Indian-European interaction during the colonial period, see James H. Merrell, " 'The Customes of Our Countrey': Indians and Colonists in Early America," in *Strangers Within the Realm: Cultural Margins of the First British Empire*, ed. Bernard Bailyn and Philip D. Morgan (Chapel Hill: University of North Carolina Press, 1991), 117–56. As far as I know, only the inimitable Roger Williams took issue with the exclusive application of the term "heathen" to Native Americans (as opposed to all those not yet truly converted). See his remarkable tract "Christenings Make Not Christians" (1645), in *The Complete Writings of Roger* Williams, ed. Perry Miller, 7 vols. (New York: Russell and Russell, 1963): 7:29–41. On the European association between Native American faiths and satanic activity, see David S. Lovejoy, "Satanizing the American Indian," *New England Quarterly* 67 (December 1994): 603–21. On the African "spiritual holocaust," see Jon Butler, *Awash in a Sea of Faith: Christianizing the American People* (Cambridge, Mass.: Harvard University Press, 1990), 153; also Eugene Genovese, *Roll Jordan Roll: The World the Slaves Made* (New York: Vintage, 1976), 184.

13. Hugh Jones, "Of the State of the Church and Clergy of Virginia" (1724) in G. MacLaren Brydon, *Virginia's Mother Church and the Political Conditions under*

Which It Grew, 2 vols. (Richmond, Va.: Virginia Historical Society, 1947–1952), 1:400. Robert Olwell estimates that between three and five percent of African slaves were baptized in South Carolina. See Olwell, *Masters, Slaves, and Subjects: The Culture of Power in the South Carolina Low Country, 1740–1790* (Ithaca, N.Y.: Cornell University Press, 1998), 118. The classic history of African American religious experiences in the eighteenth century can be found in Albert J. Raboteau, *Slave Religion: The "Invisible Institution" in the Antebellum South* (Oxford: Oxford University Press, 1978), 96–150; for a more recent account of African American Protestantism, see Sylvia R. Frey and Betty Wood, *Come Shouting to Zion: African American Protestantism in the American South and British Caribbean to 1830* (Chapel Hill: University of North Carolina Press, 1998). On the paucity of eighteenth-century discussion regarding African American beliefs and practices (not to mention their religious rights), see Butler, *Awash in a Sea of Faith*, 154–56; and Gerald R. McDermott, *Jonathan Edwards Confronts the Gods: Christian Theology, Enlightenment Religion, and Non-Christian Faiths* (New York: Oxford University Press, 2000), 6–7. For a discussion of the negative portrayals made of African American spirituality in the late eighteenth-century South, see Christine Leigh Heyrman, *Southern Cross: The Beginnings of the Bible Belt* (New York: Alfred A. Knopf, 1997), 49–52. In a rare discourse on Native American religion, the Virginian Robert Beverly wrote that they were "a Superstitious and Idolatrous people." He also likened their "Adorations and Conjurations" to the rituals of the hated Catholic Church and their shamans to its priests. See Beverly, *The History and Present State of Virginia by Robert Beverly*, ed. Louis Wright (1705; repr., Chapel Hill: University of North Carolina Press, 1947), 202. On the opportunities offered to, as well the limitations placed on, black Moravians in eighteenth- and early nineteenth-century North Carolina, see Jon Sensbach, *A Separate Canaan: The Making of an Afro-Moravian World in North Carolina, 1763–1840* (Chapel Hill: University of North Carolina Press, 1998), esp. 116 and 126.

14. Diane L. Eck, *A New Religious America: How A "Christian Country" Has Become the World's Most Religiously Diverse Nation* (San Francisco: Harper Collins, 2001). William R. Hutchison's judicious account of religious pluralism in America suggests that it only began to emerge (at least as a practice) in the late nineteenth century. See Hutchison, *Religious Pluralism in America: The Contested History of a Founding Ideal* (New Haven, Conn.: Yale University Press, 2003), esp. 6, 58, 132–38.

15. Eck, *A New Religious America*, 24; William Livingston, "Of Creeds and Systems, together with the Author's Own" (October 11, 1753) in *The Independent Reflector*, ed. Milton M. Klein (Cambridge, Mass.: The Belknap Press of Harvard University Press, 1963), 391.

16. On the influence of New England clergymen, see Peter S. Field, *The Crisis of the Standing Order: Clerical Intellectuals and Cultural Authority in Massachusetts, 1780–1833* (Amherst: University of Massachusetts Press, 1998), 16. For a thoughtful discussion of the growth in autonomy and influence exercised by the eighteenth-century New England laity, see Eric R. Seeman, *Pious Persuasions: Laity and Clergy in Eighteenth-Century New England* (Baltimore: Johns Hopkins University Press, 1999). David Hall advanced the seminal version of the argument for distinct popular interpretations

of religion in New England in *Worlds of Wonder, Days of Judgment: Popular Religious Belief in Early New England* (Cambridge, Mass.: Harvard University Press, 1989). On the transmission of ideas in early America, see Norman S. Fiering, "The Transatlantic Republic of Letters: A Note on the Circulation of Learned Periodicals to Early Eighteenth-Century America," *William and Mary Quarterly*, 3rd series, 33 (October 1976): 642–60; and David D. Hall, "Learned Culture in the Eighteenth Century," in *A History of the Book in America*, vol. 1, *The Colonial Book in the Atlantic World*, ed. Hugh Amory and David D. Hall (Cambridge: Cambridge University Press, 2000), 411–33.

17. On the predominance of women within Massachusetts and Connecticut churches, especially after the Revolutionary War, see Richard D. Shiels, "The Feminization of American Congregationalism, 1730–1835," *American Quarterly* 33 (Spring 1981): 46–62; and Harry S. Stout and Catherine A. Brekus, "Declension, Gender, and the 'New Religious History,'" in *Beliefs and Behaviors: Essays in the New Religious History*, ed. Robert P. Swierenga and Philip R. VanderMeer (New Brunswick, N.J.: Rutgers University Press, 1991), 15–37. On female preaching in early America, see Catherine A. Brekus, *Strangers and Pilgrims: Female Preaching in America, 1740–1845* (Chapel Hill: University of North Carolina Press, 1998). On the relationship between gender and evangelicalism, see Susan Juster, *Disorderly Women: Sexual Politics and Evangelicalism in Revolutionary New England* (Ithaca, N.Y.: Cornell University Press, 1994). For a discussion of the impact of the extension of religious liberty on women, see Catherine A. Brekus, "The Revolution in the Churches: Women's Religious Activism in the Early American Republic," in *Religion and the New Republic: Faith in the Founding of America*, ed. James H. Hutson (Lanham, Md.: Rowman & Littlefield, 2000), 115–36; and Brekus, *Strangers and Pilgrims*, 14–15, 123–26. On the relationship between gender and dissent in seventeenth-century Massachusetts, see Jane Kamensky, *Governing the Tongue: The Politics of Speech in Early New England* (New York: Oxford University Press, 1997), esp. 71–98; Brekus arrives at a similar conclusion in "The Revolution in the Churches," 120–21. The Anglican Charles Woodmason revealingly remarked of the Carolina frontier families he encountered that there were "very few . . . whom I can bring to join in Prayer, because most of them are of various Opinions the Husband a Churchman, Wife, a Dissenter, Children nothing at all." See Hooker, *The Carolina Backcountry on the Eve of the American Revolution*, 52.

CHAPTER I

1. My account of Leddra's experiences derives from Rufus M. Jones, *The Quakers in the American Colonies* (New York: Russell and Russell, 1962), esp. 88. My understanding of seventeenth-century hangings owes much to Frances Hill, *A Delusion of Satan: The Full Story of the Salem Witch Trials* (New York: De Capo, 1995), 171–74.

2. The most recent authoritative account of these events and their historical meaning appears in Carla Gardina Pestana, "The Quaker Executions as Myth and History," *Journal of American History* 80 (September 1993): 441–69. See also Pestana, *Quakers and Baptists in Colonial Massachusetts* (Cambridge: Cambridge University Press, 1991), 25–43.

3. Nathaniel B. Shurtleff, ed., *Records of the Governor and Company of the Massachusetts Bay in New England*, 5 vols. (Boston, 1853–54), vol. 4, pt. 1:389.

4. On the revulsion generated by the hangings, see Pestana, "The Quaker Executions as Myth and History," 469.

5. Perez Zagorin, *How the Idea of Toleration Came to the West* (Princeton, N.J.: Princeton University Press, 2003), 36. For an overview of the treatment of heretics in Catholic Europe, see Zagorin, *How the Idea of Toleration Came to the West*, 14–45; R. I. Moore, *The Formation of a Persecuting Society: Power and Deviance in Western Europe, 950–1250* (Oxford: Blackwell, 1987); Malcolm Lambert, *Medieval Heresy: Popular Movements from the Gregorian Reform to the Reformation*, 2nd ed. (Oxford: Blackwell, 1992); and Brian Tierney, "Religious Rights: A Historical Perspective," in *Religious Liberty in Western Thought*, ed. Noel B. Reynolds and W. Cole Durham Jr. (Atlanta: Scholars Press, 1996), esp. 42–45.

6. On the importance of confessionalism in seventeenth-century Europe, see James D. Tracy, "Erasmus, Coornhert, and the Acceptance of Religious Disunity in the Body Politic: A Low Countries Tradition," in *The Emergence of Tolerance in the Dutch Republic*, ed. Christiane Berkvens-Stevelinck, Jonathan Irvine Israel, and G. H. M. Posthumus Meyjes (Leiden: Brill, 1997), 49; and Wolfgang Reinhard, "Pressures towards Confessionalization? Prolegomena to a Theory of the Confessional Age," in *The German Reformation: The Essential Readings*, ed. C. Scott Dixon (Oxford: Blackwell, 1999), esp. 178–82. As Benjamin J. Kaplan points out, examples of "peaceful coexistence prevailed more widely than often supposed" in Reformation Europe, yet "the idea of tolerance suffered from a basic illegitimacy, the forms of it practiced in early modern Europe were always quite limited, bearing little resemblance to those characteristic of the West in our own day." See Kaplan, "Coexistence, Conflict, and the Practice of Toleration," in *A Companion to the Reformation World*, ed. R. Po-chia Hsia (Malden, Mass.: Blackwell, 2004). For contemporary justifications of intolerance, see Mark Goldie, "The Theory of Religious Intolerance in Restoration England," in *From Persecution to Toleration: The Glorious Revolution and Religion in England*, ed. Ole Peter Grell, Jonathan I. Israel, and Nicholas Tyacke (Oxford: Clarendon, 1991), 338–61.

7. Ernestine van der Wall, "Toleration and Enlightenment in the Dutch Republic," in *Toleration in Enlightenment Europe*, ed. Ole Peter Grell and Roy Porter (Cambridge: Cambridge University Press, 2000), esp. 117. For a comprehensive discussion of the toleration debate in the seventeenth-century Netherlands, see Jonathan Israel, "The Intellectual Debate about Toleration in the Dutch Republic," in *The Emergence of Tolerance in the Dutch Republic*, 3–36.

8. On the experimental nature of America's early religious life, see John Murrin, "Religion and Politics in America from the First Settlements to the Civil War," in *Religion and American Politics*, ed. Mark A. Noll (New York: Oxford University Press, 1990), 23. The fullest account of how this haphazard process occurred in the Middle Colonies appears in Evan Haefeli's brilliant dissertation, "The Creation of American Religious Pluralism: Churches, Colonialism, and Conquest in the Mid-Atlantic, 1628–1688" (dissertation, Princeton University, 2000).

9. John Callendar, *An Historical Discourse on the Civil and Religious Affairs of the Colony of Rhode Island and Providence* (Boston, 1739), 16, 91–92, 69. If we credit contemporary accounts, mortality rates may have been as high as ninety-five percent among the Native Americans who inhabited New England's coastline in the early seventeenth century. See David S. Jones, *Rationalizing Epidemics: Meanings and Uses of American Indian Mortality since 1600* (Cambridge, Mass.: Harvard University Press, 2004), 32.

10. Virginia legislation quoted in Charles F. James, ed., *Documentary History of the Struggle for Religious Liberty in Virginia* (New York: De Capo, 1971), 19.

11. On the Quaker dominance of Pennsylvania society and politics, see Frank Lambert, *The Founding Fathers and the Place of Religion in America* (Princeton, N.J.: Princeton University Press, 2003), 101, 116–17.

12. Jon Butler, *Awash in a Sea of Faith: Christianizing the American* People (Cambridge, Mass.: Harvard University Press, 1990), 166. On the persistence of the parochial system in both Europe and colonial America, as a practical system and an ideal, see Timothy D. Hall, *Contested Boundaries: Itinerancy and the Remaking of the Colonial American Religious World* (Durham, N.C.: Duke University Press, 1994), esp. 19–23. On the strict geographical localism that prevailed in early Massachusetts, see John D. Cushing, "Notes on Disestablishment in Massachusetts, 1780–1833," *William and Mary Quarterly*, 3rd series, 26 (April 1969): esp. 169–72. For an innovative, quantitative-based discussion of the financial limitations on religious diversity in colonial New England, see Alison G. Olson, "Rhode Island, Massachusetts, and the Question of Religious Diversity in Colonial New England," *New England Quarterly* 65 (March 1992): 93–116. This was, as William G. McLoughlin noted, more of an issue for rural than urban congregations. See McLoughlin, *New England Dissent, 1630–1833: The Baptists and the Separation of Church and State* (Cambridge, Mass.: Harvard University Press, 1971), 278.

13. [James Wetmore], *A Letter from a Minister of the Church of England to His Dissenting Parishioners* (New York, 1730), 7–10. The quotation appears on 7–8.

14. Samuel Johnson, *A Letter from a Minister of the Church of England to His Dissenting Parishioners* (New York, 1733), 7.

15. [John Graham], *Some Remarks Upon a Late Pamphlet Entitled, A Letter from a Minister of the Church of England to His Dissenting Parishioners* (Boston, 1733), 2. Another contributor to this debate, the Pennsylvania Presbyterian minister Jonathan Dickinson, asked, "[W]ho is it that dissent from the original and legal Establishment of the Country, they, or we?" See Jonathan Dickinson, *The Scripture-Bishop Vindicated* (Boston, 1733), 43–44. Mary Louise Greene noted that "[t]he terms Congregational and Presbyterian were often used interchangeably" in colonial Connecticut. See Greene, *The Development of Religious Liberty in Connecticut* (Boston: Houghton and Mifflin, 1905), 150.

16. For an excellent discussion of the "ambiguities of 'establishment' " in colonial America, see Thomas Curry, *The First Freedoms: Church and State in America to the Passage of the First Amendment* (New York: Oxford University Press, 1986), esp. 105–8; On the contemporary meaning of "orthodoxy," and James MacSparran in particular,

see Mary Sarah Bilder, *The Transatlantic Constitution: Colonial Legal Culture and the Empire* (Cambridge, Mass.: Harvard University Press, 2004), 145–167; also Peter M. Doll, *Revolution, Religion, and National Identity: Imperial Anglicanism in British North America, 1745–1795* (Madison, N.J.: Farleigh Dickinson University Press, 2000), 163–64. The Hollis incident is recounted in J. David Hoeveler, *Creating the American Mind: Intellect and Politics in the Colonial Colleges* (Lanham, Md.: Rowman & Littlefield, 2002), 215; and Samuel Eliot Morison, *Three Centuries of Harvard: 1636–1936* (Cambridge, Mass.: Harvard University Press, 1936), 66–68. The next time Hollis endowed a professorship, he would specify more clearly that Baptists should be considered, along with Congregationalists and Presbyterians. See Hoeveler, *Creating the American Mind*, 227n.

17. On the breakdown of the parish system in British North America, see Winthrop S. Hudson and John Corrigan, *Religion in America* (Upper Saddle River, N.J.: Prentice Hall, 1999), 48–49. For the first few decades of the eighteenth century, Dietmar Rothermund writes of colonial Pennsylvania, it was still possible for the various churches in that region to "mind their own business." See Rothermund, *The Layman's Progress: Religious and Political Experience in Colonial Pennsylvania, 1740–1770* (Philadelphia: University of Pennsylvania Press, 1961), 9.

18. On the importance of the passage "compel them to come in" (Luke 14:23) to seventeenth-century English justifications for persecution, see John Coffey, *Persecution and Toleration in Protestant England 1558–1689* (Harlow: Longman, 2000), 33–35. On the importance for both the individual and the community that New Englanders attached to suppressing religious error, see Timothy L. Hall, *Separating Church and State: Roger Williams and Religious Liberty* (Urbana: University of Illinois Press, 1998), 59–60.

19. Samuel Johnson, *A Second Letter from a Minister of the Church of England to His Dissenting Parishioners* (Boston, 1734), 7–8; [Arthur Browne], *The Scripture Bishop, or, The Divine Right of Presbyterian Ordination and Government* (Boston, 1733), 10.

20. The equation between heresy and disease went back at least seven centuries. R. I. Moore indicates that it was even employed by Augustine. See Moore, "Heresy as Disease," in *The Concept of Heresy in the Middle Ages (11th–13th C.): Proceedings of the International Conference, Louvain May 13–16, 1973*, ed. W. Lourdaux and D. Verhelst (The Hague: Martinus Nijhoff, 1976), esp. 9–10. On the use of the same kind of language in late sixteenth-century France, see Dalia M. Leonardo, " 'Cut off this Rotten Member': The Rhetoric of Heresy, Sin, and Disease in the Ideology of the French Catholic League," *Catholic Historical Review* 88 (April 2002): 252–54. On the Boston smallpox epidemic, see Maris A. Vinovskis, "Angels' Heads and Weeping Willows: Death in Early America," in *Studies in American Historical Demography*, ed. Maris A. Vinovskis (New York: Academic Press, 1979), 183.

21. John Cushing, ed., *Colony Laws of Virginia*, 2 vols. (Wilmington, Del.: Michael Glazier, 1978), 2:533; Hugh Jones, "Of the State of the Church and Clergy of Virginia" (1724), in G. MacLaren Brydon, *Virginia's Mother Church and the Political Conditions under Which It Grew*, 2 vols. (Richmond: Virginia Historical Society, 1947–1952), 1:399. For the penalties on Quakers, see Nathaniel B. Shurtleff, ed., *Records of the Governor*

and Company of the Massachusetts, vol. 4, pt. 1:385. For the penalties on non-Conformists generally, see Act of the Virginia House of Burgesses (March 1661/1662), reprinted in G. MacLaren Brydon, *Virginia's Mother Church and the Political Conditions under Which It Grew*, 1:457.

22. John Cotton, "A Reply to Mr. Williams His Examination, London" (1647) in *The Complete Writings of Roger Williams*, ed. Samuel L. Caldwell (New York: Russell and Russell, 1963), 2:27; *American Higher Education: A Documentary History*, ed. Richard Hofstadter and Wilson Smith, 2 vols. (Chicago: University of Chicago Press, 1961), 1:77; David D. Hall, ed., *The Antinomian Controversy, 1636–1638: A Documentary History* (Middletown, Conn.: Wesleyan University Press, 1968), 366. On the use of the contagion metaphor in early New England, see Hall, *Separating Church and State*, 59.

23. John Graham, *The Christian's duty of watchfulness against error, and establishment in the truth* (New London, Conn.: 1733), 1, 14, 5. In 1647, Nathaniel Ward wrote: "He that is willing to tolerate any Religion, or discrepant way of Religion, besides his own, unless it be in matters meerly indifferent, either doubts of his own, or is not sincere in it." See Nathaniel Ward, *The Simple Cobler of Aggawam in America*, ed. Paul M. Zall (1647; repr., Lincoln: University of Nebraska Press), 10.

24. "Instructions to the Colonists by Lord Baltimore" (1633) in *Narratives of Early Maryland, 1633–1689*, ed. Clayton C. Hall (New York: Charles Scribner's Sons, 1940), 16; John Russell Bartlett, ed., *Records of the Colony of Rhode Island and Providence Plantations, in New England*, 10 vols. (Providence, 1856–64), 2:5.

25. The quotation comes from the pamphlet's subtitle. See [John Graham], *Some Remarks Upon a Late Pamphlet Entitled, A Letter from a Minister of the Church of England to His Dissenting Parishioners*.

26. Cotton Mather, *The Way of Truth Laid Out* (Boston, 1721), miscellaneous front matter, 1–2, 5–6. The notion that the contagion of error could be contained through the use of child catechisms did not end with Mather. See, for instance, Samuel Niles, *A Vindication of Divers Important Gospel-Doctrines* (Boston, 1752), 1–2, 8.

27. [Jonathan Dickinson], *The Divine Right of Presbyterian Ordination &c. Argued* (Boston 1732), i. On the conservative quality of the early press, especially, see Daniel Boorstin, *The Americans: The Colonial Experience* (New York: Vintage, 1958), esp. 319–24.

28. Benjamin Trumbull, *A Complete History of Connecticut: Civil and Ecclesiastical, from the Emigration of Its First Planters, from England, in the Year 1630, to the Year 1764, and to the Close of the Indian Wars*, 2 vols. (1818; repr., New London, Conn.: 1898), 2:460.

29. John Bulkley, *An Impartial Account of a Late Debate at Lyme* (New London, Conn.: 1729), 4–7.

30. Ibid., 1.

31. Ibid., 134–35. It did not take long for the Baptists to respond to Bulkley's pamphlet. In 1731, printer James Franklin published the rebuttal of Rhode Island Baptist John Walton. See Walton, *Remarks on, Or, An Examination of Mr. Bulkly's Account of the Lyme Dispute* (Newport, 1731).

32. Martin Luther, "The Short Catechism, 1529," in *Documents of the Christian Church*, ed. Henry Bettenson, 2nd ed. (London: Oxford University Press, 1963), 284; Act of Uniformity quoted in Coffey, *Persecution and Toleration in Protestant England*, 83. For a remarkable piece on the architecture (and general practice) of dissent, see Benjamin Kaplan, "Fictions of Privacy: House Chapels and the Spatial Accommodation of Religious Dissent in Early Modern Europe," *American Historical Review* 107 (October 2002): 1031–64. The quote appears on 1043.

33. There is a scholarly consensus on the pragmatic origins of toleration. See, for instance, John Dunn, "The Claim to Freedom of Conscience: Freedom of Speech, Freedom of Thought, Freedom of Worship?" in Grell, Israel, and Tyacke, eds., *From Persecution to Toleration*, 172; Andrew R. Murphy, *Conscience and Community: Revisiting Toleration and Religious Dissent in Early Modern England and America* (University Park: Pennsylvania State University Press, 2001); Hugh Trevor-Roper, "Toleration and Religion after 1688," in *From Persecution to Toleration*, 390; and Richard Tuck, "Scepticism and Toleration in the Seventeenth Century," in *Justifying Toleration*, ed. Susan Mendus (Cambridge: Cambridge University Press, 1988), 21–35.

34. For general accounts of the rise of toleration in early modern Europe and America, see Henry Kamen, *The Rise of Toleration* (New York: World University Library, 1967); Hans R. Guggisberg, "The Defence of Religious Toleration and Religious Liberty in Early Modern Europe: Arguments, Pressures, and Some Consequences," *History of European Ideas* 4 (1983): 35–50; and Murphy, *Conscience and Community*. For the counterview that the ideal of toleration possessed distinctly medieval origins, see the work of Cary J. Nederman and John Christian Laursen, especially their anthology of writings on the subject, *Beyond the Persecuting Society: Religious Toleration Before the Enlightenment*, ed. Laursen and Nederman (Philadelphia: University of Pennsylvania Press, 1998). Given the evidence presented there and elsewhere, most historians would undoubtedly acknowledge that "in medieval and early modern Europe the voices favoring and the actual practices were present, both in number and in variation, on a scale hitherto unappreciated" (2). Nonetheless, there is little doubt that the late seventeenth and eighteenth century saw a turn toward the ideals of toleration and religious equality that far exceeded what occurred earlier both in breadth and scope. On the growth of the notion that error was an ineradicable element of human reasoning, see David Bates, "The Epistemology of Error in Late Enlightenment France," *Eighteenth-Century Studies* 29 (Fall 1996): 307–27. For the development of probabilistic thinking, see Barbara J. Shapiro, *Probability and Certainty in Seventeenth-Century England: A Study of the Relationships between Natural Science, Religion, History, Law, and Literature* (Princeton, N.J.: Princeton University Press, 1983); and James Tully, "Governing Conduct," in *Conscience and Casuistry in Early Modern Europe*, ed. Edmund Leites (Cambridge: Cambridge University Press, 1988).

35. Shurtleff, ed., *Records of the Governor and Company of the Massachusetts Bay*, 1:160–61. Quoted in Hall, *Separating Church and State*, 38.

36. Roger Williams, "The Bloody Tenent of Persecution" (1644) in *Complete Writings of Roger Williams*, ed. Samuel L. Caldwell, 7 vols. (New York: Russell and Russell, 1963), 3:93.

37. Quoted in Edmund S. Morgan, *The Puritan Dilemma: The Story of John Winthrop*, 2nd ed. (New York: Longman, 1999), 116, no reference given. Williams's intolerance is insightfully discussed in Hall, *Separating Church and State*, 27–33.

38. On Williams's life and thought, see Edwin S. Gaustad, *Liberty of Conscience: Roger Williams in America* (Grand Rapids, Mich.: Eerdmans, 1991); Hall, *Separating Church and State*; Jimmy D. Neff, "Roger Williams: Pious Puritan and Strict Separationist," *Journal of Church and State* 38 (Summer 1996): 529–46; and Stephen Phillips, "Roger Williams and the Two Tables of the Law," *Journal of Church and State* 38 (Summer 1996): 547–70. On Williams's lack of influence in eighteenth-century America, see Curry, *The First Freedoms*, 91; and Hall, *Separating Church and State*, 116–17.

39. On Locke's influence in America, see John Dunn, "The Politics of Locke in England and America in the Eighteenth Century," in *John Locke: Problems and Perspectives*, ed. John Yolton (Cambridge: Cambridge University Press, 1969); Steven Dworetz, *The Unvarnished Doctrine: Locke, Liberalism, and the American Revolution* (Durham, N.C.: Duke University Press, 1990); Noah Feldman, "The Intellectual Origins of the Establishment Clause," *NYU Law Review* 77 (May 2002): esp. 372–75; and Jerome Huyler, *Locke in America: The Moral Philosophy of the Founding Era* (Lawrence: University Press of Kansas, 1995). Among those who directly invoked Locke were the great proponents of religious liberty, Elisha Williams and Isaac Backus. See Williams, *A Seasonable Plea for the Liberty of Conscience and The Right of Private Judgment* (Boston, 1744), 5, 7; Backus, *A Seasonable Plea for Liberty of Conscience* (Boston, 1770), 11–13; and [Backus], *A Letter to a Gentleman in the Massachusetts General Assembly* (Boston, 1771), 20. In addition to the influence of his books, Locke had a more direct influence on colonial policies. He helped to craft the liberal constitution of Carolina, which combined an Anglican establishment with a policy of toleration. Locke also advised William Penn on the framing of his colony's charter. On Locke's role in shaping Pennsylvania's Frame of Government, see Norman K. Risjord's "William Penn," in *American Portraits: Biographies in United States History*, ed. Stephen G. Weisner and William F. Hartford, 2 vols. (Boston: McGraw-Hill, 2002),1:58.

40. J. William Frost, *A Perfect Freedom: Religious Liberty in Pennsylvania* (University Park: University of Pennsylvania Press, 1993), 26. Frost notes that "[b]y 1720 virtually all Pennsylvanians accepted the virtues of religious liberty, but now battles arose over whether the Quaker definition of religious liberty was discriminatory and a threat to security" (4).

41. For the examples cited here, see Leonard W. Levy, *The Establishment Clause: Religion and the First Amendment*, 2nd rev. ed. (Chapel Hill: University of North Carolina Press, 1994), 14–15; and Sanford H. Cobb, *The Rise of Religious Liberty in America: A History* (New York: Macmillan, 1902), 348. It took New York longer than other colonies, however, to offer full rights of incorporation to dissenting churches.

42. MS. Observations on Mr. Davies, his Letter, etc., Virginia Religious Papers of the Library of Congress—unsigned and undated. Quoted in Wesley M. Gewehr, *The Great Awakening in Virginia, 1740–1790* (Gloucester, Mass.: Peter Smith, 1965), 79; "Petition of the Hanover Presbytery, 1774–1775, Against the Proposed Toleration

Act of 1772," in Brydon, *Virginia's Mother Church and the Political Conditions under Which It Grew*, 2:554. On the treatment of Virginia dissenters from 1727 onward, see Henry R. McIlwaine, "The Struggle of Protestant Dissenters for Religious Toleration in Virginia," Johns Hopkins University Studies in Historical and Political Science (Baltimore: The Johns Hopkins Press, April 1894), 40; and John M. Mecklin, *The Story of American Dissent* (New York: Harcourt Brace, 1934), 232.

43. Curry, *The First Freedoms*, 90; Louis Wright, ed., *The History and Present State of Virginia by Robert Beverly* (Chapel Hill: University of North Carolina Press, 1947), 261.

44. The *Virginia Gazette*, 24 November 1738; the *Virginia Gazette*, 5 March 1752; the *Virginia Gazette*, 3 April 1752; and the *Virginia Gazette*, 10 April 1752. "Philo Virginia's" suggestions were endorsed by an author calling himself "Philo Bombastia," who even suggested that the colony should even open itself up to Roman Catholics. See the *Virginia Gazette*, 20 March 1752.

45. According to Rhys Isaac, "Toleration was a shibboleth in the eighteenth-century Anglo-American world; it was unthinkable to question it in the open." See Isaac, *The Transformation of Virginia, 1740–1790* (Chapel Hill: University of North Carolina Press, 1982), 152. The quotes from Mather appear in Mather, *Brethren Dwelling Together in Unity* (Boston, 1718), 37–38. Original italics removed for clarity.

46. On the strong correspondence between the content of the disputes in America and those that occurred in Scotland, see Marilyn J. Westerkamp, *The Triumph of the Laity: Scots-Irish Piety and the Great Awakening, 1625–1760* (New York: Oxford University Press, 1988), esp. 80–102, 149–56; and Patrick Griffin, *The People with No Name: Ireland's Ulster Scots, America's Scots, and the Creation of a British Atlantic World* (Princeton, N.J.: Princeton University Press, 2001), 46–60.

47. Josiah Smith, *Humane Impositions Proved Unscriptural Or, The Divine Right of Private Judgment* (Boston, 1729), ii, 11; Josiah Smith, *The Divine Right of Private Judgment Vindicated* (Boston, 1730), 36. For an excellent account of Smith's life and work, see Thomas S. Kidd, "'A Faithful Watchman on the Walls of Charlestown': Josiah Smith and Moderate Revivalism in Colonial South Carolina," *South Carolina Historical Magazine* 105 (April 2004): 82–106. For a helpful discussion of the debate in Charleston, see Curry, *The First Freedoms*, 94–95.

48. Fisher, *The Divine Right of Private Judgment, Set in a True Light* (Boston, 1731), 26, 35; Hugh Fisher, *A Preservative from Damnable Error, in the Unction of the Holy One* (Boston, 1730), 39, 18, 51–52.

49. Josiah Smith, *No New Thing to Be Slandered* (Boston, 1730).

50. Jonathan Dickinson, *A Sermon Preached at the Opening of the Synod at Philadelphia, September 19, 1722* (Boston, 1723), 2.

51. [John Thomson], *An Overture Presented to the Reverend Synod of Dissenting Ministers* (Philadelphia, 1729), 12, 7, 26.

52. *Records of the Presbyterian Church in the United States of America, 1706–1788* (1904; repr., New York: Arno, 1969), 94.

53. Benjamin Franklin, *The Autobiography of Benjamin Franklin*, ed. Louis P. Masur (Boston: Bedford, 1993), 102. Marilyn Westerkamp suggests that Hemphill's

interdenominational appeal is what brought the wrath of the Synod upon him. See Westerkamp, *The Triumph of the Laity*, 160.

54. Benjamin Franklin, "Some Observations on the Proceedings against The Rev. Mr. Hemphill; with a Vindication of his Sermons," 2nd ed. (Philadelphia, 1735) in *The Papers of Benjamin Franklin*, ed. Leonard W. Labaree, 32 vols. (New Haven, Conn.: Yale University Press, 1960), 2:49; *A Vindication of the Reverend Commission of the Synod in Answer to Some Observations on Their Proceedings against the Reverend Mr. Hemphill* (Philadelphia, 1735), 14, 5. For accounts of the Hemphill controversy, see Merton A. Christensen, "Franklin on the Hemphill Trial," William and Mary Quarterly, 3rd series 10 (July 1953): 422–40; and Melvin H. Buxbaum, *Benjamin Franklin and the Zealous Presbyterians* (University Park: Pennsylvania State University Press, 1975), 93–115. Ultimately it was well-substantiated charges of plagiarism that ended Hemphill's preaching career in the colonies.

55. [Jonathan Dickinson], *Remarks Upon a Pamphlet, Entitled, A Letter to a Friend in the Country* (Philadelphia, 1735), 4, 29.

56. *A Vindication of the Reverend Commission*, 8, 5, 2, and title page; [Jonathan Dickinson], Ibid., 12–13. Dickinson also invoked a supporting scriptural passage: *"For there are many unruly and vain Talkers and Deceivers, especially they of the Circumcision, WHOSE MOUTHS MUST BE STOPPED . . . "* (13).

57. *A Vindication of the Reverend Commission*, 1–2; Franklin, "A Defence of the Reverend Mr. Hemphill's Observations," in Labaree, ed., *The Papers of Benjamin Franklin*, 2:92, 95.

58. Robert W. T. Martin, *The Free and Open Press: The Founding of American Democratic Press Liberty, 1640–1800* (New York: New York University Press, 2001), 38–39. For a discussion of the *Courant* and its role in contemporary politics and religion, see Charles E. Clark, *The Public Prints: The Newspaper in Anglo-American Culture, 1665–1740* (New York: Oxford University Press, 1994), 123–40.

59. Curry, *The First Freedoms*, 89. On the Zenger trial, see *A Brief Narrative of the Case and Trial of John Peter Zenger*, ed. Stanley Nider Katz, 2nd ed. (Cambridge, Mass.: The Belknap Press of Harvard University Press, 1972). On the constraints placed on early eighteenth-century newspaper publication and press freedom, see James N. Green, "The Book Trade in the Middle Colonies, 1680–1720" and Richard D. Brown, "The Shifting Freedoms of the Press in the Eighteenth Century," in *A History of the Book in America*, ed. Hugh Amory and David D. Hall, vol. 1, *The Colonial Book in the Atlantic World* (Cambridge: Cambridge University Press, 2000), 199–223, 367. Not until the end of the eighteenth century would a substantive justification for criticism of civil authorities emerge. See Leonard W. Levy, *Emergence of a Free Press* (New York: Oxford University Press, 1985), 119. Larry D. Eldridge has challenged Levy's claims, insisting that while colonial law changed little during the seventeenth century, "attitudes toward it" changed dramatically, so that seditious libel was prosecuted less frequently and harshly in 1700 than it had been in previous decades. See Eldridge, *A Distant Heritage: The Growth of Free Speech in Early America* (New York: New York University Press, 1994), esp. 41.

60. *Pennsylvania Gazette*, 10 June 1731; Benjamin Franklin, "A Letter to a Friend in the Country" (Philadelphia, 1735), 84. For an extraordinary analysis of print's role in colonial America, see Michael Warner, *The Letters of the Republic: Publication and the Public Sphere in Eighteenth-Century America* (Cambridge, Mass.: Harvard University Press, 1990).

61. Statistics cited in Frank Lambert, *Inventing the "Great Awakening"* (Princeton, N.J.: Princeton University Press, 1999), table 3.1, 115.

62. On the importance of the second printer in colonial cities, see Green, "The Book Trade in the Middle Colonies, 1680–1720," 223. Not coincidentally, dissenters would find it especially hard going in Virginia where, as late as 1766, there was "still ... only one printer and one major bookstore." See Cynthia Z. Stiverson and Gregory A. Stiverson, "The Colonial Retail Book Trade in Virginia," in *Printing and Society in Early America*, ed. William L. Joyce et al. (Worcester, Mass.: American Antiquarian Society, 1983), 149. For a subtle examination of the early print trade's development, see Richard D. Brown's *Knowledge Is Power: The Diffusion of Information in Early America, 1700–1865* (New York: Oxford University Press, 1989), esp. 34, 41; and Christopher Grasso, *A Speaking Aristocracy: Transforming Public Discourse in Eighteenth-Century Connecticut* (Chapel Hill: University of North Carolina Press, 1999), esp. 8–15; Stephen Botein described how Congregationalist ministers and Congregationalist state officials kept a tight grip over the print trade in New England for the first three decades of the eighteenth century in his " 'Meer Mechanics' and an Open Press: The Business and Political Strategies of Colonial American Printers," *Perspectives in American History* 9 (1975): 170. On the relationship between print and official authority in colonial America, see David D. Hall, "The Uses of Literacy in New England, 1600–1850" in Joyce, et al., *Printing and Society in Early America*, esp. 18–19.

63. *South-Carolina Gazette*, 23 September 1732; *South-Carolina Gazette*, 7 October 1732; *South-Carolina Gazette*, 30 September 1732. For the case that the author of the 7 October piece was the Anglican Commissary, Alexander Garden, see S. Charles Bolton, *Southern Anglicanism: The Church of England in Colonial South Carolina* (Westport, Conn.: Greenwood), 134.

CHAPTER 2

1. In his seminal work on the meaning of the Great Awakening, Frank Lambert makes the convincing case that contemporaries saw the revivals as a unified series of events. See Lambert, *Inventing the "Great Awakening"* (Princeton, N.J.: Princeton University Press, 1999). Lambert also notes that, although revivals occurred almost simultaneously in New Jersey and Northampton, only the Northampton revivals were immediately publicized (56). For the plausible counterargument that the revivals were independent events, see Jon Butler, "Enthusiasm Described and Decried: The Great Awakening as Interpretive Fiction," *Journal of American History* 69 (September 1982): 305–25. Michael J. Crawford has demonstrated that New Englanders developed the "idea of a communal season of grace" as early as the 1720s. See Crawford, *Seasons of Grace: New England's Revival Tradition in Its British Context*

(New York: Oxford University Press, 1991), esp. 104–17, 123. On the connections between the revivals in Britain and those in America, see Susan O'Brien, "A Transatlantic Community of Saints: The Great Awakening and the First Evangelical Network, 1735–1755," *American Historical Review* 91 (October 1986): 811–32. Crawford also details the transatlantic characteristics of the Awakening. See *Seasons of Grace*, esp. 151–79.

2. On Mather's vision of "Reasonable Religion," see Kenneth Silverman, *The Life and Times of Cotton Mather* (New York: Welcome Rain, 1984), esp. 300–301. On Dickinson, see Bryan F. Le Beau, *Jonathan Dickinson and the Formative Years of American Presbyterianism* (Lexington: University Press of Kentucky, 1997), esp. 88–95. On the influence of rational religion in America, see Norman Fiering, "The First American Enlightenment: Tillotson, Leverett, and Philosophical Anglicanism," *New England Quarterly* 54 (September 1981): 307–44; and Henry F. May, *The Enlightenment in America* (Oxford: Oxford University Press, 1976), esp. 10–25. On the Anglicization of New England churches and ministers during the early eighteenth century, see Harry S. Stout, *The New England Soul: Preaching and Religious Culture in Colonial New England* (New York: Oxford University Press, 1986), esp. 128–37.

3. For a good account of Chauncy's intellectual life and the tempered rationalism he displayed, see John Corrigan, *The Hidden Balance: Religion and the Social Theories of Charles Chauncy and Jonathan Mayhew* (Cambridge: Cambridge University Press, 1987).

4. Charles Chauncy, *The Only Compulsion Proper to Be Made Use of in the Affairs of Conscience and Religion* (Boston, 1739), 3, 4, 10.

5. On the significance of human movement and the expansion of individual religious choice that it introduced, see Timothy H. Breen and Timothy L. Hall, "Structuring Provincial Imagination: The Rhetoric and Experience of Social Change in Eighteenth-Century New England," *American Historical Review* 103 (December 1998), esp. 1427–28. Susan Juster maintains that eighteenth-century evangelism brought about a transformation in the understanding of sacred space. See Juster, *Sexual Politics and Evangelism in Revolutionary New England* (Ithaca, N.Y.: Cornell University Press, 1994), esp. 21–24.

6. For an account of one controversial New Light, see Leigh Eric Schmidt, " 'A Second and Glorious Reformation': The New Light Extremism of Andrew Croswell," *William and Mary Quarterly*, 3rd series 43 (April 1986): 214–44.

7. T. Cutler to Z. Grey, 24 September 1743, Boston Public Library. Quoted in Susan O'Brien, "Eighteenth-Century Publishing Networks in the First Years of Transatlantic Evangelism," in *Evangelicalism: Comparative Studies of Popular Protestantism in North America, the British Isles, and Beyond, 1700–1990*, ed. Mark A. Noll, David W. Bebbington, and George A. Rawlyk (New York: Oxford University Press, 1994), 45.

8. Nathanael Eells, *A Letter to the Second Church and congregation in Scituate* (Boston, 1745), 4. For the best account of itinerancy and its meaning within the larger Anglo American world, especially during the Great Awakening, see Timothy D. Hall,

Contested Boundaries: Itinerancy and the Remaking of the Colonial American Religious World (Durham, N.C.: Duke University Press, 1994).

9. *George Whitefield's Journals* (Edinburgh: Banner of Truth Trust, 1998), 458, 414.

10. The phrase "bodily effects" appeared in *The Testimony and Advice of an Assembly of Pastors of Churches in New England, at a meeting in Boston, July 7, 1743* (Boston, 1743), 9. On the traditional association between itinerancy and heresy, see Malcolm Lambert, *Medieval Heresy: Popular Movements from the Gregorian Reform to the Reformation*, 2nd ed. (Oxford: Blackwell, 1992), 40. On the performative aspects of New Light preaching, and that of Whitefield in particular, see Harry S. Stout, *The Divine Dramatist: George Whitefield and the Rise of Modern Evangelism* (Grand Rapids, Mich.: Eerdmans, 1991).

11. *Mr. Whi—d's Soliloquy, or a Serious Debate with Himself what Course He Shall Take* (Boston, 1745), lines 69–77 (Broadside); Benjamin Prescott, *A Letter to the Reverend Mr. George Whitefield, An Itinerant Preacher* (Boston, 1745), 3; Nathanael Henchman, *Reasons Offered by Mr. Nathanael Henchman* (Boston, 1745), 7; George Gillespie, *Remarks upon Mr. George Whitefield, Proving Him a Man under Delusion* (Philadelphia, 1744), miscellaneous front matter.

12. Samuel Blair, "A Short and Faithful Narrative" (1744) in *The Great Awakening: Documents on the Revival of Religion, 1740–1745*, ed. Richard L. Bushman (Chapel Hill: University of North Carolina Press), 73; *Testimony and Advice of a Number of Laymen respecting Religion, and the Teachers of it* (Boston, 1743), 2. On the connection between Eve and the seduction of itinerancy, see Hall, *Contested Boundaries*, 57. On the close connections drawn between female behavior and eighteenth-century evangelism, see Susan Juster, *Disorderly Women*. Juster quotes Blair on 37.

13. M. Louise Greene, *The Development of Religious Liberty in Connecticut* (Boston: Houghton and Mifflin, 1905), 266; "Connecticut Expels James Davenport: *Boston Weekly News-Letter*" (1742) in Bushman, ed. *The Great Awakening*, 45–46. Gooch's instructions are reprinted in *Records of the Presbyterian Church in the United States of America, 1706–1788* (1904; repr., New York: Arno, 1969), 182–83. On the participation of African Americans in the revivals, see Sylvia R. Frey and Betty Wood, *Come Shouting to Zion: African American Protestantism in the American South and British Caribbean to 1830* (Chapel Hill: University of North Carolina Press, 1998), 94; and Frank Lambert, "'I Saw the Book Talk': Slave Readings of the First Great Awakening," *Journal of Negro History* 77 (Fall 1992): 185–98. On the implications of the revival for southern slavery, see Leigh Eric Schmidt, "'The Grand Prophet,' Hugh Bryan: Early Evangelism's Challenge to the Establishment and Slavery in the Colonial South," *South Carolina Historical Magazine* 87 (1986): 238–50.

14. William Henry Foote, *Sketches of Virginia, Historical and Biographical* (Philadelphia: 1850), 176–78; Samuel Davies, *The Impartial Trial, impartially Tried, and convicted of Partiality* (Williamsburg, 1748), 23; Samuel Davies, *The State of Religion among the Protestant Dissenters in Virginia* (Boston, 1751), 7. For a recent account of the origins of the Great Awakening among the New Light Presbyterians of Hanover County, see Robert M. Payne, "New Light in Hanover County: Evangelical Dissent in Piedmont Virginia, 1740–1755," *Journal of Southern History* 61 (November 1995):

665–94. On Davies's invocation of the Toleration Act and the eventual concessions made by the Colonial Court, see Wesley M. Gewehr, *The Great Awakening in Virginia, 1740–1790* (Gloucester, Mass.: Peter Smith, 1965), 74–76.

15. The author noted that this occurred "in the lower parts of the country" and that the offending minister was replaced by Samuel Davies. "J. T.," in "Extract of a Letter from a Gentleman of Virginia," in *The New York Journal; or, The General Advertiser*, 22 August 1771.

16. *The Diary of Ebenezer Parkman, 1703–1782: First Part, Three Volumes in One, 1719–1755*, ed. Francis G. Walett (Worcester, Mass.: American Antiquarian Society, 1974), 111, 163–64.

17. Parkman to Edwards, [unknown date] December 1741, Commonplace Book, Ebenezer Parkman Papers, Massachusetts Historical Society, 108–9.

18. Parkman Family Papers, unpublished diary entry, 16 November 1742, American Antiquarian Society.

19. Parkman Family Papers, "Psal.CXXII, 6 to 9," Box 1, Folder 3 (Sermons 1730–1739), American Antiquarian Society, 10.

20. J—. S— [Josiah Smith], "To the Rev. Dr. — in Boston," *South-Carolina Gazette*, 12 January 1740. The author himself was probably already a Whitefield supporter, and trying to get the evangelist a fair hearing. But he also seems to have been tapping into a prevailing strain of discourse. On Josiah Smith's relationship with George Whitefield, see Thomas S. Kidd, " 'A Faithful Watchman on the Walls of Charlestown': Josiah Smith and Moderate Revivalism in Colonial South Carolina," *South Carolina Historical Magazine* 105 (April 2004): 86–97.

21. *Boston Weekly Post-Boy* (unknown date); reprinted in the *South-Carolina Gazette*, 9 January 1742.

22. *The Testimony of the pastors of the churches in the province of the Massachusetts-Bay, in New-England, at their annual convention in Boston* (Boston, 1743), 8. Information on the two assemblies can be found in Bushman, *The Great Awakening*, 110–11. According to William G. McLoughlin, New England's ministerial associations, which had once been able to rely on a solid "consensus," were perpetually divided after 1740. See McLoughlin, *New England Dissent, 1630–1833: The Baptists and the Separation of Church and State* (Cambridge, Mass.: Harvard University Press, 1971), 1:345. On the theological and institutional impact of New England's revivals, see Edwin Scott Gaustad's classic *The Great Awakening in New England* (New York: Harper & Brothers, 1957).

23. *Testimony and Advice of a Number of Laymen respecting Religion, and the Teachers of It*, 2, 7.

24. [Charles Chauncy], "A Letter from a Gentleman in Boston, to Mr. George Wishart, One of the Ministers of Edinburgh, Concerning the State of Religion In New-England" (1742) in Bushman, *The Great Awakening*, 117; Richard Hofstadter and Wilson Smith, eds., *American Higher Education: A Documentary History*, 2 vols. (Chicago: University of Chicago Press, 1961), 1:72; *The Testimony and Advice of a Number of Laymen* (Boston, 1743), 6.

25. Gilbert Tennent, *The Danger of an Unconverted Ministry* (Philadelphia, 1741), 30–31, 26, 23.

26. *The Testimony and Advice of an Assembly of Pastors of Churches in New England, at a meeting in Boston, July 7, 1743* (Boston, 1743), 6; *Boston Evening-Post*, 26 July 1742; *George Whitefield's Journals*, 462n (1756 edit). In 1741, Tennent had written, somewhat less regretfully than he did in his later *Evening-Post* piece: "We own that rash Judging is a Sin against God; but we know of nothing in our Principles that leads to it." See Tennent, *Remarks Upon a Protestation Presented to the Synod of Philadelphia, June 1, 1741* (Philadelphia, 1741), 22. On Whitefield's 1744 apology, see George M. Marsden, *Jonathan Edwards: A Life* (New Haven, Conn.: Yale University Press, 2003), 309. The radical New Light Andrew Croswell was also compelled to renounce rash judging. See Schmidt, "'A Second and Glorious Reformation,'" 224.

27. John Caldwell, *An Impartial Trial of the Spirit Operating in this Part of the World* (Boston, 1742), 47–48.

28. Jonathan Edwards, "Some Thoughts Concerning the Revival in New-England," in *The Great Awakening*, ed. C. C. Goen, vol. 4 of *The Works of Jonathan Edwards*, ed. Norman Pettit (New Haven, Conn.: Yale University Press, 1972), 322. For a fuller description of Edwards's insistence on the inadequacy of language, as well as his use of the wind analogy, see Amy Schrager Lang's interpretation of the Edwards-Chauncy dispute, "A Flood of Errors: Chauncy and Edwards in the Great Awakening," in *Jonathan Edwards and the American Experience*, ed. Nathan O. Hatch and Harry S. Stout (New York: Oxford University Press, 1988), esp. 162–68. Edwards's sermon, as well as its context, is recounted in Marsden, *Jonathan Edwards*, 263–84.

29. Jonathan Dickinson, *Danger of Schisms and Contentions* (New York, 1739) 12, 34; Caldwell, *An Impartial Trial*, 6; Samuel Davies, *The Impartial Trial, impartially Tried, and convicted of Partiality* (Williamsburg, 1748). On Dickinson's sermon, see Leonard J. Trinterud, *The Forming of an American Tradition: A Re-examination of Colonial Presbyterianism* (New York: Books for Libraries Press, 1949), 84. Wesley M. Gewehr notes that Samuel Davies successfully identified Caldwell as an "imposter," fleeing from the authorities in Ireland, where he had been accused of theft. Gewehr, *The Great Awakening in Virginia*, 81–83.

30. Richard J. Hooker, ed., *The Carolina Backcountry on the Eve of the American Revolution: The Journal and Other Writings of Charles Woodmason, Anglican Itinerant* (Chapel Hill: University of North Carolina Press, 1953), 78, 101; Theodore Porter, *Trust in Numbers: The Pursuit of Objectivity in Science and Public Life* (Princeton, N.J.: Princeton University Press, 1995), 227.

31. Charles Chauncy, *Seasonable Thoughts on the State of Religion in New-England* (Boston, 1743), vi n., xiii, 369, 423. For a helpful analysis of Chauncy's opposition to the Awakening, see Charles H. Lippy, *Seasonable Revolutionary: The Mind of Charles Chauncy* (Chicago: Nelson-Hall, 1981), 25–42. Chauncy, *Seasonable Thoughts on the State of Religion in New-England*, 367, 368, 26–27.

32. Chauncy, *Seasonable Thoughts*, xxvi. I have removed the distracting italics here. On the tract's lack of popularity, see Alan Heimert and Perry Miller, eds., *The Great Awakening: Documents Illustrating the Crisis and Its Consequences* (Indianapolis: Bobbs-Merrill, 1967), 292.

33. Rhys Isaac may have been the first to point out that it was not so much the dissenting doctrines as the itinerant preaching (along with the accompanying social disruption) that truly antagonized Virginia's religious authorities. See Rhys Isaac, "Religion and Authority: Problems of the Anglican Establishment in Virginia in the Era of the Great Awakening and the Parson's Cause," *William and Mary Quarterly*, 3rd series 30 (October 1973): 26.

34. Trinterud, *The Forming of an American Tradition*, 69. As Trinterud, Elizabeth Nybakken, and Patrick Griffin have suggested, many of these differences extended back into the pre-migration past of these largely Scottish and Scots-Irish peoples. See Trinterud, *The Forming of an American Tradition*, esp. 73–85; Nybakken, "New Light on the Old Side: Irish Influences on Colonial Presbyterianism," *Journal of American History* 68 (March 1982): 813–32; and, Griffin, *The People with No Name: Ireland's Ulster Scots, America's Scots, and the Creation of a British Atlantic World* (Princeton, N.J.: Princeton University Press, 2001). The terms "New Sides" and "Old Sides" are used somewhat anachronistically in this paragraph to avoid confusion. Melvin Buxbaum notes that those appellations only came into use after the schism had occurred. See Buxbaum, *Benjamin Franklin and the Zealous Presbyterians* (University Park: Pennsylvania State University Press, 1975), 136.

35. *Records of the Presbyterian Church in the United States of America*, 157–160n. For the published version of the protest, see John Thomson, *The Government of the Church of Christ, and the Authority of Church Judicatories Established on a Scripture Foundation, and the Spirit of Rash Judging Arraigned and Condemned* (Philadelphia, 1741).

36. *Records of the Presbyterian Church in the United States of America*, 157–59. For both accounts of the event, see Trinterud, *The Forming of an American Tradition*, 105–7.

37. For the moderates' approach to the dispute, see Jonathan Dickinson's remarks before the Philadelphia Synod of 30 May 1743 in *Records of the Presbyterian Church in the United States of America*, 168.

38. Thomson, *The Government of the Church of Christ*, 80. On the doctrine of minority rights, see Patricia U. Bonomi, *Under the Cope of Heaven: Religion, Society, and Politics in Colonial America* (New York: Oxford University Press, 1986), 152–57, 262n62.

39. Thomson, ibid., 108.

40. *An Examination and Refutation of Mr. Gilbert Tennent's Remarks upon the Protestation Presented to the Synod of Philadelphia, June 1, 1741* (Philadelphia, 1742), 34–35.

41. Elisha Williams, *The essential rights and liberties of Protestants* (Boston, 1744), 7–8, 39.

42. Elisha Williams, *A Seasonable Plea for the Liberty of Conscience and The Right of Private Judgment* (Boston, 1744), 15, 49.

43. For eighteenth-century references to Williams's work, see Philemon Robbins, *Plain Narrative of the Proceedings of the Reverend Association and Consociation of New-Haven County* (Boston, 1747), 41; Israel Holly, *A Plea in Zion's Behalf* (Hartford, Conn:, 1765), 7–9; and Ebenezer Frothingham, *A Key to Unlock the Door* (Boston, 1767), 193. My claim that Williams tolerated a range of scriptural interpretations owes a debt to

Christopher Grasso's argument in *A Speaking Aristocracy: Transforming Public Discourse in Eighteenth Century Connecticut* (Chapel Hill: University of North Carolina Press, 1999), esp. 112, 142–43.

44. See *Records of the Presbyterian Church in the United States of America*, 243.

45. For a brief discussion of the millennial hope—and then disappointment—that the revivals produced, see Nathan Hatch, *The Sacred Cause of Liberty: Republic Thought and the Millennium in Revolutionary New England* (New Haven, Conn.: Yale University Press, 1977), 28–36. On the important role played by the laity in reshaping pietism on both sides of the Atlantic, see Westerkamp, *The Triumph of the Laity*.

46. Jonathan Edwards, *A Farewel-Sermon Preached at the First Precinct in Northampton* (Boston, 1751), 7–10. Edwards had been rigorously speculating on the second coming for several years prior to delivering his farewell sermon (since at least 1747). His millennial hopes seemed to have grown as the prospects for a renewed awakening dimmed. See Marsden, *Jonathan Edwards*, 333–37.

47. On the youthful quality of the Awakenings on both sides of the Atlantic, see Michael J. Crawford, *Seasons of Grace*, 7; also Bonomi, *Under the Cope of Heaven*, 146. On the discrediting of ministerial words during this period, see Peter S. Field, *The Crisis of the Standing Order: Clerical Intellectuals and Cultural Authority in Massachusetts, 1780–1833* (Amherst: University of Massachusetts Press, 1998), esp. 24.

48. Francis Allison, *Peace and Union Recommended* (Philadelphia, 1758), 48. The proposal that "all our former differences be buried in perpetual oblivion" was made several times. See, for instance, *Records of the Presbyterian Church in the United States of America*, 202, 238, 253. The first mention of the phrase that I can locate occurs in the conciliatory Old Side invitation for a return of the New Sides in 1743. See *Records of the Presbyterian Church in the United States of America*, 168.

49. On the disappointment and alienation that so many ministers felt during this time, see, for instance, Crawford, *Seasons of Grace*, 193–94. "The Great Awakening," William T. Youngs contends, "was a fulfillment both of the minister's greatest hopes for a spiritual renewal and of their worst fears of popular disrespect." See Youngs, *God's Messengers: Religious Leadership in Colonial New England, 1700–1750* (Baltimore: Johns Hopkins University Press, 1976), 10. Interestingly, one of the benefits the New York Synod saw in burying their former differences with the Philadelphia Synod was that it would enhance "the credit of our profession." See *Records of the Presbyterian Church in the United States of America*, 238.

50. C.C. Goen estimated that "almost one hundred separatist churches" emerged during New England's Great Awakening. See Goen, *Revivalism and Separatism in New England, 1740–1800: Strict Congregationalists and Separate Baptists in the Great Awakening* (New Haven, Conn.: Yale University Press, 1962), vii. Stephen Marini reports that "[b]etween 1745 and 1770 nearly one hundred congregations separated from the established church, about one quarter of all organized parishes." See Marini, *Radical Sects of Revolutionary New England* (Cambridge, Mass.: Harvard University Press, 1982), 19. The contemporary contest over the meaning of the Great Awakening is extensively developed in Lambert, *Inventing the Great Awakening*, 185–257.

51. No one has encapsulated the larger meaning of the Great Awakening better than Richard L. Bushman, who wrote: "The truly revolutionary aspect of the Awakening was the dilution of divine sanction in traditional institutions and the investiture of authority in some inward experience." See Richard L. Bushman, *From Puritan to Yankee: Character and the Social Order in Connecticut, 1690–1765* (New York: Norton, 1970), 220.

52. E. Brooks Holifield notes the use of the term "Regular Lights" by Samuel Mather. See Holifield, *Theology in America: Christian Thought from the Age of the Puritans to the Civil War* (New Haven, Conn.: Yale University Press, 2003), 93. On the sometimes debilitating ambivalence that characterized so many ministers at the time, see David C. Harlan, "The Travail of Religious Moderation: Jonathan Dickinson and the Great Awakening," *Journal of Presbyterian History* 61 (Winter 1983): 411–26.

53. The analysis here is again indebted to the work of Timothy D. Hall. "[I]tinerancy, like commerce and print," Hall writes, "mitigated individualism by opening the way for commitment to new forms of community." See Hall, *Contested Boundaries*, 136. A debt is also owed to Richard Bushman, who argues that "[b]efore the Awakening withdrawal from the Established churches marked a person as alien, while afterwards it took little effort to become a Baptist or Anglican." Bushman, *From Puritan to Yankee*, 223.

CHAPTER 3

1. For overviews of European migration to British North America, see Bernard Bailyn, *Voyagers to the West: A Passage in the Peopling of America on the Eve of the Revolution* (New York: Alfred A. Knopf, 1986); Patrick Griffin, *The People with No Name: Ireland's Ulster Scots, America's Scots Irish, and the Creation of a British Atlantic World, 1689–1764* (Princeton, N.J.: Princeton University Press, 2001); A. G. Roeber, *Palatines, Liberty, and Property: German Lutherans in Colonial British America* (Baltimore: Johns Hopkins University Press, 1998); and Marianne S. Wokeck, *Trade in Strangers: The Beginnings of Mass Migration to North America* (University Park: Pennsylvania State University Press, 1999).

2. On this point and others, this book owes much to the insights of the great historian of American religion, Sidney E. Mead. See Mead, *The Lively Experiment: The Shaping of Christianity in America* (New York: Harper & Row, 1963), esp. 2–3.

3. *The American Heritage Dictionary of the English Language*, 4th ed. (Boston: Houghton Mifflin, 2000), 567.

4. For the best account of the religious ecumenism emerging in American thought from mid-century onward, see Richard W. Pointer, *Protestant Pluralism and the New York Experience: A Study of Eighteenth-Century Religious Diversity* (Bloomington: Indiana University Press, 1988). For an excellent account of the interdenominational interaction and cooperation that took place in mid-eighteenth-century Pennsylvania, see Rothermund, *The Layman's Progress*. Also see Evan Radcliffe, "Revolutionary Writing, Moral Philosophy, and Universal Benevolence in the Eighteenth Century," *Journal of the History of Ideas* 54 (April 1993), 221–40.

5. Jonathan Edwards, *An Humble Attempt to Promote Visible Union of God's People* (Boston, 1747), 81, 185, 183. My interpretation is indebted to a brilliant analysis of Edwards's proposal and its significance by Timothy D. Hall. See Hall, *Contested Boundaries: Itinerancy and the Remaking of the Colonial American Religious World* (Durham, N.C.: Duke University Press, 1994), 105–7. The concert's transatlantic implications are developed by Michael J. Crawford. See his *Seasons of Grace: New England's Revival Tradition in Its British Context* (New York: Oxford University Press, 1991), 229–30. There, he notes that "Edwards and the Scots continued to encourage the agreement into the 1750s" (230). According to Hall, the project remained popular among revivalist preachers—and the laity who followed them—for at least another decade and a half, its reach extending as far south as Virginia. See Hall, *Contested Boundaries*, 107.

6. Gilbert Tennent, *Irenicum Ecclesiasticum, or A Humble Impartial Essay upon the Peace of Jerusalem* (Philadelphia, 1749), vi; Tennent, *Brotherly Love recommended, by the Argument of the Love of Christ* (Philadelphia, 1748), 6; also Gilbert Tennent, *The Divine Government over All Considered* (Philadelphia, 1752), 45–46.

7. Tennent, *Irenicum Ecclesiasticum*, vii. The New Lights' former opponents picked up on the new rhetoric as well. See Francis Alison, *Peace and Union Recommended* (Philadelphia, 1758), 31. I would like to thank my colleague, Karen O'Brien, for first pointing out the increasingly widespread invocation of Christ during the middle to late decades of the eighteenth century.

8. Samuel Davies, *The Impartial Trial, impartially Tried, and convicted of Partiality* (Williamsburg, 1748), 20.

9. For a contemporary definition of essentials, see *A Letter to a Clergyman, in the Colony of Connecticut, From His Friend* (New Haven, 1757), 12n–13n. Non-Anglicans seemed particularly inclined to forgive one another's differences. See John Wesley Brinsfield, *Religion and Politics in Colonial South Carolina* (Easley, S.C.: Southern Historical Press, 1983), 64. Richard W. Pointer discusses the contemporary coincidence of latitudinarian rationalism and ecumenical evangelism in *Protestant Pluralism and the New York Experience: A Study of Eighteenth-Century Religious Diversity* (Bloomington: Indiana University Press, 1988), esp. 51. Winthrop Hudson traces the move toward ecumenism to the Great Awakening. See Hudson, "Denominationalism as a Basis for Ecumenicity: A Seventeenth Century Conception," in *Denominationalism*, ed. Russell E. Richey (Nashville: Abingdon, 1977), 22. Harry S. Stout notes the ecumenical trend of post-Awakening New England religious thought. See Stout, *The New England Soul: Preaching and Religious Culture in Colonial New England* (New York: Oxford University Press, 1986), 212–16.

10. Ezra Stiles, *A Discourse on the Christian Union* (Boston, 1761), 51–52, 97. On the ultimate failure of the union, see Edmund S. Morgan, *The Gentle Puritan: A Life of Ezra Stiles, 1727–1795* (New Haven, Conn.: Yale University Press, 1962), 247. On the formation of another anti-Anglican organization, a Society of Dissenters, see Alan Tully, *Forming American Politics: Ideals, Interests, and Institutions in Colonial New York and Pennsylvania* (Baltimore: Johns Hopkins University Press, 1994), 181.

11. Francis Alison, *Peace and Union Recommended* (Philadelphia, 1758), 28, 31, 48; *Records of the Presbyterian Church in the United States of America, 1706–1788* (1904; repr., New York: Arno, 1969), 218. Alison did not include the words "of love" here, though they appear in the King James Version of the Bible.

12. Donald F. Durnbaugh, ed., *The Brethren in Colonial America: A Source Book on the Transportation and Development of the Church of the Brethren in the Eighteenth Century* (Elgin, Ill.: The Brethren Press, 1967), 278; Jane T. Merritt, "Dreaming of the Savior's Blood: Moravians and the Indian Great Awakening in Pennsylvania," *William and Mary Quarterly*, 3rd series 54 (October 1997): 728. On Zinzendorf and the Moravians, see Durnbaugh, *The Brethren in Colonial America*; A. J. Lewis, *Zinzendorf: Ecumenical Pioneer* (Philadelphia: Westminster, 1962); Stephen L. Longenecker, *Piety and Tolerance: Pennsylvania German Religion, 1700–1850* (Metuchen, N.J.: Scarecrow, 1994), 76–82; Sally Schwartz, *"A Mixed Multitude": The Struggle for Toleration in Colonial Pennsylvania* (New York: New York University Press, 1988), 135–42; and John R. Weinlick, "Moravianism in the American Colonies," in *Continental Pietism and Early American Christianity*, ed. F. Ernest Stoeffler (Grand Rapids, Mich: Eerdmans, 1976). For the tangled and often tragic story of Moravian slavery and African American Moravians in North Carolina, see Jon Sensbach, *A Separate Canaan: The Making of an Afro-Moravian World in North Carolina, 1763–1840* (Chapel Hill: University of North Carolina Press, 1998).

13. For a lucid discussion of the irenic tradition in early modern Europe, see Perez Zagorin, *How the Idea of Religious Toleration Came to the West* (Princeton, N.J.: Princeton University Press, 2003), esp. 55–56, 64, 67–68, 175–77; and Henry Kamen, *The Rise of Toleration* (New York: McGraw-Hill, 1967), esp. 24–29, 67–69, 107–10. For a discussion of dissenting latitudinarianism, see Winthrop S. Hudson, "Denominationalism as a Basis for Ecumenicity: A Seventeenth Century Conception," in Richey, ed., *Denominationalism*, 21–42. For a discussion of the latitudinarian relegation of nonessential matters to the rank of mere "probability" or "opinion," see Barbara J. Shapiro, *Probability and Certainty in Seventeenth-Century England: A Study of the Relationships between Natural Science, Religion, History, Law, and Literature* (Princeton, N.J.: Princeton University Press, 1983), esp. 104–8. For a concise description of the intolerance that often characterized seventeenth-century latitudinarians, see John Coffey, *Persecution and Toleration in Protestant England 1558–1689* (Harlow: Longman, 2000), 36–37, 53. On the problem of identifying any seventeenth-century Anglicans as self-described latitudinarians, see John Spurr, " 'Latitudinarianism' and the Restoration Church," *The Historical Journal* 31 (March 1988): 61–82. For eighteenth-century English latitudinarianism, see Martin Fitzpatrick, "Latitudinarianism at the Parting of the Ways: A Suggestion," in *The Church of England, c. 1689–1833: From Toleration to Tractarianism*, ed. John Walsh, Colin Haydon, and Stephen Taylor (Cambridge: Cambridge University Press, 1993), 209–27. For a brief but comprehensive introduction to latitudinarian thought in colonial America, see Patricia U. Bonomi, *Under the Cope of Heaven: Religion, Society, and Politics in Colonial America* (New York: Oxford University Press, 1986), 218–19. On the role of essentials at the time of the founding, see Sidney E. Mead, "Denominationalism: The Shape of Protestantism in America," in Richey, *Denominationalism*, 83.

14. William G. McLoughlin suggested that New England's Protestants, particularly those in Boston, were already on an ecumenical trajectory prior to the Awakening. See William G. McLoughlin, *New England Dissent, 1630–1833: The Baptists and the Separation of Church and State*, 2 vols. (Cambridge, Mass.: Harvard University Press, 1971), 1:287–304. Harry S. Stout points out that ecumenical understandings of Christian union had come to characterize New England preaching and writing by the beginning of the eighteenth century. See Stout, *The New England Soul*, 129–31. For evidence that this was the case, see the ecumenical discussion that took place in the *Boston Gazette* in 1734 and 1735 over the possible union of the Protestant churches there. *Boston Gazette*, 23 December 1734; *Boston Gazette*, 27 January 1735; *Boston Gazette*, 17 February 1735; *Boston Gazette*, 30 June 1735; *Boston Gazette*, 11 August 1735; *Boston Gazette*, 25 August 1735; and *Boston Gazette*, 15 September 1735. A genuinely ecumenical use of latitudinarian language was made by the renowned New England divine, Cotton Mather, at the ordination of a Baptist minister in 1717. See Cotton Mather, *Brethren Dwelling Together in Unity* (Boston, 1718), 19. Kenneth Silverman points out that Mather advanced a similar argument as early as 1692—following the passage of the English Toleration Act three years earlier. See Silverman, *The Life and Times of Cotton Mather* (New York: Welcome Rain, 1984), 140–45. For the importance of the "fundamentals of Christianity" in early eighteenth-century Pennsylvania, see Sally Schwartz, *"A Mixed Multitude,"* esp. 144–45, 157–58.

15. Thomas Barton, *Unanimity and Public Spirit* (Philadelphia, 1755), 13–14. On Protestant nationalism, see Linda Colley, *Britons: Forging the Nation 1707–1837* (New Haven, Conn.: Yale University Press, 1992), 18. A similar dynamic seems to have been at work in the colonies. See Thomas S. Kidd, " 'Let Hell and Rome Do Their Worst': World News, Anti-Catholicism, and International Protestantism in Early-Eighteenth-Century Boston," *New England Quarterly* 76 (June 2003): 287. On migration to the colonies, see Marianne S. Wokeck, *Trade in Strangers*, 44–45. For statistics on German migration, see table 2, 45. The heaviest concentration of migrants did not actually arrive in the colonies until the 1760s. From that point, the tide remained heavy until the outbreak of the American Revolution. For a discussion of the Atlantic-wide consumer revolution, see T. H. Breen, "An Empire of Goods: The Anglicization of Colonial America, 1690–1776," *Journal of British Studies* 25 (October 1986): 467–99. On the growth in colonial newspapers, see Wm. David Sloan and Julie Hedgepeth Williams, *The Early American Press, 1690–1783* (Westport, Conn.; London: Greenwood, 1994), 103–5. On the importance of communication with strangers in the development of modern public life, see Michael Warner, *Publics and Counterpublics* (New York: Zone, 2002).

16. Carl Becker, *The Heavenly City of the Eighteenth-Century Philosophers* (New Haven, Conn.: Yale University Press, 1932); Alan Heimert, *Religion and the American Mind: From the Great Awakening to the Revolution* (Cambridge, Mass.: Harvard University Press, 1966), esp. 373–79, 398, 405; George Marsden, *The Soul of the American University: From Protestant Establishment to Established Nonbelief* (New York: Oxford University Press, 1993), 50–52; and Roland Stromberg, *Religious Liberalism in Eighteenth-Century England* (Glasgow: Oxford University Press, 1954), 91–92.

17. Robert W. T. Martin, *The Free and Open Press: The Founding of American Democratic Press Liberty, 1640–1800* (New York: New York University Press, 2001), 59; *New-York Gazette*, 28 October 1734. Quoted in Stephen Botein, " 'Meer Mechanics' and an Open Press: The Business and Political Strategies of Colonial American Printers," *Perspectives in American History* 9 (1975): 179. Robert W. T. Martin notes that the "open press doctrine" was relaxed during the revolutionary period. For his discussion of the subject, see *The Free and Open Press*, 55–56, 59, 82. My own impression is that the masthead "Open to All Parties" regained popularity following the Revolutionary War. For discussions of the open press doctrine, see Botein, " 'Meer Mechanics' and an Open Press," esp. 165, 177–79; James N. Green, "The Book Trade in the Middle Colonies, 1680–1720," in *A History of the Book in America*, vol. 1, *The Colonial Book in the Atlantic World*, ed. Hugh Amory and David D. Hall (Cambridge: Cambridge University Press, 2000), 256–57; and Jeffrey A. Smith, "Impartiality and Revolutionary Ideology: Editorial Policies of the *South-Carolina Gazette*, 1732–1775" *Journal of Southern History* 49 (November 1983): 511–26.

18. Anson Phelps Stokes, *Church and State in the United States*, 3 vols. (New York: Harper & Brothers, 1950), 1:164–65. Theodore G. Tappert notes that an interdenominational charitable organization, the German Society of Pennsylvania, was established in 1764 "to protect German newcomers from injustice and cruel treatment." "Similar societies," he notes, "were organized in Charleston (1766), Baltimore (1783), and New York (1784)." See Tappert, "The Influence of Pietism in Colonial American Lutheranism," in *Continental Pietism and American Christianity*, ed. F. Ernest Stoeffler (Grand Rapids, Mich.: Eerdmans, 1976), 32. John L. Brooke discusses the growth of voluntary associations at midcentury in "Ancient Lodges and Self-Created Societies: Voluntary Association and the Public Sphere in the Early Republic," in *Launching the 'Extended Republic': The Federalist Era* (Charlottesville: University Press of Virginia, 1996), 284.

19. Steven C. Bullock, *Revolutionary Brotherhood: Freemasonry and the Transformation of the American Social Order, 1730–1840* (Chapel Hill: University of North Carolina Press, 1996), 46.

20. *Pennsylvania Gazette*, 26 June 1755; William Smith, *A Sermon Preached in Christ-Church, Philadelphia* (Philadelphia, 1755), 9. Anson Phelps Stokes stresses both the influence of the Masons and their ecumenicity in *Church and State in the United States*, 1:244–53.

21. Steven C. Bullock points to this homology in his excellent book on Freemasonry. See Bullock's *Revolutionary Brotherhood*, 57. Bullock observes that Charles Brockwell's sermon, *Brotherly Love Recommended* (cited below) was printed in Boston the same year that two other sermons on brotherly love were published, one of which—*Love to Our Neighbors Recommended*—went through a second printing before the year was through. It should also be noted that 1749 also marked the first year that Isaac Watt's classic latitudinarian tract, *Orthodoxy and Charity United* (Boston, 1749), originally printed in London (1748), was reprinted in the colonies.

22. American Catholics were not yet forbidden to participate in secret societies. See Charles H. Metzger, *Catholics in the American Revolution: A Study in Religious Climate* (Chicago: Loyola University, 1962), 210.

23. Arthur Browne, *Universal Love Recommended* (Boston, 1755), 7, 10; Thomas Pollen, *Universal Love* (Boston, 1758), 15.

24. Brockwell, *Brotherly Love Recommended*, 13–14; Browne, *Universal Love Recommended*, 22. Brockwell's language here borrowed heavily from *The Constitutions of the Free-Masons: Containing the History, Charges, Regulations, etc. of That Most Ancient and Right Worshipful Fraternity* (Philadelphia, 1734).

25. Wellins Calcott, *A Candid Disquisition of the Principles and Practices of the Most Antient and Honourable Society of Free and Accepted Masons* (Boston, 1772), 139. "Unanimity" was a common theme in Masonic writings. See, for instance, William Smith, *A Sermon Preached in Christ-Church, Philadelphia* (Philadelphia, 1755), 18, 21.

26. Henry Melchior Muhlenberg, *The Journals of Henry Melchior Muhlenberg*, trans. T. G. Tappert and J. W. Doberstein, 3 vols. (Philadelphia: Muhlenberg, 1942), 123; "To the Freeholders and Electors Of the Province of Pennsylvania" [1765], Broadside Collection, Historical Society of Pennsylvania. Quoted in Schwartz, *"A Mixed Multitude,"* 234. There is some evidence to suggest that the same process was occurring, albeit at a much more gradual pace, outside of the Middle Colonies. None of the colonies restricted officeholding to a single denomination. Moreover, it appears that minority groups were becoming more active in politics during the late colonial period and playing a prominent role in the colonial legislatures by the early 1770s. In Massachusetts, Jonathan Mayhew wrote (1764), "Episcopalians may be, and often are, chosen members of both houses of assembly in the colonies of New England; nor is there either law, or any thing else, to prevent this, if, by their qualifications and good behaviour, they can recommend themselves to the electors." See Mayhew, *Remarks on an Anonymous Tract* (Boston, 1764), 68. In Connecticut, where the Old Lights and the New Lights formed competing political parties, both groups put together coalitions with Anglican office-seekers. Bruce Steiner notes that Anglicans, who made up approximately 9 percent of the colony's population in 1774, constituted roughly 10 percent of the deputies in the Connecticut lower house. See Steiner, "Anglican Officeholding in Pre-Revolutionary Connecticut: The Parameters of New England Community," *William and Mary Quarterly*, 3rd series 31 (July 1974), esp. 370, 373, 381–88. New Jersey's legislature appears to have been as religiously diverse as Philadelphia's at midcentury. See Brendan McConville, *Those Daring Disturbers of the Peace: The Struggle for Property and Power in Early New Jersey* (Ithaca, N.Y.: Cornell University Press, 1999), 241. Regarding Virginia, Charles S. Sydnor has argued that the recusancy laws were not strictly enforced and that "as a matter of fact, dissenters seemed to have voted freely during the late-colonial period." Sydnor also contended that the "candidates cultivated the good will of dissenters with great zeal." See Sydnor, *American Revolutionaries in the Making: Political Practices in Washington's Virginia* (New York: The Free Press, 1966), 35. Until the Revolution, Virginia's Anglicans do seem to have been able to maintain their hegemony in the colony's political system. According to Paul K. Longmore, in 1759, the House of Burgesses "dissolved several vestries for including non-Anglican vestrymen." See Longmore, "'All Matters and Things Relating to Religion and Morality': The Virginia Burgesses' Committee for Religion, 1769 to 1775," *Journal of Church and State* 38 (Autumn 1996): 778. Some anecdotal evidence regarding the

North Carolina legislature suggests a large dissenter presence early in the eighteenth century. There, one Anglican missionary noted in 1711, "The Assembly was made up of a strange mixture of men of various opinions and inclinations a few Churchmen many Presbyterians Independents but most Anythingarians some out of principle others out of hopes of power and authority in the Government to the end that they might Lord it over their Neighbours...." See "From N.C. Letter Book. S.P.G. John Urmston (North Carolina)" (7 July 1711) in *Colonial Records of North Carolina, 1662–1790*, ed. W. L. Saunders, 26 vols. (Raleigh, 1886–1914), 1:769. Dissenters also seem to have been able to make significant inroads in South Carolina politics before the late eighteenth century. See Erskine Clarke, *Our Southern Zion: A History of Calvinism in the South Carolina Low Country, 1690–1990* (Tuscaloosa: University of Alabama Press, 1996), 56. It is not clear, however, what happened over the succeeding decades as the Anglican establishment was consolidated in those two southern colonies.

27. James Madison, Alexander Hamilton, and John Jay, *The Federalist Papers*, ed. Isaac Kramnick (Harmondsworth: Penguin, 1987), 128. An anonymous letter addressed to the Connecticut clergy did posit that "[t]here must be a due Balance of Power between the Clergy and the Laity." See *A Letter to the Clergy of the Colony of Connecticut* (New Haven, Conn., 1760), 14. Another exception was the prominent Rhode Island Congregationalist Ezra Stiles, who anticipated Madison's argument in his *Discourse on the Christian Union*, 96–97. William Livingston condemned factions and party divisions most directly in his essay, "Of Party-Divisions," in *The Independent Reflector*, ed. Milton M. Klein (Cambridge, Mass.: The Belknap Press of Harvard University Press, 1963), 143–50. For an excellent discussion of how religions and politics mixed across colonial America during the 1750s, 1760s, and 1770s, see Bonomi, *Under the Cope of Heaven*, 161–86.

28. William Smith, *Brief State of the Province of Pennsylvania* (1756; repr., New York, 1865), 20. For mutual charges of attempting to "turn the Hearts of the ignorant Dutch," see *The Substance of a Council* (Philadelphia, 1764), quotations on 2 and 5. See also, The Scribbler, *Being a Letter from a Gentleman in Town to his Friend in the Country* (Philadelphia, 1764). Alan Tully suggests that new German voters may have been actively recruited as early as 1740. See Tully, *Forming American Politics*, 149.

29. William Allen to Thomas Penn, 21 October 1764, Penn official correspondence, Historical Society of Pennsylvania. Reprinted in Rothermund, *The Layman's Progress*, 188; Samuel Purviance to Colonel James Burd, 20 September 1765, Shippen Papers, Historical Society of Pennsylvania. Reprinted in Rothermund, *The Layman's Progress*, 185. Alan Tully notes that the Proprietary Party gained sympathy from the colony's German population in 1764 by "plac[ing] two German churchmen on their Philadelphia County ticket, and promis[ing] more justices of the peace in the future." See Tully, *Forming American Politics*, 198. For more evidence of the kind of religious coalition building then occurring in Pennsylvania, see Richard K. MacMaster, Samuel L. Horst, and Robert F. Ulle, eds., *Conscience in Crisis: Mennonites and Other Peace Churches in America, 1739–1789: Interpretation and Documents* (Scottdale, Pa.: Herald, 1979), 199, 205. On midcentury politics generally, see Patricia U. Bonomi, "The Middle Colonies: Embryo of the New Political Order," in *Perspectives on Early American*

History: Essays in Honor of Richard B. Morris, ed. Richard Brandon Morris, Alden T. Vaughan, and George Athan Billias (New York: Harper & Row, 1973), 63–92; and Tully, *Forming American Politics*. These religious unions were not always harmonious. As Alan Tully points out, relations between Presbyterians and Anglicans were sometimes quite tense during the 1760s. See Tully, *Forming American Politics*, 195.

30. Tully, *Forming American Politics*, 156–57.

31. *Pennsylvania Gazette*, 27 November 1755.

32. Governor to Assembly, 10 January 1739–40, in Gertrude MacKinney and Charles F. Hoban, eds., *Votes and Proceedings of the House of Representatives of the Province of Pennsylvania, 1682–1776*, in *Pennsylvania Archives*, 8th series, 8 vols. (Harrisburg, Pa.: Hood, 1931–1935), 3:2535; *An Address to Those Quakers Who perversely refused to pay any Regard to the late provincial FAST, May 25, 1756* (Philadelphia, 1756), 7, 6.

33. On the relationship between politics and religion in this period, see James S. Olson, "The New York Assembly, the Politics of Religion, and the Origins of the American Revolution, 1768–1771," *Historical Magazine of the Protestant Episcopal Church* 43 (1974): 21–28.

34. *The Freeholder, No. 3. A Continuation of the Answers to the Reasons* (New York, 1769), 3. On the DeLancey electoral ticket, see Tully, *Forming American Politics*, 178.

35. *Observations on the Reasons, Lately Published, for the Malicious Combination of Several Presbyterian Dissenters* (New York, 1769), 1, 3; *The Examiner, No. III. Addressed to the Freeholders and Freemen of the City of New York* (New York, 1769), 2. According to Patricia Bonomi, the strategy appears to have succeeded. For Bonomi's account of the election, see *A Factious People: Politics and Society in Colonial New York* (New York: Columbia University Press, 1971), esp. 248–57. The Presbyterians had been facetiously accused of pursuing the same strategy. See *The Substance of a Council, Held at Lancaster August the 28th 1764* (Philadelphia, 1764), 5, 8.

36. For a good, recent overview of college education in the founding period, see J. David Hoeveler, *Creating the American Mind: Intellect and Politics in the Colonial Colleges* (Lanham, Md.: Rowman & Littlefield, 2002).

37. Richard Hofstadter and Wilson Smith, eds., *American Higher Education: A Documentary History*, 2 vols. (Chicago: University of Chicago Press, 1961), 1:45, 55. William G. McLoughlin notes the expulsion of New Lights from Yale and Harvard in *New England Dissent*, 1:363.

38. The standards for students differed from those of their teachers. According to Richard Hofstadter and Walter P. Metzger, college teachers and college officials usually still had to pass doctrinal tests before assuming their positions. See Hofstadter and Metzger, *The Development of Academic Freedom in the United States* (New York: Columbia University Press, 1955), 156. On the composition of the College of Philadelphia's student population, see Anne D. Gordon, *The College of Philadelphia, 1747–1779: Impact of an Institution* (New York: Garland, 1989), 100. Most, it should be noted, were Anglicans from the Philadelphia area. At King's College, members of Dutch Reformed and Presbyterian churches generally stayed away.

39. Dr. Smith's Manuscript Notes, Commencement, 17 November 1767, Rev. William Smith Papers, VI, 141–42. Historical Society of Pennsylvania. Quoted in

Schwartz, "A Mixed Multitude," 265; John Witherspoon, *Address in Behalf of the College of New-Jersey* (Philadelphia, 1772), 25–26 (the address was later reprinted in *The New-York Gazette, and The Weekly Mercury,* 28 December 1772); *The New-York Gazette,* 7 December 1772; [John Vardill or Thomas Bradbury Chandler], *Candid Remarks on Dr. Witherspoon's Address to the Inhabitants of Jamaica, And the other West-India Islands, &c.* (Philadelphia, 1772), 53, 56–57. In some cases, assertions of educational non-sectarianism were greeted by outright disdain. See "A Looking Glass &c., Number II" (publication date not given) in John R. Dunbar, ed., *The Paxton Papers* (The Hague: Martinus Nijhoff, 1957), 309–10.

40. *Boston Evening-Post,* 23 March 1747; *Boston Evening-Post,* 9 February 1747. For the argument that the colonial colleges were primarily induced to tolerate different faiths by "competition among the colleges for students," see Hofstadter and Metzger, *The Development of Academic Freedom in the United States,* 152. Marsden discusses the composition of college boards in *The Soul of the American University,* 57. The example of Brown University is cited on 65–66. On Stiles's efforts to create a less Baptist-dominated college, see Herbst, *From Crisis to Crisis: American College Government, 1636–1819* (Cambridge, Mass.: Harvard University Press, 1982), 124–25; and Herbst, "The Charter for a Proposed College in Newport, Rhode Island: A Chapter in the History of Eighteenth Century Higher Education in America," *Newport History* 49 (Spring 1976): 25–49. According to Walter C. Bronson, Harvard had never imposed religious tests on its students. See Bronson, *The History of Brown University, 1764–1914* (Providence, R.I.: Brown University, 1914), 4. However, non-Congregationalist worship was clearly restricted at Harvard. Not until 1760 did the college's overseers begin to "permit Anglican scholars to go to their own services," though, even then, only with "a written application to the president and faculty." See Charles Akers, *Called unto Liberty: A Life of Jonathan Mayhew, 1720–1766* (Cambridge, Mass.: Harvard University Press, 1964), 169–70.

41. Dartmouth charter quoted in Herbst, *From Crisis to Crisis,* 130. On Wheelock's charity school and the founding of Dartmouth, see James Axtell, *Natives and Newcomers: The Cultural Origins of North America* (New York: Oxford University Press, 2001), 174–88.

42. Thomas Clap, *The Religious Constitution of Colleges* (New Haven, 1754), 12–14, 19; Clap, *A Brief History and Vindication of the Doctrines Received and Established in the Churches of New-England* (Boston, 1757), 13. On Clap's prohibition against off-campus worship, see Hoeveler, *Creating the American Mind,* 73. Clap's rejection of the Baptist merchant's donation is discussed in David D. Hall, "Learned Culture in the Eighteenth Century," in *A History of the Book in America,* vol. 1, *The Colonial Book in the Atlantic World,* ed. Hugh Amory and David D. Hall (Cambridge: Cambridge University Press, 2000), 430–31.

43. Thomas Clap, *The Religious Constitution of Colleges* (New Haven, 1754), 16. "Persons of all Denominations of Protestants are allowed the Advantage of an Education here," Clap would later write, "and no Inquiry has been made, at their Admission or afterwards, about their particular Sentiments in Religion." Only if an individual "should take Pains to infect the Minds of their Fellow-Students with such

pernicious Errors, as are contrary to the Fundamentals of Christianity, and the special Design of founding this College" would action be taken against them. See Clap, *The Annals or History of Yale-College* (New York, 1766), 83–84. Information on the Yale apostasy is derived from Peter Doll, *Revolution, Religion, and National Identity: Imperial Anglicanism in British North America, 1745–1795* (Madison, N.J.: Farleigh Dickinson University Press, 2000), 161. On the hostility displayed toward Clap, see Hofstadter and Metzger, *The Development of Academic Freedom*, 174–76; and Marsden, *The Soul of the American University*, 56. Among the complaints lodged against him was that he drew an unjustified, and uncharitable, distinction between "Primary and Secondary" matters of faith and worship. See [Shubael Conant], *A Letter to a Friend* (New-Haven, 1757), 16, 19, 52.

44. David C. Humphrey, *From King's College to Columbia 1746–1800* (New York: Columbia University Press, 1976), 26. It does appear that most of the trustees were awarded their position in virtue of offices they already possessed. On the composition of the original board and the Anglicans' position in the city, see Nancy L. Rhoden, *Revolutionary Anglicanism: The Colonial Church of England during the American Revolution* (New York: New York University Press, 1999), 30.

45. Thomas Jones, *History of New York during the Revolutionary War*, ed. Edwin Floyd De Lancey, 2 vols. (New York, 1879), 1:7. Quoted in Milton M. Klein, ed., *The Independent Reflector* (Cambridge, Mass.: The Belknap Press of Harvard University Press 1963), 5.

46. William Livingston, "Remarks on Our Intended College" (29 March 1753) in Klein, ed., *The Independent Reflector*, 180–82.

47. *New-York Mercury*, 16 April 1753; Livingston, "A Prayer" (31 May 1753) in Klein, ed., *The Independent Reflector*, 242–49; Benjamin Nicoll, *A Brief Vindication of the Proceedings of the Trustees Relating to the College* (New York, 1754), 4–5; *New-York Mercury*, 30 July 1753. On this matter at least, Anglican beliefs lined up with their Dutch Reformed counterparts. Writing under a pseudonym, the prominent Dutch Reformed minister Theodore Frelinghuysen argued that it was a good idea for each tolerated group to have its own institution of higher learning. See David Marin Ben Jesse [Theodore Frelinghuysen], *A Remark on the Disputes and Contentions in this Province*, 11. For a discussion of the Dutch Reformed position, see Pointer, *Protestant Pluralism and the New York Experience*, 57–58. Frelinghuysen's identity as author of the piece is persuasively argued in Beverly McAnear's "American Imprints Concerning King's College," *Papers of the Bibliographical Society of America* 44 (1950): 327–28.

48. William Livingston, "Primitive Christianity short and intelligible, modern Christianity voluminous and incomprehensible" (28 June 1753) in Klein, ed., *The Independent Reflector*, 270–77. The quotations appear on 271.

49. Humphrey, *From King's College to Columbia*, 47, 49. The quotation appears on 47; Livingston's maneuverings are discussed in McAnear, "American Imprints Concerning King's College," 316; and Humphrey, *From King's College to Columbia*, 47.

50. *New York Gazette*, 3 June 1754. Quoted in Humphrey, *From King's College to Columbia*, 48. On the composition of the board stipulated by the King's College charter, see Humphrey, *From King's College to Columbia*, 48; and Mary Augustina Ray,

American Opinion of Roman Catholicism in the Eighteenth Century (New York: Columbia University Press, 1936), 150. In Johnson's case at least, the ecumenical sentiments were probably not insincere. He was one of Yale's Apostates who had converted to Anglicanism in 1722 and had recently campaigned against Thomas Clap's policy of prohibiting students from attending a local Anglican church. See Humphrey, *From King's College to Columbia*, 48.

51. *New-York Mercury*, 22 October 1753. Alan Tully points out that Anglican assemblymen proved more conciliatory than their ordained counterparts. Some even publicly distanced themselves from the campaign to make King's College into an Anglican institution because of opposition from their Quaker and Presbyterian constituents. See Tully, *Forming American Politics*, 139–40.

52. *New-York Mercury*, 30 April 1753. Tully notes, however, that Livingston and his allies did not succeed in turning this sentiment into actual votes. See Tully, *Forming American Politics*, 141.

53. Isaac Backus, "Policy as well as Honesty, Forbids the use of Secular Force in Religious Affairs" (1779), in William G. McLoughlin, *Isaac Backus: On Church, State, and Calvinism, Pamphlets 1754–1789* (Cambridge, Mass., 1968), 376–77.

54. *A Speech Said to have been Delivered some Time before the Close of the Late Sessions* (New-York, 1755), 4, 20. The pamphlet was signed anonymously: "By a Member Dissenting from The Church." Beverly McAnear posits that its author was Archibald Kennedy. See McAnear, "American Imprints Concerning King's College," 326. Similar points about the importance of children making unbiased decisions regarding religious affiliation appeared in two college-related tracts of the period, both probably penned by New York Anglicans. See *The New-York Gazette*, 7 December 1772; and *Candid Remarks on Dr. Witherspoon's Address*, 56.

55. Hermon Husbands, *Some Remarks on Religion, With the Author's Experience in Pursuit thereof* (Philadelphia, 1761), esp. 3–4, 24. Amid a heated dispute over the massacre committed by Pennsylvania's Paxton Boys, an anonymous writer (probably another Quaker) also drew upon the father-son analogy to suggest the contingent nature of religious identity. See "The Quaker Vindicated; Or, Observations on a Late Pamphlet, Entituled, The Quaker Unmask'd, Or, Plain Truth" (1764) in Dunbar, ed., *The Paxton Papers*, 237.

56. *A True Copy of a Genuine Letter* (New-York, 1761), 3, 7, 16; *A Second Letter to the Congregations of the Eighteen Presbyterian (or New-Light) Ministers* (Philadelphia, 1761), 8.

57. Thomas Fitch, *An Explanation of Say-Brook Platform* (Hartford, 1765), 6, 8; Catholicus, *A Letter to a Clergyman, in the Colony of Connecticut, From His Friend* (New Haven, 1757), 17; [Hart, William], *A Letter to Paulinus, Containing an Answer to His Three Questions, Lately proposed to the Public, In the Connecticut Gazette* (New Haven, 1760), 10n. According to Richard Bushman, "the Platform was silently dropped from the colony's statue book in 1784." See Bushman, *From Puritan to Yankee*, 174.

58. Franklin, *The Autobiography of Benjamin Franklin*, ed. Louis P. Masur (Boston: Bedford, 1993), 108; Gilbert Tennent to George Whitefield, 5 June 1742. Reprinted in Rothermund, *The Layman's Progress*, 148. George Whitefield to the Trustees of

the New Building, 19 September 1742. Reprinted in *The Layman's Progress*, 148–49. The quote comes from Gilbert Tennent's letter to Whitefield (*Layman's Progress*, 148), though Whitefield also used the term "Bable" in his own epistle to the building's trustees. On nondenominational churches, see Jon Butler, *Becoming America: The Revolution before 1776* (Cambridge, Mass.: Harvard University Press, 2000), 203. For New Building's history, see Rothermund, *Layman's Progress*, 28–29, 115–17.

59. New Building's history, Rothermund acutely observed, marked an important change: "Liberalism had replaced Pietism as the agent of interdenominational activity." See *The Layman's Progress*, 117.

60. Davies to the Bishop of London [unsubmitted letter], in William Henry Foote, *Sketches of Virginia, Historical and Biographical* (Philadelphia, 1850), 193, 199. For the best discussion of religious identity and its relationship to religious diversity in America, see Moore, *Religious Outsiders and the Making of Americans* (New York: Oxford University Press, 1986), esp. 208.

61. On the difference between sectarianism and denominationalism, and for some seminal discussions of denominationalism in America, see Will Herberg, *Protestant-Catholic-Jew: An Essay in American Religious Sociology* (Chicago: University of Chicago Press, 1980), 85–86; Winthrop S. Hudson, "Denominationalism as a Basis for Ecumenicity," esp. 19; Winthrop S. Hudson and John Corrigan, *Religion in America: An Historical Account of the Development of American Religious Life*, 6th ed. (Upper Saddle River, N.J.: Prentice Hall, 1999), 100–101; Sidney E. Mead, "The Fact of Pluralism and the Persistence of Sectarianism," in *The Religion of the Republic*, ed. Elwyn A. Smith (Philadelphia: Fortress, 1971), 247–66; Timothy Smith, "Congregation, State, and Denomination: The Forming of the American Religious Structure," *William and Mary Quarterly*, 3rd series 25 (April 1968): 155–76.

62. Samuel Pike, *A Plain and Full Account of the Christian Practices Observed By the Church in St. Martin-le-grand, London* (Boston, 1766), 23, 25. On the Sandemanians, see John Howard Smith, "'Sober Dissent' and 'Spirited Conduct': The Sandemanians and The American Revolution, 1765–1781," *Historical Journal of Massachusetts* 28 (Summer 2000): 142–66.

63. Samuel Pike, *A Plain and Full Account*, 23–24; Pike, *A Letter Wrote By Mr. Samuel Pike to Mr. Robert Sandeman* (Portsmouth, 1766), 4–5.

64. Franklin, *The Autobiography of Benjamin Franklin*, 88–89.

65. Ibid. Franklin did, as Melvin H. Buxbaum points out, dislike the brand of Calvinism espoused by American Presbyterians and often expressed resentment toward Presbyterian theology and politics. See Buxbaum, "Franklin Looks for a Rector: 'Poor Richard's' Hostility to Presbyterians," *Journal of Presbyterian History* 48 (1970): 176–88. Moderate Anglicanism was considerably more appealing to him. By the end of the 1740s, Buxbaum notes, Franklin held a pew in Philadelphia's (Anglican) Christ Church. Buxbaum, "Franklin Looks for a Rector," 180.

66. *Pennsylvania Gazette*, 5 September 1754.

67. "Rom.XII.18," Parkman Family Papers Box 1, Folder 5 (Sermons 1750–1759), 13, 10, 16. American Antiquarian Society. On the increasingly intimate and harmonious

relations between Congregationalists and Anglicans in late eighteenth-century Connecticut, see Steiner, "Anglican Officeholding in Pre-Revolutionary Connecticut," 396–401.

CHAPTER 4

1. As reprinted in Herbert L. Osgood, "The Society of Dissenters founded at New York in 1769," *American Historical Review* 6 (April 1901): 504. Quoted in Richard W. Pointer, *Protestant Pluralism and the New York Experience: A Study of Eighteenth-Century Religious Diversity* (Bloomington: Indiana University Press, 1988), 64.

2. Pierre Bourdieu, *Language and Symbolic Power*, ed. John B. Thompson, trans. Gino Raymond and Matthew Adamson (Cambridge, Mass.: Harvard University Press, 1982), 40.

3. Ira Berlin, "Two Concepts of Liberty," in *Four Essays on Liberty* (London: Oxford University Press, 1969); also Quentin Skinner, "The Idea of Negative Liberty," in *Philosophy in History*, ed. Richard Rorty, J. B. Schneewind, and Quentin Skinner (Cambridge: Cambridge University Press, 1984). Steven D. Smith discusses the various meanings of religious freedom and religious liberty during the founding period in *Foreordained Failure: The Quest for a Constitutional Principle of Religious Freedom* (New York: Oxford University Press, 1995), 3–43.

4. My account of Apthorp's personal life and Apthorp House is indebted to Wendell D. Garrett, *Apthorp House 1760–1969* (Cambridge, Mass.: Adams House, 1960), 3–19, 22–35.

5. Charles Akers, *Called unto Liberty: A Life of Jonathan Mayhew, 1720–1766* (Cambridge, Mass.: Harvard University Press, 1964). Akers refers to Mayhew's characteristic "impetuosity" on 110.

6. For a brief discussion of the growing Anglican presence in New England, see Carl Bridenbaugh, *Mitre and Sceptre: Transatlantic Faiths, Ideas, Personalities, and Politics, 1689–1775* (New York: Oxford University Press, 1962), 179. On the growing religious diversity within New England towns, see John M. Murrin, "Review Essay" *History and Theory* 11 (1972): 248–50.

7. East Apthorp, *The Constitution of a Christian Church, Illustrated in a Sermon at the Opening of Christ-Church in Cambridge* (Boston, 1762), 17–18; Apthorp, *Considerations on the institution and conduct of the Society for the Propagation of the Gospel in Foreign Parts* (Boston, 1763), 23–24.

8. Apthorp, *Considerations on the institution and conduct,* 13–14.

9. Jonathan Mayhew, *Observations on the Charter and Conduct of the Society for the Propagation of the Gospel* (Boston, 1763), 13, 21; Mayhew, *Remarks on an Anonymous Tract* (Boston, 1764), 43, 17. For an earlier accusation that the SPG had done a poor job of proselytizing anyone but white Protestants, see the *Boston Evening-Post,* 27 April 1747.

10. Thomas Secker, *An Answer to Dr. Mayhew's Observations, On the Charter and Conduct of the Society for the Propagation of the Gospel in Foreign Parts* (Boston, 1764), 12, 30–31, 50.

11. One of the remarks that aggravated Boston's Congregationalists in the early 1760s was the suggestion made by an Anglican writer—after acknowledging the construction of Christ's Church—that Harvard's commencement services might be held there, as well as at the local "Independent *Meeting House.*" See *The Boston Gazette; and the Country Journal,* 12 January 1761.

12. On the interest taken across the Atlantic in the missionary controversy, see Akers, *Called unto Liberty,* 191–93; also the *Boston-Gazette,* 28 November 1763.

13. For a discussion of representation and its associated problems during this period, see Edmund Morgan, *Inventing the People* (New York: W. W. Norton, 1988), esp. 240–42.

14. On Chandler's role in the King's College dispute, see Beverly McAnear, "American Imprints on King's College," 311n.19, 324.

15. Thomas Bradbury Chandler, *An Appeal to the Public, in Behalf of the Church of England in America* (New York, 1767), 82, 40, 93. Technically, the campaign began earlier that year when John Ewer, bishop of Landaff, publicly recommended a colonial bishop in a sermon before the SPG. See Ewer, *A Sermon Preached Before the Incorporated Society for the Propagation of the Gospel in Foreign Parts* (New York, 1768).

16. Chandler, *An Appeal to the Public,* 42, 82. Bishop Thomas Secker had framed the argument for an Anglican bishop in similar fashion in his 1764 tract. Secker argued that Mayhew and his fellow dissenters could not oppose the occasional presence of such an officer and still "call themselves Patrons of religious Liberty." See Secker, *An Answer to Dr. Mayhew's Observations,* 57. For a similar conception of religious liberty, see the *Boston Evening-Post,* 28 February 1763.

17. Charles Inglis, *A Vindication of the Bishop of Landaff's Sermon* (New York, 1768), 82. Quoted in Nancy L. Rhoden, *Revolutionary Anglicanism: The Colonial Church of England during the American Revolution* (New York: New York University Press, 1999), 56. On the pluralistic bent of the Anglican argument, see Pointer, *Protestant Pluralism and the New York Experience,* 61.

18. Thomas Bradbury Chandler, *An Appeal Defended or the Proposed American Episcopate vindicated* (New York, 1769), 14–15; Chandler, *An Appeal to the Public,* 26–27. Seconding Chandler's pragmatism, the pro-Anglican essayist, "A Whip for the American Whig," insisted that "the only fair Way for Men to judge of this Case is, to consider it upon the Principles of the Church, and not of those who differ from it." See *A Collection of Tracts from the Late News Papers* (New York, 1769), 301.

19. The *Virginia Gazette,* 15 August 1771; and the *Virginia Gazette,* 11 July 1771 [Purdie and Dixon]. For similar references to religious liberty, see the *Virginia Gazette,* 22 August 1771; the *Virginia* Gazette, 10 October 1771; the *Virginia* Gazette, 2 January 1772; the *Virginia Gazette,* 9 January 1772; and the *Virginia* Gazette, 16 January 1772 [Purdie and Dixon].

20. Charles Chauncy, *A Reply to Dr. Chandler's Appeal Defended* (Boston, 1770), 174; Barnabas Binney, *An Oration Delivered on the Late Public Commencement at Rhode-Island College* (Boston, 1774), 23.

21. *An Address to the Merchants, Freeholders and All Other The Inhabitants of the Province of Pennsylvania* (Philadelphia, 1768) [Broadside]; *To the Freeholders and*

Freemen of the City and County of New-York, in Communion with the Reformed Dutch Church (New York, 1769) [Broadside].

22. Thomas B. Chandler, *An Appeal Farther Defended* (New York, 1771), 226–27; the *Virginia Gazette*, 5 September 1771 [Rind]. The word was "ye."

23. Centinel XV (30 June 1768) in *The Centinel: Warning of a Revolution*, ed. Elizabeth Nybakken (Newark: University of Delaware Press, 1980), 166; Centinel I, 24 March 1768, 85. "[M]ust all these be termed Dissenters because the Doctor and they differ?" the authors of the Centinel asked. See Centinel I, 87.

24. Centinel XIV, 23 June 1768, 151, 158.

25. Thomas Bradbury Chandler, *The Appeal Defended* (New York, 1769), 3; *The Freeholder, No. 3. Conclusion of the Answers to the Reasons* (New York, 1769), 2–3.

26. Thomas Bradbury Chandler complained that the "Church of England, and the Society for the Propagation of the Gospel, ha[d] been violently forced into this Controversy, and *violently* treated." Their plan, he remarked earlier in the same tract, had been greeted "with Violence." See Chandler, *The Appeal Defended* (New York, 1771), 238, 1. Charles Chauncy was not far off the mark when he argued that Chandler was incapable of distinguishing between the denial of privileges and the imposition of physical punishment. See Chauncy, *A Reply to Dr. Chandler's Appeal Defended* (New York, 1770), 140. John Camm thought that if given the chance, his opponents would stop "appeal[ing] to Argument," and turn "to Violence, or to one of the severest Methods of Persecution, namely, that of letting loose the inflamed Mob." See the *Virginia Gazette*, 15 August 1771 [Purdie and Dixon]. The Centinel expressed the fear that "the Spirit of persecution" would reemerge "with its native Violence," as soon as the opportunity presented itself. See Centinel IV, 14 April 1768, 108. Religious establishments, The Centinel wrote on another occasion, generate "pride" that "easily proceed[s] to inquisitions, tortures, and death." See Centinel III, 7 April 1768, 102.

27. Ezra Stiles, *A Discourse on the Christian Union* (Boston, 1761), 114; Benjamin Franklin, "Observations Concerning the Increase of Mankind, Peopling of Countries, etc." (1751) in *The Papers of Benjamin Franklin*, ed. Leonard W. Labaree, 35 vols. (New Haven, Conn.: Yale University Press), 4:234. Carl Bridenbaugh should be credited with initially reprinting Stiles's table. My account of Stiles is heavily indebted to his chapter on the minister. See *Mitre and Sceptre*, esp. 12, 22. On Stiles's propensity for quantification, see Patricia Cline Cohen, *A Calculating People: The Spread of Numeracy in Early America* (New York: Routledge, 1982), 110–12. Roger Finke and Rodney Starke note that there were only about 449,000 people living in all of New England at the time. See Finke and Starke, *The Churching of America, 1776–1990: Winners and Losers in Our Religious Economy* (New Brunswick, N.J.: Rutgers University Press, 1992), 23. Stiles's calculations may have built as much upon the numerical claims of the Society for the Propagation as much as it was built on Franklin's calculations. According to Bridenbaugh, "The clergy of the Northern Colonies wrote regularly to [the SPG's] secretary, and once a year submitted reports of numbers, membership gains, the state of churches and parishes, and other pertinent information, which was abstracted and published as an appendix to the Society's annual sermon." See Bridenbaugh, *Mitre and Sceptre*, 186.

28. *The Literary Diary of Ezra* Stiles, ed. Franklin Bowditch Dexter, 3 vols. (New York: Charles Scribner, 1901): 1:8–9, quoted in Cohen, *A Calculating People*, 111.

29. *A Collection of Tracts from the Late News Papers*, 390; *The Freeholder, No. 3. Conclusion of the Answers to the Reasons*, 1. Frank Lambert has noted that the Awakening-era revivalists were careful arithmeticians when it came to the calculation of audiences. See Lambert, *Inventing the "Great Awakening"* (Princeton, N.J.: Princeton University Press, 1999), 105.

30. William Tennent, *Mr. Tennent's Speech on the Dissenting Petition* (Charleston, 1777), 12.

31. Boucher, "On the American Episcopate," *A View of the Causes and Consequences of the American Revolution in thirteen discourses, preached in North America between the years 1763 and 1775, with an historical preface* (1797; repr., New York: Russell and Russell), 109, 100; Richard J. Hooker, ed., *The Carolina Backcountry on the Eve of the American Revolution: The Journal and Other Writings of Charles Woodmason, Anglican Itinerant* (Chapel Hill: University of North Carolina Press, 1953), 43.

32. Centinel XIV, 23 June 1768, 162; Charles Chauncy, *A Letter to a Friend* (Boston, 1767), 46.

33. Centinel XIV, 163–64.

34. The advertisement for the conventions can be found in a number of issues of both Rind and Purdie and Dixon's *Virginia Gazette* during April and May of 1771. See, for instance, the *Virginia Gazette*, 16 May 1771 [Rind]. For the fullest account of these events, see George W. Pilcher, "Virginia Newspapers, and the Dispute Over the Proposed Colonial Episcopate, 1771–1772," *The Historian* 23 (November 1960): 98–113; also Pilcher, "The Pamphlet War on the Proposed Virginia Anglican Episcopate, 1767–1775," *Historical Magazine of the Protestant Episcopal Church* 30 (1961): 266–79.

35. The *Virginia Gazette*, 6 June 1771; the *Virginia Gazette*, 25 June 1771 [Purdie and Dixon]. Gwatkin and Henley's protest was also reprinted in *To the Public* (New York, 1771). "A Real Layman" voiced the same objections, noting again that only twelve clergymen attended the convention, and that four of them were appointed to serve on a committee that would address the king on behalf of *"the Majority of the Clergy in the Colony."* See the *Virginia Gazette*, 25 June 1771 [Purdie and Dixon].

36. The *Virginia Gazette*, 13 June 1771 [Purdie and Dixon]; *New York Journal; or, The General Advertiser*, 5 September 1771; the *Virginia Gazette*, 21 November 1771 [Purdie and Dixon]. According to the author of the *New-York Journal* article, the only true opponents of an episcopacy were the legislators who had been elected by the Scots-Irish of the Virginia frontier and who "would not amount to a tenth part of the Assembly." Northern opponents of an episcopate picked up on this controversy, once again equating slave ownership and pro-Episcopal notions of religious representation. Challenging the advertisement issued by the "eight clergymen," an anonymous author refuted Chandler's suggestion that resistance was confined to a "few" "Non-Episcopalians." Indeed, he asserted, *support* for a bishop was actually confined to the men who signed the advertisement—and their slaves. "Doctor *Chandler*," the author wryly noted, "ought to deduct from the number of Episcopalians, whom he suppose were for an American Bishop, all the white people in that dominion, except eight, and (as all

negroes, according to his Argument, are presumed to be of their masters religion) all the blacks in that province, except those belonging to the said eight." See *To the Public* (New York, 1771) (Broadside).

37. The *Virginia Gazette*, 26 March 1772 [Rind].

38. John Leland, *The Virginia Chronicle* (Norfolk, 1790), 8.

39. These events are carefully detailed in Paul K. Longmore, " 'All Matters and Things Relating to Religion and Morality': The Virginia Burgesses' Committee for Religion, 1769 to 1775" *Journal of Church and State* 38 (Autumn 1996): 784–85. On the ambiguity of Virginia's toleration policy, see Rhys Isaac, *The Transformation of Virginia, 1740–1790* (Chapel Hill: University of North Carolina Press, 1992), 153; and Longmore, " 'All Matters and Things Relating to Religion and Morality' ": 782–83.

40. Longmore, " 'All Matters and Things Relating to Religion and Morality' ": 794. Rhys Isaac, " 'The Rage of Malice of the Old Serpent Devil': The Dissenters and the Making and Remaking of the Virginia Statute for Religious Freedom," in *The Virginia Statute for Religious Freedom: Its Evolution and Consequences in American History*, ed. Merrill D. Peterson and Robert C. Vaughan (Cambridge: Cambridge University Press, 1988), 143.

41. For a discussion of the change from toleration to religious equality, see Isaac, *The Transformation of Virginia*, 279–82; William L. Miller, *The First Liberty: Religion and the American Public* (New York: Knopf, 1986), 3–16; Irving Brant, "Madison: On Separation of Church and State," *The William and Mary Quarterly*, 3rd series 8, James Madison, 1751–1836: Bicentennial Number (January 1951), 5–6. For an excellent short overview of church-state developments in Virginia from 1776 to 1786, see Daniel L. Dreisbach, "Church-State Debate in the Virginia Legislature: From the Declaration of Rights to the Statute for Establishing Religious Freedom," in *Religion and Political Culture in Jefferson's Virginia*, ed. Garrett Ward Sheldon and Daniel L. Dreisbach (Lanham, Md.: Rowman & Littlefield, 2000): 135–65. For the discussion of the Declaration of Rights and subsequent developments, see 138–44. The best and most comprehensive account of events during the founding period can be found in Thomas E. Buckley, *Church and State in Revolutionary Virginia, 1776–1787* (Charlottesville: University Press of Virginia, 1977). The developments that occurred in 1776 are discussed on 17–37.

42. William Waller Hening, ed., *Statutes at Large Being a Collection of all the Laws of Virginia, from the first session of the Legislature, in the Year 1619*, 13 vols. (Richmond, 1821), 9:164, quoted in Isaac, *The Transformation of Virginia*, 281.

43. Charles F. James, ed., *Documentary History of the Struggle for Religious Liberty in Virginia* (1900; repr., New York: De Capo, 1971), 69. On the assertion that one petition garnered ten thousand signatures, see James, *Documentary History*, 74.

44. The *Virginia Gazette*, 11 October 1776 [Dixon and Hunter]; the *Virginia Gazette*, 24 April 1778 [Dixon and Hunter]. For other examples of both charitable and uncharitable rhetoric from the period, see the *Virginia Gazette*, 18 October 1776 [Dixon and Hunter]; the *Virginia Gazette*, 1 November 1776 [Purdie]; the *Virginia Gazette*, 6 December 1776 [Purdie]; and the *Virginia Gazette*, 13 December 1776 [Dixon and Hunter]. Thomas Buckley notes the uncharitable language used against the evangelical

sects in at least three 1778 petitions to the legislature. See Buckley, *Church and State in Revolutionary Virginia*, 42–43. Buckley discusses the 24 April 1778 *Virginia Gazette* article on 43–44. Rhys Isaac discusses the conflict between evangelicals and Anglicans in "Evangelical Revolt: The Nature of the Baptists' Challenge to the Traditional Order in Virginia, 1765 to 1775," *William and Mary Quarterly*, 3rd series 31 (July 1974), esp. 365. On the centrality of "equality" to the contemporary meaning of religious liberty, see Philip A. Hamburger, *Separation of Church and State* (Cambridge, Mass.: Harvard University Press, 2002), 96. Also see Hamburger's notes on 97n14. For examples, see the *Virginia Gazette*, 8 November 1776 [Purdie]; and *The Freeman's Remonstrance against an Ecclesiastical Establishment* (Williamsburg, 1777), 10.

45. The *Virginia Gazette*, 18 October 1776 [Purdie].

46. William Lee Miller offers an incisive account of Madison's intellectual development, especially his views on church-state relations, in *The First Liberty*, esp. 87–106. On the intellectual direction offered to early Princetonians, see Francis L. Broderick, "Pulpit, Physics and Politics: The Curriculum of the College of New Jersey, 1746–1794," *William and Mary Quarterly*, 3rd series 6 (January 1949): 42–68. For the fullest discussion of Madison's education, see Irving Brant, *James Madison: The Virginia Revolutionist*, 4 vols. (Indianapolis: Bobbs-Merrill, 1941), 1:56–85.

47. Madison to William Bradford, December 1, 1773, in *James Madison on Religious Liberty*, ed. Robert S. Alley (Buffalo: Prometheus, 1985), 46.

48. "Madison's Remonstrance" in James, ed. *Documentary* History, 260, 258. Defenders of religious establishments made use of the language of equality themselves. See, for instance, the *Virginia Gazette*, 18 September 1779 [Dixon and Nicholson].

49. Madison to George Mason, 14 July 1826, Virginia Historical Society, Richmond, Virginia, quoted in Dreisbach, "Church-State Debate in the Virginia Legislature," 152. Dreisbach wisely notes that in the Virginia Bill of Rights (1776), the "language rests on two important assumptions: first, the rights of conscience envisioned by the Virginia Convention were to be exercised in a theistic context, and, second, that it involves not only a relationship between on man and his God, but also the relationship of each man to his neighbor." See Dreisbach, "Church-State Debate in the Virginia Legislature," 140.

50. For the denials of an establishment in Massachusetts, see the *Boston Gazette*, 14 December and 2 November 1778. For affirmations, see the *Independent Chronicle*, 17 December 1778 and 25 February 1779.

51. Peter S. Field points out that with the Massachusetts Religious Act of 1760, the "General Court now granted tax support solely to ministers who had a formal college education or the 'testimony of the clergy in his county that his learning was sufficient.'" See Field, *The Crisis of the Standing Order: Clerical Intellectuals and Cultural Authority in Massachusetts, 1780–1833* (Amherst: University of Massachusetts Press, 1998), 24.

52. Examples can be drawn from both Massachusetts and Connecticut. See *An Essay on Education* (New Haven, 1772), esp. 3–4, 7; Zabdiel Adams, "An Election Sermon" (Boston, 1782) in *American Political Writing during the Founding Era*,

1760–1785, ed. Charles S. Hyneman and Donald S. Lutz, 2 vols. (Indianapolis: Liberty, 1983), 556; Joseph Fish, *The Examiner Examined* (New London, 1771), 4; Joseph Huntington, *Demonstration of the Duty and Importance of Infant Baptism* (Norwich, 1783), 25; and Samuel Locke, *A Sermon Preached Before the Ministers of the Province of the Massachusetts-Bay* (Boston, 1772), esp. 26, 36.

53. "Address of the Convention, March 1780" in *The Popular Sources of Political Authority. Documents on the Massachusetts Constitution of 1780*, ed. Oscar Handlin and Mary Handlin (Cambridge, Mass.: Harvard University Press, 1966), 436, 435. These sentiments are perhaps all the more notable given that only five of the 293 delegates at the convention were Baptists. See John Witte Jr., "'A Most Mild and Equitable Establishment of Religion': John Adams and the Massachusetts Experiment," in *Religion and the New Republic: Faith in the Founding of America*, ed. James H. Hutson (Lanham, Md.: Rowman & Littlefield), 9. However, as Charles H. Lippy notes, the committee chosen to redraft Article Three "consisted of five Congregationalists and two Baptists and included one clergyman of each denomination." See Lippy, "The 1780 Massachusetts Constitution: Religious Establishment or Civil Religion?" *Journal of Church and State* 20 (1978): 537.

54. "Address of the Convention, March 1780," 435.

55. Amos Adams, *Religious Liberty an Invaluable Blessing* (Boston, 1768), 8, 52.

56. The fullest general account of Backus's life can be found in William McLoughlin, *Isaac Backus and the American Pietistic Tradition* (Boston: Brown, 1967). The quote appears on 21. For a concise account of Backus's career, see "Isaac Backus and the Separation of Church and State in America," *American Historical Review* 73 (June 1968): 1393.

57. Drawing a direct analogy to the ongoing civil rights movement, William G. McLoughlin wrote that there was "a clear social prejudice attached to being 'a certificate man' in a small New England town." McLoughlin also noted the revealing example of a Congregational deacon who, in 1770, "told two young girls in his church who had attended a Baptist service that 'he should rather court a Negro than a girl who had been to a Baptist meeting.'" See McLoughlin, "Massive Civil Disobedience as a Baptist Tactic in 1773," *American Quarterly* 21 (Winter 1969): esp. 712, 718, 721. The quotes appear on 712 and 721.

58. Isaac Backus, "A Fish Caught in His Own Net" (Boston 1768) in *Isaac Backus on Church and State: Pamphlets, 1754–1789*, ed. William G. McLoughlin (Cambridge, Mass.: Harvard University Press, 1968), 255, 219, 260, 215. For Backus's argument that the accidents of birth cannot condemn an individual to a particular church, see Backus, "A Door Opened for Equal Christian Liberty" (Boston, 1783), 6.

59. Backus, "An Appeal to the Public for Religious Liberty" in *Isaac Backus: On Church, State, and Calvinism*, 335, 325. For a similar perspective on religious liberty, see Ebenezer Frothingham, *A Key to Unlock the Door* (Boston, 1767). The orthodox Hieronymous maintained that no harm was done when governments simply compelled people to be "instructed in their duty," since everyone was permitted "to choose their own mode of worship." See *Boston Gazette*, 18 January 1779. "Hieronymous," according to Evans, was probably Robert Treat Paine.

60. Backus, "A Fish Caught in His Own Net," 218, 273; Backus, *True Faith will Produce Good Work* (Boston, 1767), 90.

61. Backus, "A Fish Caught in His Own Net" 280–81; Backus, "An Appeal to the Public for Religious Liberty," 324; *Independent Chronicle; and Universal Advertiser*, 2 December 1779.

62. McLoughlin, "Isaac Backus and the Separation of Church and State in America," 1401–9. A broadside petition from the State Baptist Association did state that it was the work of "inhabitants . . . of various religious denominations." I have not, however, found any evidence to counter McLoughlin's insistence on Backus's parochialism. For a reprint of the broadside's opening page, see Samuel Eliot Morison, "The Struggle over the Adoption of the Constitution of Massachusetts, 1780," *Massachusetts Historical Society Proceedings* 50 (1917): 377. The New Light Separate Ebenezer Frothingham was downright uncharitable to non-Calvinist dissenters. "I think I have a just Right to exclude out of the Controversy that is between me and my Author," he wrote, "the Quakers, Moravians, Separate-Baptists, Rogerenes, and other Enthusiasts; and leave them to vindicate themselves, as they see fit." See Frothingham, *A Key to Unlock the Door* (Boston, 1767), 34.

63. On the general tenor of the reactions to Article Three, see Lippy, "The 1780 Massachusetts Constitution," 546–47. On the possibility that the article did not receive the necessary two-thirds majority, see John Witte Jr., " 'A Most Mild and Equitable Establishment of Religion'," 15.

64. Samuel Eliot Morison may have been the first to point out that "[t]he Word 'orthodox' . . . and the word 'Congregational' are not found in Article III." See Morison, "The Struggle over the Adoption of the Constitution of Massachusetts, 1780," 370n. According to John Witte Jr., this represented "the first formal statement in Massachusetts history of religious equality before the law not only for individuals but also for groups." See Witte, " 'A Most Mild and Equitable Establishment of Religion'," 14.

65. Isaac Backus, "An Appeal to the Public for Religious Liberty," 324; Backus, *A History of New England with Particular reference to the Baptists* (New York, 1871), 226, quoted in Field, *The Crisis of the Standing Order*, 34. In 1777, the "Freeman of Virginia" observed, "[f]ormerly when any of the nations made the least attempt to recover, or to maintain their liberty, the prevailing outcry was the CHURCH, the CHURCH is in danger! But now it is the STATE, the STATE is in danger!" See *The Freeman's Remonstrance*, 11. For a good discussion of these issues, see Philip Hamburger, *Separation of Church and State*, esp. 67. On the percentage of Congregationalists in Massachusetts, see Field, *The Crisis of the Standing Order*, 36.

66. *Independent Ledger*, 17 April 1780. "Irenaeus," Peter Field notes, "was Boston minister, Samuel West." See Field, *The Crisis of the Standing Order*, 40. This mode of argument emerged at least four years earlier with the writings of "Worcestriensis." See, for example, *Massachusetts Spy*, 4 September 1776. For other instances of religious liberty being conflated with a church establishment, see Irenaeus's pieces in the *Independent Ledger*, 15 May 1780, and in the *Independent Chronicle*, 9 March 1780.

67. *Boston Gazette*, 28 December 1778; *Independent Chronicle*, 9 March 1780. Irenaeus was also careful to note that "the mention of the German Anabaptists [during

the convention's debate] was not designed as a reflection upon any sect or party of men among us, for it was presumed that there were no persons of such a character among us." See *Independent Ledger*, 22 May 1780. On the contemporary understanding of what constituted an establishment in Massachusetts, see Thomas J. Curry, *The First Freedoms: Church and State in America to the Passage of the First Amendment* (New York: Oxford University Press, 1986), 174.

68. John Adams purportedly maintained that "[t]here is, indeed, an ecclesiastical establishment in our province; but a very slender one, hardly to be called an establishment." See Backus, *History of New England*, 202n, quoted in Field, *The Crisis of the Standing Order*, 37. Isaac Backus expressed his own optimism in 1783: "All former taxes to support worship, were imposed in each government by a particular sect, who held all others in subordination thereto; which particularly is now expressly excluded from among us." See Backus, *A Door Opened for Equal Christian Liberty* (Boston, 1783), 11.

69. "Charter of Liberties and Frame of Government of Pennsylvania" (25 April–5 May 1682) in *Foundations of Colonial America: A Documentary History*, ed. W. Keith Kavenagh, 3 vols. (New York: Chelsea House, 1973), 2:1144.

70. For a brief survey of the history of religious liberty throughout Pennsylvania's early history, see J. William Frost, "Pennsylvania Institutes Religious Liberty, 1682–1860," *Pennsylvania Magazine of History and Biography* 112 (July 1988): 327–47. For a more detailed analysis, see Frost, *A Perfect Freedom: Religious Liberty in Pennsylvania* (University Park: University of Pennsylvania Press, 1993).

71. Richard K. MacMaster, Samuel L. Horst, and Robert F. Ulle, eds., *Conscience in Crisis: Mennonites and Other Peace Churches in America, 1739–1789: Interpretation and Documents* (Scottdale, Pa.: Herald, 1979), 70–72; also Herman Wellenreuther, "The Quest for Harmony in a Turbulent World: The Principle of 'Love and Unity' in Colonial Pennsylvania Politics," *Pennsylvania Magazine of History and Biography* 107 (1983), esp. 556.

72. "The Conduct of the Paxton-men, Impartially Represented" (1764) in *The Paxton Papers*, ed. John R. Dunbar (The Hague: Martinus Nijhoff, 1957), 294. In the fall of 1755, a bill for a volunteer military force finally passed. A year later, the British Parliament overruled the bill and the Assembly sought an alternative. See MacMaster, et al., *Conscience in Crisis*, 76.

73. Samuel Finley, *The Curse of Meroz* (Philadelphia, 1757), 8, 26; "The Quaker Unmask'd; Or, Plain Truth: Humbly address'd to the Consideration of all the Freeman of Pennsylvania" (1764) in Dunbar, *Paxton Papers*, 209, 211, 214. Quote appears on 209. Samuel Finley had grossly simplified the Friends' position. Some Quakers were committed to unqualified pacifism, but they resigned their offices when the war began. The majority of Quaker assemblymen took a more moderate stance. They were willing to appropriate funds for the defense of the colony during this provincial emergency. They were not, however, willing to relinquish control of the colony's purse strings to the proprietor. Nor would they allow for the creation of a more vigorous military establishment. See Tully, *Forming American Politics: Ideals, Interests, and Institutions in Colonial New York and Pennsylvania* (Baltimore: Johns Hopkins University

Press, 1994), 149–50, 195. For extensive accounts of the role that Pennsylvania's Quakers played in provincial politics, as well as the divisions that beset them, see Richard Bauman, *For the Reputation of Truth: Politics, Religion, and Conflict among the Pennsylvania Quakers, 1750–1800* (Baltimore: Johns Hopkins University Press, 1971); Ralph L. Ketcham, "Conscience, War, and Politics in Pennsylvania, 1755–1757," *William and Mary Quarterly*, 3rd series 20 (July 1963), 416–39; and, Jack D. Marietta, "Conscience, the Quaker Community, and the French and Indian War," *Pennsylvania Magazine of History and Biography* 95 (January 1971): 3–17.

74. The preceding account benefited from the descriptions of the crisis included in Dunbar, ed., *The Paxton Papers*, 4–48; Sally Schwartz, *"A Mixed Multitude": The Struggle for Toleration in Colonial Pennsylvania* (New York: New York University Press, 1988), 225–29; and Alan Tully, *Forming American Politics: Ideals, Interests, and Institutions in Colonial New York and Pennsylvania* (Baltimore: Johns Hopkins University Press, 1994), 182–96. For an analysis of the accompanying print debate, see Alison Olson, "The Pamphlet War over the Paxton Boys," *Pennsylvania Magazine of History and Biography* 123 (January/April 1999): 31–55.

75. "[Benjamin Franklin], A Narrative of the Late Massacres in Lancaster County" (1764) in Dunbar, *The Paxton Papers*, 72; "The Author of Quaker Unmask'd Strip'd Start Naked" (1764) in *The Paxton Papers*, 263; "An Answer to the Pamphlet Entituled the Conduct of the Paxton Men, impartially represented" (1764), in *The Paxton Papers*, 324; "The Plain Dealer: Or, A few Remarks upon Quaker Politicks, And their Attempts to Change the Government of Pennsylvania," (1764) in *The Paxton Papers*, 341; "The Conduct of the Paxton-men, Impartially Represented" (1764) in *The Paxton Papers*, 274. Sally Schwartz notes the religious orientation of the Paxton print dispute in *"A Mixed Multitude,"* 226.

76. "The Quaker Unmask'd; Or, Plain Truth: Humbly address'd to the Consideration of all the Freeman of Pennsylvania," (1764) in Dunbar, ed., *The Paxton Papers*, 214; "The Address of the People call'd Quakers," (1764) in *The Paxton Papers*, 135; "The Quaker Vindicated; Or, Observations on a Late Pamphlet, Entitluled, The Quaker Unmask'd, Or, Plain Truth," in *The Paxton Papers*, 239.

77. "The MEMORIAL of the Officers of the Military Association of the City and Liberties of *Philadelphia"* (30 October 1775) in Gertrude MacKinney and Charles F. Hoban, eds., *Votes and Proceedings of the House of Representatives of the Province of Pennsylvania, 1682–1776*, in *Pennsylvania Archives*, 8th series, 8 vols. (Harrisburg, Pa.: Hood, 1931–1935), 8:7338.

78. "The MEMORIAL," 8:7339; *Pennsylvania Gazette*, 27 November 1755. Another bill passed in the Pennsylvania Assembly in June 1777 was described as an act "for rendering the burthen of the defence of the State more equal." See MacMaster, et al., *Conscience in Crisis*, 282. As J. William Frost puts it, "Pluralism and toleration were good, but a religious dissent that threatened the war effort would not be acceptable." See Frost, *A Perfect Freedom*, 66.

79. *Maryland Gazette*, 29 May 1777. Statement of the Philadelphia Whig Society reprinted in MacMaster, et al., *Conscience in Crisis*, 408. These sentiments were echoed by a group of petitioners in Virginia. See "The Humble Petition of the

Committee of the County of Dunmore" (23 July 1776), in *Conscience in Crisis*, 273. Likewise, Maryland's Committees of Observation were instructed "to make a difference between such persons as may refuse from religious principles, or other motives." See *Conscience in Crisis*, 341.

80. Peter Brock, *Pacifism in the United States: From the Colonial Era to the First World War* (Princeton, N.J.: Princeton University Press, 1968), 248.

81. Edwin S. Gaustad, *Faith of Our Fathers: Religion and the New Nation* (San Francisco: Harper & Row, 1987) appendix B, 163, 167, 170, 173. Similarly, affirmations (rather than oaths) were permitted by the U.S. Constitution and some state governments. On the Second Amendment, see Richard Wilson Renner, "Conscientious Objection and the Federal Government, 1787–1792," *Military Affairs* 38 (December 1974): 143.

82. Washington to Reverend Samuel Langdon, 28 September 1789, in *The Writings of George Washington*, ed. John C. Fitzpatrick, 39 vols. (Washington, D.C.: U.S. Government Printing Office, 1931–1944), 30:416n.

83. On the legal status of pacifism during the revolutionary period, see Derek H. Davis, *Religion and the Continental Congress, 1774–1789: Contributions to Original Intent* (New York: Oxford University Press, 2000), 165–66.

84. Depending on how the issue is defined, it can be argued that Massachusetts, Connecticut, and New Hampshire maintained exclusive establishments. For a lucid summary of changes in the state constitutions during this period, see John K. Wilson, "Religion Under the State Constitutions, 1776–1800," *Journal of Church and State* 32 (Autumn 1990): 753–74.

85. [Charles Plowden], *A Short Account of the Establishment of the New See of Baltimore in Maryland, and of Consecrating the Right Reverend Dr. John Carroll* (Philadelphia, 1791), 4.

86. *An Appeal to the Impartial Public, By the Society of Christian Independents Congregating in Glocester* (Boston, 1785), 29.

87. John Leland, *The Virginia Chronicle* (Norfolk, 1790), 38.

88. *American Museum, or Repository of Ancient and Modern Fugitive Pieces Prose and Poetical* 4 (July 1790), 404. Anson Phelps Stokes speculates that the author was Tench Coxe. See Stokes, *Church and State in the United States*, 3 vols. (New York: Harper & Brothers, 1950), 1:275.

89. Barnabas Binney, *An Oration Delivered on the Late Public Commencement at Rhode-Island College* (Boston, 1774), 9, 12. An anti-Episcopal Virginia Anglican put it to his pro-Episcopal counterparts in a less abstract way: "Who, in this protestant country, this land of liberty, gave you a right to catechize me upon such a subject?" See the *Virginia Gazette*, 18 July 1771 [Rind].

90. William Livingston, "Remarks on liberty of conscience" (January 1778) in the *American Museum* 4 (July 1788), 493, 495. A footnote to this piece and a footnote to the larger history of religious pluralism in America should be recognized. In 1788 Mathew Carey, publisher of the *American Museum*, took Livingston to task for his defense of New Jersey's constitution. " 'Are protestants the only capable or upright men in this state?' asked Carey. 'Is not the Roman Catholic hereby disqualified? Why

so? Will not every argument in defense of his exclusion, tend to justify the intolerance and persecutions of Europe?'" Livingston's essay and Carey's response are discussed in Morton Borden, *Jews, Turks and Infidels* (Chapel Hill: University of North Carolina Press, 1984), 19.

CHAPTER 5

1. Hannah Adams, *An Alphabetical compendium of the various sects which have appeared in the world from the beginning of the Christian era to the present day* (Boston, 1784). The volume proved extremely popular. It would be reprinted three more times in the United States and twice in England. In the United States, the encyclopedia later appeared as *A View of Religions, in two parts* (1791, 1801) and *A Dictionary of All Religions and Religious Denominations Jewish, Heathen, Mahometan, Christian, Ancient and Modern* (1817). The publisher of the third edition planned to sell two thousand copies. With each revision of the original, Adams added more religious groups. However, she retained the same ecumenical tone (as well as the opening advertisement), and generally omitted the harsher language of previous encyclopedists. Adams' innovative approach to religious differences is insightfully discussed in Gary D. Schmidt, *A Passionate Usefulness: The Life and Literary Labors of Hannah Adams* (Charlottesville: University of Virginia Press, 2004), esp. 32–35. For a helpful introduction to Adams's life and work, see Hannah Adams, *A Dictionary of All Religions and Religious Denominations Jewish, Heathen, Mahometan, Christian, Ancient and Modern*, ed. Thomas A. Tweed (Atlanta: Scholars Press, 1992). Also see Adams's revealing account of her life, *A Memoir of Miss Hannah Adams, Written By Herself with Additional Notices by a Friend* (Boston, 1832). The same spirit would appear in nineteenth-century religious histories. In 1844, I. D. Rupp published a revised edition of his earlier religious encyclopedia. The author characterized his book as an act of contrition for his previous work on the same subject. "[C]omplaints by ministers and lay members of different denominations" persuaded Rupp that he had "unjustly represented their religion" in that earlier volume. So this time Rupp solicited "the history of each denomination from the pen of . . . its most distinguished ministers or professors; thus affording each sect the opportunity of giving its own history." Although traditional Native American and African American faiths were again ignored, the bounds of Rupp's book extended broadly. The author included selections from five Methodist churches, the Church of Latter Day Saints (by no less a personage than Joseph Smith, its founder), and the Moravians, as well as the old-line Protestant denominations. Roman Catholics were allotted over fifty pages to describe their faith. See Rupp, *An Original History of the Religious Denominations at Present Existing in the United States, Etc.* (Philadelphia, 1844), v.

2. Hannah Adams, *An Alphabetical Compendium*, ii. On the overwhelming support for, if not the actual practice of, the Bible's use in the nineteenth-century common schools, see R. Laurence Moore, "Bible Reading and Nonsectarian Schooling: The Failure of Religious Instruction in Nineteenth-Century Public Education," *Journal of American History* 86 (March 2000): 9.

3. Gertrude MacKinney and Charles F. Hoban, eds., *Votes and Proceedings of the House of Representatives of the Province of Pennsylvania, 1682–1776*, in *Pennsylvania Archives*, 8th series, 8 vols. (Harrisburg, Pa.: Hood, 1931–1935), 8:7371, quoted in *A Mixed Multitude: The Struggle for Toleration in Colonial Pennsylvania* (New York: New York University Press, 1988), 279. "[T]heir religion, freed from minute ceremonies, resembles a sentiment," a later French visitor observed, "as much as their love of liberty resembles a creed." See Milton Powell, ed., *The Voluntary Church: American Religious Life (1740–1865) Seen through the Eyes of European Visitors* (New York: Macmillan, 1967), 64. Gordon Wood draws the comparison between the foundational role played by the Bible and the foundational role played by republican constitutions in his essay, "Religion and the American Revolution," in *New Directions in American Religious History*, ed. Harry S. Stout and D. G. Hart (New York: Oxford University Press, 1997), 195. Also see William G. McLoughlin, "The Role of Religion in the Revolution: Liberty of Conscience and Cultural Cohesion in the New Nation" in *Essays on the American Revolution*, ed. Stephen G. Kurtz and James H. Hutson (Chapel Hill: University of North Carolina Press, 1973), 192–255. On the unusually strong affinity that late eighteenth-century American believers had for republican ideals, see Mark A. Noll, *America's God: From Jonathan Edwards to Abraham Lincoln* (Oxford: Oxford University Press, 2002), esp. 64–92.

4. Samuel Stillman, *A Sermon Preached before the Honorable Council, and the Honorable House of Representatives of the State of Massachusetts-Bay* (Boston, 1779), 10, 25, 30. The novelty of Stillman's selection as the speaker is noted in Stephen A. Marini, *Radical Sects of Revolutionary New England* (Cambridge, Mass.: Harvard University Press, 1982), 23.

5. Robert Annan, *Brief Animadversions on the Doctrine of Universal Salvation* (Philadelphia, 1787), 52. For an example of the religious reductionism described here, see the essay of the South Carolina Presbyterian, Thomas Reese, printed in *The American Museum, or The Universal Magazine* 7 (January 1790), 31ff. I take the founding generation's understanding of religion to be broader than does Philip Hamburger, whose analysis of church-state thought in America maintains that this generation embraced "an astonishingly broad view of Protestantism and a remarkably narrow conception of religion." See Hamburger, *Separation of Church and State* (Cambridge, Mass.: Harvard University Press, 2002), 205. For an example of a broader conception of "religion" being employed, see the very interesting debate between "Ireneaus" and "Philanthropos" in the Boston newspapers (March–April 1780). See especially the *Independent Ledger*, 1 May 1780.

6. Washington to the General Committee, Representing the United Baptist Churches in Virginia, May 1789, in *The Writings of George Washington*, ed. Jared Sparks, 12 vols. (Boston, 1834–1837), 12:155. For examples of Washington's correspondence with different churches, see 12:152–153, 156, 166–69, 177–79. Paul Boller notes that, following his inauguration, Washington participated in twenty-two "exchanges . . . with the major religious bodies of his day." See Boller, "George Washington and Religious Liberty," *William and Mary Quarterly*, 3rd series 17 (October 1960): 497. For an insightful discussion of the relationship between essentials of

faith and republican citizenship, see Sidney E. Mead, *The Lively Experiment: The Shaping of Christianity in America* (New York: Harper & Row, 1963), 64–67. As Mark Noll puts it, the Founders "wanted [religious] influence to remain implicit, to be an indirect force in guiding public policy rather than an institutionalized agency participating directly in public affairs." See Noll, *One Nation Under God: Christian Faith and Political Action in America* (San Francisco: Harper & Row, 1988), 65. For an indispensable general discussion, see Jon Butler, "Why Revolutionary America Wasn't a 'Christian Nation'," in *Religion and the New Republic: Faith in the Founding of America*, ed. James H. Hutson (Lanham, Md.: Rowman & Littlefield, 2000), 187–202.

7. Robert Bellah, "Civil Religion in America," *Daedalus* 96 (Winter 1967): 1–21; Samuel Williams, *The Influence of Christianity on Civil Society* (Boston, 1780), 20–21, 9. On civil religion, see also John Wilson, "The Status of 'Civil Religion' in America," in *The Religion of the Republic*, ed. Elwyn A. Smith (Philadelphia: Fortress, 1971), 1–21; and Colin Kidd, "Civil Theology and Church Establishments in Revolutionary America," *The Historical Journal* 42 (December 1999): 1007–26. The text of the Northwest Ordinance related to religion appears in Derek H. Davis, *Religion and the Continental Congress, 1774–1789: Contributions to Original Intent* (New York: Oxford University Press, 2000), 169. The religious policies of the Continental Congress are thoroughly discussed in *Religion and the Continental Congress, 1774–1789*; and Ronald A. Smith, "Freedom of Religion and the Land Ordinance of 1785," *Journal of Church and State* 24 (Autumn 1982): 589–602.

8. [Timothy Dwight], "Address to the ministers of the gospel of every denomination in the united states," *American Museum* 4 (July 1788), 33, 30. This tract was published anonymously under the pseudonym "Z." But Dwight's biographer, John R. Fitzmier, attributes it to him. See Fitzmier, *New England's Moral Legislator: Timothy Dwight, 1752–1817* (Bloomington: Indiana University Press, 1998), 51–52.

9. For an especially thoughtful analysis of this development, see Edwin S. Gaustad, "Colonial Religion and Liberty of Conscience," in *The Virginia Statute for Religious Freedom: Its Evolution and Consequences in American History*, ed. Merrill D. Peterson and Robert C. Vaughan (Cambridge: Cambridge University Press, 1988), 40. Even the ecumenical Hannah Adams had difficulty avoiding such reductionism. As Thomas A. Tweed notes, "more than eighty-five percent of the more than seven hundred entries deal with 'orthodox' or 'heretical' Christian groups or ideas." See Tweed, "Introduction: Hannah Adams's Survey of the Religious Landscape," in Adams, *A Dictionary of All Religions*, xvi.

10. William T. Hutchinson and William M. E. Rachal, eds., *The Papers of James Madison*, 17 vols. (Chicago: University of Chicago Press, 1962–1991), 7:46, quoted in Thomas E. Buckley, *Church and State in Revolutionary Virginia, 1776–1787* (Charlottesville: University Press of Virginia, 1977), 75; " 'A Bill concerning Religion,' " (1779), reprinted in Buckley, *Church and State in Revolutionary Virginia*, appendix I, 185–86. The provisions of the proposed measure are discussed in Buckley, *Church and State in Revolutionary Virginia*, 56–58.

11. "A Bill 'Establishing a Provision for Teachers of the Christian Religion'," (1784) reprinted in Buckley, *Church and State in Revolutionary Virginia*, appendix I,

188. For a discussion of Madison's role in defeating the general assessment measure, see Irving Brant, *James Madison: The Nationalist, 1780–1787* (Indianapolis: Bobbs-Merrill, 1948), 343–55. The differences between the 1779 and 1784 establishment bills are insightfully discussed in Buckley, *Church and State in Revolutionary Virginia*, 108.

12. "Madison's Notes on Debate" in *James Madison on Religious Liberty*, ed. Robert S. Alley (Buffalo: Prometheus, 1985), 54–55; Madison to Jefferson, 9 January 1785 *James Madison on Religious Liberty*, 67. The argument that religious liberty (or toleration) should be extended to non-Christians went back at least to 1773. See the *Virginia Gazette*, 3 June 1773 [Rind]. On the transformation of what "religion" meant during this period, see Jon Butler, *Awash in a Sea of Faith: Christianizing the American People* (Cambridge, Mass.: Harvard University Press, 1990), 260, 263–65. On the transformed meaning of "religion" in the eighteenth century, see Wilfred Cantwell Smith, *The Meaning and End of Religion: A New Approach to the Religious Traditions of Mankind* (New York: New American Library, 1964), esp. 40–43; also see Peter Harrison, *"Religion" and Religions in the English Enlightenment* (New York: Cambridge University Press, 1990).

13. Madison to Jefferson, 9 January 1785, *James Madison on Religious Liberty*, 67; "Madison's Remonstrance," in *Documentary History of the Struggle for Religious Liberty in Virginia*, ed. Charles F. James (New York: De Capo, 1971), appendix G, 257; Buckley, *Church and State in Revolutionary Virginia, 1776–1787*, 60. On the proposed compromise, see Daniel L. Dreisbach, "Church-State Debate in the Virginia Legislature: From the Declaration of Rights to the Statute for Establishing Religious Freedom," in *Religion and Political Culture in Jefferson's Virginia*, ed. Garrett Ward Sheldon and Daniel L. Dreisbach (Lanham, Md.: Rowman & Littlefield, 2000), 151. Madison's cause was also helped by that fact that he conceded to the incorporation of the former Church of England as the Protestant Episcopal Church and lent his support to Henry's successful bid for the governorship. See Brant, *James Madison: The Nationalist, 1780–1787* (Indianapolis: Bobbs-Merrill, 1948), 345–49.

14. Oscar Handlin and Mary Handlin, eds., *The Popular Sources of Political Authority: Documents on the Massachusetts Constitution of 1780* (Cambridge, Mass.: The Belknap Press of Harvard University Press, 1966), 529, 693; "Philanthropos," *Continental Journal*, 23 March 1780 (Supplement). The phrase "very ambiguously expressed" is cited in Samuel Eliot Morison, "The Struggle over the Adoption of the Constitution of Massachusetts, 1780," *Massachusetts Historical Society Proceedings* 50 (1917): 372. Both Morison and Peter S. Field comment on the Raynham response. See Morison, "The Struggle over the Adoption of the Constitution of Massachusetts," 371–72; and, Field, *The Crisis of the Standing Order: Clerical Intellectuals and Cultural Authority in Massachusetts, 1780–1833* (Amherst: University of Massachusetts Press, 1998), 38. Morison notes that Philanthropos's newspaper pieces were widely read and highly regarded. His "arguments," Morison notes, "are found in the returns of towns as widely scattered as Boston, Framingham, Gorham (Maine), Granville, and New Providence in the northwest corner of the state." See Morison, "The Struggle over the Adoption of the Constitution of Massachusetts," 379. Field points out that "Philanthropos has never been identified." See Field, *The Crisis of the Standing Order*, 40.

15. On the problems endured by orthodox Congregationalists because of Article Three's ambiguous wording, see Field, *The Crisis of the Standing Order*, 39.

16. Washington to George Mason, 3 October 1785, *The Writings of George Washington*, ed. John C. Fitzpatrick, 39 vols. (Washington, D.C.: U.S. Government Printing Office, 1931–1944), 28:285. For a helpful interpretation of this letter, see Paul F. Boller, "George Washington and Religious Liberty," *William and Mary Quarterly*, 3rd series 17 (October 1960): 490. For a thorough account of George Washington's views on church-state relations and religious freedom, see Boller, "George Washington and Religious Liberty," 486–506.

17. Thomas Jefferson, *Notes on the State of Virginia*, ed. William Peden (Chapel Hill: University of North Carolina Press, 1982), 159.

18. Jefferson, ibid., 160; "A Bill 'for Establishing Religious Freedom,'" in Buckley, *Church and State in Revolutionary Virginia*, appendix I, 190–91. On the weight given the mind over the body in Jefferson's statute, see J. G. A. Pocock, "Religious Freedom and the Desacralization of Politics: From the English Civil Wars to the Virginia Statute," in *The Virginia Statute for Religious Freedom*, esp. 61. The idea that truth would subdue error in any open contest had a long heritage, dating at least to the seventeenth century. The principle was central to the libertarian arguments of both John Milton's *Areopagitica* and John Locke's *Letter Concerning Toleration*. For a full analysis of this tradition, see Richard W. Pointer, "Freedom, Truth, and American Thought, 1760–1810," in *Liberty and Law: Reflections on the Constitution in American Life and Thought*, ed. Ronald A. Wells and Thomas A. Askew (Grand Rapids, Mich.: Eerdmans, 1987). The meaning, context, and legacy of Jefferson's Statute are imaginatively discussed by various authors in *The Virginia Statute for Religious Freedom*. Thomas E. Buckley, "The Political Theology of Thomas Jefferson" (75–107) is particularly useful for understanding the development of Jefferson's thought; Rhys Isaac, "'The Rage of Malice of the Old Serpent Devil': The Dissenters and the Making and Remaking of the Virginia Statute for Religious Freedom" (139–70) does an especially nice job of explaining the bill's social and intellectual context.

19. *Notes of Debates in the Federal Convention of 1787 Reported by James Madison* (New York: W. W. Norton, 1987), 561; Max Farrand, ed., *The Records of the Federal Convention*, 4 vols. (New Haven, 1966), 3:227. For an excellent general discussion of the debate surrounding Article VI, as well as its context and implications, see Daniel L. Dreisbach, "The Constitution's Forgotten Religious Clause: Reflections on the Article VI Religious Test Ban," *Journal of Church and State* 38 (Spring 1996): 261–97.

20. John Swanwick, *Considerations on an Act of the Legislature of Virginia* (Philadelphia, 1786), iii, 25.

21. State constitutions quoted in Edwin S. Gaustad, "Religious Tests, Constitutions, and 'Christian Nation'," in *Religion in a Revolutionary Age*, ed. Ronald Hoffman and Peter J. Albert (Charlottesville: University Press of Virginia, 1994), 219–20. For a discussion of contemporary concerns about infidelity, see Moore and Kramnick, *The Godless Constitution*, 29–36. On Backus, see Thomas J. Curry, *The First Freedoms: Church and State in America to the Passage of the First Amendment*

(New York: Oxford University Press, 1986), 170–71. On revisions to, or eliminations of, religious tests in the states following the U.S. Constitution's passage, see Dreisbach, "The Constitution's Forgotten Religion Clause," 272–73.

22. William Tennent, *An Address Occasioned by the Late Invasion of the Liberties of the American Colonies by the British Parliament* (Philadelphia, 1774), 11, quoted in Lambert, *The Founding Fathers and the Place of Religion in America* (Princeton, N.J.: Princeton University Press, 2003), 217; Henry Pattillo, *Sermons &c.* (Wilmington, 1788), 275–76. What James Turner said of the seventeenth century could be said of the eighteenth as well. "[L]acking a tradition of open unbelief, contemporaries also lacked the vocabulary to describe it. Thus the word 'atheism' could apply to everything from denial of the Trinity to gross immorality—and did." Contemporaries understood, Turner adds, that deism could easily slip into atheism. See Turner, *Without God, Without Creed: The Origins of Unbelief in America* (Baltimore: Johns Hopkins University Press, 1985), 26, 46. One exception was Ethan Allen, whose *Reason the Only Oracle of Man* (Bennington, 1784) came in for criticism. Perhaps chastened by so much hostility, Allen seemed reluctant to attach the appellation "Deism" to his deistic beliefs. Instead, he noted that his acquaintances had generally "denominated" him "a Deist." In good liberal fashion, Allen would not say whether they were correct or not. But, he continued, he knew that was not a Christian. See Allen, *Reason the Only Oracle of Man*, unpaginated preface. On the animus toward deists and for an explanation of eighteenth-century deistic principles, see Herbert M. Morais, *Deism in Eighteenth Century America* (New York: Russell & Russell, 1960). The closest thing I have seen to an indiscriminate condemnation of all conventional churches appeared in the *Virginia Gazette*, 13 December 1776 [Purdie].

23. Marini, *Radical Sects of Revolutionary New England*, 69. In the early 1780s, a slew of pamphlets debated Charles Chauncy's *Salvation for All Men, Illustrated and Vindicated as a Scripture Doctrine* (Boston, 1782). Charles Hanson describes the response to Chauncy's pamphlet in his *Necessary Virtue: The Pragmatic Origins of American Liberty* (Charlottesville: University Press of Virginia, 1999), 162ff. See also Timothy Allen, *Salvation for All men, Put Out of All Dispute* (Hartford, 1783); Isaac Backus, *The Doctrine of Universal Salvation Examined and Refuted* (Providence, 1782); George Beckwith, *An Attempt to Shew and maintain The Wisdom, Justice, Equity and Fitness of God's Annexing Eternal Rewards and Punishments to His Righteous Laws* (Norwich, 1783); William Gordon, *The Doctrine of Final Universal Salvation Examined and Shewn to be Unscriptural* (Boston, 1783).

24. J. Hector St. John Crèvecoeur, *Letters from an American Farmer and Sketches of Eighteenth-Century America*, ed. Albert E. Stone (New York: Penguin, 1986), 75–76.

25. Jacob Duché, *Observations on a Variety of Subjects, Literary, Moral and Religious* (Philadelphia, 1774), 62. For an extensive account of the rise of "liberality" as a late eighteenth-century Anglo American ideal, see Philip Hamburger, "Liberality," *Texas Law Review* 78 (May 2000), 1216–85.

26. Ezra Stiles, *The United States Elevated to Glory and Honor* (New Haven, 1783), 70. It was indeed common to suggest, as one contemporary put it, that "the [religious] principles [which] do not subvert the foundation of good government; may be safely

tolerated; but the man of no religion is the most dangerous, and in fact is not a fit subject of moral government." See *Brief Animadversions on the Doctrine of Universal Salvation* (Philadelphia, 1787), 48.

27. Pattillo, *Sermons &c.*, 42; Field Horne, ed. *The Diary of Mary Cooper: Life on a Long Island Farm, 1768–1773* (Oyster Bay, N.Y.: Oyster Bay Historical Society, 1981), 35. On the early national movement from church to church, see Nathan O. Hatch, *The Democratization of American Christianity* (New Haven, Conn.: Yale University Press, 1989), 64. The accusation of "indifference" was not new. Seventeenth-century critics of John Locke leveled the charge against him. See James Tully, "Governing Conduct," *Conscience and Casuistry in Early Modern Europe*, ed. Edmund Leites (Cambridge: Cambridge University Press, 1988), 24.

28. Richard J. Hooker, ed., *The Carolina Backcountry on the Eve of the American Revolution: The Journal and Other Writings of Charles Woodmason, Anglican Itinerant* (Chapel Hill: University of North Carolina Press, 1953), 13.

29. Timothy Dwight, "Libertines and Deists," *Norwich Packet; and The Country Journal*, 26 July 1787. For the details of Dwight's struggles, see Fitzmier, *New England's Moral Legislator*. For an analysis of Dwight's "Triumph of Infidelity" in its historical context, see Colin Wells, "Timothy Dwight's American *Dunciad: The Triumph of Infidelity* and the Universalist Controversy," in *Early American Literature* 33 (September 1998): 173–91. For other nostalgic invocations of doctrinal scrupulosity, see John Bisset, *A Sermon Delivered in St. Paul's* (Philadelphia, 1791), 9; Thomas Beveridge, *The Difference Briefly Stated* (Philadelphia, 1789), 6–7; and Alexander Miller, *A Sermon Preached at Schenectady, December 27, 1774* (New York, 1775), 5.

30. Will Herberg, *Protestant-Catholic-Jew: An Essay in American Religious Sociology* (Chicago: University of Chicago Press, 1980), 89; John Leland, *The Bible-Baptist* (Baltimore, 1789), unpaginated preface. Hannah Adams, *A Memoir of Miss Hannah Adams, Written By Herself with Additional Notices by a Friend* (Boston, 1832), 13–16. On church adherence rates throughout American history, see Starke and Finke, *The Churching of America*. For a concise statement of the belief that religious imposition was worse than religious error, see Aaron Bancroft, *A Discourse Delivered at Windsor, in the State of Vermont* (Worcester, 1790), 13; also "MEANWELL," "To the People of Maryland," *Maryland Gazette*, 19 June 1777.

31. Gaustad, "Religious Tests, Constitutions, and 'Christian Nation'," 223. For a cogent argument against the assertion of religious "indifference" in eighteenth-century America, see Patricia U. Bonomi and Peter R. Eisenstadt, "Church Adherence in the Eighteenth-Century British American Colonies," *William and Mary Quarterly*, 3rd series 39 (April 1982): 247. For other insightful discussions of the issue, see Richard Pointer, *Protestant Pluralism*, 37; and Wood, "Religion and the American Revolution," 176. Some anecdotal evidence from the perspective of a visiting Venezuelan suggests the same conclusion. See Roy M. Peterson, "A South American's Impressions of New England after Yorktown," *New England Quarterly* 4 (October 1931): 718. On the disruption of churches and churchgoing at the time, see the *American Museum* 7 (January 1790), appendix II, 2; and Robert M. Calhoon, "Religion, Politics, and Ratification," in Hoffman and Albert, *Religion in a Revolutionary Age*.

32. *A Draught of an Overture, Prepared and Published By a Committee of the Associate Reformed Synod* (Philadelphia, 1787), 107.

33. Adams to Jefferson, 28 June 1813, *The Adams-Jefferson Letters: The Complete Correspondence between Thomas Jefferson and Abigail and John Adams*, ed. Lester J. Cappon, 2 vols. (Chapel Hill: University of North Carolina Press, 1959), 2:339; John Carmichael, *A Self-Defensive War Lawful, Proved in a Sermon, Preached at Lancaster* (Lancaster, 1775), 29, 34. Quoted in Karen Elizabeth O'Brien, "Pragmatic Toleration: Lived Religion, Obligation, and Political Identity in the American Revolution" (PhD diss., Northwestern University, 2005), 221; *Pennsylvania Gazette*, 20 September 1775, quoted in Schwartz, *"A Mixed Multitude,"* 279. The discussion of pacifism during the war elicited similar statements. See Richard K. MacMaster, Samuel L. Horst, and Robert F. Ulle, eds., *Conscience in Crisis: Mennonites and Other Peace Churches in America, 1739–1789: Interpretation and Documents* (Scottdale, Pa.: Herald, 1979), esp. 235, 237–38.

34. Ezra Stiles, *The United States Elevated to Glory and Honor* (New Haven, 1783), 54–55.

35. Samuel MacClintock, *The Artifices of Deceivers Detected and Christians Warned Against Them* (Portsmouth, 1770), 5; *The Act of Incorporation of the Benevolent Congregational Society* (Providence, 1771), nonpaginated introduction; Devereux Jarratt, *The Life of the Reverend Devereux Jarratt* (Cleveland: Pilgrim, 1995), 32, 61. For a traditionalist attack on "error" during this same period, see Joseph Fish, *The Examiner Examined* (New London, 1771).

36. Dan Foster in Isaac Foster, *A Defence of Religious Liberty* (Worcester, 1780), appendix, 168, 171. John Tucker, *A Reply to the Rev. Mr. Chandler's Answer* (Boston, 1768), 42. These were not marginal figures. John Tucker was asked to present "the annual address to the convention of the Congregational clergy of Massachusetts" in 1768 and Dan Foster was invited to deliver Massachusetts' annual election sermon in 1790. Information on John Tucker can be found in Elizabeth Carroll Reilly, "The Boston Book Trade of Jeremy Condy," in *Printing and Society in Early America*, ed. William L. Joyce, David D. Hall, Richard D. Brown, and John B. Hench (Worcester, Mass.: American Antiquarian Society, 1983), 101.

37. *An Appeal to the Impartial Publick* (Boston, 1785), 23–24. Another, more typical example, can be found in the 1784 petition of the Presbytery of Hanover, Virginia, where that body expressed its willingness "to allow a full share of credit to our fellow-citizens, however distinguished in name from us, for their spirited exertions" during the Revolutionary War. See Charles F. James, ed., *Documentary History of the Struggle for Religious Liberty in Virginia* (New York: De Capo, 1971), 231. One of the things that set Hannah Adams to writing her own encyclopedia of religion was her encounter with less charitable predecessors. "I soon became disgusted with the want of candor in the authors I consulted," she wrote, "in giving the most unfavorable descriptions of the denominations they disliked, and applying to them the names of heretics, fanatics, enthusiasts, &." See Adams, *A Memoir of Miss Hannah Adams*, 11.

38. *Laws of the State of New York: Passed at the Sessions of the Legislature Held in the Years 1777–1801*, 5 vols. (Albany, 1886–1887), 1:687–89; Edward Potts Cheyney, *History*

of the University of Pennsylvania 1740–1940 (Philadelphia: University of Pennsylvania Press, 1940), 130; "Correspondence of Ezra Stiles, President of Yale College, and James Madison, President of William and Mary College, 1780," *William and Mary Quarterly*, 2nd series 7 (October 1927): 294. The measures related to Columbia College are discussed in David C. Humphrey, *From King's College to Columbia 1746–1800* (New York: Columbia University Press, 1976), 272; and Mark D. McGarvie, *One Nation Under Law: America's Early National Struggles to Separate Church and State* (DeKalb: Northern Illinois Press, 2004), 114. Interestingly, however, in 1785, Maryland assemblymen published a piece that warned of Presbyterian designs on the state's proposed colleges and insisted that these "seminaries" were designed to be *"liberal and catholic,"* where "equal privileges and advantages are secured to all religious denominations and persuasions." They cited the College of Philadelphia's troubles, particularly the Presbyterians' role in them, as negative examples. See *Maryland Gazette*, 29 September 1785. On the plans for a nonsectarian national university that would not have discriminated on the basis of religion, see Lorraine Smith Pangle and Thomas L. Pangle, *The Learning of Liberty: The Educational Ideas of the American Founders* (Lawrence: University Press of Kansas, 1993), esp. 149.

39. The debate was primarily conducted in the pages of the *Maryland Journal and Baltimore Advertiser* from late January to early April 1785.

40. *Maryland Gazette*, 29 September 1785. The planners of the proposed college were John Carroll, William Smith, and Patrick Allison.

41. *Maryland Journal*, 8 February 1785; *Maryland Journal*, 15 February 1785. "Marylander" was not quite as effusive about the Episcopalians, but his remarks were nonetheless positive.

42. The ever-controversial subject of infant baptism remained one of the few sources of serious theological disputation in the late eighteenth century. But even here, proponents of this practice (that is, non-Baptists) were careful to profess their inclination "to avoid all harsh reflections upon those of opposite sentiments," or their reluctance to "fix opprobrious epithets on those of different denominations." Instead, they merely claimed to offer "a fair and rational vindication" of their own principles. See Samuel Taggart, *A Calm Impartial Inquiry into, and Vindication of the Divine Right of Infants to Baptism* (Northampton, 1789); and David Bostwick, *A Fair and Rational Vindication of the Right of Infants to the Ordinance of Baptism* (New Brunswick, 1790), 11. If Baptists framed adult baptism as an essential particularity of their church, their opponents framed it as a particular principle that had been raised to essential status. See Bostwick, *A Fair and Rational Vindication of the Right of Infants to the Ordinance of Baptism*, 11–12; and, Noah Worcester, *A Friendly Letter to the Reverend Thomas Baldwin, Concerning an Answer to His Brief Defence of the Practice of the Close Communionists* (Concord, 1791), 8, 47.

43. For remarks on the Quebec Act, linking Roman Catholicism and despotism, see James Dana, *A Sermon, Preached Before the General Assembly of the State of Connecticut* (Hartford, 1779), 15. On the extent of anti-Catholic rhetoric unleashed by the Quebec Act, see Charles H. Metzger, *Catholics and the American Revolution: A Study in Religious Climate* (Chicago: Loyola University Press, 1962), 24–47. Anti-Catholic

prejudice afflicted even the most liberal minded in early America. See, for instance, George Whitefield, *George Whitefield's Journals* (Edinburgh, Scotland: The Banner of Truth Trust, 1960), 136; Jonathan Mayhew, *Remarks on an Anonymous Tract* (Boston, 1764), 71; and *Massachusetts Spy*, 21 August 1776.

44. John Lathrop, *A Discourse on the Errors of Popery* (Boston, 1793), 5–6. My understanding of the Dudleian lectures is indebted to Pauline Maier, who provides an excellent overview. See Maier, "The Pope at Harvard: The Dudleian Lectures, Anti-Catholicism, and the Politics of Protestantism," *Proceedings of the Massachusetts Historical Society* 97 (1986): 17–41.

45. Lathrop, *A Discourse on the Errors of Popery*, 7. Lathrop's surprisingly lenient approach to contemporary Roman Catholics—and the representative quality of such deference—is noted in both Maier, "The Pope at Harvard," 28; and Hanson, *Necessary Virtue*, 177. For changing views of Catholics, see Barnabas Binney's 1774 injunction for religious liberty, even for "Papists." Binney, *An Oration Delivered on the Late Public Commencement at Rhode-Island College* (Boston, 1774), 24; Nathaniel Hooker, *Six Discourses on Different Subjects* (Hartford, 1771), 50; and Jonathan Boucher, "On the Toleration of Papists," *A View of the Causes and Consequences of the American Revolution in thirteen discourses, preached in North America between the years 1763 and 1775, with an historical preface* (1797; repr., New York: Russell and Russell, 1967).

46. On the role that the war played in diminishing anti-Catholicism, see John T. McGreevy, *Catholicism and American Freedom: A History* (New York: W. W. Norton, 2003), 11. On New England's stance toward Catholicism during the Revolution, see Hanson's *Necessary Virtue*; Francis D. Cogliano, *No King, No Popery: Anti-Catholicism in Revolutionary New England* (Westport, Conn.: Greenwood, 1995). Cogliano argues that "[d]espite elite attempts to eradicate anti-popery, anti-Catholic feeling was never entirely eliminated there." Nonetheless, he does maintain that the Revolution "permanently undermined the foundation of anti-popery" in New England (3, 155). According to Hanson, some even took comfort from the knowledge that Catholic France had been secularized by Deistic Philosophes. See Hanson, *Necessary Virtue*, 122, 132–35.

47. [Benjamin Rush], *Information to Europeans Who Are Disposed to Migrate to the United States* (Philadelphia, 1790), 11; "Address of the Convention" (March 1780) in Handlin and Handlin, *The Popular Sources of Political Authority*, 440. Samuel Eliot Morison notes that a "great many towns" requested "the addition of the word 'Protestant' at some or all places in the constitution when the word 'Christian' was mentioned." See Morison, "The Struggle over the Adoption of the Constitution of Massachusetts, 1780," 381.

48. General Orders, 5 November 1775, in *The Writings of George Washington*, ed. Fitzpatrick, 4:65. Pope's Day is also called Guy Fawkes Day. For discussions of early Pope's Day celebrations, see Ray Allen Billington, *The Origins of Nativism in the United States 1800–1844* (1933; repr., New York: Arno, 1974), 32–33; Mary Augustina Ray, *American Opinion of Roman Catholicism in the Eighteenth Century* (New York: Columbia University Press, 1936), 256–58; William Pencak, "Play as Prelude to Revolution: Boston, 1765–1776," in *Riot and Revelry in Early America*, ed. William Pencak, Matthew Dennis, and Simon P. Newman (University Park: Pennsylvania

State University Press, 2002), 133–34; and Peter Shaw, *American Patriots and the Rituals of Revolution* (Cambridge, Mass.: Harvard University Press, 1981), 15–18.

49. For Arnold's critique, see Thomas O'Gorman, *A History of the Roman Catholic Church in the United States* (New York: Christian Literature, 1895), 256; also Cogliano, *No King, No Popery*, 83. For useful contextual information, see Ray, *American Opinion of Roman Catholicism in the Eighteenth Century*, 335–38. Derek H. Davis notes that "[t]he members of Congress attended mass on four occasions." See Davis, *Religion and the Continental Congress*, 259n44.

50. Carroll's letter is reprinted in Peter Guilday, *The Life and Times of John Carrol, Archbishop of Baltimore, 1735–1815* (Westminster, Md.: Newman Press, 1954), 172–73. The quotation appears on 172. On Adams's invitation to Carroll, see Thomas A. Tweed, introduction to Hannah Adams, *A Dictionary of All Religions*, x. A concise account of Carroll's life and historical significance can be found in Stokes, *Church and State in the United States*, esp. 1:327–32.

51. [Charles Henry Wharton], *A Letter to the Roman Catholics of the City of Worcester* (Philadelphia, 1784), 4; Charles Henry Wharton, *A Reply to an Address to the Roman Catholics of the United States of America* (Philadelphia, 1785), 97.

52. [John Carroll], *An Address to the Roman Catholics of the United States of America* (Annapolis, 1784), 13, 16, 10.

53. *Gazette of the United States*, 9 May 1789; *Gazette of the United States*, 10 June 1789. The anonymous "E.C." also wondered how "dangerous" religions "may be counteracted, consistent with the just and generous principles of toleration." Guilday discusses the controversy in *The Life and Times of John Carroll*, 128.

54. Thomas O'Brien Hanley, ed., *The John Carroll Papers*, 2 vols. (Notre Dame, Ind.: University of Notre Dame Press, 1976), 1:158; Guilday, *The Life and Times of John Carroll*, 458. For Carroll's insistence on the importance of even so-called "non-essentials," see *An Address to the Roman Catholics of the United States of America*, 34, 50–51. For the removal of the phrase *exterminare Haereticos*, see Stokes, *Church and State in the United States*, 1:331; and Guilday, *Life and Times of John Carroll*, 375. On early Georgetown College, especially its religious provisions, see Robert Emmett Curran, *The Bicentennial History of Georgetown University*, vol. 1, *From Academy to University, 1789–1889* (Washington, D.C.: Georgetown University Press, 1993), esp. 26.

55. *Columbian Magazine*, [Date Unspecified] December 1787. Reprinted in Guilday, *Life and Times of John Carroll*, 114; "An Answer to Strictures on an Extraordinary Signature" (21 November 1792) in Hanley, *The John Carroll Papers*, 2:69–71.

56. *A Documentary History of the Jews in the United States, 1654–1875*, ed. Morris U. Schappes, ed., 3rd ed. (New York: Shocken), 65. William McLoughlin once wrote, without citing any sources, but certainly with a vast knowledge of the period that "even Roman Catholics and Jews, the most extreme outsiders, found themselves included in the new nation. Many even talked as though Buddhists and Mohammedans would have been equally welcome." See McLoughlin, "The Role of Religion in the Revolution: Liberty of Conscience and Cultural Cohesion in the New Nation" in *Essays on the American Revolution*, ed. Stephen G. Kurtz and James H. Hutson (Chapel Hill: University of North Carolina Press, 1973), 208. For an understanding of religious liberty

that extended well beyond Protestants, see the *Independent Ledger*, 8 May 1780. A supporter of the establishment in Maryland similarly indicated that the proposed bill to support Christian teachers so "far from compelling either Jews, Turks, or Infidels, to embrace Christianity, that it does not even compel them to contribute to the support of it." See "CIVIS," *Maryland Journal*, 11 February 1785. For the estimated Jewish population in the United States, see Sydney Ahlstrom, *A Religious History of the American People* (New Haven, Conn.: Yale University Press, 1972), 573; Jonathan D. Sarna, "The Impact of the American Revolution on American Jews," *Modern Judaism* 1 (1981): 149; and Morton Borden, *Jews, Turks and Infidels* (Chapel Hill: University of North Carolina Press, 1984), 6.

57. For a lucid discussion of Jewish civil rights throughout early American history, see Stanley F. Cheyt, "The Political Rights of the Jews in the United States: 1776–1840," *American Jewish Archives* 10 (1958): 14–73. For a broader discussion of the status of Jews in post-revolutionary America, see Borden, *Jews, Turks, and Infidels*. For a brief, relatively sanguine account of Jews in revolutionary America, including Christian assistance to them, see Jonathan D. Sarna, *Judaism in America: A History* (New Haven, Conn.: Yale University Press, 2004), 36–41. For an earlier and less sanguine account, see Sarna, "The Impact of the American Revolution on American Jews."

58. [Samuel Seabury], *An Address to the Ministers and Congregations of the Presbyterian and Independent Persuasions in the United States* (New Haven, 1790), 33.

59. [William White], *The Case of the Episcopal Churches in the United States Considered* (Philadelphia, 1782), 11, unpaginated preface, 6, 8–9. Jon Butler notes that "[i]n parish after parish supporters of the Revolution stripped American churches of their royal coat of arms, although usually they left the buildings and other fittings intact." See Butler, *Awash in a Sea of Faith*, 207.

60. [Patrick Allison], *Candid Animadversions Respecting a Petition to the Late General Assembly of Maryland* (Baltimore, 1783), ii, 5, 4. On the post-revolutionary Anglican/Episcopal Church and for specific information regarding the debate in Maryland, see Clara O. Loveland, *The Critical Years: The Reconstitution of the Anglican Church in the United States of America: 1780–1789* (Greenwich, Conn.: Seabury Press, 1956), 26–27.

61. Robert Greenhalgh Albion and Leonidas Dodson, eds., *Philip Vickers Fithian: Journal, 1775–1776: Written on the Virginia-Pennsylvania Frontier and in the Army around New York* (1934; repr., Princeton, N.J.: Princeton University Press, 1979), 118. For an example of anti-Episcopalian evangelicalism, see the otherwise ecumenical work of the Baptist John Leland, *The Virginia Chronicle* (Norfolk, 1790).

62. For examples of anti-Methodist invective, see "To the People of Maryland," *Maryland Gazette*, 19 June 1777; *A Methodist's Remonstrance Addressed to a Certain Clergyman* (Yorktown, 1790); and Jarratt, *The Life of the Reverend Devereux*, 72–74. Cynthia Lynn Lyerly notes that criticism of Methodists did not diminish until the next century. But she also notes that the Methodists had, by that time, moderated their doctrines, become less distinctive in their practices, and that their opposition to slavery had become less conspicuous. It did not hurt that the denomination became wealthier and its leaders more respectable by that time. See Lyerly, *Methodism and the Southern*

Mind, 1770–1810 (New York: Oxford University Press, 1998), 176–77. For accounts of southern evangelicalism and the challenges it posed to traditional culture, see Christine Leigh Heyrman, *Southern Cross: The Beginnings of the Bible Belt* (New York: Knopf, 1997); Lyerly, *Methodism and the Southern Mind*; and, Rhys Isaac, *The Transformation of Virginia, 1740–1790* (Chapel Hill: University of North Carolina Press, 1982). Anti-Methodism may not have been as prevalent in the early national north, but it was by no means absent. See Richard D. Shiels, "The Methodist Invasion of Congregational New England," in *Methodism in American Culture*, eds. Nathan O. Hatch and John H. Wigger (Nashville: Kingswood, 2001), 266; and Curtis D. Johnson, *Islands of Holiness: Rural Religion in Upstate New York, 1790–1860* (Ithaca, N.Y.: Cornell University Press, 1989), 45.

63. The preceding description is especially indebted to Marini, *Radical Sects of Revolutionary New England*, 75–80, 92–94. The quotation appears on 93. For the fullest account of early Shaker history, see Stephen J. Stein, *The Shaker Experience in America: A History of the United Society of Believers* (New Haven, Conn.: Yale University Press, 1992). Another nuanced account that explores the gendered implications of Ann Lee's leadership can be found in Catherine A. Brekus, *Strangers & Pilgrims: Female Preaching in America, 1740–1845* (Chapel Hill: University of North Carolina Press, 1998), 97–112.

64. Amos Taylor, *A Narrative of the Strange Principles, Conduct, and Character of the People Known by the Name of Shakers* (Worcester, 1782), 3.

65. On Quaker separatism, see Stein, *The Shaker Experience in America*, 37.

66. John Huntington, *Letters of Friendship to Those Clergymen Who Have Lately Renounced Communion with the Ministers and Churches of Christ in General* (Hartford, 1780), 40.

67. Examples of creeds published by marginal groups include *A Form of Discipline For the Ministers, Preachers, and members of the Methodist Episcopal Church in America, Considered and Approved at a Conference* (1784; New York, 1789); *Articles of Faith, and Plan of Church Government, Composed and Adopted by the Churches Believing in the Salvation of All Men, Met in Philadelphia on the 25th of May, 1790* (Philadelphia, 1790); and [Joseph Meacham or James Whittaker], *A Concise Statement of the Principles of the Only True Church, According to the Gospel, of the Present Appearance of Christ as Held to and practiced by the Followers of the Living Saviour, at New Lebanon, &c.* (Bennington, 1790). In a February 15, 1785, article that appeared in the *Maryland Journal*, "A Protestant" advised his readers that *"If the Reader is desirous to know what the office of a Superintendent is, he is referred to the Liturgy of the Methodists.—They are sold at the store in Market-street, the corner of Public-Alley, near the Printing-Office."*

68. *A Draught of an Overture*, 107; John Adams to James Sullivan, 26 May 1776, in *Papers of John Adams*, ed. Robert Joseph Taylor, 12 vols. (Cambridge, Mass.: The Belknap Press of Harvard University Press, 1977), 4:208. For perspectives similar to that of the Associate Reformed Synod, see [Benjamin Thurston], *An Address to the Public, Containing Some Remarks on the Present Political State of the American Republicks, &c.* (Exeter, N.H., 1787), 29–30; and *"An ADDRESS to the ANABAPTISTS imprisoned in CAROLINE County,"* Virginia Gazette, 20 February 1772 [Purdie and Dixon].

69. Farrand, *The Records of the Federal Convention of 1787*, 2:642–43. On the ideal of unanimity embodied in the Constitution, see Jay Fliegelman, introduction to *Wieland and Memoirs of Carwin the Biloquist* by Charles Brockden Brown (New York: Penguin, 1991); and Julia Stern, *The Plight of Feeling: Sympathy and Dissent in the Early American Novel* (Chicago: The University of Chicago Press, 1997). On Jefferson's zeal for "unanimity," see Peter Onuf, *Jefferson's Empire: The Language of American Nationhood* (Charlottesville: University Press of Virginia, 2000), 106–7. The founders themselves were a religiously diverse bunch, though heavily weighted toward both Episcopalianism and Congregationalism. Of the forty delegates whose religious affiliation can be identified, nineteen were Episcopalian, eight Congregationalist, seven Presbyterian, two Quaker, two Roman Catholic, one Dutch Reformed, and one Methodist. There were no Baptists in attendance. See Ralph E. Pyle and James D. Davidson, "The Origins of Religious Stratification in Colonial America," *Journal for the Scientific Study of Religion* 42 (March 2003): table 2, 69.

70. William Gordon, *A Discourse Preached December 15th 1774* (Boston, 1775), 26; Timothy Dwight, *A Valedictory Address to the Young Gentlemen, Who Commenced Bachelors of Arts* (New Haven, 1776), 10. For other invocations of unanimity, see *To the Free and Respectable Mechanicks, and Other Inhabitants of the City and County of New-York* (New York, 1775); and "An ADDRESS to the Inhabitants of the City of New York," *The New-York Gazette and Weekly Mercury* (2 July 1770), signed by "A true Friend to Liberty and Unanimity."

71. Isaac Mansfield, *A Sermon, Preached in the Camp at Roxbury, November 23, 1775* (Boston, 1776), 21. Sometimes the claim of unanimity revealed itself to be a product of delusion or just plain fabrication. See the revealing example cited in Schwartz, "A Mixed Multitude," 272–73.

72. *A Letter to a Gentleman; containing a Plea for the Rights of Conscience, in Things of a Religious Nature* (Boston, 1753), 6; "Hieronymous," *The Boston Gazette*, 18 January 1779. Perhaps the most radical anti-majoritarian critiques of the Massachusetts establishment flowed from the pens of the Reverend Isaac Foster and his brother Dan. See Isaac Foster, *A Defence of Religious Liberty* (Worcester, 1780), 23–24, 31. For other attacks on majoritarianism in religious matters, see *To the General Court of the Massachusetts, Assembled at Boston* (Boston, 1780); *An Appeal to the Impartial Publick* (Boston, 1785), 32–33; and Israel Holly, *A Plea in Zion's Behalf* (Hartford, 1765), 9.

73. On the concept of unanimity in contemporary French thought, see Mona Ozouf, " 'Public Opinion' at the End of the Old Regime," *Journal of Modern History* 60, Supplement (September 1988): S11.

74. See Pattillo, *Sermons*, iii, x, 40–41.

75. For the best account of the relationship between religious differences and Americanness, see R. Laurence Moore, *Religious Outsiders and the Making of Americans* (New York: Oxford University Press, 1986).

76. "The Text of Eisenhower Speech," *The New York Times*, 23 December 1952, quoted in Herberg, *Protestant-Catholic-Jew*, 84. Isaac Kramnick and R. Laurence Moore argue that God is conspicuously absent from the Founder's writings,

particularly the Constitution. See *The Godless Constitution: The Case against Religious Correctness* (New York: W. W. Norton, 1996). For a particularly poignant example of such sentiments, see Benjamin Rush, *A Plan for the Establishment of Public Schools and The Diffusion of Knowledge in Pennsylvania* (Philadelphia, 1786), 17, 27.

77. A Layman, *The Claims of Christianity to the Presidency Examined at the Bar of Christianity* (Philadelphia, 1800), 10, quoted in Charles F. O'Brien, "The Religious Issue in the Presidential Campaign of 1800," *Essex Institute Historical Collections* 107 (January 1971), 89.

78. On the charges of infidelity leveled against Jefferson during the presidential campaign of 1800, see O'Brien, "The Religious Issue in the Presidential Campaign of 1800," 82–93; and Constance B. Schulz, " 'Of Bigotry in Politics and Religion': Jefferson's Religion, the Federalist Press, and the Syllabus," *Virginia Magazine of Biography and History* 91 (January 1983): 73–91. For a good overview of the religious issues in the campaign, see Lambert, *The Founding Fathers and the Place of Religion in America*, 276–84, and Mark A. Noll, *One Nation Under God*, 75–82. Also see Merrill D. Peterson, *Thomas Jefferson and the New Nation* (New York: Oxford University Press, 1970), 637–40.

79. Boucher, "On the Toleration of Papists," in *A View of the Causes and Consequences of the American Revolution*, 257.

80. Washington to the Hebrew Congregations of Philadelphia, New York, Charleston, and Richmond, in *The Papers of George Washington: Presidential Series*, ed. Dorothy Twohig, 9 vols. (Charlottesville: University Press of Virginia, 1996), 7:61.

81. Hooker, *The Carolina Backcountry on the Eve of the American Revolution*, 93–94. According to Hooker, the local Presbyterian Kirk did not permit this sermon to be delivered before its intended audience.

82. East Apthorp, *The Constitution of a Christian Church* (Boston, 1762), 24–25. Likewise, according to James Axtell, Doctor Eleazer Wheelock, founder of college called Dartmouth that aimed to educate Native Americans, "said that his educational goal was to 'cure the Natives . . . of their Savage Temper' and to 'purge all the Indian out' of his students." Axtell, *Natives and Newcomers: The Cultural Origins of North America* (New York: Oxford University Press, 2001), 180.

83. James Axtell, *Natives and Newcomers: The Cultural Origins of North America* (New York: Oxford University Press, 2001), 146–47. There were a few exceptions to the indifference displayed toward traditional Indian faiths. For instance, Thomas Jefferson proposed a bill during the Revolution that would have obliged William and Mary's faculty to "appoint, from time to time, a missionary of approved veracity, to the several tribes of Indians, whose business shall be to investigate their laws, customs, religions, traditions, and more particularly their languages, constructing grammars thereof." *Papers of Thomas Jefferson*, ed. Julian P. Boyd, 31 vols. (Princeton, N.J.: Princeton University Press, 1960), 2:542, quoted in J. David Hoeveler, *Creating the American Mind: Intellect and Politics in the Colonial Colleges* (Lanham, Md.: Rowman & Littlefield, 2002), 292–93.

84. Elias Smith, *Five Letters* (Boston, 1804), quoted in William G. McLoughlin, *New England Dissent, 1630–1833: The Baptists and the Separation of Church and State*, 2 vols. (Cambridge, Mass.: Harvard University Press, 1971), 1:765.

85. On early segregationism, see Milton C. Sernett, *Black Religion and American Evangelicalism: White Protestants, Plantation Missions, and the Flowering of Negro Christianity, 1787–1865* (Metuchen, N.J.: Scarecrow, 1975), 115. Even the inclusive Moravians, Jon Sensbach notes, designated separate burial plots for blacks and whites. See Sensbach, *A Separate Canaan: The Making of an Afro-Moravian World in North Carolina, 1763–1840* (Chapel Hill: University of North Carolina Press, 1998), 186, 202–3. For a brief overview of African American treatment in southern churches, see John B. Boles, introduction to *Masters & Slaves in the House of the Lord: Race and Religion in the American South, 1740–1870* (Lexington: University Press of Kentucky, 1988), 1–18. For an excellent account of African American religious life in the eighteenth-century northern colonies, see John Wood Sweet, *Bodies Politic: Negotiating Race in the American North, 1730–1830* (Baltimore: Johns Hopkins University Press, 2003), esp. 104–23; and Carol V. R. George, *Segregated Sabbaths: Richard Allen and the Emergence of Independent Black Churches* (New York: Oxford University Press, 1973). For the classic discussion of the relationship between early republican evangelicalism and African American religious life, especially southern missionary efforts, see Sernett, *Black Religion and American Evangelicalism.*

86. Richard Allen, *The Life Experience and Gospel Labors of the Rt. Rev. Richard Allen: To Which Is Annexed The Rise and Progress of the African Methodist Episcopal Church in the United States* (New York: Abingdon, 1960), 25.

87. The account offered here relies upon Gary B. Nash, *Forging Freedom: The Formation of Philadelphia's Black Community, 1720–1840* (Cambridge, Mass.: Harvard University Press, 1988), 100–133; Julie Winch, *Philadelphia's Black Elite: Activism, Accommodation, and the Struggle for Autonomy, 1787–1848* (Philadelphia: Temple University Press, 1988), esp. 10–14; and Sernett, *Black Religion and American Evangelicalism,* 116, 120–23. On the formation of a separate black church out of Samuel Stillman's church, see McLoughlin, *New England Dissent, 1630–1833,* 1:765.

88. Allen, *The Life Experience and Gospel Labors,* 27. On the accusation of pride made against Allen's group, see Winch, *Philadelphia's Black Elite,* 10. The classic work on the emergence of race and racism in early America remains Winthrop Jordan's *White Over Black: American Attitudes toward the Negro, 1550–1812* (Baltimore: Pelican, 1969), esp. 403–569. For an incisive reevaluation of the book's argument, see James Campbell and James Oakes, "The Invention of Race: Rereading *White Over Black,*" *Reviews in American History* 21 (March 1993): 172–83. An excellent recent appraisal of northern attitudes toward race can be found in John Wood Sweet, *Bodies Politic,* especially 271–311.

89. Charles Taylor, *Philosophical Arguments* (Cambridge, Mass.: Harvard University Press, 1995), 234; William Tennent, *Mr. Tennent's Speech on the Dissenting Petition* (Charleston, 1777), 16. The exceptions to the nineteenth century's anatomic racism were those missionaries who continued to think of Native Americans as benighted souls, cursed by a pagan culture that suppressed their godly characteristics. See Michael C. Coleman, "Not Race, But Grace: Presbyterian Missionaries and American Indians, 1837–1893," *Journal of American History* 67 (June 1980): 41–60. Reginald Horsman notes that contemporary missionaries preferred to think of Native

Americans as handicapped by their culture, though essentially equal. See Horsman, "Scientific Racism and the American Indian in the Mid-Nineteenth Century," *American Quarterly* 27 (May 1975), esp. 167.

90. "Madison's Remonstrance," in James, *Documentary History of Struggle for Religious Liberty in Virginia,* appendix G, 258; Hughes, quoted in John R. G. Hassard, *Life of the Most Reverend John Hughes, D.D.* (1866; repr., New York: Arno, 1969), 20.

CONCLUSION

1. Washington to the Hebrew Congregation in Newport, Rhode Island, 18 August 1790, *The Papers of George Washington: Presidential Series,* ed. Dorothy Twohig, 9 vols. (Charlottesville: University Press of Virginia, 1996), 6:286n., 285. It is also possible that Thomas Jefferson "originally drafted the president's reply." See *The Papers of George Washington: Presidential Series* 285n. The estimate of twenty-five Jewish families in Newport also comes from *The Papers of George Washington: Presidential Series* 6:286n.

2. A list of important and generally representative works on both sides of the question would include Gerald V. Bradley, *Church-State Relationships in America* (New York: Greenwood, 1987); Robert L. Cord, *Separation of Church and State: Historical Fact and Current Fiction* (New York: Lambeth, 1982), esp. 3–63; Philip A. Hamburger, *Separation of Church and State* (Cambridge, Mass.: Harvard University Press, 2002); Isaac Kramnick and R. Laurence Moore, *The Godless Constitution: The Case against Religious Correctness* (New York: W. W. Norton, 1996); Leonard W. Levy, *The Establishment Clause: Religion and the First Amendment,* 2nd ed. (Chapel Hill: University of North Carolina Press, 1994); Michael J. Malbin, *Religion and Politics: The Intentions of the Authors of the First Amendment* (Washington, D.C.: American Enterprise Institute for Public Policy Research, 1978); Leo Pfeffer, *Church, State, and Freedom* (Boston: Beacon, 1967), esp. 71–180.

3. Washington to the Hebrew Congregation in Newport, 6:285.

4. On the popularity of oral debate in nineteenth-century America, see E. Brooks Holifield, "Theology as Entertainment: Oral Debate in American Religion" *Church History* 67 (September 1998): 499–520. On the competitive character of religion in the early republic, and especially on the animus between Methodists and Baptists in the south and west, see Richard Carwardine, "Unity, Pluralism, and the Spiritual Market-Place: Interdenominational Competition in the Early Republic," in *Unity and Diversity in the Church,* ed. Robert Swanson, *Studies in Church history,* no. 32 (Oxford: Blackwell, 1996), 297–335; and Mark A. Noll, introduction to *God and Mammon: Protestants, Money, and the Market, 1790–1860,* ed. Mark A. Noll (Oxford: Oxford University Press, 2002), 12. Curtis D. Johnson's research on early nineteenth-century Cortland County, New York, suggests that rural communities witnessed the same pattern of revival-inspired division, competition, and appeals for unity that occurred earlier in urban areas. See Johnson, *Islands of Holiness: Rural Religion in Upstate New York, 1790–1860* (Ithaca, N.Y.: Cornell University Press, 1989).

5. Washington to George Mason, 6 July 1789, *Writings of George Washington,* ed. John C. Fitzpatrick, 39 vols. (Washington: U.S. Government Printing Office,

1931–1944), 30:355n47; David Austin, ed., *The American Preacher*, 3 vols. (Elizabeth-town, N.J.: 1791), 1:iii, v–vi. For analyses of cooperative religious enterprises during the period, see Richard R. Pointer, *Protestant Pluralism and the New York Experience: A Study of Eighteenth-Century Religious Diversity* (Bloomington: Indiana University Press, 1988), esp. 114, 121–23, 139, and 144; Terry D. Bilhartz, *Urban Religions and the Second Great Awakening: Church and Society in Early National Baltimore* (Rutherford, N.J.: Farleigh Dickinson University Press, 1986), esp. 100–106, 116; Candy Gunther Brown, *Word in the World: Evangelical Writing, Publishing, and Reading in America, 1789–1880* (Chapel Hill: University of North Carolina Press, 2004), esp. 27–45; and, David Paul Nord, *Faith in Reading: Religious Publishing and the Birth of Mass Media in America* (New York: Oxford University Press, 2004).

   6. "Isaac Harby on Religious Equality: A Letter to Secretary of State James Monroe," *American Jewish Archives* 7 (January 1955): 70–71. For a discussion of Christian attitudes toward Jews in the early republican and antebellum periods, see Robert K. Whalen, "Christians Love the Jews! The Development of American Philo-Semitism, 1790–1860," *Religion and American Culture* 6 (Summer 1996): 225–60. On the cooperative efforts needed to establish and maintain nonsectarian common schools, see Timothy L. Smith, "Protestant Schooling and American Nationality, 1800–1850," *Journal of American History* 53 (March 1967), esp. 685, 693–95; also David Tyack, "The Kingdom of God and the Common School; Protestant Ministers and the Education Awakening in the West," *Harvard Educational Review* 36 (Fall 1966), esp. 448, 455. On the difficulty in maintaining shared meetinghouses, see John H. Wigger, *Taking Heaven by Storm: Methodism and the Rise of Popular Christianity in America* (New York: Oxford University Press, 1998), 37. On the surprising levels of acceptance of intermarriage between Protestants, Catholics, and Jews in the nineteenth century, see Anne C. Rose, *Beloved Strangers: Interfaith Families in Nineteenth-Century America* (Cambridge, Mass.: Harvard University Press, 2001).

   7. Milton Powell, ed., *The Voluntary Church: American Religious Life (1740–1865) Seen Through the Eyes of European Visitors* (New York: Macmillan, 1967), 162, 173; Richard Hofstadter and Wilson Smith, eds., *American Higher Education: A Documentary History*, 2 vols. (Chicago: University of Chicago Press, 1961), 1:437–38; Jefferson to Thomas Cooper, 2 November 1822, in *The Writings of Thomas Jefferson*, ed. H. A. Washington, 9 vols. (New York, 1859), 7:267. It appears that Jefferson's proposal did not go anywhere. Merrill D. Peterson suggests that evangelical groups simply were not taken with this conciliatory gesture of Jefferson's. See Peterson, *Thomas Jefferson and the New Nation: A Biography* (New York: Oxford University Press, 1970), 980. On the nonsectarian character of many smaller colleges in the early nineteenth century, see Daniel Walker Howe, "Church, State, and Education in the Young American Republic," *Journal of the Early Republic* 22 (Spring 2002): 15; David B. Potts, "American Colleges in the Nineteenth Century: From Localism to Denominationalism," *History of Education Quarterly* 11 (Winter 1971): 363–80; and Potts, "College Enthusiasm! as Public Response, 1800–1860," *Harvard Educational Review* 47 (February 1977): 30. On the general religious shape of nineteenth-century colleges, see George Marsden, *The Soul of the American University: From*

Protestant Establishment to Established Nonbelief (New York: Oxford University Press, 1993), esp. 84–85.

8. R. Laurence Moore, *Selling God: American Religion in the Marketplace of Culture* (New York: Oxford University Press, 1994), 86. On the mutual expansion of denominational and nondenominational publishing, see Brown, *Word in the World*, 39. On the moderation of rhetoric among mainline Christians in early national (*ca.* 1790–1830) Baltimore, see Bilhartz, *Urban Religions and the Second Great Awakening*, esp. 100, 106, 117.

9. For a representative and important sample of anti-Catholicism, see "An American" [Samuel F. B. Morse], *Imminent Dangers to the Free Institutions of the United States Through Foreign Immigration, and the Present State of the Naturalization Laws* (New York, 1854), esp. 11–13. Terry D. Bilhartz points out that, in Baltimore, there was only one "major Protestant-Catholic conflict before 1830" and that "occurred early in the century when several local Protestants castigated the administrators of St. Mary's College for admitting Protestant pupils and then requiring them to attend Catholic mass." See Bilhartz, *Urban Religions and the Second Great Awakening*, 122. For the discussion of anti-Catholic urban bookstores, see Ray Allen Billington, *The Origins of Nativism in the United States 1800–1844* (1933; repr., New York: Arno, 1974), 458.

10. On Roman Catholic tensions with republican government in the early republic, see Hamburger, *Separation of Church and State*, 211; and, John T. McGreevy, *Catholicism and American Freedom: A History* (New York: W. W. Norton, 2003), 13. For a brief overview of the traditionalism that flourished among nineteenth-century Catholics, see Jay Dolan, "Catholicism and American Culture: Strategies for Survival," in *Minority Faiths and the American Protestant Mainstream*, ed. Jonathan D. Sarna (Urbana: University of Illinois Press, 1998), 63–71.

11. John Hancock Lee, *The Origin and Progress of the American Party in Politics: Embracing a Complete History of the Philadelphia Riots in May and July, 1844, etc.* (1855; repr., Freeport, N.Y.: Books for Libraries, 1970), 31; Walter Colton, "The Bible in Public Schools," *The Quarterly Review of the American Protestant Association* 1 (January 1844), 21. Colton's text was first printed as a pamphlet. On its wide distribution, see Vincent P. Lannie and Bernard C. Diethorn, "For the Honor and Glory of God: The Philadelphia Bible Riots, 1840" *History of Education Quarterly* 8 (Spring 1968): 63. Regarding the differences between Catholics and Protestants, Orestes Brownson wrote (with the distinct air of triumphalism) that "Protestantism has virtually yielded the question as a theological question, and now debates it as a question lying within the secular order," that is, on the alleged incompatibility of Catholicism with republicanism, capitalism, and American nationalism. See Brownson, "The Know-Nothings," *Brownson's Quarterly Review* (October 1854), 469.

12. Lyman Beecher, *A Plea for the West* (Cincinnati, 1835), 139, 63–64. Throughout this tract, Beecher repeatedly noted that "odium" was not to be leveled upon Catholics (e.g., 157). More ominously, he went on to note that the Catholics' "use of invidious terms" and their incivility generally was rapidly exhausting both the sympathy and the patience of the community in their behalf" (64).

13. Ibid., 60–61, 145, 83, 160.

14. Ibid., 66–68, 156.

15. Horace Mann, "Religious Education" (1841) in *Cornerstones of Religious Freedom in America*, ed. Joseph L. Blau (Boston: Beacon, 1950), 181, 191; W. M. Oland Bourne, ed., *History of the Public School Society* (1869; repr., New York: Arno, 1971), 185, 247. For an account of Catholic educational practices during the mid-nineteenth century, see Jay P. Dolan, *The Immigrant Church: New York's Irish and German Catholics, 1815–1865* (Notre Dame, Ind.: University of Notre Dame Press, 1983), 99–120. On the debate surrounding religion and the public schools across the country, see Dolan, *The American Catholic Experience: A History from Colonial Times to the Present* (Garden City, N.Y.: Doubleday, 1985), esp. 262–78. For an excellent account of the relevant ideological convictions behind the common school movement, see Vincent P. Lannie, *Public Money and Parochial Education: Bishop Hughes, Governor Seward, and the New York School Controversy* (Cleveland: Case Western Reserve University Press, 1968), esp. 2–4; also Diane Ravitch, *The Great School Wars, New York City, 1805–1973: A History of the Public Schools as Battlefield of Social Change* (New York: Basic, 1974), esp. 33–76; and Robert Michaelsen, *Piety and the Public Schools: Trends and Issues in the Relationship between Religion and the Public School in the United States* (London: Macmillan, 1970). On Bible reading (or the lack thereof) in the Common Schools, as well as the confusion that increasingly afflicted those who used the terms "sectarian" and "nonsectarian," see R. Laurence Moore, "Bible Reading and Nonsectarian Schooling: The Failure of Religious Instruction in Nineteenth-Century Public Education," *Journal of American History* 86 (March 2000): 1581–99. On the subject of (religious and ethnic) diversity in the common schools during this period, see James W. Fraser, *Between Church and State: Religion and Public Education in a Multicultural America* (New York: St. Martin's, 1999), esp. 23–65.

16. Peter K. Guilday, ed., *The National Pastorals of the American Hierarchy (1792–1919)* (Westminster, Md.: Newman, 1954), 134; Lawrence Kehoe, ed., *Complete works of the Most Rev. John Hughes, D.D.*, 2 vols. (New York: Lawrence Kehoe, 1866), 1:102–6. Catholic advocates went too far, however, when they appealed for public funds on the grounds that the peculiar tenets of their church—like those of Quaker pacifists— should be accorded equal treatment by the state. New York's Public School Society reminded them that Friends paid a fine or a tax in lieu of their military service. The Society also reprimanded the bishops for their "illiberal" discussion of Quaker influences on the educational system and replied to Catholic complaints of marginality by noting that there were just two Quaker teachers in the system—one-third the number of Catholics. The Catholics were demanding preferential treatment for their sect, Protestant advocates argued, not mere equality. For a discussion of the Quaker analogy and its rejection by the Public School Society, see Lannie, *Public Money and Parochial Education*, 69; and Bourne, *History of the Public School Society*, 200, 197.

17. For a detailed recent account of Hughes's life, see Richard Shaw, *Dagger John: The Unquiet Life and Times of Archbishop John Hughes of New York* (New York: Paulist, 1977). For a less objective, older account that also includes primary sources, see John R. G. Hassard, *Life of the Most Reverend John Hughes, D.D.* (1866; repr., New York: Arno, 1969).

18. Kehoe, *Complete works of the Most. Rev. John Hughes*, 1:92. For the argument that the schools were both less religious and more sectarian than their proponents admitted, see Hughes's speech in Kehoe, *Complete works of the Most Rev. John Hughes*, 1:103.

19. Bourne, *History of the Public School Society*, 321. Absent Catholic cooperation, new editions of the offensive texts included the same old anti-Catholic dogmas, and the Public Society's heavy-handed, albeit well intentioned, editing was blamed on Hughes's alleged inquisitorial methods. On the committee's work, see Lannie, *Public Money and Parochial Education*, 97. On the specifics of the textbook controversy, see *Public Money and Parochial Education*, 103–18. On the resolution that was finally reached, see Michaelsen, *Piety and the Public Schools*, 88.

20. Horace Bushnell, "Common Schools," in *Building Eras in Religion* (New York: Charles Scribner's Sons, 1903), 99, 92, 78, 87, 97.

21. John England, "Address Before Congress," in *The Works of the Right Reverend John England, First Bishop of Charleston*, ed. Sebastian G. Messmer, 7 vols. (Cleveland: Arthur H. Clark, 1908), 7:43. The contemporary use of the phrase "mixed education" is evident in David Gartner, "The Growth of a Catholic Educational System in Providence and the Protestant Reaction, 1848–1876," *Rhode Island History* 55 (1997): 135. One of Orestes Brownson's essays suggests that the phrase "mixed schools" was indeed used by Catholics in a negative sense. See Brownson, "Catholic Schools and Education," *Brownson's Quarterly Review* (January 1862), 78. On the development of a Catholic parochial school system, see Gartner, "The Growth of a Catholic Educational System," 133–45. On the important distinction between Catholic and Protestant understandings of freedom in the nineteenth century, see McGreevy, *Catholicism and American Freedom*, esp. 36–37.

22. Joseph Smith, *History of the Church of Jesus Christ of Latter-day Saints*, ed. B. H. Roberts, 7 vols. (Salt Lake City: Church of Jesus Christ of Latter-day Saints, 1932–1951), 1:3–4, 5–6, quoted in Richard L. Bushman, *Joseph Smith and the Beginnings of Mormonism* (Urbana: University of Illinois Press, 1984), 55, 58. On the existential crisis brought about by the diversity of religious alternatives in the western New York town where Joseph Smith grew up, see Bushman, *Joseph Smith and the Beginnings of Mormonism*, esp. 4–6. According to the leading authorities on Mormon history, Leonard J. Arrington and Davis Bitton, these existential concerns were shared by many early adherents. See Arrington and Bitton, *The Mormon Experience: A History of the Latter-Day Saints*, 2nd ed. (Urbana: University of Illinois Press, 1992), esp. 28, 37.

23. On the possible role of primitivist thought in shaping early Mormonism, see Kenneth H. Winn, *Exiles in a Land of Liberty: Mormons in America, 1830–1846* (Chapel Hill: University of North Carolina Press, 1989), 50–51; and Arrington and Bitton, *The Mormon Experience*, 26–27.

24. Francis W. Kirkham, *A New Witness for Christ in America: The Book of Mormon*, rev. ed., 2 vols. (Salt Lake City: Utah Printing, 1967, 1959), 2:30–31, quoted in Bushman, *Joseph Smith and the Beginnings of Mormonism*, 111.

25. Terry L. Givens points out that both print and personal attacks on the Mormons began soon after Smith made his visions public. And he suggests that the object

of, as well as the motivation for, this persecution could only have been Smith's un-orthodox doctrines. See *The Viper on the Hearth: Mormons, Myths, and the Construction of Heresy* (New York: Oxford University Press, 1997), 43. For an acute analysis of the reasons behind Mormon persecution, see Arrington and Bitton, *The Mormon Experience*, esp. 62–63. Jan Shipps also stresses the importance of secular causes in the hostility aimed at Mormonism. See Shipps, "Differences and Otherness: Mormonism and the American Religious Mainstream," in Sarna, *Minority Faiths and the American Protestant Mainstream*, esp. 88–91. As William R. Hutchinson points out, anti-Mormonism rapidly faded once polygamy was official renounced. See Hutchison, *Religious Pluralism in America: The Contested History of a Founding Ideal* (New Haven, Conn.: Yale University Press, 2003), 54.

26. On the links between the rhetoric of anti-Mormonism and anti-Catholicism, see David Brion Davis, "Some Themes of Counter-Subversion: An Analysis of Anti-Masonic, Anti-Catholic, and Anti-Mormon Literature," *Mississippi Valley Historical Review* 47 (September 1960), esp. 211–13. Givens qualifies Davis's argument in *The Viper on the Hearth*, 47–49. The liberal Roman Catholic Bishop John England stated the Catholic understanding of their church's position with regard to the truth: "We know nothing of speculation, we know nothing of opinion. Opinions form no part of our religion. It is all a statement of facts." See *The Works of the Right Reverend John England*, 22.

27. Kehoe, *Complete Works of the Most Rev. John Hughes*, 1:112; Bourne, *History of the Public School Society*, 273–74.

28. Kehoe, *Complete works of the Most Rev. John Hughes*, 2:101, 99. Hughes's critique was shared by the German Reformed theologian, Philip Schaff, who critiqued the elements in reformed Calvinism (especially Congregationalism) that led to "full atomism" and the "disease" of the "sect system." See Schaff, *The Principle of Protestantism*, ed. Bard Thompson and George H. Bricker (1845; repr., Philadelphia: United Church Press, 1964), 148, 141.

29. Excerpt from the New York *Journal of Commerce*, in *The American and Foreign Christian Union* 1 (December 1850): 550; Orestes A. Brownson, "Native American-ism," *Brownson's Quarterly Review* (January 1845), 84. Brownson, whose sophisticated opinions often changed, would later contend that anti-Irish hostility (which he himself shared by that point) was the chief cause of nativist sentiment. See Brownson, "Of Native Americanism," *Brownson's Quarterly Review* (July 1854), 337; also Brownson, "The Know-Nothings," *Brownson's Quarterly Review* (October 1854), 448.

30. Horace Mann, "Religious Education," 163–201; Bourne, *History of the Public School Society*, 229, 243; and Guilday, *The National Pastorals of the American Hierarchy*, 36.

31. Robert Baird, *Religion in the United States of America* (1844; repr., New York: Arno, 1969), 613, 607, 342.

32. William R. Hutchison notes the significance of the rise of biblical literalism, or Biblicism, in *Religious Pluralism in America*, 64–65.

33. Voltaire, *Letters on England*, trans. Leonard Tancock (New York: Penguin, 1980), 37, 41. On the eighteenth-century importance of, as well as the meaning of,

"politeness," see Lawrence E. Klein, *Shaftesbury and the Culture of Politeness: Moral Discourse and Cultural Politics in Early Eighteenth-Century England* (Cambridge: Cambridge University Press, 1994), esp. 3–14. For Bushnell's reference to Dutch and Irish examples, see "The Common Schools," 93n, 95. For a fuller account of the European (especially the Prussian) precedents that American Common School reformers drew upon, see Charles Leslie Glenn, *The Myth of the Common School* (Oakland, Calif.: Institute for Contemporary Studies Press, 2002), esp. 86–88.

34. Philip Hamburger, "Liberality," *Texas Law Review* 78 (May 2000): 1215–85. Drawing upon the insights of Mickey Kaus as well as his own substantial research, Gordon Wood argued that Revolutionary-era Americans manifested a peculiarly "equal sense of self-worth and dignity among people." See Wood, "Equality and Social Conflict in the Revolution," *William and Mary Quarterly*, 3rd series 51 (October 1994): 710.

35. On the persistence of religious discrimination in England in the late seventeenth century and eighteenth century, see Mark Goldie, "The Theory of Religious Intolerance in Restoration England," *From Persecution to Toleration: The Glorious Revolution and Religion in England*, ed. Ole Peter Grell, Jonathan I. Israel, and Nicholas Tyacke (Oxford: Clarendon, 1991); and Richard Ashcraft, "Latitudinarianism and Toleration: Historical Myth Versus Political History," in *Philosophy, Science, and Religion 1640–1700*, ed. Richard Kroll, Richard Ashcraft, and Perez Zagorin (Cambridge: Cambridge University Press, 1992), 155. For an excellent, nuanced overview of the condition of dissenters in eighteenth-century England, see James E. Bradley, *Religion, Revolution and English Radicalism: Non-Conformity in Eighteenth-Century Politics and Society* (Cambridge: Cambridge University Press, 1990), esp. 49–90; and Richard Burgess Barlow, *Citizenship and Conscience: A Study in the Theory and Practice of Religious Toleration in England during the Eighteenth Century* (Philadelphia: University of Pennsylvania Press, 1962). England's Test and Corporation Acts, which limited civil and military offices to Anglicans, remained in force until 1829.

36. Powell, *The Voluntary Church*, 69; *New-York Mercury*, 16 April 1753; "To the Congregation of Boston" (Baltimore, April 30, 1790) in *The John Carroll Papers*, ed. Thomas O'Brien Hanley, 2 vols. (Notre Dame, Ind.: University of Notre Dame Press, 1976), 1:441, quoted in Cogliano, *No King, No Popery*, 142. Sacvan Bercovitch makes a similar point in his work on American Romanticism. See Bercovitch, "The A-Politics of Ambiguity in The Scarlet Letter," *New Literary History* 19 (Spring 1988): 629–54. Trollope's insistence on the importance of attaching oneself to a particular denomination should be considered in light of John Robert Godley's contention that "numbers, especially among the more wealthy and educated classes, openly profess to belong to no particular church, at the same time assuming to be 'Christians'." See Powell, *The Voluntary Church*, 164–65.

37. Michael Walzer, "What Does It Mean to Be an 'American'?" in *The American Intellectual Tradition: A Sourcebook*, ed. David A. Hollinger and Charles Capper, 3rd ed., 2 vols. (1997), 2:447. The best and most thorough discussion of the relationship between religious identity and American identity can be found in R. Laurence Moore, *Religious Outsiders and the Making of Americans* (New York and Oxford: Oxford

University Press, 1986); R. Laurence Moore, *Touchdown Jesus: The Mixing of Sacred and Secular in American History* (Louisville: Westminster John Knox, 2003), 5, 108; and Ruth Alden Doan, *The Miller Heresy, Millennialism, and American Culture* (Philadelphia: Temple University Press, 1987), 26. On the development of Catholic liberalism in the United States, see McGreevy, *Catholicism and American Freedom*, 118–26; and Philip Gleason, "American Catholics and Liberalism, 1789–1960," in *Catholicism and Liberalism: Contributions to American Public Philosophy*, ed. R. Bruce Douglass and David Hollenbach (Cambridge: Cambridge University Press, 1994), 45–55. For the liberal Catholic argument that Irish Americans should trade their original national characteristics for American ones, while preserving their Catholic religious traditions, see Orestes Brownson, "The Know-Nothings," esp. 473, 486. Catholicism was compatible with different nationalities, he contended, but different nationalities were not compatible with one another (463).

38. *Brown v. Board of Education*, 347 U.S. 483 (1954). Available at http://www.nationalcenter.org/brown.html (accessed February 9, 2006).

39. *Maryland Journal and Baltimore Advertiser*, 21 January 1785.

40. Habermas's seminal argument is developed in *The Structural Transformation of the Public Sphere: An Inquiry into a Category of Bourgeois Society*, trans. Thomas Burger (Cambridge: MIT Press, 1989). On the long-standing resistance to party politics in early America, see Richard Hofstadter, *The Idea of a Party System: The Rise of Legitimate Opposition in the United States, 1780–1840* (Berkeley: University of California Press, 1969); and William G. Shade, "Political Pluralism and Party Development: The Creation of a Modern Party System: 1815–1852," in *The Evolution of American Electoral Systems*, ed. Paul Kleppner (Westport, Conn.: Greenwood, 1981), esp. 79. On the centrality of religious "distinctions" (and the "secondary" importance of ethnic distinctions) to New York politics in the 1760s, see Alan Tully, *Forming American Politics: Ideals, Interests, and Institutions in Colonial New York and Pennsylvania* (Baltimore: Johns Hopkins University Press, 1994), 205. On the use of federalism as a justification for dissent, see Richard R. Beeman, *The Old Dominion and the New Nation, 1788–1801* (Lexington: University Press of Kentucky, 1972), 191. On the political culture of the time and the limits placed on political opposition, see Joanne B. Freeman, "Explaining the Unexplainable: The Cultural Context of the Sedition Act," in *The Democratic Experiment; New Directions in American Political History*, ed. Meg Jacobs, William J. Novak, and Julian E. Zelizer (Princeton, N.J.: Princeton University Press, 2003), esp. 40. Early National "Partisans," Rosemarie Zagarri writes, "embraced their views with an almost religious intensity." See Zagarri, "Women and Party Conflict in the Early Republic" in *Beyond the Founders: New Approaches to the Political History of the American Republic*, eds. Jeffrey L. Pasley, Andrew W. Robertson, and David Waldstreicher (Chapel Hill: University of North Carolina Press, 2004), 118.

41. Thomas Jefferson, "First Inaugural Address" (4 March 1801) in *Thomas Jefferson: Writings*, ed. Merrill D. Peterson (New York: Library of America, 1984), 493–95. For a subtle interpretation of this document, see Peter Onuf, *Jefferson's Empire: The Language of American Nationhood* (Charlottesville: University Press of Virginia, 2000), 106–7.

Index

Academy of Philadelphia, 111
Act of Toleration. *See* Toleration Act
Act of Uniformity (1559), 18, 31
Adams, Amos, 139
Adams, Hannah, 157–58, 173–74, 183
Adams, John, 175, 192
African Americans
  civil rights movement, 223
  in eighteenth century, 11–12
  independent churches, 200
  missionary activity among, 85, 119
  Moravian proselytizing, 85
  as objects of evangelization, 197–98
  segregation in churches, 199–200
African Episcopal Church of St. Thomas, 199
Alison, Francis, 74, 84, 98
Allen, Richard, 199–200
Allen, William, 92
Allison, Patrick, 188–89
American colonies. *See* colonial America; *specific colonies*

Amos (prophet), 25
Anabaptists, 141
Anglican Church
  attempts to bolster membership, 128–29
  colonial bishop controversy, 119–26, 130, 154
  demography, 129
  dissenters, 22–23
  in England, 18–19
  King's College controversy, 100–103
  in Maryland, 188
  in Massachusetts, 6, 115–19
  missionary controversy, 116–19
  in New York, 21–22, 34, 94–95
  officeholders among, 128
  suspicions concerning loyalism, 187
  and taxation, 31, 34
  in Virginia, 20, 26, 57, 123, 130, 132, 133, 135
Anglo-Saxons, 127
Antinomians, 65
Apthorp, East, 115–18, 198

Arnold, Benedict, 183
atheism, 169, 196–97

Backus, Isaac, 104, 139–44, 168, 194
Baird, Robert, 219
baptism, 11, 21, 24
Baptists
  and baptism, 21
  Bulkley on, 30
  in Connecticut, 29
  criticism of, 189
  evangelical ecumenism, 205
  in Massachusetts, 6, 35, 140
  in New England, 24
  and taxation, 31, 34, 35
  varieties in nineteenth-century
    U.S., 8
  in Virginia, 24, 35
Barton, Thomas, 86
Beecher, Lyman, 209–10, 213
Bellah, Robert, 160
Benevolent Congregational Society,
  176–77
Berlin, Ira, 115
Bethel African Methodist Episcopal
  Church, 199
Bible, 28, 158, 168, 206, 211, 213,
  218, 219
bigotry, 5, 51, 104, 110, 170–71, 176,
  186, 204, 209, 214
Billington, Ray Allen, 209
Bill of Rights, 204
Binney, Barnabas, 153
Blair, Samuel, 68
body, 52, 66, 141
Bolingbroke, Lord, 92
Bonomi, Patricia, 69, 93
Book of Common Prayer, 31
Book of Mormon, 215
Boston (Mass.), 3, 5, 26, 182, 199
Boston Gazette, 46
Boston Weekly News-Letter, 46
Boucher, Jonathan, 128
Bourdieu, Pierre, 114

Bradford, William, Jr., 136
Brekus, Catherine, 13
Brock, Peter, 150
Brockwell, Charles, 90
Browne, Arthur, 89, 90
Brownson, Orestes, 218
Brown University, 97, 127
Brown v. Board of Education, 223
Buckley, Thomas E., 165
Buddhists, 12
Buell, Samuel, 58, 60
Bulkley, John, 29–31
Bullock, Stephen, 89
Bushnell, Horace, 213–14, 221
Butler, Jon, 107

Caldwell, John, 63, 64
Callendar, John, 19–20
Calvinism, 33, 37, 118, 138
Cambridge (Mass.), 115
Camm, John, 123, 130, 144
Campbell, Alexander, 211
Canada, 180, 183
Carmichael, John, 175
Carroll, John, 3, 5, 12, 183, 184–86,
  222
Catholics and Catholicism
  alleged affiliation with foreign
    powers, 180
  Beecher on, 209–10
  change in attitude toward, 181–86
  in eighteenth century, 4, 10
  in England, 19, 31–32
  liberal, 223
  in Maryland, 28
  in Massachusetts, 6, 182
  in nineteenth century, 12, 208–14
  Protestant hostility, 10, 86, 91,
    111–12, 180, 209, 217–20
  and suppression of religious
    dissent, 17
Catholicus (pseudonym), 106
Chandler, Thomas Bradbury,
  120–25, 129, 144, 154

charity, 197
Charles II (king), 16, 21
Charleston (S.C.), 37–38, 40, 46–47, 59, 128
Chauncy, Charles, 52, 54, 61, 63, 65–66, 72, 123, 129, 138, 169, 173
Checkley, John, 44
Chesterfield, Lord, 173
children, 27, 28
Christian Independents, 178
Christianity, 102, 116, 117, 160, 162–64, 167
Christian Primitivism, 215
Church of England. *See* Anglican Church
Church of Jesus Christ of Latter-Day Saints. *See* Mormons
church separations, 67–73, 75, 77, 82
church-state relations, 136–37, 163, 166–67
civil peace, 9
civil rights movement, 223
Clap, Thomas, 99–100, 105
Clarke, Samuel, 51
Clinton, George, 206
College of New Jersey, 97, 98, 102, 135–36
College of Philadelphia, 97, 98, 107, 111
College of Rhode Island, 97
College of William and Mary, 96, 130, 178
colleges, 96–103, 207–8
colonial America
    colleges in, 96–103
    congregations in, 7–8
    English theology in, 87
    integration of institutions, 87–90
    integration of politics, 91–96
    migrants to, 86
    population, 127
    religious boundaries in, 53
    religious settlement of, 17–25

toleration in, 6
    See also specific colonies and states
Columbia College, 178
Columbia University, 100
concert of prayer, 81, 110
Conestoga raids, 148
Congregationalist churches
    and Anglicans in Massachusetts, 116–18
    in Connecticut, 105–6, 161
    in Massachusetts, 137–38, 140, 142–45
    in New England, 8, 24, 34, 35, 138
    Puritan origins, 20
    and taxation, 31, 34
Connecticut
    Congregationalists in, 105–6, 161
    dissent in, 20–21, 29, 31
    and Great Awakening, 56
    Presbyterians in, 23
    Saybrook Platform, 105–6
    taxation in, 34
conscience, 21, 31, 32, 36, 41, 43, 52, 71–72, 141
Constitution (U.S.), 167, 168, 193, 204–5
Continental Congress, 181, 183
Cooper, Mary, 171–72
cooperative endeavors, 9
Cotton, John, 26
Crèvecoeur, Hector Saint John, 170, 171, 175, 222
Curry, Thomas J., 35
Cutler, Timothy, 54

Danger of an Unconverted Ministry, The (Tennent), 67
Dartmouth College, 97, 98–99
Davenport, James, 55, 56
Davies, Samuel, 57, 64, 83
de Beauvoir, Simone, 30
deism, 87, 166, 169, 170, 171
DeLancey family, 94–95
Delaware, 10

Delaware Valley, 21
demography, 126–31
denominationalism, 107–8
Dickinson, Jonathan, 29, 39–43, 51, 54, 64, 65, 66
Discourse on the Christian Union (Stiles), 83, 126, 127
discrimination, 12, 186, 199
disease, 19–20, 26, 27
disestablishment, 128, 133, 137, 139, 168, 171, 192
dissent
  in Anglican Church, 22–23
  in Connecticut, 20–21, 29, 31
  in Europe, 152
  Fisher on, 38
  in Massachusetts, 20–21, 141–43
  plague of, 15–48
  and private judgment, 31–48
  Protestant, 132
  public expressions of, 35
  and religious settlement of British America, 17–25
  in Rhode Island, 17
  as subversive activity, 25
  suppression of, 17, 47
  unprecedented degree of, 76
  in Virginia, 6, 35–36, 131, 132, 134
divine right of private judgment, 31–36
Dixon, James, 207
doctrine of innate ideas, 32
Douglass, William, 44
DuBois, W.E.B., 30
Duché, Jacob, 171
Dudleian lecture series, 180–81
Dudley, Paul, 180
Dutch Reformed Church, 18, 94, 95
Dwight, Timothy, 161, 172–73, 174, 194

Eck, Diana L., 12
ecumenism, 169, 171, 180, 220
  definition of, 80

King's College controversy, 100–103
  and opening of colleges, 96
  and religious identity, 103–8
  rise of, 81–87
education, 136, 211–14, 217, 221
Edwards, Jonathan, 50, 59, 63, 65, 73, 74, 81, 110, 172
Eells, Nathanael, 54
egalitarianism, 9, 200, 221
eighteenth-century revivals. *See* Great Awakening
Eisenhower, Dwight D., 196
Elizabeth I (queen), 18, 31
England
  Anglican Church in, 18–19
  Catholics in, 19, 31–32
  liberalism in, 32
  religious settlement of British America, 17–25
  and Revolutionary War, 175
  and right to private judgment, 31–32
  toleration in, 152
  Voltaire on, 220–21
  wars with France and Spain, 86
England, John, 214
epidemics, 26
Episcopalians, 121, 122, 187–88, 189
equality, 6–7, 31, 152, 157–201
essential rights and liberties of Protestants, The (Williams), 71
essentials. *See* fundamentals
evangelism, 12, 57, 58, 63, 139, 142, 189
exclusion, 6
excommunication, 177

faith, 173–74, 196
Fay, Stephen, 59
Federalism, 224
Finley, Samuel, 147
First Amendment, 204–5

First Great Awakening. *See* Great Awakening

Fisher, Hugh, 37, 38, 40, 45

Fitch, Thomas, 106

Fithian, Philip Vickers, 189

Foster, Dan, 177

France, 86, 112, 146, 181

Franklin, Benjamin, 41, 42–47, 66, 107, 110–11, 148, 193, 225

Franklin, James, 44, 46

fraternal societies, 88–90

freedom, 31

Freemasons, 88–90, 106, 110, 170

fundamentals, 83–86, 87, 111, 159–67

Gaustad, Edwin, 174

Germany, 84, 86

Givens, Terry L., 215

Glasites, 108

Godley, John Robert, 207

Gordon, Thomas, 91–92

Graham, John, 23, 24, 27, 28, 42

Great Awakening, 49–77, 81, 83, 87, 116, 139, 197

Great Britain. *See* England

Green, James N., 46

Gwatkin, Thomas, 130

Habermas, Jürgen, 224

Hancock, John, 182

Hanover Presbytery of Virginia, 34

Harby, Isaac, 207

Harvard College, 23–24, 61, 62, 96, 98, 180

Hatch, Nathan, 171

Hemphill, Samuel, 40–45, 47, 65, 67, 72

Henchman, Nathaniel, 56

Henley, Samuel, 130

Henry, Patrick, 163, 165, 166, 187

Henry VIII (king), 18

heresy, 17, 19, 28, 33

Hieronymous (pseudonym), 144, 194

Hindus, 12

Hollis, Thomas, 23–24

Hopkinson, Francis, 4

House of Burgesses, 131, 132–33

Hughes, John, 201, 212–13, 216–17

Humphrey, David C., 102

Huntington, John, 191

Husbands, Hermon, 104–5

Hutchinson, Anne, 27, 65

Independent Reflector, The, 101–2, 103, 110, 136

Indians, American. *See* Native Americans

indifference, 170, 171, 172, 175

intermarriage, 170

Irenaeus (Samuel West), 144

irenic tradition, 85

Irish Catholics, 209, 218

itinerant ministers, 53–56, 58, 60, 62, 71, 72, 128, 172

Jarratt, Devereux, 177

Jefferson, Thomas, 134, 137, 163, 164, 166–67, 197, 201, 208, 225

Jesus Christ, 52, 82

Jews and Judaism
    appointment of Jews to office, 207
    change in attitude toward, 186–87
    discrimination against, 186
    in eighteenth century, 4
    in Newport, 203–4
    in Pennsylvania, 186
    in twentieth century, 12

Johnson, William Samuel, 23, 24, 25, 102, 116, 120

Jones, Hugh, 11, 26

Kennedy, Archibald, 104

King's College, 100–103, 104, 116, 178, 222

language, 35, 42, 152, 154–55, 165, 223–24

Lathrop, John, 181
latitudinarianism, 85, 86, 87, 102,
    138, 146
law, 5–6
Leddra, William, 15–16
Lee, Ann, 190, 220
Leland, John, 132, 153, 173
liberalism, 32
liberty, religious. *See* religious liberty
liberty of conscience, 21, 31, 32, 36,
    41, 43, 72, 141
literacy, 24
Livingston, William, 12, 94, 101–5,
    110, 136, 153, 206, 222
Livingston family, 94–95
Locke, John, 32, 33, 42, 47, 52, 65, 71,
    104, 140, 220
Luther, Martin, 18, 31

Macclintock, Samuel, 176
MacSparran, James, 23
Madison, James (college president),
    178
Madison, James (U.S. president),
    91, 92, 133, 135–37, 163–64,
    166, 201
majority rights, 73, 192–95
Mann, Horace, 211, 218
Martin, Luther, 167, 168
Martin, Robert W.T., 88
Maryland, 10, 28, 168, 179, 186, 188
*Maryland Journal and Baltimore
    Advertiser*, 179, 224
Mason, George, 133
Masons. *See* Freemasons
Massachusetts
    Catholics in, 6, 182
    Congregationalists in, 137–38, 140,
        142–45, 165
    constitution, 142–43, 153, 165, 178,
        182, 194
    dissent in, 20–21, 141–43
    financial support for religion, 162
    and Great Awakening, 60

heretics in, 19
immigration into, 79
intolerance in, 16, 153
missionary controversy in,
    116–18
religious liberty in, 137–45
religious minorities in, 205
schools, 211, 218
Stillman's plea for religious
    equality, 159
system of exclusion, 26
taxation in, 6, 34, 35, 142, 144, 145,
    178, 194
Massachusetts Bay Colony, 27
Massachusetts Bay Company, 20
Mather, Cotton, 28, 29, 36, 45, 51
Mayhew, Jonathan, 116, 117–19
measurement, 126–27
Methodists, 12, 196, 205, 220
Middleborough (Mass.), 139
Middle Colonies, 8, 54, 62, 93, 103
mind, 52, 66, 141
minority rights, 70, 72
Molasses Act, 119
Monroe, James, 207
Moore, R. Laurence, 208
morality, 52, 102, 169
Moravians, 84–85, 101, 106–7,
    122, 206
Mormons, 12, 214–16
Muhlenberg, Henry Melchior, 91
multiculturalism, 9
Murray, John, 169–70
Muslims, 12

names, 177–78
Native Americans
    in eighteenth century, 11
    European-borne diseases, 19–20
    missionary activity among, 85, 117,
        119, 206
    Moravian proselytizing, 85
    as objects of evangelization,
        197–98

racism against, 200
  schooling, 98
natural religion. *See* deism
negative liberty, 115
New Brunswick Presbytery, 67
New Building (Phila., Pa.), 107
New England
  anti-Catholicism, 180
  Baptists in, 24, 160
  church separations, 71, 75
  Congregational churches in, 24,
    34, 35, 138
  denominational divisions in, 8
  dissent in, 47, 54
  and Great Awakening, 60, 62,
    70, 72
  missionary controversy, 116–19
  Puritans in, 17, 20, 26
  Quakers in, 24
  religious competition in, 115–19
New-England Courant, 44
New Hampshire, 97
New Jersey, 21, 62, 97, 98, 153
New Lights, 116, 134
  at Princeton, 97
  commitment to Protestant doc-
    trine, 76, 105
  conflict with Episcopalians, 189
  and ecumenism, 81, 82
  and itinerant ministers, 53–54
  and partial judgments, 61–66
  and Philadelphia Synod, 68, 69
  "rash judging," 68
  and religious liberty in
    Massachusetts, 139–40
  revolutionary propensities, 56–57
New London (Ct.), 29
Newport (R.I.), 203–4
New Siders, 67–70, 73
newspapers, 44, 46, 86, 87–88, 135
New York
  Anglicans in, 21–22, 34, 94–95
  King's College, 100–103, 178
  New Siders in, 73

politics, 91, 94–95
  Presbyterians in, 34
  schools, 211–13, 217, 218
  1769 Assembly election, 94–95
  teachers in, 56
  toleration of dissent in, 21
New-York Mercury, 101
non-forbearance, 109
Northampton (Mass.), 50, 63, 73
Northwest Ordinance, 160–61
Notes of the State of Virginia
  (Jefferson), 166, 167

Occasional Conformity and Schism
  Acts, 34
Old Lights, 54, 63, 66, 68, 69, 76,
  82, 105, 189
Old Siders, 67–68, 70, 72
open-mindedness, 170

pacifism, 145–51
Parkman, Ebenezer, 58–59, 64, 76, 112
partial judgments, 58–67
Pattillo, Henry, 195–96
Paxton Boys, 148
Peace of Augsburg, 18
Penn, John, 148
Penn, William, 21, 145
Pennsylvania
  as asylum for persecuted
    minorities, 17
  Catholics in, 10
  colleges in, 97, 178
  designs for military association,
    159
  immigration into, 79
  itinerant preachers in, 62
  and liberty of conscience, 21, 41
  pacifism in, 145–51
  Quakers in, 21, 24, 92–94, 145–51
  religious considerations in poli-
    tics, 91, 92–94
  requirements for legislators, 168
Pequot Indians, 19

persecution, 5, 6, 17, 115, 121–22, 137,
    141–42, 186
Philadelphia (Pa.), 3–4, 5, 12, 37,
    39–40, 45, 95, 171
Philadelphia Synod, 40–42, 45,
    66–70, 74, 82, 84, 92, 192, 195
Philanthropos (pseudonym), 165
Pietists, 24, 84
Pike, Samuel, 109
Pinckney, Charles, 167
Plea for the West, A (Beecher), 209
Plowden, Charles, 152
pluralism
    of Adams (Hannah), 158
    Christian, 12
    denominationalism as measure
        of, 108
    origins of, 5, 7
    religion and American, 220–25
    religious, after founding of
        republic, 203–25
    religious, during founding of
        republic, 157–201
    in schooling, 98
political egalitarianism, 9
politics, 91–96, 224–25
Pollen, Thomas, 89
population, 127, 129
Porter, Theodore, 64
positive liberty, 115
prayer, 162
prejudice, 6, 115, 198, 200, 209
Prentiss, Thomas, 158
Presbyterians
    in Connecticut, 23
    in Middle Colonies, 8
    in New York, 34
    in Philadelphia, 39–40, 41, 67, 69
    and Quaker pacifism, 148–49
    and religious liberty, 37
    tolerationist consensus, 37
    in Virginia, 24, 34, 35
press liberty, 87–88
Princeton University, 97, 136

printing, 44–47, 54, 87–88
private judgment, 53, 59, 65–66, 70
    Binney on, 153
    divine right of, 31–36
    early eighteenth-century debates
        over, 37–40
    and Great Awakening, 63,
        65–66, 75
    and Hemphill dispute, 40–43
    inviolability of, 76
    as sacrosanct, 52, 61
    Williams (Elisha) on, 71, 72
Protestantism
    dissent in Virginia, 132
    hostility toward Catholicism, 10,
        86, 91, 111–12, 180, 209,
        217–20
    liberal, 223
    and Mormons, 214–16
    and pluralistic ideals, 12
    in southern colonies, 17
    as species of Christianity, 162, 164
    and toleration for private religious
        judgment, 36
Protestant Reformation, 18, 31, 221
publishing industry, 43–44, 86,
    87–88
Puritans, 17, 20

Quakers
    Graham on, 27, 42
    hanging of, 15–16, 17
    Husbands' denomination
        hopping, 104–5
    in Massachusetts, 6, 35
    missionaries, 16
    in New England, 24
    pacifism, 146–51
    in Pennsylvania, 21, 24, 92–94,
        145–51
    and taxation, 31, 34, 35, 36
    in Virginia, 26, 35, 36
Quebec Act (1774), 180
Queen's College, 97

"rash judging," 68, 197, 204
rationalist thought, 51, 52
reductionism, 162–64
Regular Lights, 76
religion
   changing affiliations, 171
   church-state relations, 136–37, 163,
      166–67
   compulsory support of, 171
   congregations in American
      colonies, 7–8
   contemporary importance of, 8
   disestablishment, 128, 133, 137,
      139, 168, 171, 192
   divided churches, 67–73, 75, 77, 82
   multiple establishments, 162,
      163
   and pluralism, 7, 9, 220–25
   as preserver of order, 159–60
   and private judgment, 31–48, 52,
      53, 59, 61, 63, 65–66
   religious settlement of British
      America, 17–25
   See also religious liberty; specific
      religions
religious identity, 103–8, 110, 222
religious integration, 79–112
religious liberty, 6, 31
   Adams on, 139
   Anglican pleas for, 123
   Backus on, 140–41
   Callendar on, 19
   Chandler's invocation of, 121–22
   Chauncy's defense of, 52–53
   constitutional provisions for, 205
   limits of, 145–51
   Macclintock on, 176
   in Massachusetts, 137–45
   in Pennsylvania, 145–51
   and Presbyterians, 37
   and public civility, 175
   rise of, 113–55
   and slaves, 132
   in Virginia, 135

Religious Liberty an Invaluable
   Blessing (Adams), 139
religious pluralism. See pluralism
religious reductionism, 162–64
representation, 120, 126, 130–31
Revolutionary War, 174, 175, 181,
   182, 193
Rhode Island
   colleges in, 97, 98, 127
   as dissenting refuge, 17
   founding of, 33
   Jews in, 186
   MacSparran case, 23
   religious liberty in, 19, 28
   voluntary religious support, 22
right of private judgment. See private
   judgment
Roman Catholics. See Catholics and
   Catholicism
Rush, Benjamin, 4, 5, 182
Rutgers University, 97

saints, 63
salvation, 53, 169–70
Sandeman, Robert, 108
Sandemanianism, 108–9, 191
Sarna, Jonathan D., 187
Saybrook Platform, 105–6
science, 51
Scott, John Morin, 103
Seabury, Samuel, 187
Seasonable Plea (Williams), 71
Seasonable Thoughts on the State of
   Religion in New-England
   (Chauncy), 65, 66
Secker, Thomas, 118–19
sectarians, 29–31, 36
sects, 107, 157–58, 161, 171, 178, 220
sedition, 44
self-definition, 177–78
Separate Baptists, 12, 189
Seven Years' War, 86, 147
Seward, William H., 212
Shakerism, 190–91, 220

Sherman, Roger, 167
slaves and slavery, 11, 129, 131, 132
Smith, Joseph, 215, 216
Smith, Josiah, 37–38, 43
Smith, Thomas, 175–76
Smith, William, 89, 92, 97, 98, 111
social contract, 32, 71
Society for Useful Knowledge,
    88, 110
*Some Thoughts Concerning the Revival
    in New-England* (Edwards),
    63, 65
Sons of Liberty, 193
South Carolina, 79, 172, 200
South-Carolina Gazette, 46, 60
Southern Methodists, 189
Spain, 86
Stamp Act, 120, 125
statistics, 126–31
Stiles, Ezra, 83–84, 98, 116, 126–27,
    129, 171, 176, 178, 197
Stiles, Isaac, 63
Stillman, Samuel, 159, 160, 199
Sullivan, James, 192
Swanwick, John, 168

taxation
    in American colonies, 6
    in Connecticut, 31, 34
    in Massachusetts, 34, 35, 142, 144,
        145, 178, 194
    in Virginia, 35, 36, 134
Taylor, Amos, 190
Taylor, Charles, 10
Tennent, Gilbert, 62, 63, 67, 68, 72,
    82–84, 87, 107
Tennent, William, 128, 169, 200
Tennessee, 174
theory of the social contract, 32
Thomson, John, 39–40, 45,
    69–70, 72
Tillotson, John, 51, 52
toleration
    Chauncy on, 52, 54

decline of, 114
    in eighteenth century, 6, 52
    end of, 119–26, 131–37, 152–55
    in Europe, 152
    language of, 35, 42, 152
    in Massachusetts, 16, 153
    in Pennsylvania, 21
    and print trade, 46
    for private judgment and worship,
        32, 36, 43
    in Virginia, 131–37, 153
    Williams on, 33
Toleration Act (1689), 23, 34, 35, 57,
    118, 132
Trenchard, John, 91
Trollope, Frances, 222
truth, 38, 43, 167
Tucker, John, 177
Two Treatises on Civil Government
    (Locke), 32

unanimity, 192–95
Union Society, 88
Unitarians, 166
unity, 80, 83, 110
Universalism, 169–70, 178
University of Pennsylvania, 97
University of Virginia, 208

*Vindication of the Reverend
    Commission of the Synod, A,*
    41, 42
Virginia
    Anglicans in, 20, 24, 26, 57, 123,
        130, 132, 133, 135
    Baptists in, 24, 35
    definition of Christianity, 163–64
    dissent in, 6, 35–36, 131, 132, 134
    end of toleration in, 131–37, 153
    Henry's general assessment bill,
        163, 166
    immigration into, 79
    Jefferson's proposal for religious
        freedom, 166–67, 225

move toward disestablishment, 166, 168

New Light faith in, 57, 189

Presbyterians in, 24, 34, 35

Quakers in, 26, 35, 36

religious minorities in, 205

religious reductionism in, 162–64

system of exclusion, 26

taxation in, 35, 36, 134

Virginia Company, 20

Virginia Gazette, 35–36

Voltaire, 220–21

voluntary consent, 32, 33

Walzer, Michael, 222

warfare, 146

Washington, George, 151, 160, 166, 182–83, 187, 197, 203–6, 225

Wesley, John, 196, 220

Westborough (Mass.), 58, 59

Westminster Confession of Faith, 37, 38, 39, 42, 67, 68

Wetmore, James, 22–23, 24

Wharton, Charles Henry, 184

Wheelock, Eleazar, 99

White, William, 188

Whitefield, George, 54–58, 60–63, 81–83, 104, 107, 141, 190

Whittelsey, Chauncey, 102

Wigglesworth, Edward, 61

Wightman, Valentine, 29

Williams, Elisha, 71–72, 141

Williams, Roger, 26, 33

Williams, Samuel, 160

Winthrop, John, 27, 33, 38

Witherspoon, John, 97, 136

women, 13–14, 196

Woodmason, Charles, 8, 64, 129, 172, 198

words. *See* language

Yale College, 96, 99–100, 172

Zagorin, Perez, 17

Zenger, John Peter, 44

Zinzendorf, Nicholas von, 84–85